POCKET BOOK OF

BRITAIN'S WALKS

120 THEMED WALKS EXPLORING THE DIVERSITY OF BRITAIN

Produced by AA Publishing

First published with *The Book of Britain's Walks* 1999
Published in this edition January 2000
Reprinted 2000, 2001, 2002

Published by AA Publishing (a trading name of Automobile Association Developments Limited, whose registered office is Millstream, Maidenhead Road, Windsor, Berkshire SL4 5GD; registered number 1878835)

Visit the AA Publishing Web site at www.theAA.com

ISBN 0 7495 35008

A01365

A CIP catalogue record for this book is available from the British Library.

Colour separation by Leo Reprographic Ltd., Hong Kong
Printed and bound by Fratelli Spada SpA, Italy

POCKET BOOK OF

BRITAIN'S WALKS

120 THEMED WALKS EXPLORING THE DIVERSITY OF BRITAIN

Thurso
114
Wick
113
Ullapool
Gairloch
Tain
Uig
Dingwall
Banff
Portree
115
Inverness
Elgin
Peterhead
112
Kyle of Lochalsh
Aviemore
116
Aberdeen
Mallaig
117
Fort William
111
110
Pitlochry
Montrose
118
Crianlarich
Oban
109
Perth
Dundee
108
119
Stirling
120
107
Glasgow
99
Edinburgh
Largs
101
100
68
Berwick-upon-Tweed
Kilmarnock
Peebles
67
Campbeltown
Ayr
106
102
Alnwick
Moffat
Dumfries
103
104
Newcastle upon Tyne
66
Stranraer
105
Workington
Carlisle
62
63
64
Penrith
58
61
Middlesbrough
60
59
65
70
Kendal
69
Thirsk
Scarborough
73
71
Settle
Lancaster
York
75
77
74
78
Blackpool
Burnley
76
Leeds
Hull
72
79
Grimsby
Liverpool
Manchester
Sheffield
Holyhead
Colwyn Bay
46
48
95
97
45
49
50
51
Lincoln
56
Caernarfon
Chester
47
Newark-on-Trent
96
94
98
Stoke-on-Trent
52
93
90
92
44
Stafford
Nottingham
Boston
57
Dolgellau
80
Shrewsbury
54
King's Lynn
91
89
41
Leicester
Norwich
88
Newtown
40
Birmingham
53
Peterborough
37
Great Yarmouth
42
Aberystwyth
Coventry
55
39
Ludlow
Northampton
Bury St Edmunds
87
38
21
86
Worcester
Cambridge
Ipswich
Hereford
43
Bedford
Fishguard
84
82
20
Brecon
19
35
Luton
22
Carmarthen
81
Gloucester
Abergavenny
Oxford
85
Pembroke
Swansea
83
18
Watford
Chelmsford
17
33
Swindon
36
LONDON
Cardiff
Reading
Bristol
32
14
16
23
Bath
15
Guildford
Sevenoaks
Maidstone
9
11
10
12
13
34
24
Dover
Barnstaple
Taunton
Salisbury
Southampton
26
28
25
Yeovil
Chichester
Brighton
Hastings
30
3
1
Bournemouth
29
27
Exeter
2
31
4
Weymouth
Truro
Plymouth
7
8
5
6

Contents

Northern England

Wales

Scotland

Using this Book

Each walk is shown on an illustrated map. Many of these will stand up to being used alone to navigate your way around the walk, and the book is specially designed for you to use in this way. However, some detail is lost because of the restrictions imposed by scale. Particularly in the upland areas, we recommend that you use them in conjunction with a more detailed map, produced for walkers by, for example, Ordnance Survey or Harvey Map Services. In poor visibility, you should not attempt the walks in upland areas unless you are familiar with bad weather navigation in the hills.

Using the illustrated maps is simple, just read off the numbered instructions around the edge. Remember the countryside, and especially towns, are changing all the time, and with the seasons, so features mentioned as landmarks may alter or disappear.

Information Each walk has a coloured panel giving information about the distance, total ascent, terrain, gradients, conditions under foot and where to park a vehicle. All the walks are suitable for motorists who wish to return to their cars at the end. There is also information here about any special conditions which apply to the walk, for example restricted access or access/entrance fees. The parking suggestions given have been chosen to minimise the impact of leaving cars parked in the countryside. They do not imply that motorists have a guaranteed right to park in the places suggested. Please park your vehicle with due consideration for other traffic and countryside users, especially agricultural access. Refreshment places mentioned in the text are suggestions by field researchers for their convenience to the route. Listing does not imply that they are AA inspected or recognised, though they may coincidentally carry an AA classification.

Grading The walks have been graded simply to give an indication of their relative difficulty. Easier walks, such as those around towns, or with little total ascent and over shorter distances have one boot. The hardest walks, either because they include a lot of ascent, greater distances, or are in mountainous or otherwise difficult terrain, are given three boots. Moderate walks have two boots. These gradings are relative to each other and for guidance only.

Access All the walks in this book are on rights of way, permissive paths or on routes where de facto access for walkers is accepted. On routes in England and Wales which are not on legal rights of way, but where access for walkers is allowed by local agreements, no implication of a right of way is intended.

Safety Although each walk here has been researched with a view to minimising the risk to the walkers who follow its route, no walk in the countryside can be considered to be completely free from risk. Walking in the outdoors will always involve a degree of common sense and judgement to ensure that it is as safe as possible.

- Be particularly careful on cliff paths and in mountainous terrain, where the consequences of any slip can be very serious.
- Remember to check tidal conditions before walking on the seashore.
- Some sections of route are by or cross busy roads, so take care here and remember traffic is a danger even on minor country lanes.
- Be careful around farm machinery and livestock, especially if you have children with you.
- Be aware of the consequences of changes in the weather and know the weather forecast for the day of your walk.

Introduction by Roly Smith

Why Walk? Walking is the number one outdoor activity in Britain, with many more participants than angling, golf or even watching football. According to the official figures, as many as 15 million people regularly take a walk of 2 miles or more every month, either individually, in families, or in organised groups or clubs. That's a staggering 180 million rambles a year – over 40 times the number of anglers' outings and seven times the total annual football attendances in Britain each season. So we can safely say that Britain is a nation of walkers. Or, to be more strictly accurate, we are a nation of ramblers, and the use of that gentler, more ambulatory and very British term is significant. In America, walkers are known as hikers or backpackers, and in continental Europe excursionists or wanderers, signifying a much more worthy and serious enterprise. Rambling, on the other hand, means to wander where you fancy, to generally rove about, sometimes with no particular destination in mind.

This book is aimed at those ramblers who want to find out more, to seek out the relatively undiscovered corners, and delve behind the usual tourist board clichés so often glibly trotted out to describe this country. There is no doubt that the best way to see and really experience Britain is on foot. Fleeting coach- or car-bound tourists can only expect to receive a sanitised view. It is left to the walker to really explore the warp and weft of the land.

But what is the attraction? There are many reasons, of course, apart from the sheer physical and mental pleasure of getting away from it all. Hippocrates is credited with first coming up with the maxim that walking is the best medicine. And in a famous essay on walking published in 1913, the great English historian George Macaulay Trevelyan claimed that when his mind or body was out of sorts, he knew he only had to call in his two doctors – his left leg and his right.

It is now generally accepted that walking has great therapeutic properties, both mentally and physically. Unlike more vigorous exercise such as running or jogging, which put unnatural strains on joints and muscles, with walking you are always in control and can set your pace according to your own personal levels of fitness and commitment. You can ramble, in fact.

Where to Walk Apart from its health-giving qualities, another aspect that makes walking so attractive a prospect in Britain is the wonderfully varied and outstandingly beautiful scenery with which our islands are blessed. There are few other countries in the world where, during the course of a day's walk, you can pass from airy coastal cliffs, sand dunes, through lovely riverside meadows and woods to towering crag-bound lakes and mountains. But it remains perfectly possible in places like the English Lake District, Wales or Scotland. In this book there are many walks to these spectacular natural showplaces, from the awesome rift of Hell's Mouth on the wild north Cornish coast to the ice-carved splendour of the Cuillin Hills on the Isle of Skye. In between are the apparent wildernesses of Hampshire's lovely New Forest and the forbidding moorland wastes of Cross Fell in the North Pennines and the Kinder plateau in Derbyshire.

Britain is a land rich in history and folklore. Some sites visited in these pages still hold on to their age-old secrets. For example, no one can be sure why and by whom the uninhibited Cerne Abbas Giant was carved on a Dorset hillside, or what strange ceremonies were enacted around Long Meg and her enigmatic 'Daughters' in Cumbria.

Humans have so shaped the land over the 10,000 years of their history that there are few places left which can truly be termed wilderness. Only the steepest mountain crags or coastal cliffs have not felt the influence of their hand in one way or another. Even the wide, barren moorlands of the north of England, Wales and Scotland – which many people would regard as wildernesses – are only that way because they have been cleared of woodland and used for grazing by farmers since the Stone Age.

The whole British landscape has been described as a palimpsest – a living manuscript which has been written on over and over again. And the first thing that a landscape historian discovers, as Professor W G Hoskins pointed out nearly 50 years ago, is that everything is older than you think. Those dimples in a clearing of the conifers in Norfolk's Breckland mark the neolithic flint mines which were among the first industrial sites in Britain. That insignificant mound on a Peak District hilltop may be the last resting place of a Bronze Age prince, buried some 4,000 years ago. And those strange corrugations which mark so many Midland pastures, or the step-like lynchets on the slopes of the southern chalk downs, show where every available piece of land had to be cultivated to counter the threat of starvation in the early medieval period.

Other sites give hints of a violent past, such as the sylvan water meadows round Tewkesbury, where the fate of the Crown was decided in a series of medieval battles, and the Elizabethan defences of Berwick-upon-Tweed, for so long a bulwark against the Scots. A network of ancient trackways crosses our countryside, from the prehistoric Ridgeway across the Wessex downs to the paved packhorse routes of the Pennines, these once important arteries of commerce and industry now offering quiet highways rich in history for the observant walker.

Many other areas remain treasured havens for wildlife, and the nature walks in this book introduce you to a few of the most special.

Practicalities There are 140,000 miles (225,300km) of public rights of way in England and Wales, and in most mountain areas and Scotland there is a *de facto* right of access above the enclosed foothills. In some hill areas access agreements are in force which allow the walker the virtually unlimited right to roam, and the Government has announced that it intends to introduce this right to all mountains, moorlands and uncultivated land in due course.

Elsewhere, it is the law of the land that you should stick to those rights of way which, it should be noted, have the same status in law as a public highway like the M1 motorway. Therefore, if you find one that is blocked, you have the right to clear it to allow your free passage, although we do not reccomend that you argue or try to force a way. It is better to report the blockage to the responsible authority, (usually the county council or unitary authority highways department). If you stray from a right of way, technically you will be trespassing, but unless you do damage you cannot be prosecuted, despite what some signs still say.

When out in the country, you should respect the life of the people who live and work there, especially the farmers, who have to such a large extent created the landscapes we know and love today

Walking Safely Finally, a word should be said about equipment and safety. The most important single item of equipment required for country walking is a good pair of boots or sturdy walking shoes – your feet need to be kept warm and dry in all conditions.

Britain's climate is nothing if not unpredictable, so warm and waterproof clothing is the next essential, but you don't need to spend a fortune on an Everest-specification jacket for strolling in the Cotswolds. There are many efficient and breathable alternatives which need not cost the earth. Waterproof trousers or gaiters are also a good idea, and as up to 40 per cent of body heat is lost through the head, a warm hat is essential. Some of the mountain walks in this book should not be attempted in winter conditions unless you have previous experience and the technical knowledge of winter walking techniques.

If you get into trouble, fall or are injured on a country walk, particularly in the hills, the rule is to send someone for help and alert the emergency services by ringing 999. They will ascertain the extent of the injury and whether it is appropriate for the mountain rescue service to be called, for an evacuation of the casualty. A careful note should be made of your exact location, and ideally, someone should stay with the injured party, keeping the person warm and dry until help comes.

Above all, enjoy your walking. After all, 15 million people can't be wrong!

Southwest England

The southwest of England tapers into a long and remarkably varied peninsula, stretching from the rural heart of England to the broken cliffs and coves of the Lizard and Land's End. Tiny fishing coves and smugglers' haunts contrast with bustling seaside resorts such as Newquay and Penzance, and the rolling farmland of central Devon. Despite the extensive granite uplands rising inland, you're never far from the sea, which means this corner of England gets its fair share of mist and rain – but the warming effects of the Gulf Stream also give the region more hours of sunshine than almost anywhere else.

The Southwest is blessed with a continuous coastal path from Minehead to Poole Harbour, no mere seaside stroll but one of the most varied and interesting walks in Britain. Trodden by excisemen and smugglers over the centuries, this path takes in a succession of rugged cliffs and coves.

The area boasts two national parks: the wild upland bogs of Dartmoor and the coastal cliffs and rolling heaths of Exmoor. Further protected areas encompass large stretches of the Cornish coast, Bodmin Moor, parts of Devon and Dorset, as well as the Quantock Hills and North Wessex Downs. There's a wealth of natural history to explore in the uncultivated land of the Cotswold escarpment, or the rugged gorges of the Mendips.

This is an area rich in legend. To the east the hills of the Dorset and Wessex Downs are scored by ancient earthworks and decorated with chalk figures. Cornwall was a last bastion of Celtic culture in England, and this is also the legendary homeland of King Arthur. Our ancient forebears trod along the crest of the downs when Britain was a wild and wooded place, and so there is no shortage of footpaths and trackways. At the opposite end of the scale, attractive historic towns offer the walker a rich urban landscape to discover.

The literary tradition is strong in the Southwest, and Thomas Hardy's novels contain some of the best descriptions ever of the English countryside. Other literary works lead you through Exmoor in search of Lorna Doone and Tarka the Otter, or almost anywhere in Cornwall after Daphne du Maurier's characters.

Best of the Rest

Lyme Regis and Dorset Coast Meryl Streep brought the image of the Cobb in Lyme Regis to cinema screens all over the world. The Dorset seaside town is the setting for John Fowles' international bestseller *The French Lieutenant's Woman,* and was used extensively in the film version. From Lyme walks extend along the beautiful coast in both directions, with nearby Golden Cap, the highest point on the south coast, a notable highlight.

Tintagel The north Cornish coast is rich in Arthurian legend, and at Tintagel the dramatic cliffs are surmounted by the brooding ruins of a plausible Camelot. Whether or not the British hero really lived in the castle here will seem irrelevant as you explore the rugged coastline, traced by the excellent South-West Way.

Forest of Dean A remote corner of Gloucestershire, nestling up to the Welsh border, it became rich through the exploitation of its mineral wealth. Now time has healed its industrial scars, leaving a legacy of excellent footpaths and bridleways through beautiful forest and, at Symond's Yat, a breathtaking view of the River Severn meandering along a wooded gorge.

Bath The Romans understood the importance of Bath's therapeutic waters, but it took the commercial savvy and aesthetic brilliance of the Georgians to create this upmarket watering hole of the 18th century. There are famous tourist sights in Bath, but it is a walk around the lesser known parts which will bring the true history of the city to life. The squalor of the servants' living quarters and the expedient shortcuts in construction are shown up by a walk around the passages and alleys.

Slaughters For many the Cotswolds are epitomised by the chocolate-box images of Upper and Lower Slaughter. But away from the tourist coaches a network of excellent paths connect these idyllic settlements and gives the walker a unique view of this most English of landscapes.

The Somerset Coal Canal Hidden in the valleys which connect with the Avon near Bath is a lost industrial relic, a testament to a time when the Industrial Revolution touched every remote corner. To extricate coal from the Somerset coalfield for industrialising Bristol, a branch was built from the great Kennet and Avon waterway up the Cam valley to Paulton. Geology made the coal hard won, and railways soon slashed the price of heavy transport. A walk along the canal's remnants is a reminder of a bygone pioneering spirit.

The Mystery of the Cerne Abbas Giant

High on a Dorset hillside a strange figure is carved in the chalk

1 In Cerne Abbas, make your way to the church, which stands in Abbey Street and walk along the street with the church to your right. To your left is an elegant row of timbered houses complete with overhangs.

2 Go past the village pond, to the right. Ahead now is beautiful Abbey Farm.

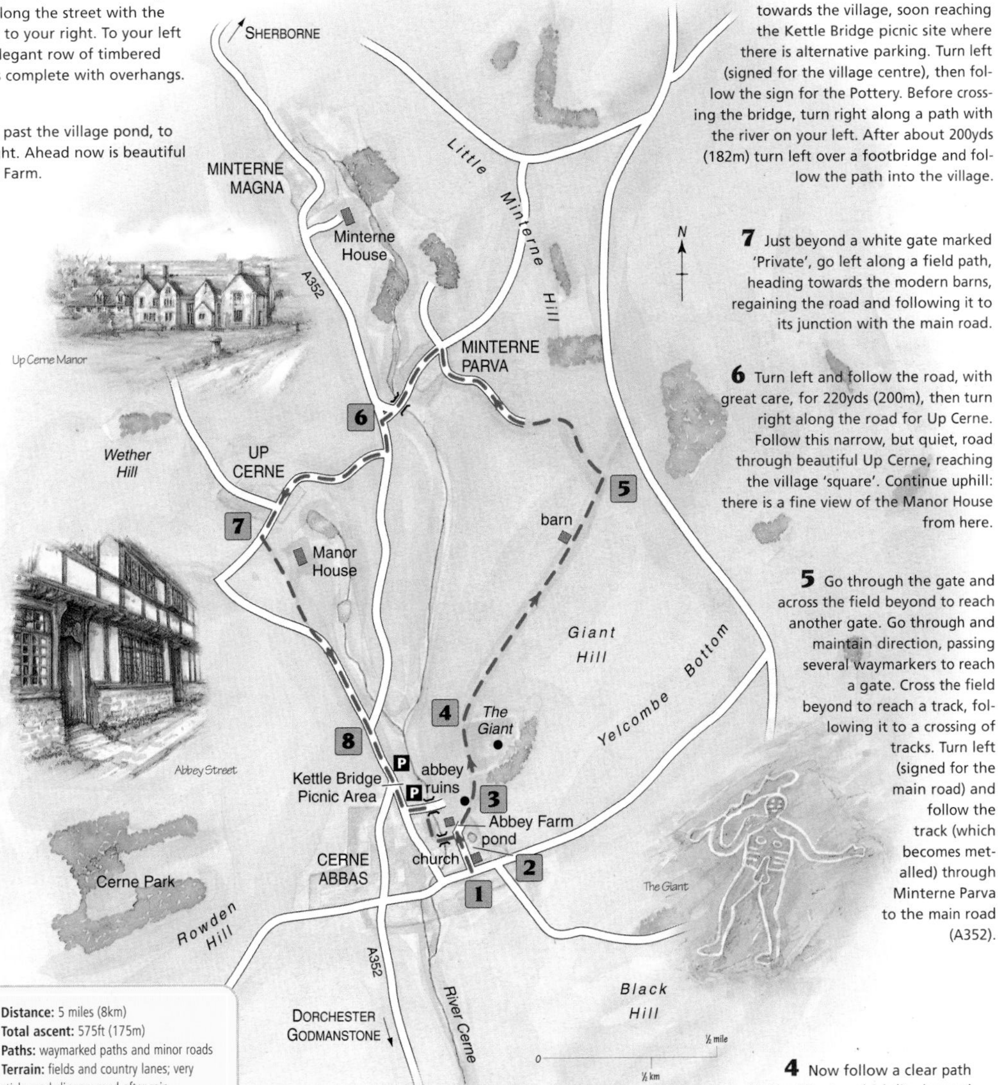

3 Just beyond the pond, go right, under an arch and diagonally across the cemetery – the site of Cerne Abbey. Leave the cemetery through another arched gateway and cross the field diagonally beyond – the abbey ruins are to your left. Go over a stile to reach the base of Giant Hill.

4 Now follow a clear path beneath the Giant – which lies beyond the fence on your right. When the fence ends, continue along the obvious path, eventually crossing a stile and then maintaining direction to reach a waymarker near a barn. Go to the right past the barn, and follow the hedge on the left for about 380yds (346m) to reach a gate, also on the left.

5 Go through the gate and across the field beyond to reach another gate. Go through and maintain direction, passing several waymarkers to reach a gate. Cross the field beyond to reach a track, following it to a crossing of tracks. Turn left (signed for the main road) and follow the track (which becomes metalled) through Minterne Parva to the main road (A352).

6 Turn left and follow the road, with great care, for 220yds (200m), then turn right along the road for Up Cerne. Follow this narrow, but quiet, road through beautiful Up Cerne, reaching the village 'square'. Continue uphill: there is a fine view of the Manor House from here.

7 Just beyond a white gate marked 'Private', go left along a field path, heading towards the modern barns, regaining the road and following it to its junction with the main road.

8 Cross the main road with care, bearing right and then left along the minor road towards the village, soon reaching the Kettle Bridge picnic site where there is alternative parking. Turn left (signed for the village centre), then follow the sign for the Pottery. Before crossing the bridge, turn right along a path with the river on your left. After about 200yds (182m) turn left over a footbridge and follow the path into the village.

Up Cerne Manor

Abbey Street

The Giant

Distance: 5 miles (8km)
Total ascent: 575ft (175m)
Paths: waymarked paths and minor roads
Terrain: fields and country lanes; very sticky and slippery mud after rain
Gradients: gradual
Refreshments: several possibilities in Cerne Abbas; on the A352 at Godmanstone, the Smith Arms is claimed to be Britain's smallest pub
Park: limited parking available in Cerne Abbas, and also at the viewpoint of the figure beside the A352

Among the Tors of Dartmoor

A spectactular walk among the granite tors of this last southern wilderness

1 From the car park, cross the road and head up the wide grassy path to reach Haytor. Despite the forbidding face first reached, the tor can be easily climbed up a series of big steps at the back.

2 Walk past the rock mass, with it on your right, and pause. Ahead is an area of western Dartmoor, one of the most accessible, but beautiful, sections of the moor. In the distance, slightly left, is Hound Tor, with Greator Rocks to its right. Beyond Haytor Down, which spreads out in front of you, is the wooded valley of the River Bovey. Down and right (northeast) you will see the remains of Haytor Quarry. To continue the walk, aim for the quarry's perimeter fence and pick up the rough track just to the right.

3 After skirting the right hand edge of the quarry bear left to follow the clear granite tramway. Go past the quarry entrance and continue on the tramway as it bears right across a stone embankment to a T-junction. Turn left and follow the tramway to bear right at a fork. After a few paces take one of the many paths that head off right across open moorland towards Smallacombe Rocks.

4 There are excellent views of the surrounding moor from the rocks. Turning to face Haytor, lower and to the right you will see a quarry set in the back of Holwell Tor. Take the path from Smallacombe Rocks which heads just to the left of the quarry. This will take you back to the tramway.

5 Turn right along the tramway, passing a ruined building and the main quarry, then continuing round the back of the quarry, crossing a ruined bridge. Just over the bridge, head left up to the top of Holwell Tor.

6 From Holwell Tor take a direct line across the moor – there is a rough and indistict path – heading for Low Man, the cliff to the right of Haytor. From Haytor reverse the outward route back to the start.

7 The walk can be extended, in fine style, by heading onwards from Holwell Tor south across the moor to Saddle Tor, then turning left across the wide and low ridge back to Haytor.

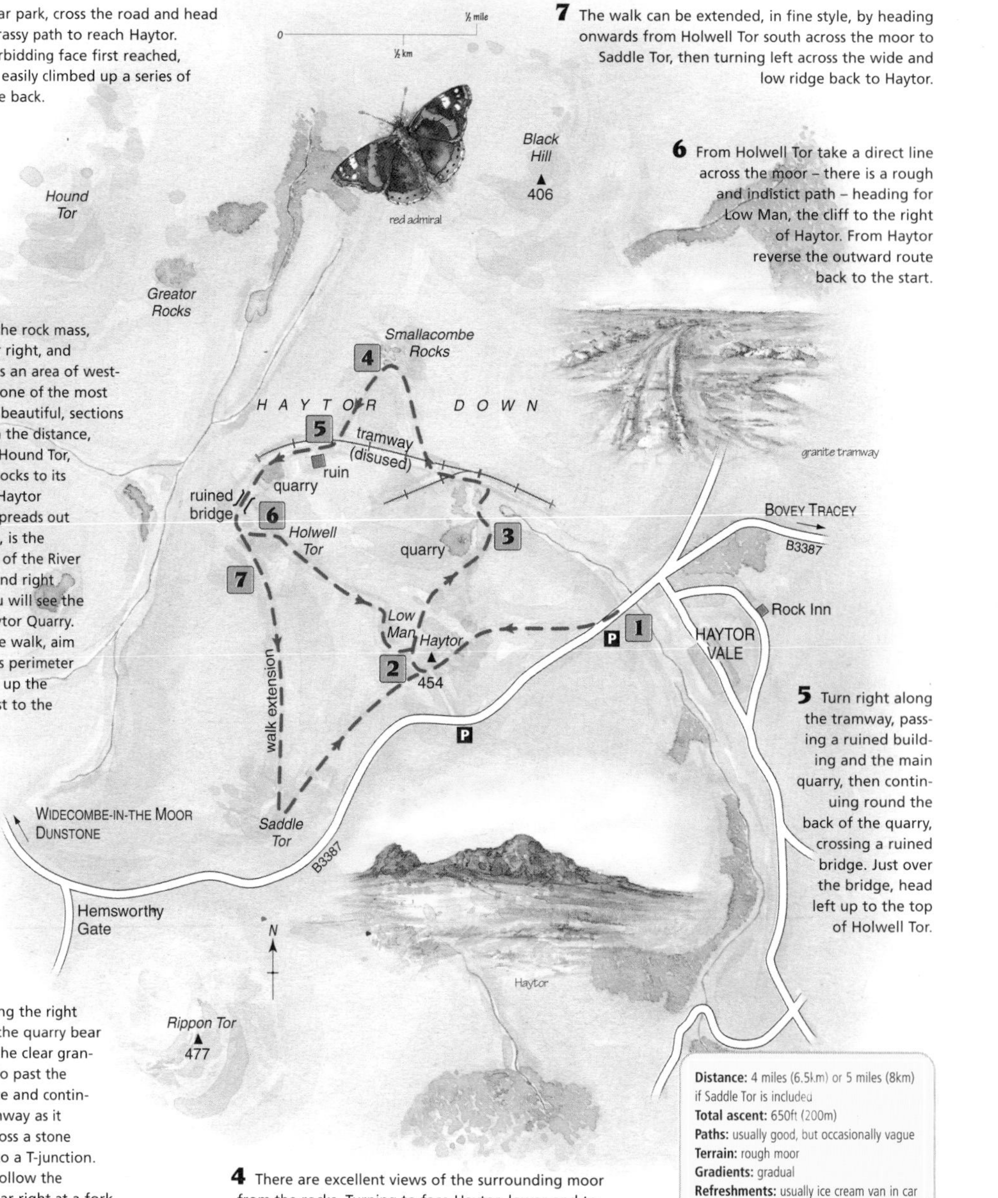

0 ½ mile ½ km
red admiral
Black Hill 406
Hound Tor
Greator Rocks
Smallacombe Rocks
HAYTOR DOWN
tramway (disused)
ruin
quarry
ruined bridge
Holwell Tor
quarry
Low Man
Haytor 454
walk extension
Saddle Tor
granite tramway
BOVEY TRACEY
B3387
Rock Inn
HAYTOR VALE
WIDECOMBE-IN-THE MOOR DUNSTONE
B3387
Hemsworthy Gate
N
Rippon Tor 477
Haytor

Distance: 4 miles (6.5km) or 5 miles (8km) if Saddle Tor is included
Total ascent: 650ft (200m)
Paths: usually good, but occasionally vague
Terrain: rough moor
Gradients: gradual
Refreshments: usually ice cream van in car park, otherwise Widecombe-in-the-Moor
Park: car park and information centre (seasonal) on B3387 ½ mile (800m) west of Haytor Vale

Bolt Head's Wartime Secrets

From prehistoric times to the Cold War this South Devon headland has kept watch over the sea

Distance: 7 miles (11.3km)
Total ascent: 700ft (215m)
Paths: cliff and field paths, farm tracks, short stretch of metalled road; mostly good but occasionally muddy
Terrain: cliff top, open grassland
Gradients: two steep ascents on cliff path
Refreshments: Port Light Hotel, Bolberry Down (limited winter opening)
Park: Bolberry Down car park, seaward of the Port Light Hotel and reached by following signs from the A381 at Malborough

1 From the boulders at the end of the car park, follow the coast path with the sea on your right for about ½ mile (800m) to where the track drops down and then cuts back inland to the floor of a steep valley.

2 Continue down the valley and over a footbridge spanning a stream. Ascend steeply along the path right, skirting the pinnacled ridge to seaward. After a stile, descend into a small valley, cross a footbridge and ascend straight to just before the ridge. Turn inland onto the plateau of The Warren.

3 Follow the clifftop for 1 mile (1.6km) to a wall and stile. At the next wall take the right-hand stile, signed for Bolt Head. Continue up over the open top of Bolt Head, bearing right to a wall and stile.

4 Descend rightwards via a small valley to the headland with its ruined lookout.

5 Return to the stile and continue downhill with the wall on your left. Turn left over a stile (signed Soar Mill Cove) and just before the next wall turn right (signed South Sands) down to a stile.

6 Cross the stream and take the lane to a stone barn. Go through the gate, uphill for 50yds (46m) and right, through another gate, to a fingerpost. Turn left, up the valley to East Soar Farm, left through a gate, then through the farm gate to follow the farm track past the farmhouse and the nuclear bunker with its radio mast, to East Soar car park.

7 Follow the road to the white cottages, going straight on to where the Soar Mill road joins from the left. 100yds (91m) on, at Rew Cross, take the footpath which strikes left over fields to Southdown Farm.

8 Cross the road via two stiles and bear right, then left around the barn to take a path beside a bramble hedge for ¼ mile (400m) to a stile in the corner of the field. Cross this, turn left along the tree-lined Jacob's Lane for ½ mile (800m) to the road and follow this left past radio masts to the car park.

0 ½ mile ½ km

Bolt Tail
Hope Cove
HOPE
GALMPTON
coastguard lookout
SW Coast Path
Slippery Point
Bolberry Down
Portlight Hotel
BOLBERRY
N
radio masts
KINGSBRIDGE
A381
West Cliff
Lantern Rock
Southdown Farm
MALBOROUGH
Soar Mill Cove
Rew Cross
SOAR
COLLATON
REW
Steeple Cove
Lloyds Signal Station
BATSON
COMBE
The Warren
bunker
East Soar Farm
radio mast
Off Cove
caravan park
SALCOMBE
Soar Mill Cove
North Sands
South Sands
Overbecks (NT Museum & Gardens)
Kingsbridge Estuary
ferry
Starehole Bay
Bolt Head
SW Coast Path
gate and stile

Smugglers' Tales from the Helford River

Following the tracks of excise men and 'free traders' around this idyllic Cornish inlet

Distance: 7 miles (11km)
Total ascent: 900ft (275m)
Paths: can be very muddy in places, particularly in winter
Terrain: fields, farm tracks, coast path
Gradients: undulating; several steep sections
Refreshments: Shipwright's, Helford
Park: by the church in St Anthony-in-Meneage, 8 miles (12.9km) from Helston

FALMOUTH
MAWNAN SMITH
kissing gate
PORTH NAVAS
MAWNAN
DURGAN
HELFORD PASSAGE
Polgwidden Cove
Parson's Beach
Toll Point
HELFORD RIVER
Penarvon Cove
cottage
Bosahan Cove
Groyne Point
Shipwright's PH
ruins
The Gew
sailing club
ST ANTHONY
Frenchman's Creek
HELFORD
church
Dennis Head
St Anthony's Church
Kestle Cottage
Gillan Harbour
Gillan Creek
MANACCAN church
CARNE
GILLAN
N
ST MARTIN'S GREEN
ST KEVERNE
NEWTOWN
Frenchman's Creek
0 ½ mile ½ km

1 From the front of the church, facing the water, turn left up the hill, bearing right at a pebbly wall, to a lane and kissing gate. Walk to a stile where the field narrows and cross it to take the path around the headland and returning to the stile.

2 Follow the right side of the field through a kissing gate. After 3 stiles go through another kissing gate on the right, and continue along the wooded path above the estuary, past several coves, to a cottage and stables.

3 Bear right between the ruins and the cottage and then left up a track. Fork downhill at the top of the track and turn left up some steps just before a white cottage. Continue past the sailing club and a kissing gate on the right and go through another one straight ahead.

4 Turn left, then immediately right, to follow the road down through the village to a footbridge. Cross this, turn right and continue to the Shipwright's pub. Go left up the hill out of the pub car park, ignoring the path on the right to the ferry, and after l00yds (91m), turn right at a footpath sign.

5 Take the footpath to Penarvon Cove. Cross the beach and take the track left and uphill, away from the cottages. Join the road and after another l20yds (110m) turn right at a cattle grid.

6 Follow signs for Frenchman's Creek, to a stile on the left by a gateway. Cross the stile and take the path above the creek to a small car park. Turn left up the lane to the road opposite Kestle Cottage.

7 Cross into the cottage's farmyard and at the bottom take the right gate. Turn right and follow the edge of the field to a gate. Turn left through this and descend to a stile. Cross the stile, bear right and cross two streams, continuing uphill through woods, across two stiles until the path opens out into a field. Bear right diagonally uphill across the field to a stile between two trees.

8 Turn left and cross the road. After 15yds (14m), take the path on the right to some houses. Continue to the main road, turn right, then immediately left, downhill to Manaccan church.

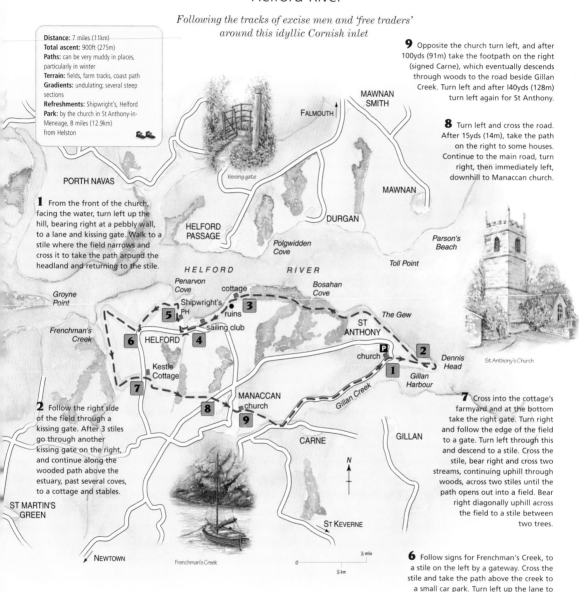

9 Opposite the church turn left, and after 100yds (91m) take the footpath on the right (signed Carne), which eventually descends through woods to the road beside Gillan Creek. Turn left and after l40yds (128m) turn left again for St Anthony.

WALK 7

Zenner and the Spectacular Coast Path

Traverse the Cornish coast's front line, defiantly facing the mighty Atlantic Ocean

Distance: 5½miles (9km)
Total ascent: 800ft (244m)
Paths: mostly good but can be very muddy, particularly between Tregerthen and Wicca
Terrain: fields, farm tracks, coast path
Gradients: steep in places on the coast path
Refreshments: Tinners Arms and Old Chapel Café, Zennor
Park: car park, Zennor, on B3306 betweeen St Ives and St Just

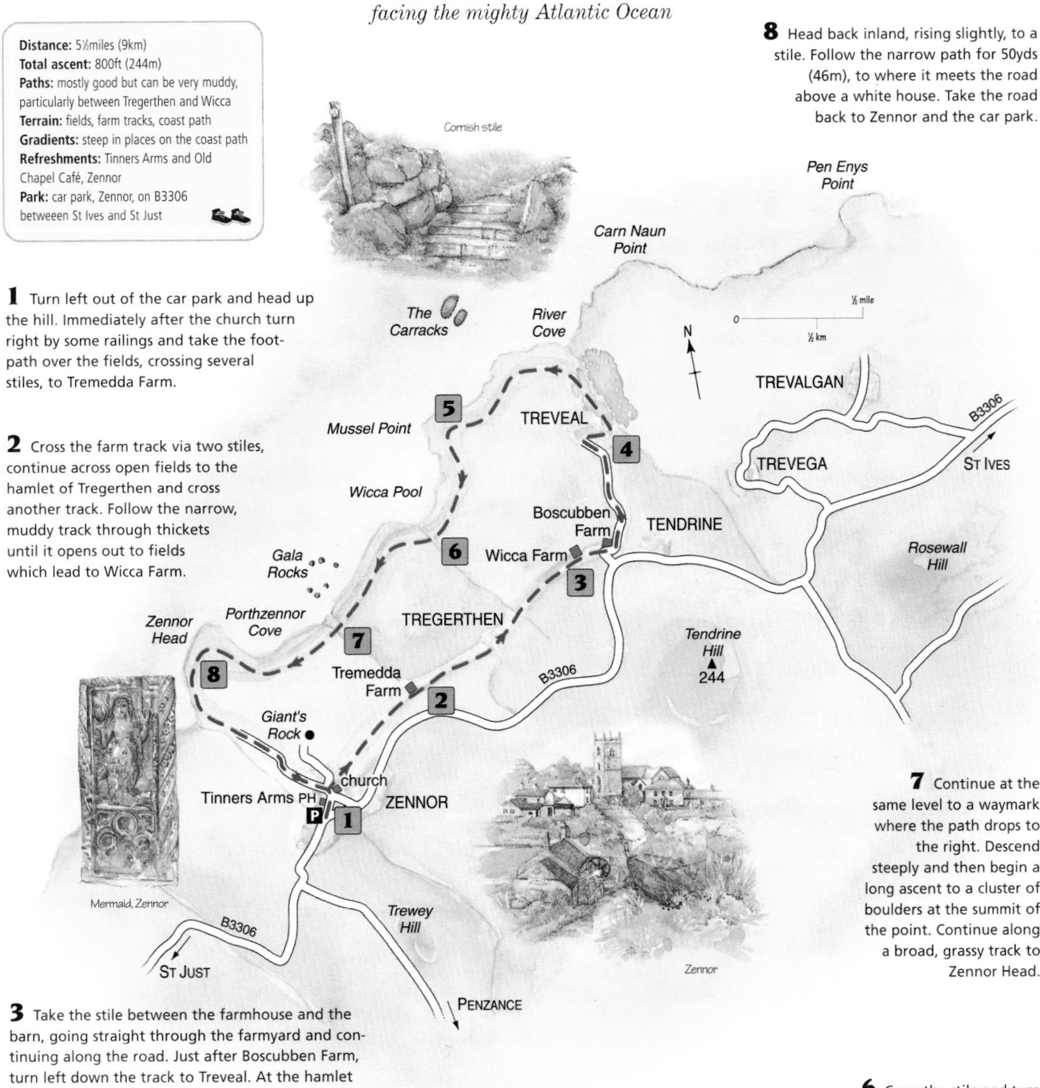

1 Turn left out of the car park and head up the hill. Immediately after the church turn right by some railings and take the foot-path over the fields, crossing several stiles, to Tremedda Farm.

2 Cross the farm track via two stiles, continue across open fields to the hamlet of Tregerthen and cross another track. Follow the narrow, muddy track through thickets until it opens out to fields which lead to Wicca Farm.

3 Take the stile between the farmhouse and the barn, going straight through the farmyard and continuing along the road. Just after Boscubben Farm, turn left down the track to Treveal. At the hamlet take the right-hand fork at the footpath sign, where the track turns back on itself and leads down to a cattle grid.

4 Take the path signed River Cove down the wooded valley to the stream, where the path starts to rise and then descends to the coast. Veer left and follow the coast path, which eventually rises steeply to some prominent rocks at the summit of Mussel Point.

5 Continue round the point and follow the path across the open, grassy hillside. After a prominent boulder on the right the path drops steeply into a small valley. Cross the stream on stepping stones to a stile.

6 Cross the stile and turn right, following the coast and descending slightly before ascending to a small point. The path then zigzags steeply down, almost to sea level. Continue along a flatter section for ½ mile (800m), then bear inland and uphill steeply, over one stream and on to another.

7 Continue at the same level to a waymark where the path drops to the right. Descend steeply and then begin a long ascent to a cluster of boulders at the summit of the point. Continue along a broad, grassy track to Zennor Head.

8 Head back inland, rising slightly, to a stile. Follow the narrow path for 50yds (46m), to where it meets the road above a white house. Take the road back to Zennor and the car park.

Hell's Mouth and the North Cornwall Coast

On the rollercoaster of headlands and clifftops around Godrevy Point

Distance: 5½ miles (8.8km)
Total ascent: 700ft (213m)
Paths: mostly good but can be muddy; short stretch of metalled road
Terrain: cliff top, open grassland
Gradients: two steep ascents on cliff path
Refreshments: café and Sand Sifters Hotel, Godrevy car park; Hell's Mouth café
Park: Godrevy National Trust car park, reached from the B3301, 2½ miles (4km) north of Hayle. Do not park adjacent to the café

1 Turn left out of the car park and walk up the road to the coast of St Ives Bay.

2 Follow the cliff-top road for ½ mile (800m), passing Godrevy Farm. St Ives is visible on the opposite side of the bay. Just before the toilets (seasonal only) on your right, bear left across open, springy turf to a stile.

3 The path now climbs around the hill over tussocky grassland to the very tip of the point and a couple of benches. The handsome little Godrevy Island with its octagonal white lighthouse lies ¼ mile (400m) offshore.

4 Continue round the cliff top, with magnificent views up the coast. On a clear day you can see the faint outline of Trevose Head, nearly 30 miles (48km) up the coast. Follow the path over some very impressive (unfenced) cliffs for ¾ mile (1.2km), to a kissing gate.

5 Take the track, rising gently, over the downland of The Knavocks to the highest point of the bleak headland and a trig point. Continue, descending slightly, through an area of gorse to two stiles.

6 Cross a field to another stile and turn left along the lane, which becomes a narrow path after 100yds (91m). Follow the path through thickets to two granite gateposts.

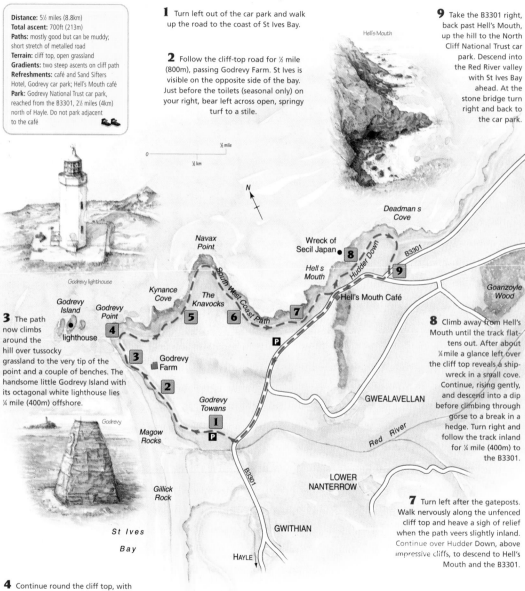

7 Turn left after the gateposts. Walk nervously along the unfenced cliff top and heave a sigh of relief when the path veers slightly inland. Continue over Hudder Down, above impressive cliffs, to descend to Hell's Mouth and the B3301.

8 Climb away from Hell's Mouth until the track flattens out. After about ¼ mile a glance left over the cliff top reveals a shipwreck in a small cove. Continue, rising gently, and descend into a dip before climbing through gorse to a break in a hedge. Turn right and follow the track inland for ¼ mile (400m) to the B3301.

9 Take the B3301 right, back past Hell's Mouth, up the hill to the North Cliff National Trust car park. Descend into the Red River valley with St Ives Bay ahead. At the stone bridge turn right and back to the car park.

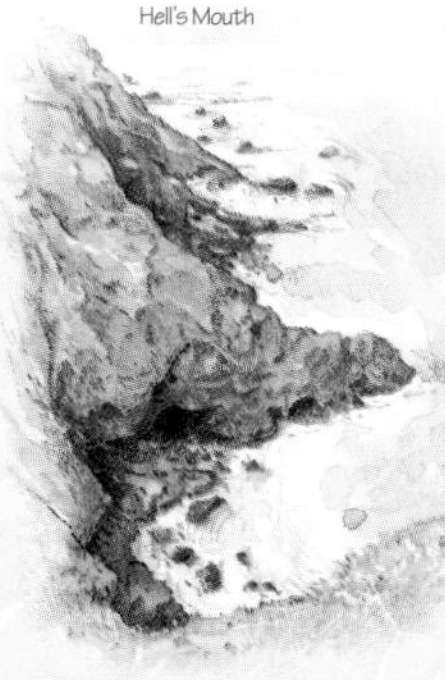

Hell's Mouth

Godrevy lighthouse

Godrevy

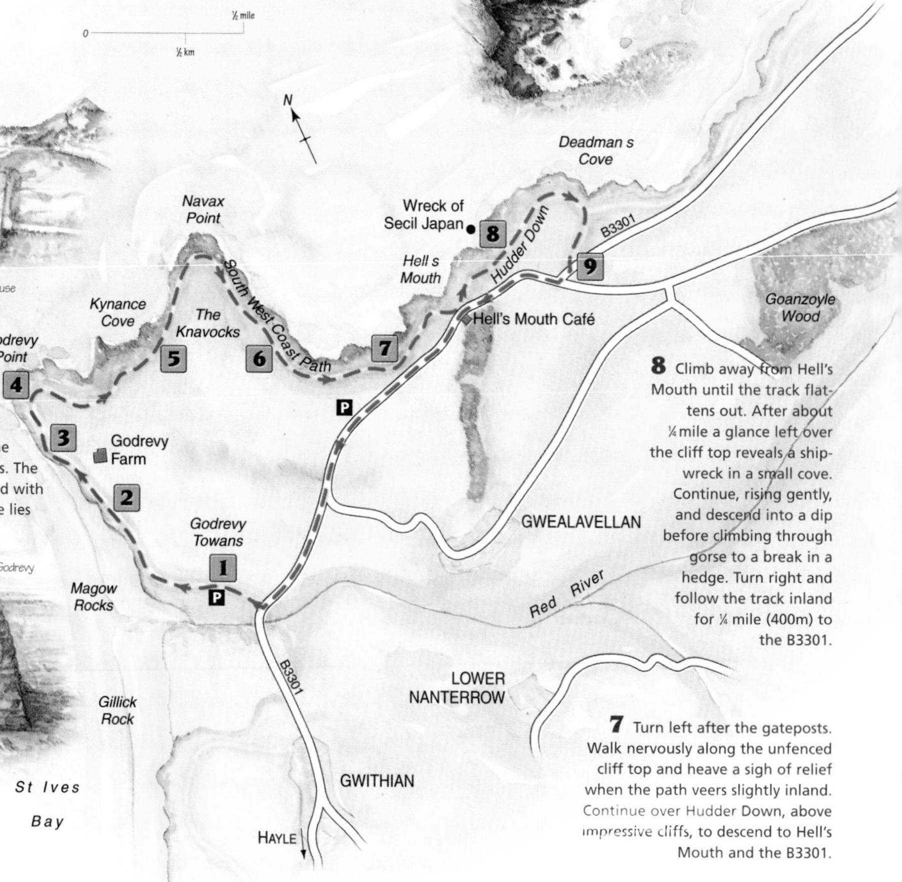

The Rocky Coast beyond Woolacombe

The North Devon coast becomes spikier as the sands give way to clifftop paths

1 From either car park turn left, following the South West Coast Path alongside the road to Mortehoe. It's possible to walk nearer to the sea in places but you must return to the road before the bend at the foot of the hill up to Mortehoe.

Rockham Bay

2 Follow the coast path signs to cut out the bend in the road and follow the road a short distance up the hill towards Mortehoe. About 300yds (273m) up the hill turn left. Follow the coast path signs for the next 3 miles (4.8km). The path keeps close to the coast all around Morte Point, down into a little valley below Mortehoe and another behind the beach at Rockham and up to Bull Point lighthouse.

Woolacombe

3 At the entrance to the lighthouse compound turn right up the tarmac drive. However, it's worth continuing on the coast path to the seat on the hillock above the lighthouse for the view along the coast to Ilfracombe and returning to the drive. The drive ascends 1 mile (1.6km) to the edge of the village at Mortehoe.

4 Pass through the signed gateway at the end of the drive and take the second footpath signposted to the left, passing through a thicket alongside a house. Take the stile into the field, carrying straight on across the middle of the field and coming out by a stile onto a bend in a tarmac drive. Keep right, going up the drive past the golf course and from the bend onto a road at the top.

5 Turn right down the road towards Mortehoe and take the first field gateway on the left. Keep straight ahead with the bank on your right and cross a stile onto a drive in a caravan site. Turn left, following the drive to a footpath by a stream. Cross the stream at the bottom and go up to the junction with a footpath. Bear right along the path and take the first turning left. Keep straight ahead between the caravans.

6 At the end of the caravan site drive, find a path descending through the trees and crossing the stream at the bottom. Ascend to the path junction and turn right and over a stile by a National Trust sign. The path descends the valley side for nearly a mile (1.6km). Just before the bottom there is a small gate at a sharp bend in the path. Take the gate and follow the road straight down to the coast road. Turn left to return to the start.

Distance: 6 miles (9.6km)
Total ascent: 650ft (200m)
Paths: generally good; grass slippery when wet
Terrain: coastal grass and heathland, fields
Gradients: gradual and fairly short
Refreshments: Woolacombe
Park: either of two car parks by beach in Woolacombe village; can be busy in summer, but there is plenty of other parking

High Moors above the River Exe

Never tamed by human industry, The Chains retain the wildness that impressed Exmoor's earliest settlers

1 From the lay-by walk along road towards Simonsbath for 350yds (319m). Turn right down drive signed to Mole's Chamber (follow blue waymarked signs all the way to Wood Barrow). Follow bridleway off the drive at point where it becomes private, and go through gate at bend after bridge. After next gate take smaller path straight ahead, keeping slightly right and following top of steep valley side, gradually descending to stream. Follow path through gate at Mole's Chamber.

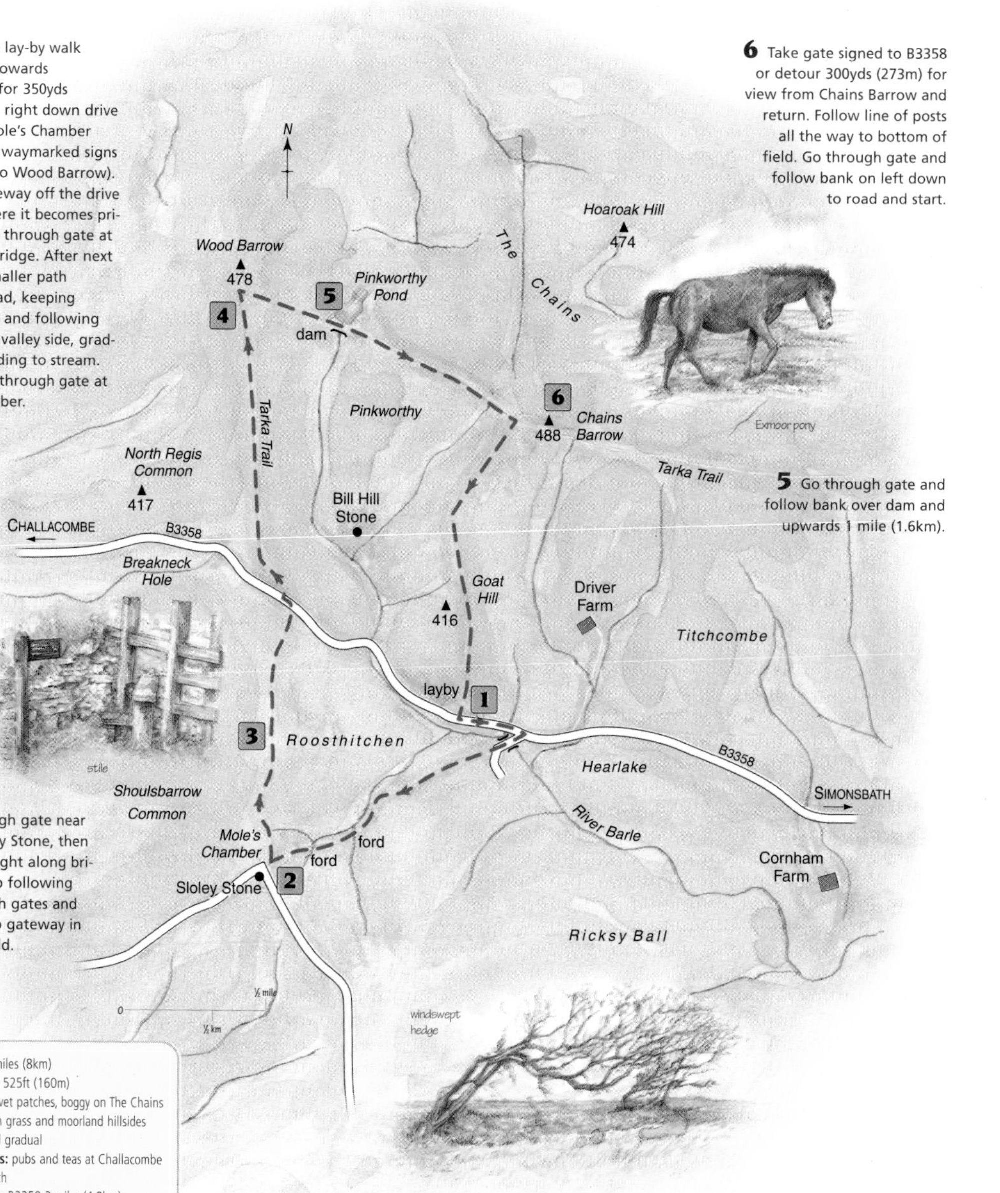

2 Go through gate near road at Sloley Stone, then sharp back right along bridleway. Keep following track through gates and over fields to gateway in corner of field.

3 Keeping fence to left, follow track signed to Wood Barrow (follow pawprint waymarks all the way to near Chains Barrow). Cross road and continue following track uphill with bank on left.

4 At barrow do not take gate but turn right and follow path signed to Pinkworthy Pond, running slightly away from bank.

5 Go through gate and follow bank over dam and upwards 1 mile (1.6km).

6 Take gate signed to B3358 or detour 300yds (273m) for view from Chains Barrow and return. Follow line of posts all the way to bottom of field. Go through gate and follow bank on left down to road and start.

Exmoor pony

stile

windswept hedge

Distance: 5 miles (8km)
Total ascent: 525ft (160m)
Paths: some wet patches, boggy on The Chains
Terrain: rough grass and moorland hillsides
Gradients: all gradual
Refreshments: pubs and teas at Challacombe and Simonsbath
Park: lay-by on B3358 3 miles (4.8km) W of Simonsbath (first lay-by after drive to Driver Farm) and 2½miles (4km) E of Challacombe (second lay-by after drive to Pinkery Farm)

WALK 11

In Search of Lorna Doone on Exmoor

R D Blackmore's heroine lived among these charming combes and peaceful moors

1 Cross the road from the car park entrance and take the bridleway along the heath, signed to Broomstreet Farm.

2 Turn right up the drive past Yenworthy Lodge. Cross the road, take the stile and follow a yellow waymarked path down to Oare. Skirt through trees around a farm at Oare House then turn left onto a road, over a bridge and up to Oare church. Turn left, then take the gate to left of churchyard, signed to Larkbarrow. Follow the blue waymarks straight up over fields, keeping the field perimeter on your right.

Distance: 9 miles (14.5km)
Total ascent: 920ft (280m)
Paths: vary from wide tracks to open moor; boggy in patches
Terrain: valley, fields, moor and heath
Gradients: mostly easy with short steep parts
Refreshments: teas at Cloud Farm and Malmsmead, cold drinks at County Gate (all seasonal)
Park: National Park car park, toilets and visitor centre at County Gate, 7miles (11.3km) west of Porlock on A39

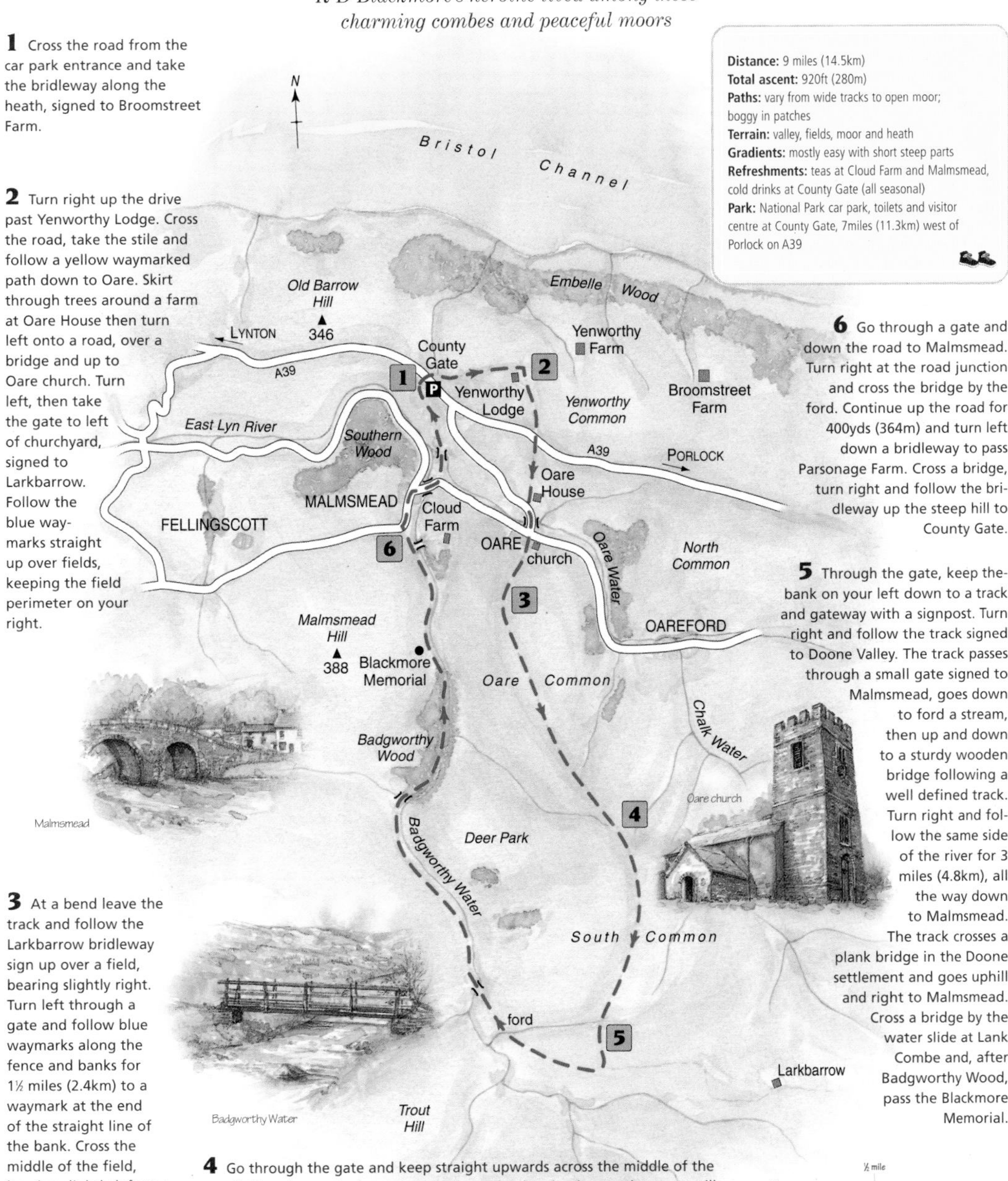

Malmsmead

Oare church

Badgworthy Water

6 Go through a gate and down the road to Malmsmead. Turn right at the road junction and cross the bridge by the ford. Continue up the road for 400yds (364m) and turn left down a bridleway to pass Parsonage Farm. Cross a bridge, turn right and follow the bridleway up the steep hill to County Gate.

5 Through the gate, keep the bank on your left down to a track and gateway with a signpost. Turn right and follow the track signed to Doone Valley. The track passes through a small gate signed to Malmsmead, goes down to ford a stream, then up and down to a sturdy wooden bridge following a well defined track. Turn right and follow the same side of the river for 3 miles (4.8km), all the way down to Malmsmead. The track crosses a plank bridge in the Doone settlement and goes uphill and right to Malmsmead. Cross a bridge by the water slide at Lank Combe and, after Badgworthy Wood, pass the Blackmore Memorial.

3 At a bend leave the track and follow the Larkbarrow bridleway sign up over a field, bearing slightly right. Turn left through a gate and follow blue waymarks along the fence and banks for 1½ miles (2.4km) to a waymark at the end of the straight line of the bank. Cross the middle of the field, bearing slightly left to a gate in the fence.

4 Go through the gate and keep straight upwards across the middle of the next field and over the top to a gate through a low bank onto the moor, still following Larkbarrow bridleway signs. Cross the moor straight ahead and bearing slightly left. Keep straight on and do not be misled by numerous tracks. In ½ mile (800m) you should have rounded the head of a small combe and come to a gate in a bank with a bridleway sign.

WALK 12

Spectacular Views from the Quantock Hills

Last of the southwest moorlands, the Quantocks boast fine views over Somerset and the Bristol Channel

Distance: 7 miles (11.3km)
Total ascent: 820ft (250m)
Paths: mostly good but muddy after rain; shallow stream to ford in Holford Combe
Terrain: mostly open heath or wooded valley
Gradients: gradual, but one short, steep downhill section
Refreshments: Plough Inn, Holford, and teas in village in season
Park: car park in old quarry by bowling green at Holford, on minor road between Holford village and Alfoxton Park

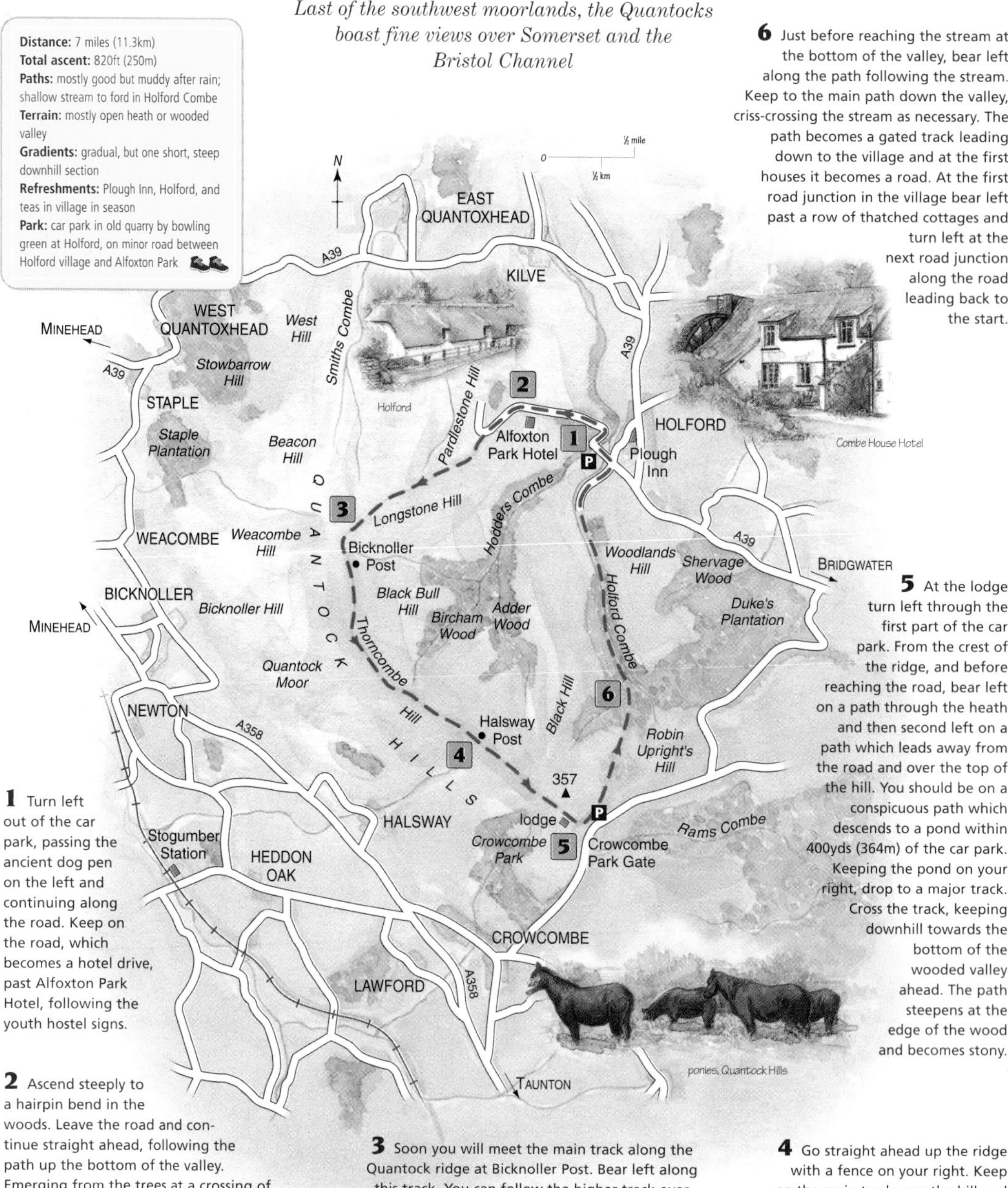

Holford

Combe House Hotel

ponies, Quantock Hills

1 Turn left out of the car park, passing the ancient dog pen on the left and continuing along the road. Keep on the road, which becomes a hotel drive, past Alfoxton Park Hotel, following the youth hostel signs.

2 Ascend steeply to a hairpin bend in the woods. Leave the road and continue straight ahead, following the path up the bottom of the valley. Emerging from the trees at a crossing of tracks on the heath, keep straight ahead, bearing slightly right and gradually uphill, following the sign for West Quantoxhead. Keep uphill on the main track. At the top of the hill turn left, descending slightly.

3 Soon you will meet the main track along the Quantock ridge at Bicknoller Post. Bear left along this track. You can follow the higher track over Thorncombe Hill or the lower one along the left-hand side of it, but continue ahead along the ridge. Keep slightly to the left along the top of the hill to join the main track, which drops to a tall post and crossing of tracks at Halsway Post.

4 Go straight ahead up the ridge with a fence on your right. Keep on the main track over the hill and down to a dip in the ridge and lodge at Crowcombe Park Gate.

5 At the lodge turn left through the first part of the car park. From the crest of the ridge, and before reaching the road, bear left on a path through the heath and then second left on a path which leads away from the road and over the top of the hill. You should be on a conspicuous path which descends to a pond within 400yds (364m) of the car park. Keeping the pond on your right, drop to a major track. Cross the track, keeping downhill towards the bottom of the wooded valley ahead. The path steepens at the edge of the wood and becomes stony.

6 Just before reaching the stream at the bottom of the valley, bear left along the path following the stream. Keep to the main path down the valley, criss-crossing the stream as necessary. The path becomes a gated track leading down to the village and at the first houses it becomes a road. At the first road junction in the village bear left past a row of thatched cottages and turn left at the next road junction along the road leading back to the start.

The Other Sides to Cheddar Gorge

A fine circuit of nature proves there is more to Cheddar than cheese and tourists

1 From car park turn right towards the Gorge. Cross the bridge and take the next road on the right, keeping uphill. Just before the brow of the hill turn left up behind cottages. At the end of the lane follow the bridleway up to the left. Keep following the Gorge Walk waymarks along the edge of the gorge for 1¼ miles (2km). The path ascends to the top of a ridge and descends through woodland to the road at the head of the Gorge.

2 Cross the road and take the gate and track ahead into Black Rock reserve. Follow the main track up the bottom of the valley for ⅔ mile (1km). After the National Trust sign turn right over a wall and follow the waymarks up the bottom of the valley for another mile (1.6km).

6 Cross a stile from fields into a scrubby area. Bear left, then right, to pick up the Gorge Walk waymarks. Keep dowhill with the Gorge on your left. It is worth the detour down a steep flight of steps to a viewpoint. Returning, the path steepens to descend through woods to a track. Turn left down the track, then right and down the road through the Gorge to return to the start.

5 Turn right along the road and take the next turn to the left, down a farm drive. Keep right of Charterhouse and Piney Sleight Farms, then follow the yellow waymarks ahead across fields, keeping close to the walls on your right.

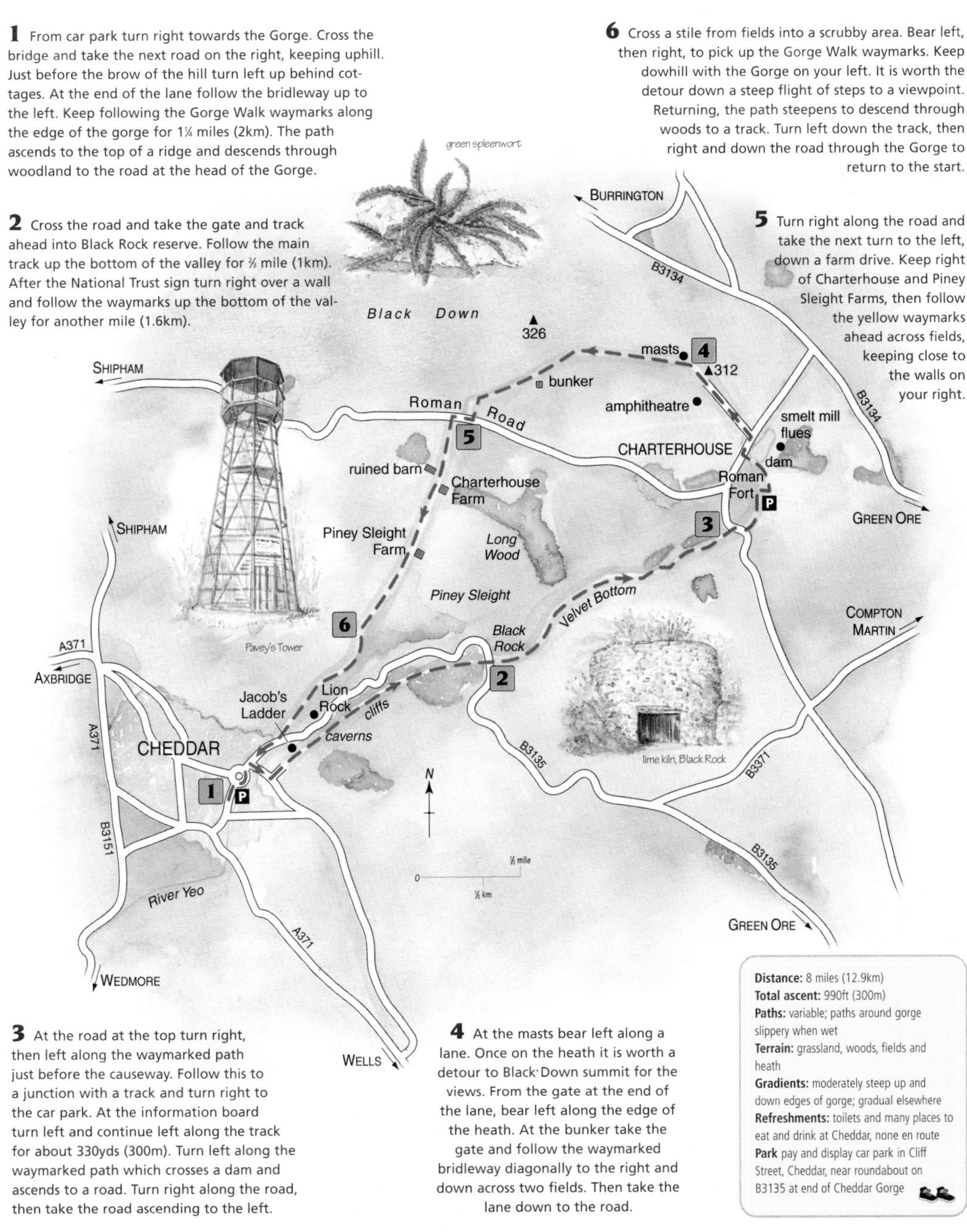

3 At the road at the top turn right, then left along the waymarked path just before the causeway. Follow this to a junction with a track and turn right to the car park. At the information board turn left and continue left along the track for about 330yds (300m). Turn left along the waymarked path which crosses a dam and ascends to a road. Turn right along the road, then take the road ascending to the left.

4 At the masts bear left along a lane. Once on the heath it is worth a detour to Black Down summit for the views. From the gate at the end of the lane, bear left along the edge of the heath. At the bunker take the gate and follow the waymarked bridleway diagonally to the right and down across two fields. Then take the lane down to the road.

Distance: 8 miles (12.9km)
Total ascent: 990ft (300m)
Paths: variable; paths around gorge slippery when wet
Terrain: grassland, woods, fields and heath
Gradients: moderately steep up and down edges of gorge; gradual elsewhere
Refreshments: toilets and many places to eat and drink at Cheddar, none en route
Park pay and display car park in Cliff Street, Cheddar, near roundabout on B3135 at end of Cheddar Gorge

WALK 14

Lansdown – a Civil War Battle for Bath

Where Sir Beville Grenville led his Cornishmen in a heroic charge

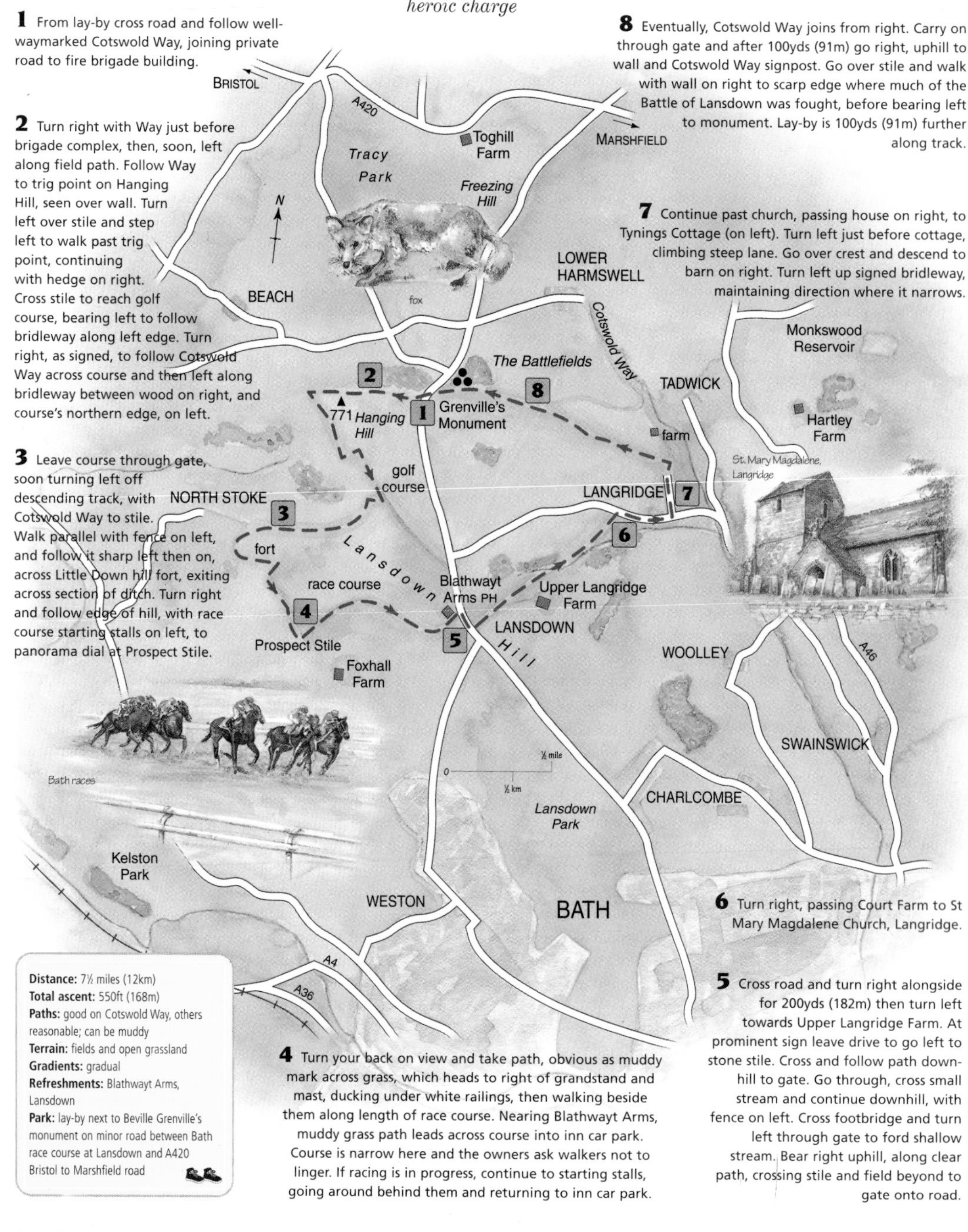

1 From lay-by cross road and follow well-waymarked Cotswold Way, joining private road to fire brigade building.

2 Turn right with Way just before brigade complex, then, soon, left along field path. Follow Way to trig point on Hanging Hill, seen over wall. Turn left over stile and step left to walk past trig point, continuing with hedge on right. Cross stile to reach golf course, bearing left to follow bridleway along left edge. Turn right, as signed, to follow Cotswold Way across course and then left along bridleway between wood on right, and course's northern edge, on left.

3 Leave course through gate, soon turning left off descending track, with Cotswold Way to stile. Walk parallel with fence on left, and follow it sharp left then on, across Little Down hill fort, exiting across section of ditch. Turn right and follow edge of hill, with race course starting stalls on left, to panorama dial at Prospect Stile.

4 Turn your back on view and take path, obvious as muddy mark across grass, which heads to right of grandstand and mast, ducking under white railings, then walking beside them along length of race course. Nearing Blathwayt Arms, muddy grass path leads across course into inn car park. Course is narrow here and the owners ask walkers not to linger. If racing is in progress, continue to starting stalls, going around behind them and returning to inn car park.

5 Cross road and turn right alongside for 200yds (182m) then turn left towards Upper Langridge Farm. At prominent sign leave drive to go left to stone stile. Cross and follow path downhill to gate. Go through, cross small stream and continue downhill, with fence on left. Cross footbridge and turn left through gate to ford shallow stream. Bear right uphill, along clear path, crossing stile and field beyond to gate onto road.

6 Turn right, passing Court Farm to St Mary Magdalene Church, Langridge.

7 Continue past church, passing house on right, to Tynings Cottage (on left). Turn left just before cottage, climbing steep lane. Go over crest and descend to barn on right. Turn left up signed bridleway, maintaining direction where it narrows.

8 Eventually, Cotswold Way joins from right. Carry on through gate and after 100yds (91m) go right, uphill to wall and Cotswold Way signpost. Go over stile and walk with wall on right to scarp edge where much of the Battle of Lansdown was fought, before bearing left to monument. Lay-by is 100yds (91m) further along track.

Distance: 7½ miles (12km)
Total ascent: 550ft (168m)
Paths: good on Cotswold Way, others reasonable; can be muddy
Terrain: fields and open grassland
Gradients: gradual
Refreshments: Blathwayt Arms, Lansdown
Park: lay-by next to Beville Grenville's monument on minor road between Bath race course at Lansdown and A420 Bristol to Marshfield road

Frome's Medieval Highlights

Discover the faded charm and surprising medieval wealth of this once great Somerset town

Distance: 4½ miles (7.2km)
Total ascent: 200ft (61m)
Paths: town streets and good paths
Terrain: town streets and fields
Gradients: gradual, though the ascent of Gentle Street belies its name
Refreshments: numerous opportunities in Frome
Park: car park beside the tourist information centre

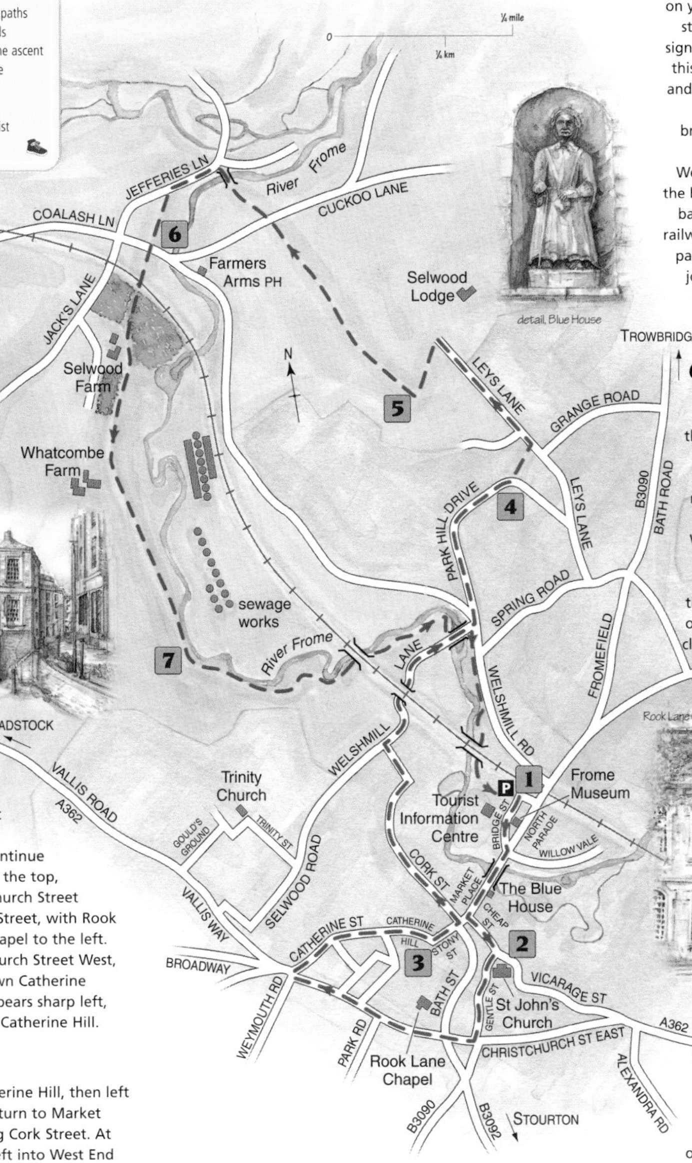

1 From the courtyard of the tourist information centre, turn right, then right again, to the main street into town. To the left is the town museum. Turn right over the bridge, looking left to see the Blue House. Continue along Market Place, then turn left up Cheap Street.

Catherine Hill

2 At the top of the street turn right and go up the steps; left is the Via Crucis by the churchyard entrance. Continue up Gentle Street and, at the top, turn right along Christchurch Street West. First right is Bath Street, with Rook Lane Congregational Chapel to the left. Continue along Christchurch Street West, turning fourth right down Catherine Street. Where the road bears sharp left, continue down cobbled Catherine Hill.

3 Bear right with Catherine Hill, then left down Stony Street to return to Market Place and turn left along Cork Street. At the Coach House bear left into West End (unsigned). Turn right along Welshmill Lane. Bear left to go under the railway bridge and continue along Welshmill Lane, crossing the River Frome. Cross into Park Hill Drive, following it around to the right.

4 Take a footpath on the left, between Numbers 39 and 41, maintaining direction along Packsaddle Way for a few steps before turning left into Leys Lane. Continue to reach a gate for Selwood Lodge. Follow the drive beyond, but where it bears right, go left over a stile and follow the hedge on the right.

5 Go over a stile and follow the signed path over a stone stile and onto a road. Cross the stile opposite and head for a metal bridge. Cross this, reaching a lane soon after. Turn left for 100yds (91m) then turn left along a signed path across a field to a road.

6 Cross the road and the stile opposite. Cross the railway with care, go through a kissing gate and follow a path through a small copse to reach a metal stile. Cross and continue, with elegant Whatcombe Farm on your right. Go through a V-shaped stile and head for the pylon; Trinity Church is on the horizon. Follow the clear path with the sewage works on your left.

Rook Lane Chapel

7 Go through another stile and continue with the river on your left, crossing another stile. Continue to reach the signed Riverside Walk. Follow this to reach a concrete road and a metal bridge. Cross the road and go under the bridge, following a sign for the town centre to reach Welshmill Bridge. Now cross the bridge and follow the left bank of the river, under the railway bridge back to the car park or reverse the outward journey to Cork Street and turn left at Market Place.

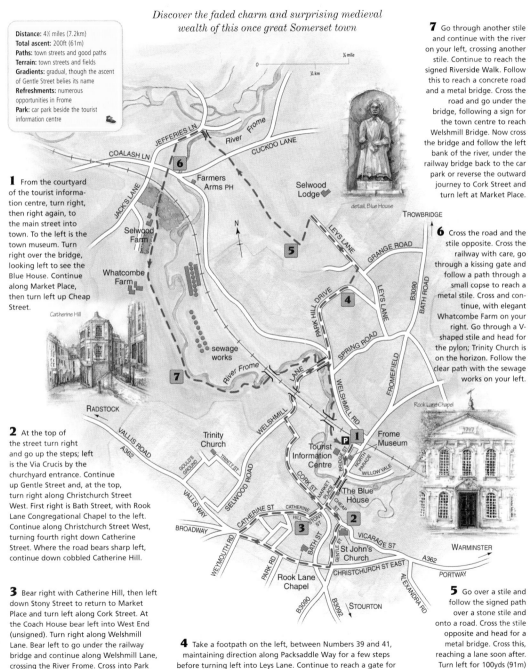

detail, Blue House

Old Ways on the Wiltshire Downs

Prehistoric pathways, Saxon defences and a Georgian canal towpath span this quiet corner of Wiltshire

Distance: 8 miles (12.9km)
Total ascent: 519ft (158m)
Paths: mainly good; lower paths and towpath can be very wet
Terrain: downland, linear earthwork, gentle farmland, canal towpath
Gradients: one lengthy climb, though not steep
Refreshments: Kings Arms, All Cannings; Barge Inn, Honey Street
Park: on roadside by Alton Barnes church, in Vale of Pewsey between Devizes and Marlborough

1 From Alton Barnes church, go through the turnstile to follow the paved path towards Alton Priors church. Keep left of the tower, go through a kissing gate and turnstile and follow the road between houses. Cross over at the next road junction, follow the Ridgeway up to the next road and turn right. Turn left through a gate into Pewsey Downs National Nature Reserve, up the grassy track parallel to the road. Approaching a fence, bear left up to the summit of Walker's Hill.

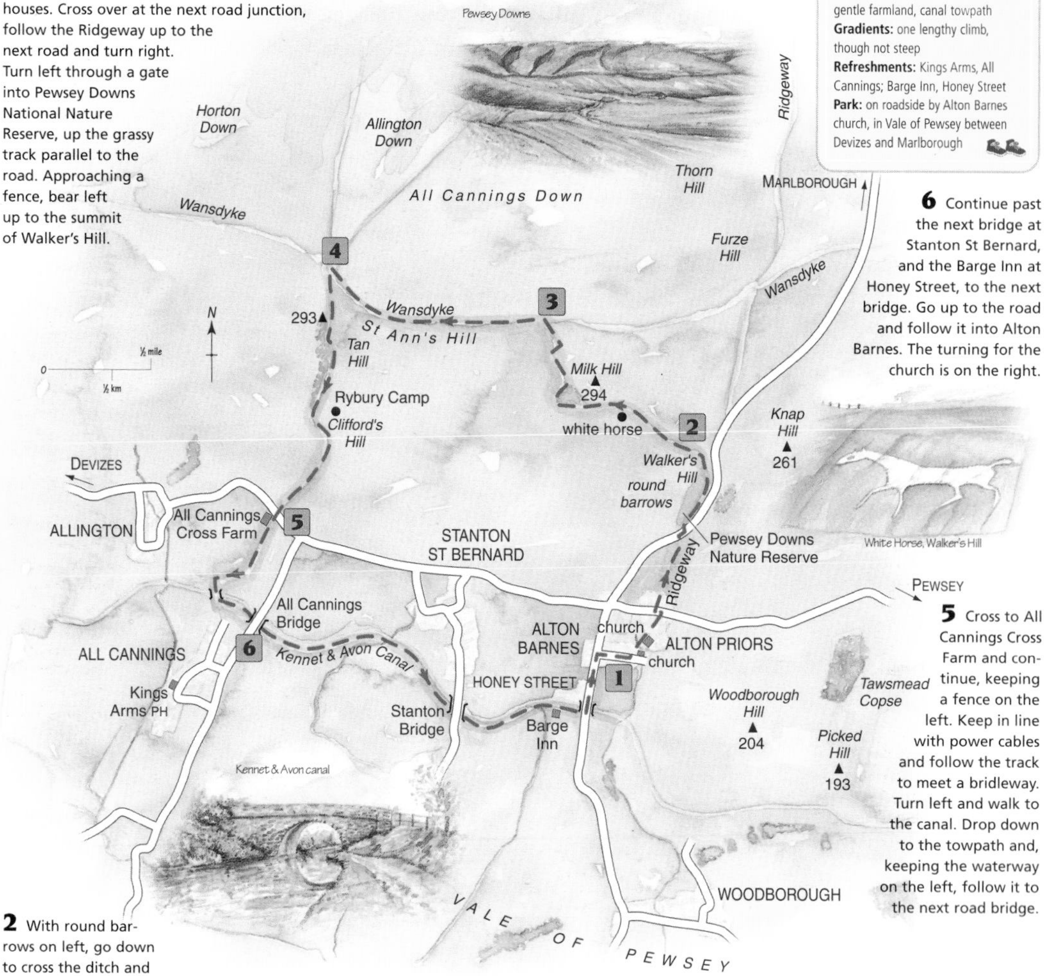

Pewsey Downs

White Horse, Walker's Hill

Kennet & Avon canal

2 With round barrows on left, go down to cross the ditch and follow the path towards the White Horse. Continue above the chalk carving, through a gate and on to a fence on the right. Follow the fence, making for a gate round the far side of the woodland. Follow the track across open downland to a gate. Continue ahead with a fence on the right to the next gate. Go through it and, with a fence on the right, drop down the field to a gate and stile.

3 Turn left and follow the track down to the Wansdyke at the foot of the hill. Keep the ditch on the right and follow the linear earthwork in a westerly direction for about 1½ miles (2.4km).

4 At a fence by a gate and bridleway sign turn left, with the fence on the right and head south over Tan Hill. At the summit make for a stile in the field corner. Head down to the next stile and gate, then turn left and drop down to the field corner. Cross a stile and turn immediately right. Keep the fence on your right and follow the path to the next gate and stile. Don't cross it, but turn left and follow the path along the foot of the escarpment. Turn right at the fence corner and follow the path to a stile in the right-hand boundary; step over and join a path south through trees. Follow it to a grassy track running to the road.

5 Cross to All Cannings Cross Farm and continue, keeping a fence on the left. Keep in line with power cables and follow the track to meet a bridleway. Turn left and walk to the canal. Drop down to the towpath and, keeping the waterway on the left, follow it to the next road bridge.

6 Continue past the next bridge at Stanton St Bernard, and the Barge Inn at Honey Street, to the next bridge. Go up to the road and follow it into Alton Barnes. The turning for the church is on the right.

Uley Bury and Hetty Pegler's Tump

Strange earthworks abound on this walk through the Cotswold fringe

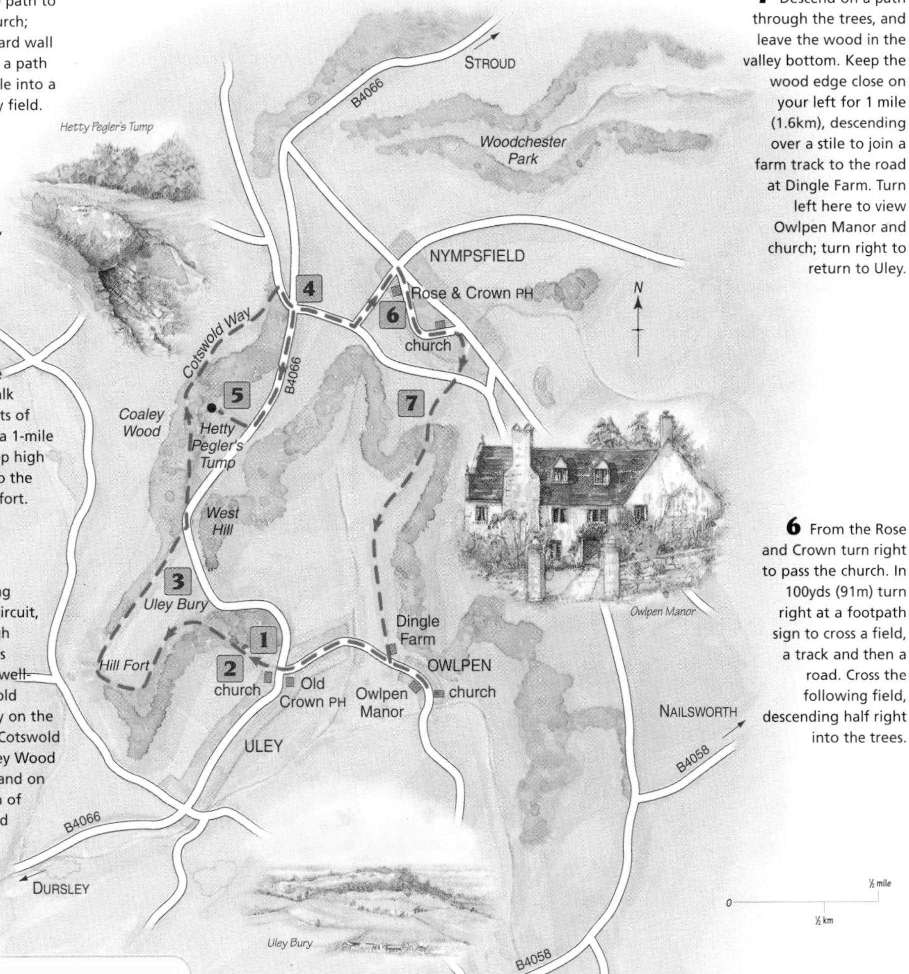

1 In Uley take the path to the right of the church; before the churchyard wall ends, bear right up a path which leads to a stile into a steeply rising grassy field.

2 Climb the slope, aiming diagonally left, up to a gate into the woods. Follow the path up through the woods to another stile. Cross the gate and bear left to walk around the ramparts of Uley Bury hill fort, a 1-mile (1.6km) circuit. Keep high up when you get to the second side of the fort.

3 After completing three sides of the circuit, keep ahead through the trees for 200yds (182m) to join the well-waymarked Cotswold Way below a lay-by on the B4066. Follow the Cotswold Way through Coaley Wood for 1 mile (1.6km) and on reaching a junction of path, bridleway and road end, take a sharp right, ascending to meet the B4066.

4 Turn right along the grass verge of the road. In ⅓ mile (535m), turn right off the road on a signposted track to Hetty Pegler's Tump, a green grassy mound lying by the edge of the wood.

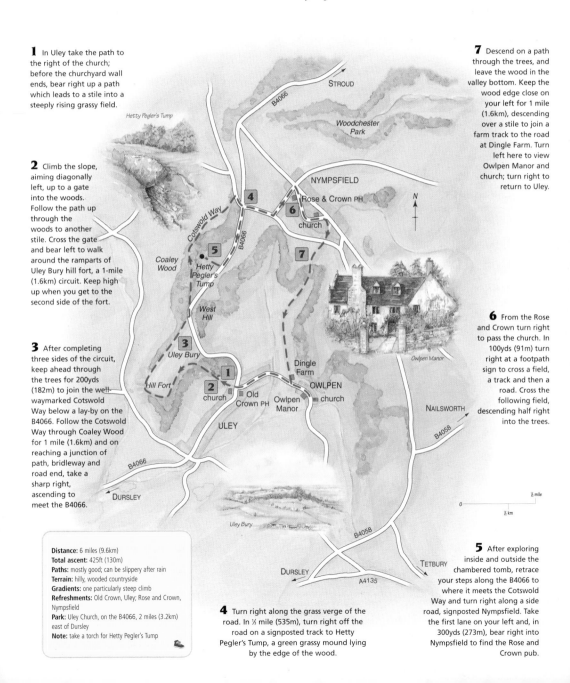

5 After exploring inside and outside the chambered tomb, retrace your steps along the B4066 to where it meets the Cotswold Way and turn right along a side road, signposted Nympsfield. Take the first lane on your left and, in 300yds (273m), bear right into Nympsfield to find the Rose and Crown pub.

6 From the Rose and Crown turn right to pass the church. In 100yds (91m) turn right at a footpath sign to cross a field, a track and then a road. Cross the following field, descending half right into the trees.

7 Descend on a path through the trees, and leave the wood in the valley bottom. Keep the wood edge close on your left for 1 mile (1.6km), descending over a stile to join a farm track to the road at Dingle Farm. Turn left here to view Owlpen Manor and church; turn right to return to Uley.

Distance: 6 miles (9.6km)
Total ascent: 425ft (130m)
Paths: mostly good; can be slippery after rain
Terrain: hilly, wooded countryside
Gradients: one particularly steep climb
Refreshments: Old Crown, Uley; Rose and Crown, Nympsfield
Park: Uley Church, on the B4066, 2 miles (3.2km) east of Dursley
Note: take a torch for Hetty Pegler's Tump

Birdlip and the Cotswolds

A walk through woodland and farmland shows the Cotswold escarpment at its best

Distance: 7½ miles (12km)
Total ascent: 400 ft (120m)
Paths: Waymarked section of the Cotswold Way on good paths, together with reasonable field paths
Terrain: fields and open grassland
Gradients: gradual
Refreshments: The Air Balloon Inn
Park: Barrow Wake viewpoint car park on A417 near the Air Balloon Inn

1 From the panorama board and memorial in the car park bear left along the Cotswold Way to a stile into beech woodland. There is a fine view to the right, but it is even better if the short detour is taken to The Peak. From here return to the Cotswold Way and follow it through the wood. After passing a high bank on the left a distinct path goes off left.

2 Turn left, bearing left at a fork to a gate. Follow the wall on the right across the field beyond to reach a road (the B4070). Cross the road, footbridge and waymarked stile and cross the field beyond to another stile (don't cross). Turn left along field edge to a stile on to the A417.

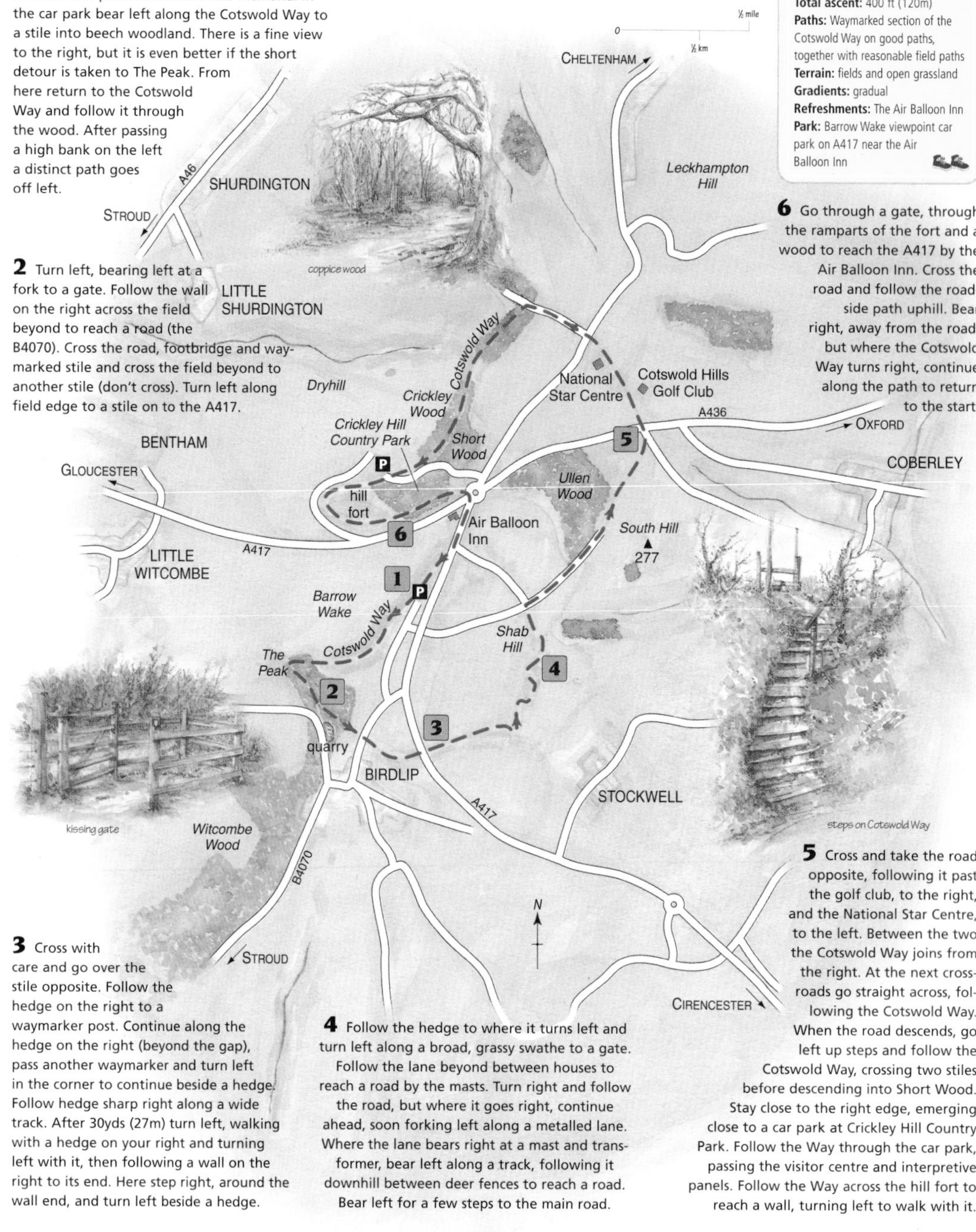

3 Cross with care and go over the stile opposite. Follow the hedge on the right to a waymarker post. Continue along the hedge on the right (beyond the gap), pass another waymarker and turn left in the corner to continue beside a hedge. Follow hedge sharp right along a wide track. After 30yds (27m) turn left, walking with a hedge on your right and turning left with it, then following a wall on the right to its end. Here step right, around the wall end, and turn left beside a hedge.

4 Follow the hedge to where it turns left and turn left along a broad, grassy swathe to a gate. Follow the lane beyond between houses to reach a road by the masts. Turn right and follow the road, but where it goes right, continue ahead, soon forking left along a metalled lane. Where the lane bears right at a mast and transformer, bear left along a track, following it downhill between deer fences to reach a road. Bear left for a few steps to the main road.

5 Cross and take the road opposite, following it past the golf club, to the right, and the National Star Centre, to the left. Between the two the Cotswold Way joins from the right. At the next crossroads go straight across, following the Cotswold Way. When the road descends, go left up steps and follow the Cotswold Way, crossing two stiles before descending into Short Wood. Stay close to the right edge, emerging close to a car park at Crickley Hill Country Park. Follow the Way through the car park, passing the visitor centre and interpretive panels. Follow the Way across the hill fort to reach a wall, turning left to walk with it.

6 Go through a gate, through the ramparts of the fort and a wood to reach the A417 by the Air Balloon Inn. Cross the road and follow the roadside path uphill. Bear right, away from the road, but where the Cotswold Way turns right, continue along the path to return to the start.

Turmoil at Tewkesbury

A walk across the Bloody Meadow from Tewkesbury recalls its bitter role in the Wars of the Roses

1 From the Abbey Lawns car park go through the gate, along the north of the abbey and leave by the main gateway, turning left. Pass the long-stay car park then turn right along Lower Lode Lane. Go left at the Battle Trail sign (crossed swords).

2 Go over a stile to the right and follow the hedge to a plinth commemorating the battle. Turn right along the lane, through the golf club gates and along the drive, veering left along the signed footpath, and following further waymarks to reach a stile.

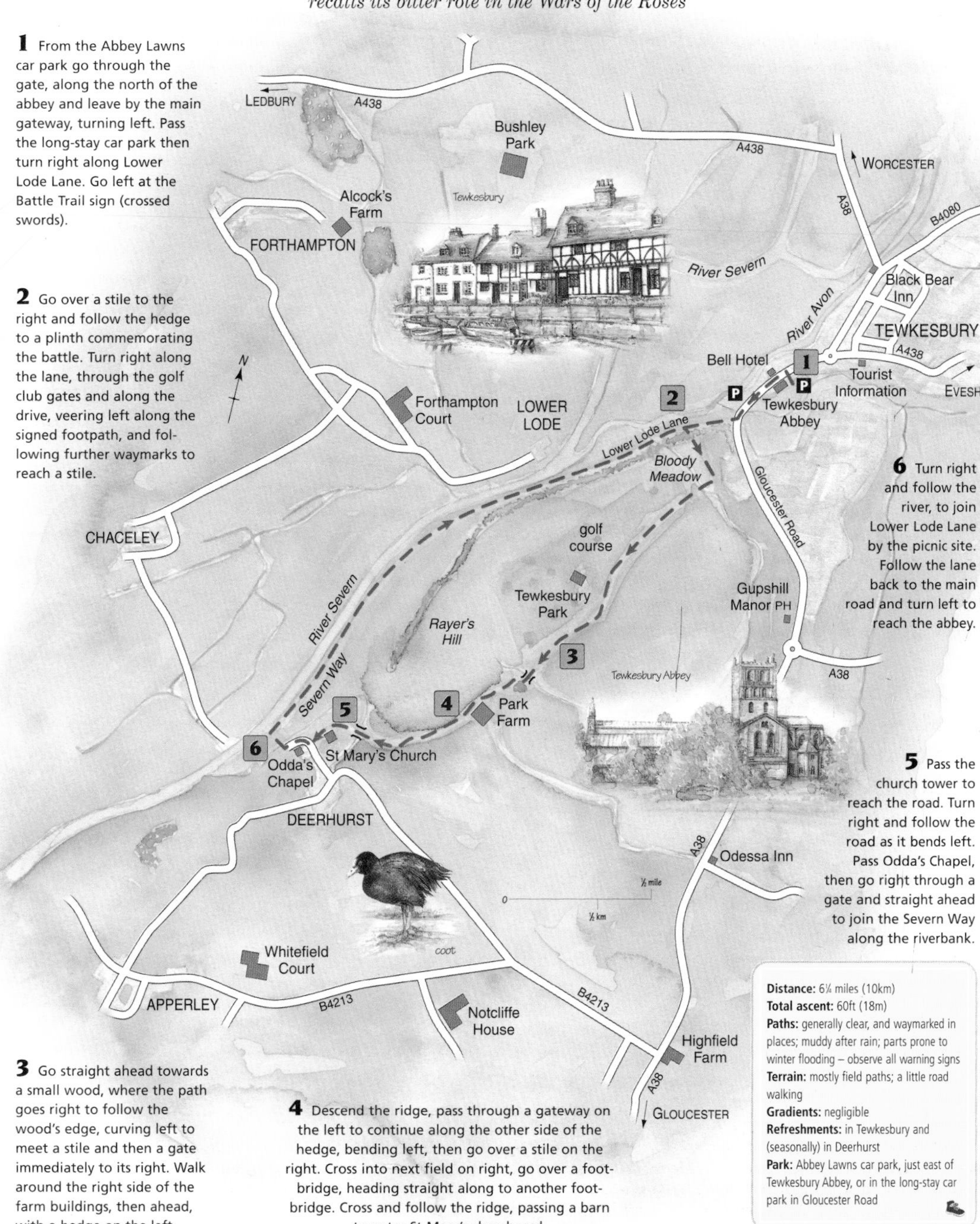

3 Go straight ahead towards a small wood, where the path goes right to follow the wood's edge, curving left to meet a stile and then a gate immediately to its right. Walk around the right side of the farm buildings, then ahead, with a hedge on the left.

4 Descend the ridge, pass through a gateway on the left to continue along the other side of the hedge, bending left, then go over a stile on the right. Cross into next field on right, go over a footbridge, heading straight along to another footbridge. Cross and follow the ridge, passing a barn to enter St Mary's churchyard.

5 Pass the church tower to reach the road. Turn right and follow the road as it bends left. Pass Odda's Chapel, then go right through a gate and straight ahead to join the Severn Way along the riverbank.

6 Turn right and follow the river, to join Lower Lode Lane by the picnic site. Follow the lane back to the main road and turn left to reach the abbey.

Distance: 6¼ miles (10km)
Total ascent: 60ft (18m)
Paths: generally clear, and waymarked in places; muddy after rain; parts prone to winter flooding – observe all warning signs
Terrain: mostly field paths; a little road walking
Gradients: negligible
Refreshments: in Tewkesbury and (seasonally) in Deerhurst
Park: Abbey Lawns car park, just east of Tewkesbury Abbey, or in the long-stay car park in Gloucester Road

Southeast England

There is an air of busy industriousness in the southeast of England. Road and rail routes hum with activity, and even the sky is seldom free from aircraft. All the conurbations, and especially London, are in a constant state of motion. Amid the hustle and bustle there are green oases of peace and calm to discover, an immensely long and complex history to unravel, ancient ways to travel, mysteries to ponder – and the best way to see it all is on foot. It's a gentle, rolling landscape with no towering heights, essentially agricultural but well wooded in places, threaded by a fine assortment of paths and tracks. As you tread in the footsteps of packmen and pilgrims, warriors and wayfarers, you glimpse a landscape that has altered little, despite centuries of change.

The white cliffs of Dover, the Seven Sisters and other chalk cliffs form England's southern bulwark. The eastern coast is altogether gentler and lower-lying, often crumbling into the sea. Sand and shingle are constantly on the move, and the region is rich in maritime history.

Between the Thames and the English Channel the landscape rises and falls according to the underlying geology, forming ridges such as the North Downs, Weald and South Downs. Away from the high downs you could enjoy a tour of little towns and villages. By the time you reach the ancient royal capital of Winchester you are in Hampshire and within easy reach of the bountiful walking opportunities of the New Forest.

North of the Thames and London the only high ground is formed by the chalk escarpment of the Chilterns, famous for their well-established beech woods. You can traverse a stretch of the ancient Icknield Way along their foot or climb to Ivinghoe Beacon, Combe Hill or other notable heights to enjoy the view.

It's possible to drive across Suffolk and Norfolk and be aware only of the vast prairie-like fields, but take a walk through the landscape and you will be astounded by its variety and complexity. The ancient underground warren of Grime's Graves and the lingering remains of huge, isolated airfields are just two intriguing stories waiting to be told.

Best of the Rest

Dover During World War II the white cliffs of Dover came to symbolise the free world, beyond the yoke of Nazi occupation. This is a fascinating landscape, deeply pitted with the scars of its strategic importance. A walk out on the high cliffs is the perfect foil to an exploration of this historic town, and of the defences dubbed 'Hellfire Corner' for their proximity to German guns across the Channel.

Beacon Hill North Hampshire's landscape of gently rolling hills and crystal clear rivers tops out in a fine ridge of downland, mirroring the Ridgeway on the opposite side of the Kennet Valley. At Beacon Hill, above Highclere near Newbury, the views become far reaching and spectacular. The strategic vantage point was not lost on the local Iron Age population, who built a mighty hill fort here.

Thames Path From the Thames Barrier to its Cotswold source, the Thames Path follows England's greatest river. Around Kew and Richmond, London's more opulent suburbs show their back-garden style and hundreds of pleasure craft line the banks.

Essex marshes This small corner of Essex from Burnham to Bradwell-on-Sea is closer in spirit to the deserted shores of Suffolk than the brashness of Southend-on-Sea. Bradwell has an intriguing history – an ancient barn near by has been found to be a Saxon church, part of what must have been impressive fortifications built on the edge of the sea.

Norfolk Coast Lashed by the North Sea and prey to ungovernable tides, the Norfolk coastline seems wilder and more remote than most – and a birdwatcher's paradise. The perfect way to explore it is on the Norfolk Coast Path, from Hunstanton to Cromer, which threads its way through dunes and salt-marshes, and takes in stately Holkham.

Suffolk Coast Cut off from the rest of the country by the road and rail lines running 5 miles (8km) inland, this is one of the most isolated and unspoilt stretches of coast in the country. The variety of habitats means that you can see a great diversity of wildlife, and seaside towns like Southwold and Aldeburgh are good start and end points for walks.

Epping Forest The 6,000 surviving acres of this once mighty forest make a great day out for the family, only a Tube ride away from central London. Pick up a hiking leaflet at the visitors' centre and choose a walk through stands of ancient pollarded oak, beech and hornbeam, or picnic on a grassy heath.

Constable's Suffolk Landscapes

From 'Dedham Vale' to 'The Haywain', the Suffolk countryside was a constant theme in the artist's work

1 Turn left out of the car park and up to T-junction. The church and old grammar school are opposite. Turn left and where the road bends sharp right, take the path signed Flatford, diagonally to the left. Keep right at the farm.

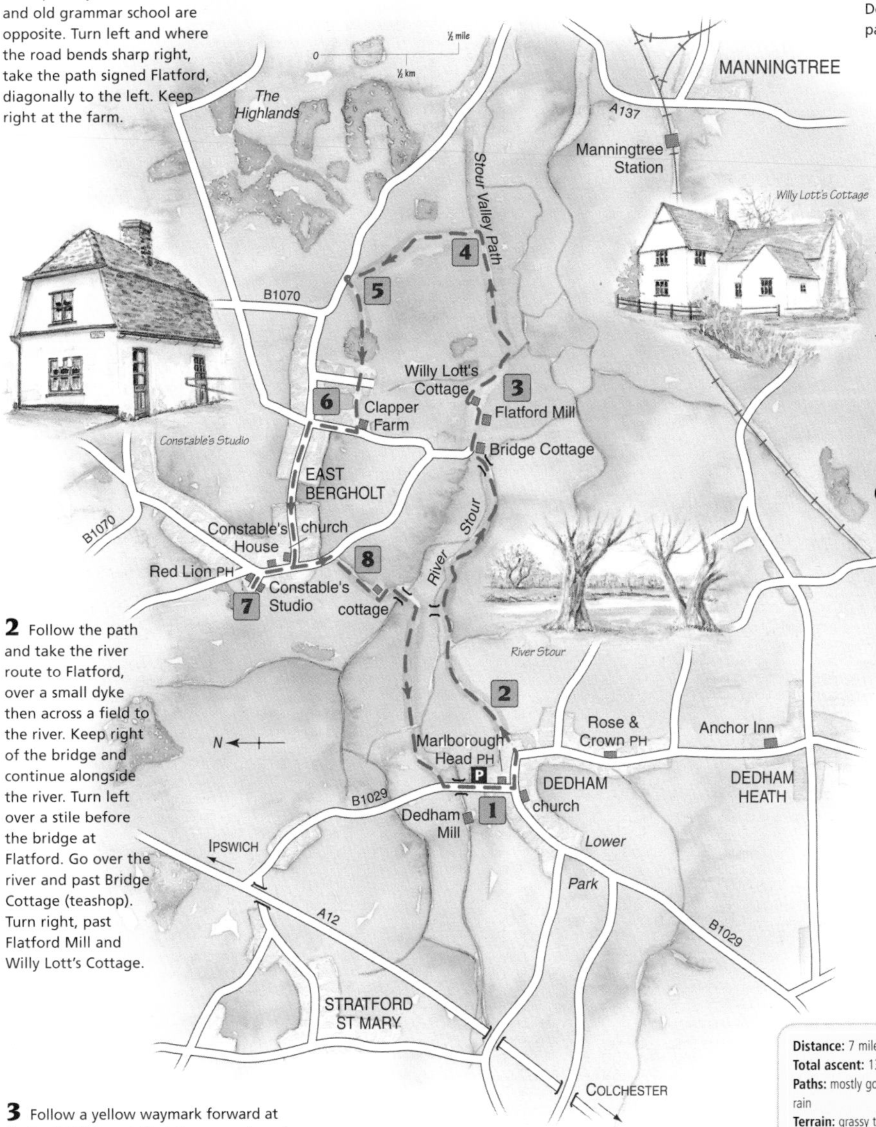

2 Follow the path and take the river route to Flatford, over a small dyke then across a field to the river. Keep right of the bridge and continue alongside the river. Turn left over a stile before the bridge at Flatford. Go over the river and past Bridge Cottage (teashop). Turn right, past Flatford Mill and Willy Lott's Cottage.

3 Follow a yellow waymark forward at Flatford Mill then left at the car park and take the public footpath to the right. At a double finger post take the Stour Valley path left. Cross the stile and keep by the fence, to the right side of a pylon, to a stile. Continue, crossing over two more stiles.

4 Continue to a double stile. Go straight over the field and continue by a hedge. Go over a stile then take the lane on left. Continue uphill about 600yds (546m) to road and turn left. After 40yds (36m) take the very narrow public footpath to left.

5 Proceed to an open field and go straight over to a waymark. Go through the wood, past houses to a gate. Cross over the lane, through a field and over a stile. Continue to the left of next field, towards a farm. Go down the hill and turn right into a lane, then up hill to East Bergholt.

6 Turn left at the cross-roads and follow the road for ¾ mile (1.2km) to the church, turning right. Continue past the Constable birthplace plaque on the fence to the right. Turn left at the no-through road by a shop to see his studio, on the left.

7 Retrace your steps to the war memorial opposite the church. Take the no through road right. After 300yds (273m) take a footpath to right, signed private road. Continue down the track, past a cottage, keeping left, then right to a bridge. Go over bridge.

8 After 75yds (68m) take right fork, signed to Dedham. Follow a narrow path to a gate and cross a field with the river to left. Follow the path across a field to a road. Turn left, over the bridge, past the mill and back to the car park on the left.

Distance: 7 miles (11.3km)
Total ascent: 130ft (40m)
Paths: mostly good; can be very muddy after rain
Terrain: grassy tracks and fields
Gradients: mainly flat, some gradual ascents
Refreshments: numerous in Dedham and East Bergholt; teashop at Flatford Mill
Park: free public car park in Mill Lane, Dedham

Atomic Secrets of Orford Ness

This remote shingle spit on the Suffolk coast was once the scene of historic military experiments

1 From Orford Quay take the National Trust ferry to Orford Ness jetty. The Red Trail leads off up the road for ½ mile (800m) to a T-junction. Immediately on your right is the Old Telephone Exchange display building.

2 Leaving the display, turn right to pass the NT offices and workshops. In ½ mile (800m) bear right across a Bailey bridge over Stony Ditch. Bear immediately left, aiming for the lighthouse, to reach the Bomb Ballistic Building (display).

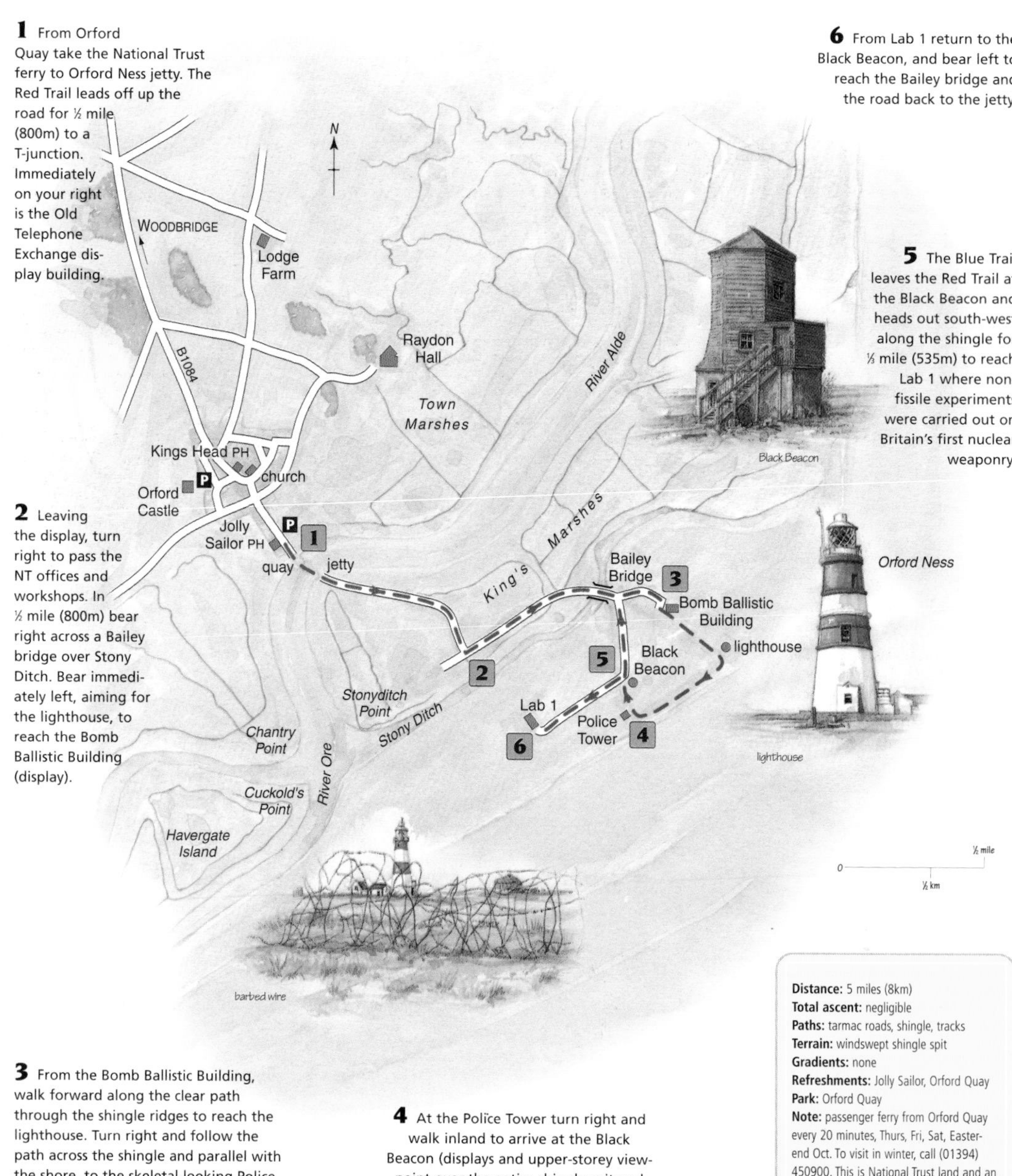

3 From the Bomb Ballistic Building, walk forward along the clear path through the shingle ridges to reach the lighthouse. Turn right and follow the path across the shingle and parallel with the shore, to the skeletal-looking Police Tower.

4 At the Police Tower turn right and walk inland to arrive at the Black Beacon (displays and upper-storey viewpoint over the entire shingle spit and surrounding countryside).

5 The Blue Trail leaves the Red Trail at the Black Beacon and heads out south-west along the shingle for ⅓ mile (535m) to reach Lab 1 where non-fissile experiments were carried out on Britain's first nuclear weaponry.

6 From Lab 1 return to the Black Beacon, and bear left to reach the Bailey bridge and the road back to the jetty.

Distance: 5 miles (8km)
Total ascent: negligible
Paths: tarmac roads, shingle, tracks
Terrain: windswept shingle spit
Gradients: none
Refreshments: Jolly Sailor, Orford Quay
Park: Orford Quay
Note: passenger ferry from Orford Quay every 20 minutes, Thurs, Fri, Sat, Easter-end Oct. To visit in winter, call (01394) 450900. This is National Trust land and an entrance fee is payable

Village Ways in Coggeshall

Exploring an Essex village which has retained its medieval charm

Distance: 8½ miles (13.7km)
Total ascent: 100ft (30m)
Paths: good, some can be very muddy after rain
Terrain: pavements, fields, woodland tracks
Gradients: few, very gradual
Refreshments: numerous in village; Compasses, Pattiswick; teashop, Marks Hall
Park: public car park, Stoneham Street, Coggeshall

1 Leave the car park by the clock tower. Cross the road diagonally and turn left into Church Street. Continue to Woolpack Inn and church on the left. Cross road opposite the end of the church and take marked Essex Way path on the right.

2 Continue past the school into the recreation ground to the left-hand corner and turn left into East Street. Follow a footpath then cross over and take the Essex Way to right at the end of houses. Follow hedge to a stile and continue by fence following Essex Way towards farmyard.

3 Turn right and pass a mill on the left, through the farmyard with abbey ruins on right. Continue past the chapel to T-junction (Grange Barn opposite). Turn right down the hill. Beyond a bridge, turn left then shortly left again into West Street. (Paycocke's is on left). Cross over, taking the path by an old school.

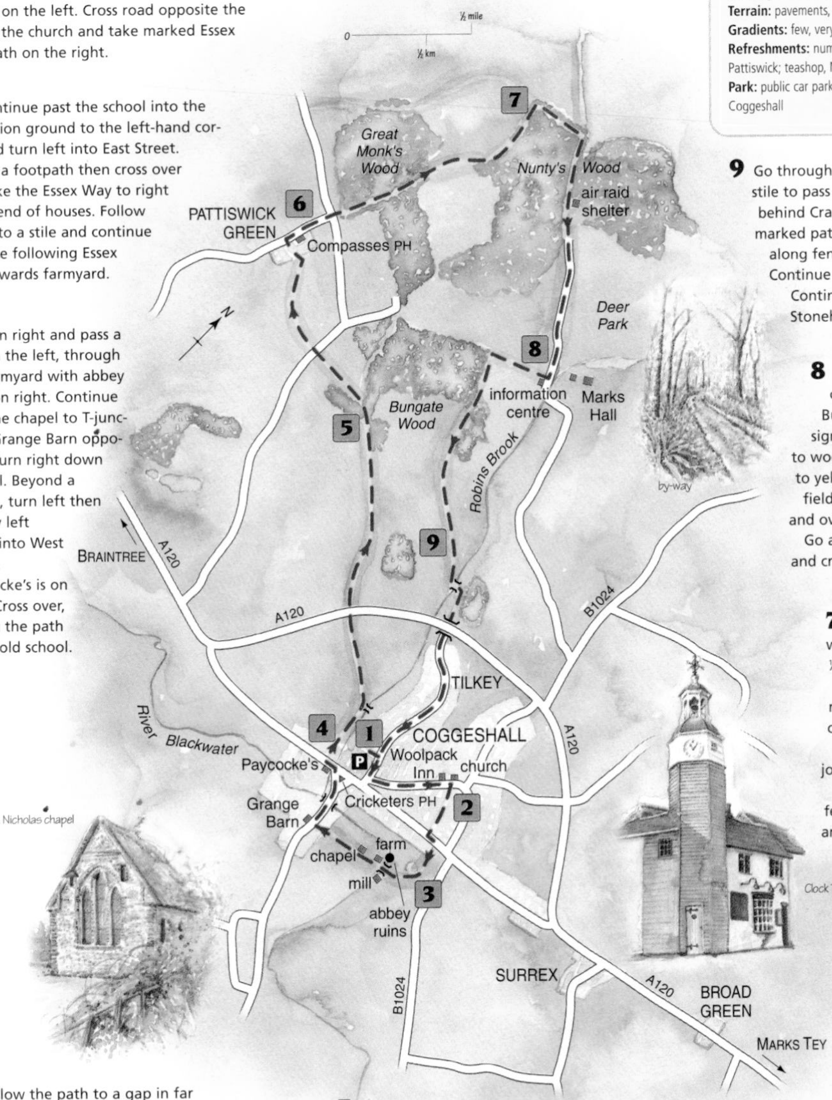

4 Follow the path to a gap in far right of field, continue, then go left by a little bridge. Go ½ mile (800m) up lane, approaching the busy A120. Cross over, taking no-through road. Continue ¾ mile (1.2km) to Bungate Wood.

5 Continue through the wood and after 300yds (274m) follow the yellow waymark left, diagonally across the field. Cross a lane and go straight over field by pylon. Follow to waymark and go along hedge. Turn left, then right into lane, passing the Compasses pub.

6 Continue to a T-junction. Take the path diagonally opposite. Follow it into Great Monk's Wood, bearing slightly right. After ¼ mile (400m), find an open area and bear slightly left. Cross a stile and go over the field towards Nunty's Wood.

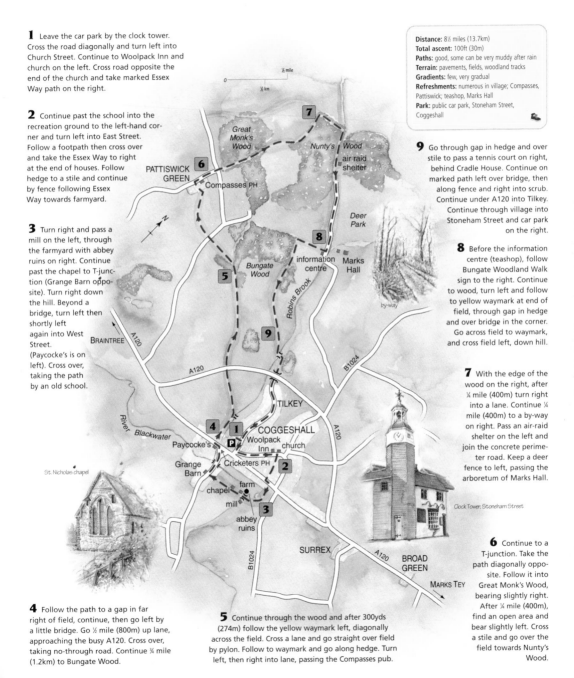

7 With the edge of the wood on the right, after ¼ mile (400m) turn right into a lane. Continue ¼ mile (400m) to a by-way on right. Pass an air-raid shelter on the left and join the concrete perimeter road. Keep a deer fence to left, passing the arboretum of Marks Hall.

8 Before the information centre (teashop), follow Bungate Woodland Walk sign to the right. Continue to wood, turn left and follow to yellow waymark at end of field, through gap in hedge and over bridge in the corner. Go across field to waymark, and cross field left, down hill.

9 Go through gap in hedge and over stile to pass a tennis court on right, behind Cradle House. Continue on marked path left over bridge, then along fence and right into scrub. Continue under A120 into Tilkey. Continue through village into Stoneham Street and car park on the right.

St. Nicholas chapel

by-way

Clock Tower, Stoneham Street

WALK 23

Historic Medway Towns

A rich and varied past is all around you on the historic streets of Rochester and Chatham

Distance: 5½ miles (8.8 km)
Total ascent: 100ft (30m)
Paths: good
Terrain: city streets
Gradients: gentle
Refreshments: available throughout
Park: Rochester Station

1 From Rochester Station turn left, go under the rail bridge and walk right, down to the main road. Turn left along Medway Street, follow the road round, then turn left again up Dock Road, signposted to Historic Dockyard.

2 Keep walking up this busy road. Go straight on at the roundabout, then left into the Historic Dockyard. After exploring the dockyard come out and turn left. Go over the roundabout, then past the Medway Tunnel. Cross the road at the next roundabout and walk up to the submarine Ocelot.

3 Follow the road back into town. At the clock, cross over to the Pentagon Shopping Centre. Turn right up a pedestrianised street, then go right along a quiet part of Chatham High Street. Keep going straight ahead, back to Rochester Station.

4 Pass the station, walk up to the main road, cross over and walk down the pedestrianised High Street. Just after Eastgate House turn left, up Crow Lane. Cross over at Restoration House and follow the sign for Centenary Walk, which leads over a small park.

5 Turn right at the end, go down the hill, then left at the bottom. Pass the cathedral, cross the road and turn left round the castle, following Centenary Walk signs. Pass Satis House, turn right at the river, then right again by the bridge.

6 Walk right along the High Street, exploring the small alleys and passageways.Cross the road at the end and walk back to the station.

Following the Pilgrims through Kent

At Hollingbourne, medieval pilgrims bound for Canterbury found hospitality in a pleasing village

1 From the street opposite the manor house walk up the road by the house. Turn right where the path forks. You will pass a converted oast house. Follow the byway sign. At the electricity sub-station, go right and up to the Pilgrims' Way.

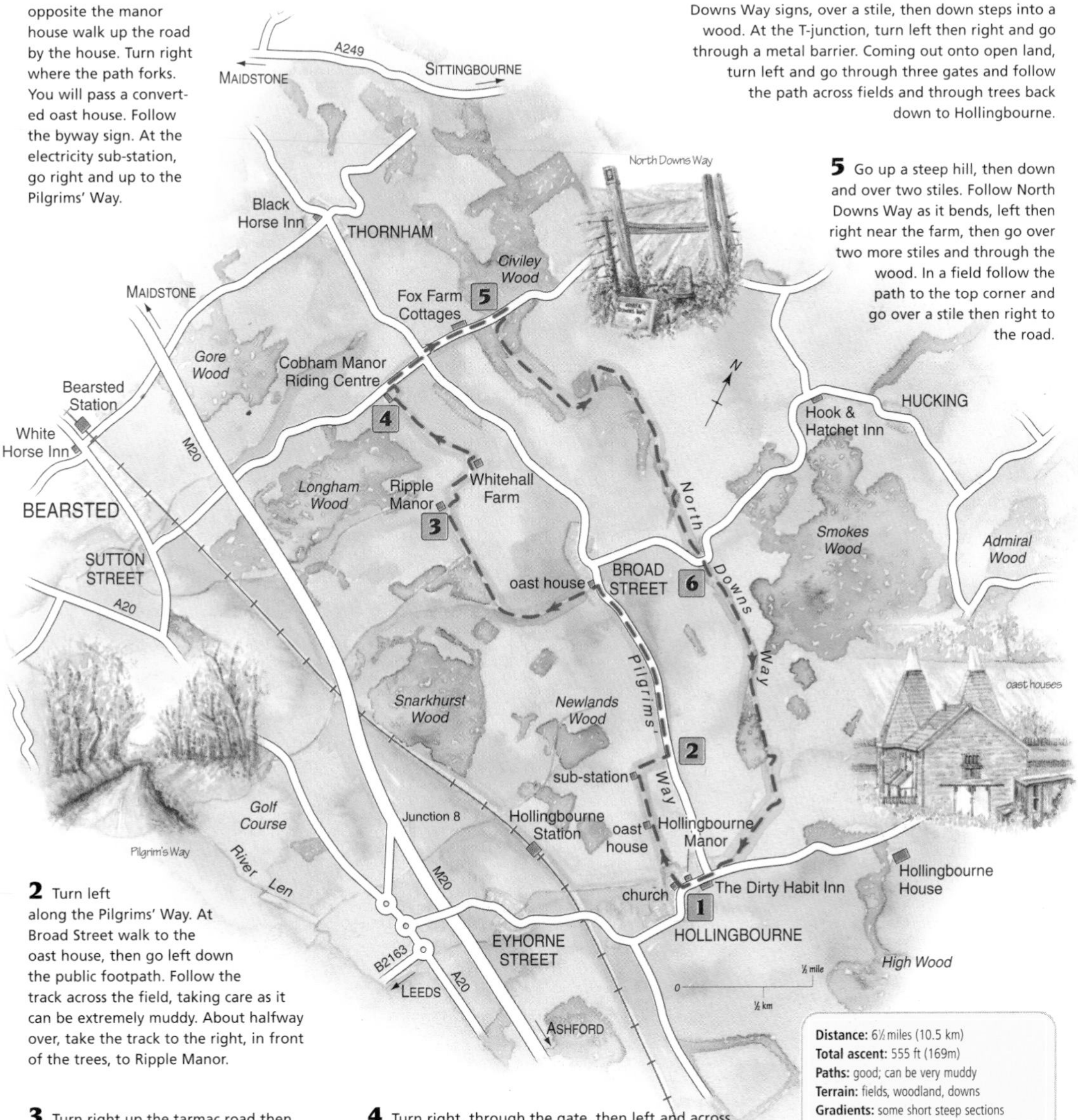

2 Turn left along the Pilgrims' Way. At Broad Street walk to the oast house, then go left down the public footpath. Follow the track across the field, taking care as it can be extremely muddy. About halfway over, take the track to the right, in front of the trees, to Ripple Manor.

3 Turn right up the tarmac road then, just before the farmhouse, take the path on the left signposted Cobham Manor. You keep following the footpath signs over several stiles until you come out at the stables.

4 Turn right, through the gate, then left and across the stableyard to the tarmac road. Turn right, up Water Lane and straight over at the crossroads (signposted Hucking). Go up the lane, past Fox Farm Cottages and turn right at the sign for the North Downs Way, which you now follow.

5 Go up a steep hill, then down and over two stiles. Follow North Downs Way as it bends, left then right near the farm, then go over two more stiles and through the wood. In a field follow the path to the top corner and go over a stile then right to the road.

6 Cross Broad Street then go up steps following North Downs Way signs, over a stile, then down steps into a wood. At the T-junction, turn left then right and go through a metal barrier. Coming out onto open land, turn left and go through three gates and follow the path across fields and through trees back down to Hollingbourne.

Distance: 6½ miles (10.5 km)
Total ascent: 555 ft (169m)
Paths: good; can be very muddy
Terrain: fields, woodland, downs
Gradients: some short steep sections
Refreshments: Dirty Habit Inn and Windmill Inn, Hollingbourne
Park: in street, opposite Hollingbourne Manor, Hollingbourne, 1 mile (1.6km) north of A20 Maidstone-Ashford road

'Mad Jack's' Brightling Follies

A tour of the charming landmarks built by 'Mad Jack' Fuller, a Sussex eccentric

1 From crossroads follow Willingford Lane (signed Burwash Weald) with Obelisk on left. Pass Barn Farm right and take bridleway left along concrete track. At junction, just beyond cottage, turn left over a stile and follow left-hand edge of field to another stile.

2 Bear half-right downhill to bridge and stile. Head straight uphill, then down to stile and descend to cross bridge. Climb steps and stile, then head uphill to gate and turn right at junction, following hedge to stile. Proceed to stile on edge of woodland, turning left at fingerpost on path parallel with woodland. Shortly, turn right at junction.

3 Cross forest track and descend through gorse. Ignore path on left and continue down sunken bridleway to cross stream. Follow path left to track and turn sharp left on bridleway, passing two posts. Ascend for ¼ mile (400m), past two houses.

4 Follow lane uphill. Disregard first footpath left and take second arrowed path, beyond two houses. Go through gate, pass right of pond to fingerpost by hedge ahead. Keep straight on path towards Sugar Loaf. Cross double stile and bear half-left to gap in hedge near end of houses.

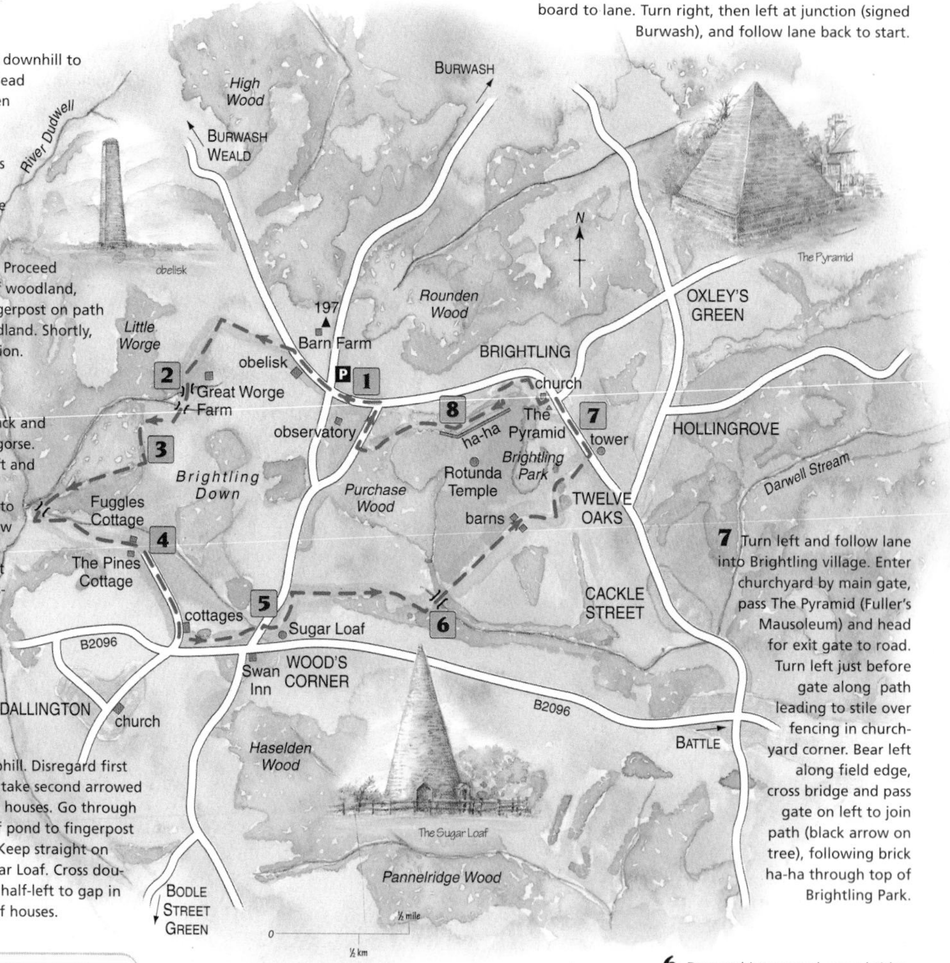

5 Turn left along road to entrance to salvage yard. To view Sugar Loaf, enter yard (yellow arrow), pass gates to first yard and follow markers uphill along fenced path to gate. Return to yard entrance and follow white arrows on right into Purchase Wood. Ignore path to Brightling, left, and keep ahead on path (signed The Tower), eventually merging with gravel track. ½ mile (800m) into woodland look for arrowed post left for The Tower.

6 Descend into wood, cross bridge and pass through gate into Brightling Park. Proceed through gate ahead and follow path through edge of woodland to gate. Keep left along field edge (The Temple clearly visible to left - no access), eventually reaching gate by barns. Turn right on track and keep left at junction to follow track to lane. Turn right to view The Tower.

7 Turn left and follow lane into Brightling village. Enter churchyard by main gate, pass The Pyramid (Fuller's Mausoleum) and head for exit gate to road. Turn left just before gate along path leading to stile over fencing in churchyard corner. Bear left along field edge, cross bridge and pass gate on left to join path (black arrow on tree), following brick ha-ha through top of Brightling Park.

8 Ignore arrowed path right through trees and keep to ha-ha. Proceed at end through small copse and large gate into field. Turn left along field edge to gate and follow path signed The Sugar Loaf through woodland to forest drive. Bear right and keep right by Forestry Commission board to lane. Turn right, then left at junction (signed Burwash), and follow lane back to start.

Distance: 6 miles (9.7km)
Total ascent: 650ft (198m)
Paths: good; muddy after rain
Terrain: fields, woodland, open parkland
Gradients: gradual
Refreshments: Swan Inn, Wood's Corner
Park: on verge near Fuller's Obelisk and Observatory on Brightling Down, between Wood's Corner and Burwash, 1 mile (1.6km) north of B2096 at Wood's Corner

A Wealth of Wildlife in the Arun Valley

A walk across the wetlands of the Arun Valley and up onto the Down reveals why this area is affectionately known as the Sussex Camargue

1 From the car park turn right across the bridge and over the stile (Wey-South Path) immediately right. Walk along the river bank, pass through a gate and bear right on reaching a track. Bear sharp left beyond Limekiln house and follow the track through farm buildings, ignoring the path right by metal barns. At a fork bear right and descend past Hayles Barn.

2 Turn left along the field edge to a gate in the corner. Turn right following Wey-South Path marker to go through a gate and across a bridge on the left. Turn right beside the ditch and soon cross the wooden bridge into Amberley Wild Brooks. Keep to the path, heading south through marshland, over a stile to open pasture and on to another stile, joining the track to Amberley village. Turn right at the lane then right again at the T-junction towards the church. Drop down to pass Rock Cottage and follow the track beneath the walls of Amberley Castle.

3 Bear right at a gate and follow the path to the railway line. Cross via stiles and remain on the path towards Bury Church. Climb a stile and bear left to cross a bridge over a dyke. Keep ahead, cross a further bridge and water meadow to join the raised path beside the River Arun. Turn left and follow the river bank, bearing left to a gate beyond the footbridge over the river. Now on the South Downs Way (SDW), soon follow the fenced path right to reach the B2139.

4 Turn right and, shortly, cross the road, soon to reach a metalled lane. Turn left with SDW marker and gradually ascend the South Downs. Keep right at the junction, pass High Down house, then bear left up a steep stony track to a gate. Continue ascending on SDW, then at the crossing of bridleways at the top of Rackham Hill, turn left and descend on a winding path through woods to the B2139.

5 Turn left, then right in 50 yds (46m) to join narrow Rackham Street. Walk through Rackham, passing the lane to Amberley and soon taking the path left by houses to a gate. Pass a house and skirt woodland to a junction of paths by a footbridge. Bear right along the edge of woodland, ignore the path on your right and keep left, eventually passing through woods to a metalled lane.

6 Turn left and continue to a T-junction at Greatham. Turn left and follow the road for just over ½ mile (800m) back to the car park.

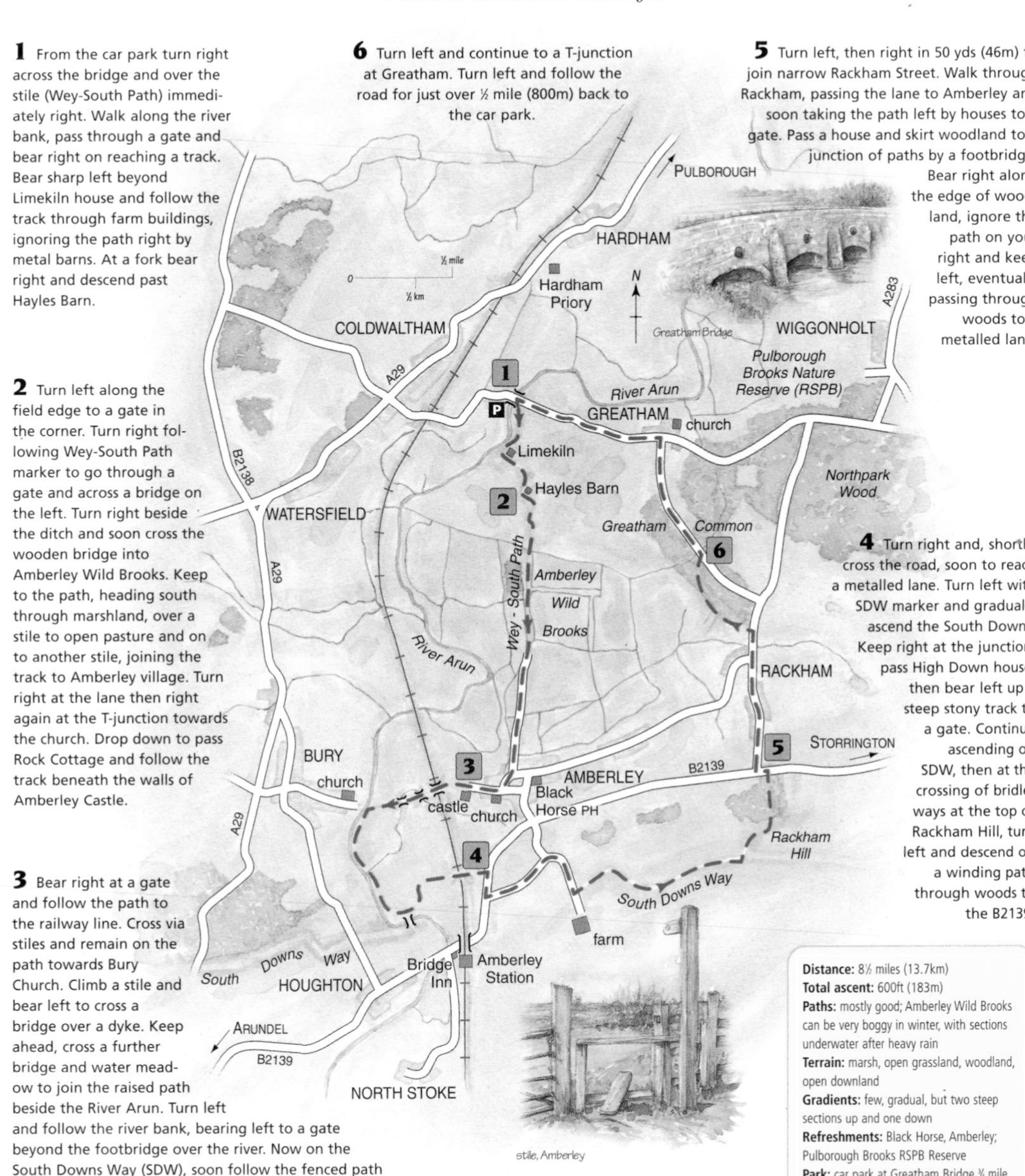

stile, Amberley

Distance: 8½ miles (13.7km)
Total ascent: 600ft (183m)
Paths: mostly good; Amberley Wild Brooks can be very boggy in winter, with sections underwater after heavy rain
Terrain: marsh, open grassland, woodland, open downland
Gradients: few, gradual, but two steep sections up and one down
Refreshments: Black Horse, Amberley; Pulborough Brooks RSPB Reserve
Park: car park at Greatham Bridge ¾ mile (1.2km) east off the A29 at Coldwaltham

Up and Down on the Seven Sisters

White cliffs epitomise the South Coast and there is no better place to walk on them than the Seven Sisters

1 From the car park cross the road, and with the visitor centre on your left, walk up the grassy hill, on the South Downs Way, to a flint wall at the top. Climb over the wall, turn slightly to the right and take the Friston Forest Forestry Commision signpost. The path soon leads steeply to steps down to Westdean Pond.

2 Take the road on the right of the pond, signposted Friston and Jevington, and continue on into Friston Forest. Follow the ride between the trees until it curves left. Do not follow this, but take the wide fork straight ahead and continue until this meets a narrow track.

Distance: 7 miles (11.3km)
Total ascent: 250ft (76m)
Path: wide forest rides; good field paths
Terrain: forest, fields, downland
Gradients: some steep sections on Seven Sisters
Refreshments: Seven Sisters Restaurant and Tea Rooms, Exceat
Park: car park at Exceat, on A259 opposite Seven Sisters Country Park Visitor Centre

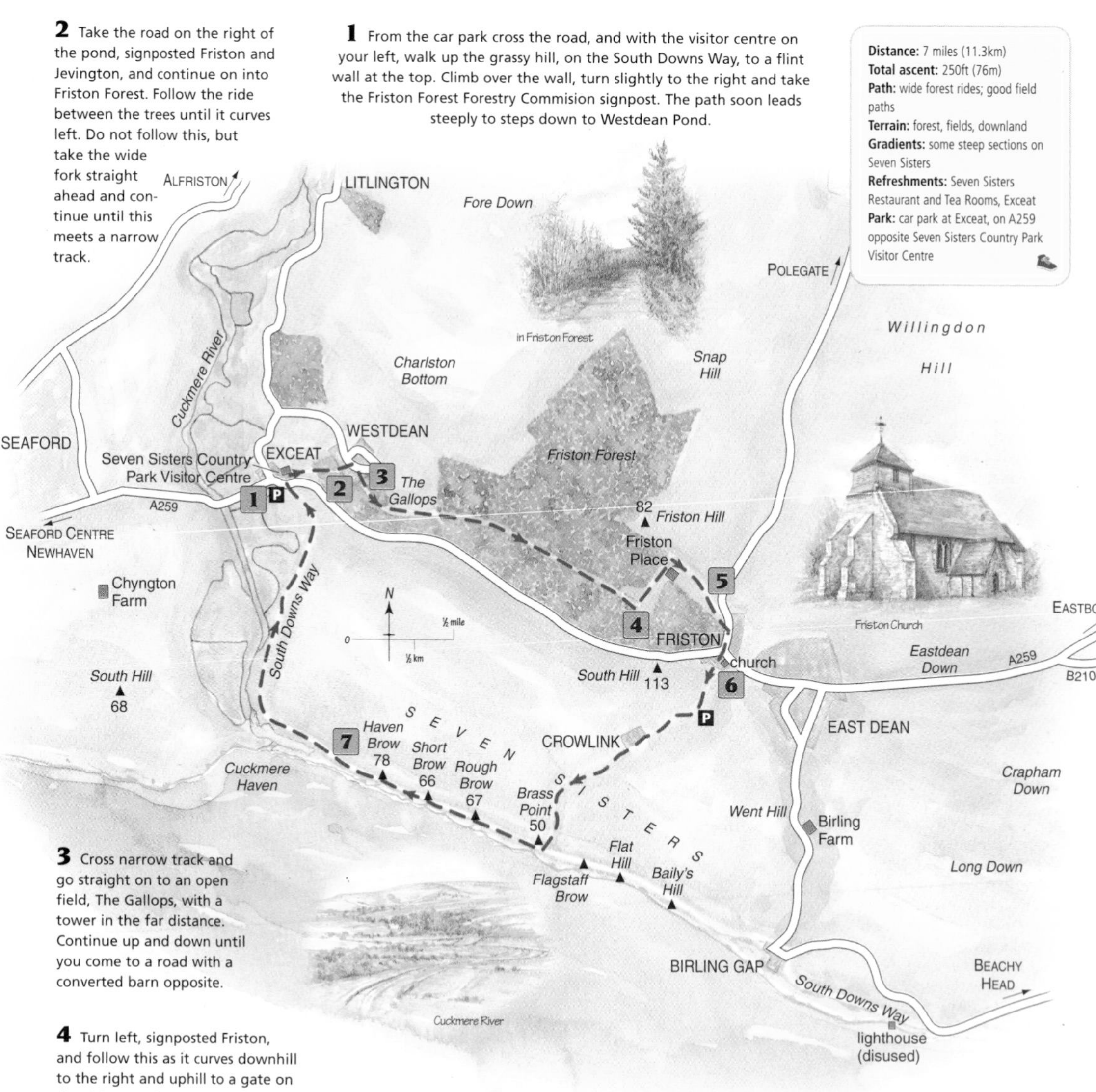

3 Cross narrow track and go straight on to an open field, The Gallops, with a tower in the far distance. Continue up and down until you come to a road with a converted barn opposite.

4 Turn left, signposted Friston, and follow this as it curves downhill to the right and uphill to a gate on the right. Go through this into a field, with an electric fence on your right, and walk to the gate at the far end.

5 Walk diagonally across the next field. Climb over the stile at the end, up some steps onto a minor road which leads to the A259 at Friston church and pond. Cross the road.

6 Follow the no-through road next to the church, past the National Trust car park, and down the tarmac path to the hamlet of Crowlink. Walk through a gate to a grassy path and follow this until the Downs open up. Bear right up the hillside to tackle Brass Point 160ft (50m), Rough Brow 216ft (67m), Short Brow, 214ft (66m), and the last Sister before Cuckmere Haven, Haven Brow (also, the highest at 253ft/78m).

7 At a signpost follow the South Downs Way down to Cuckmere Haven, with a wire fence on your left. Turn right along a concrete path which leads back alongside the river to Exceat car park.

Lewes – Birthplace of the English Parliament

Walking through the ancient streets of this Sussex county town

Distance: 7 miles (11.3km)
Total ascent: 100ft (30m)
Paths: good, mostly paved; some muddy sections
Terrain: town streets and riverside
Gradients: moderate
Refreshments: wide choice
Park: car park at railway station

1 With your back to Lewes railway station, turn left. Turn first left into Mountfield Road and almost immediately right into narrow path. Continue to end of path and turn right alongside playing fields. Bear right by brick lock-up workshops through to priory ruins. Follow grass path with ruins on right to tennis club on left.

2 Leave priory grounds, turn right at Priory Cottage on corner into Cockshut Road and follow this under low-arched bridge to Southover High Street. Turn left. Anne of Cleves House is a little way along on right. Retrace steps back along Southover High Street with Southover parish church on right, to King's Head and turn left.

3 At corner of Eastport Lane (right) is entrance to Southover Grange gardens. Explore gardens but return to this point. On leaving gardens, turn right. Walk past 16th-century Southover Grange, continue up steep, cobbled Keere Street to 15th-century bookshop at top. Turn right into High Street. Follow High Street to Castlegate on left and walk to castle.

4 Turn left up through 14th-century Barbican arch, continue past 300-year-old bowling green to Battle of Lewes memorial plaque on left under trees. Go down steps (on right, if facing plaque), down Castle Banks, and cross road into Abinger Place. Continue to end. Fork left at church (St John sub Castro), down to The Pells, an L-shaped canal.

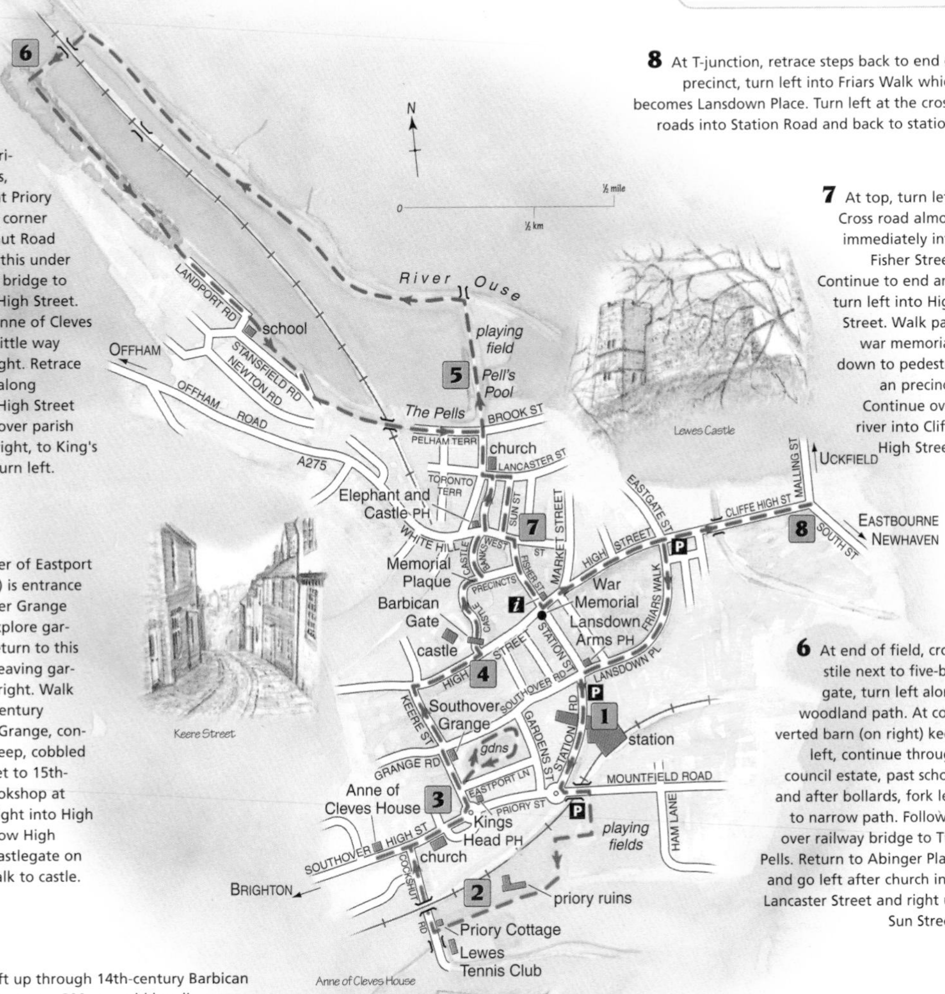

5 Continue along path (canal on left) to white, railed bridge. Turn left just before bridge, and walk along river path. Ignore first rail bridge and at third stile, just past a small concrete building, turn left. Cross another stile, walk under railway bridge into meadow, with stream on left.

6 At end of field, cross stile next to five-bar gate, turn left along woodland path. At converted barn (on right) keep left, continue through council estate, past school and after bollards, fork left to narrow path. Follow it over railway bridge to The Pells. Return to Abinger Place and go left after church into Lancaster Street and right up Sun Street.

7 At top, turn left. Cross road almost immediately into Fisher Street. Continue to end and turn left into High Street. Walk past war memorial, down to pedestrian precinct. Continue over river into Cliffe High Street.

8 At T-junction, retrace steps back to end of precinct, turn left into Friars Walk which becomes Lansdown Place. Turn left at the crossroads into Station Road and back to station.

Keere Street

Lewes Castle

Anne of Cleves House

WALK 29

The South Downs and the Bloomsbury Set

A fine downland walk introduces the landscape which inspired a Bohemian generation

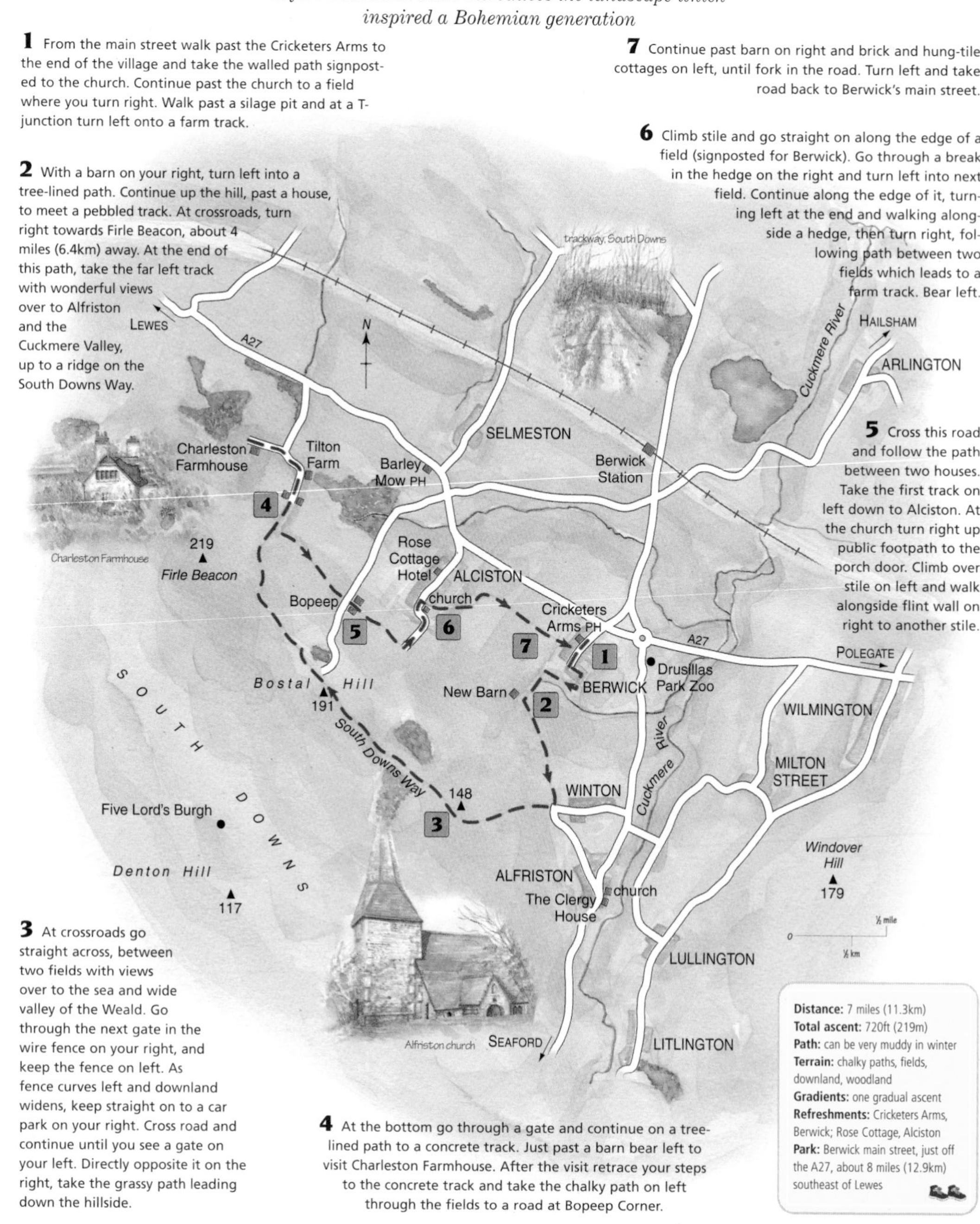

1 From the main street walk past the Cricketers Arms to the end of the village and take the walled path signposted to the church. Continue past the church to a field where you turn right. Walk past a silage pit and at a T-junction turn left onto a farm track.

2 With a barn on your right, turn left into a tree-lined path. Continue up the hill, past a house, to meet a pebbled track. At crossroads, turn right towards Firle Beacon, about 4 miles (6.4km) away. At the end of this path, take the far left track with wonderful views over to Alfriston and the Cuckmere Valley, up to a ridge on the South Downs Way.

3 At crossroads go straight across, between two fields with views over to the sea and wide valley of the Weald. Go through the next gate in the wire fence on your right, and keep the fence on left. As fence curves left and downland widens, keep straight on to a car park on your right. Cross road and continue until you see a gate on your left. Directly opposite it on the right, take the grassy path leading down the hillside.

4 At the bottom go through a gate and continue on a tree-lined path to a concrete track. Just past a barn bear left to visit Charleston Farmhouse. After the visit retrace your steps to the concrete track and take the chalky path on left through the fields to a road at Bopeep Corner.

5 Cross this road and follow the path between two houses. Take the first track on left down to Alciston. At the church turn right up public footpath to the porch door. Climb over stile on left and walk alongside flint wall on right to another stile.

6 Climb stile and go straight on along the edge of a field (signposted for Berwick). Go through a break in the hedge on the right and turn left into next field. Continue along the edge of it, turning left at the end and walking alongside a hedge, then turn right, following path between two fields which leads to a farm track. Bear left.

7 Continue past barn on right and brick and hung-tile cottages on left, until fork in the road. Turn left and take road back to Berwick's main street.

Distance: 7 miles (11.3km)
Total ascent: 720ft (219m)
Path: can be very muddy in winter
Terrain: chalky paths, fields, downland, woodland
Gradients: one gradual ascent
Refreshments: Cricketers Arms, Berwick; Rose Cottage, Alciston
Park: Berwick main street, just off the A27, about 8 miles (12.9km) southeast of Lewes

The New Forest – a Royal Hunting Ground

In Hampshire's special Heritage Area a king once died in mysterious circumstances

1 With Rufus Stone opposite, turn right and walk along to Sir Walter Tyrrell Inn. Veer left at 'Except for Access' sign and cross turf, keeping to right-hand half of open grassy area. Cross several little streams and make for obvious gap in trees. Negotiate shallow ford here and follow indistinct path ahead. Cross winter ford and simple water meadow bridge spanning gully. Keep left when path forks just beyond bridge and follow it through trees to join concrete track leading to Long Beech Caravan Park. Pass several barriers to reach water tower.

2 Pass concrete track immediately beyond tower and continue for about 50 yds (46m) to barrier. Veer right here and make for some wooden posts. Follow path between bracken and gorse bushes and head for corner of King's Garn Gutter Inclosure. Continue on path, keeping inclosure boundary fence on right. Avoid gate in fence and look for Janesmoor Pond up ahead. Make for next corner of inclosure and turn right.

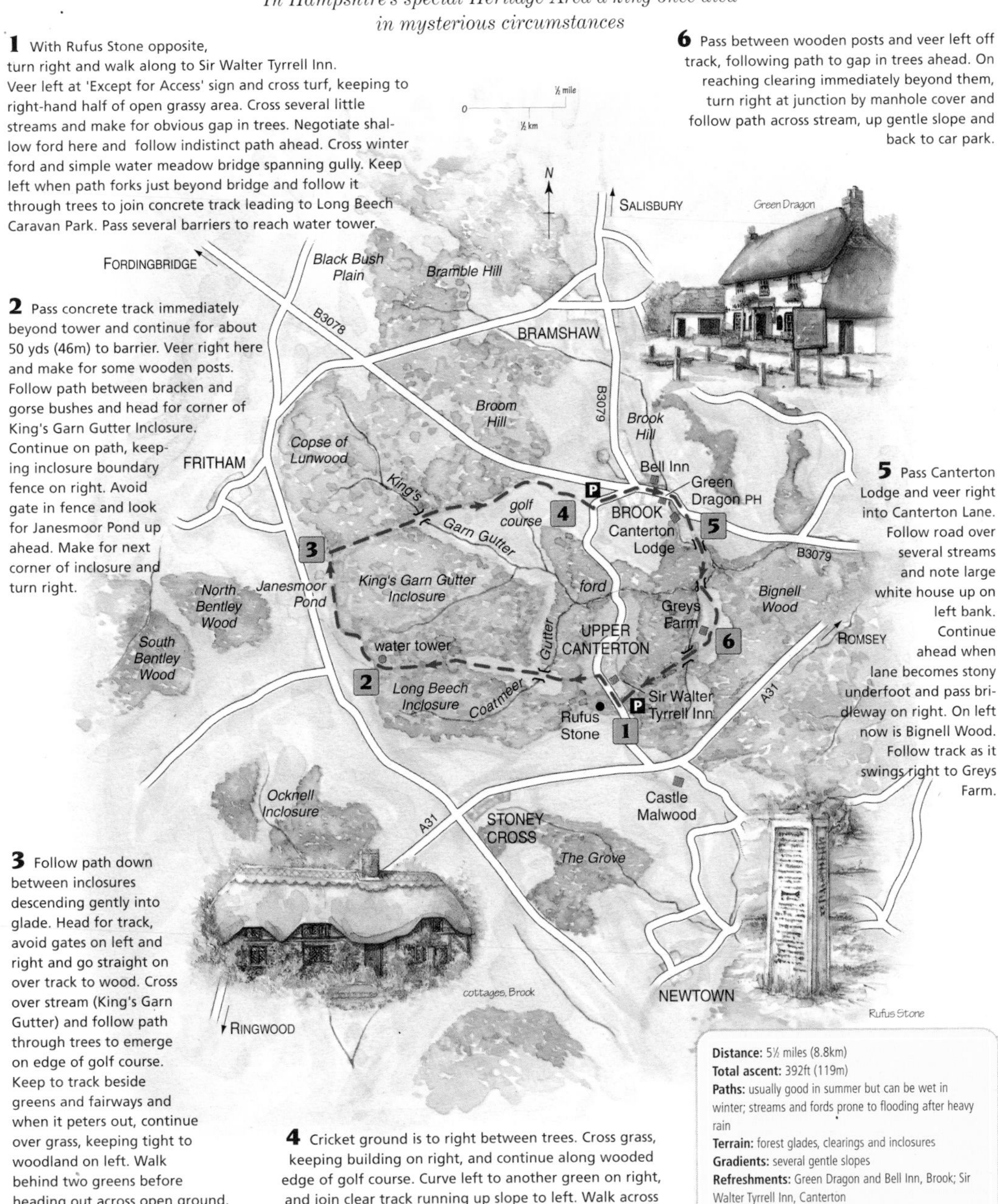

3 Follow path down between inclosures descending gently into glade. Head for track, avoid gates on left and right and go straight on over track to wood. Cross over stream (King's Garn Gutter) and follow path through trees to emerge on edge of golf course. Keep to track beside greens and fairways and when it peters out, continue over grass, keeping tight to woodland on left. Walk behind two greens before heading out across open ground, dotted with gorse bushes and fringed by woodland on left, towards car park on far side.

4 Cricket ground is to right between trees. Cross grass, keeping building on right, and continue along wooded edge of golf course. Curve left to another green on right, and join clear track running up slope to left. Walk across car park and continue to road. Turn left and head for Brook. Follow road through village, pass The Bell Inn and The Green Dragon and avoid footpath on left just beyond.

5 Pass Canterton Lodge and veer right into Canterton Lane. Follow road over several streams and note large white house up on left bank. Continue ahead when lane becomes stony underfoot and pass bridleway on right. On left now is Bignell Wood. Follow track as it swings right to Greys Farm.

6 Pass between wooden posts and veer left off track, following path to gap in trees ahead. On reaching clearing immediately beyond them, turn right at junction by manhole cover and follow path across stream, up gentle slope and back to car park.

Distance: 5½ miles (8.8km)
Total ascent: 392ft (119m)
Paths: usually good in summer but can be wet in winter; streams and fords prone to flooding after heavy rain
Terrain: forest glades, clearings and inclosures
Gradients: several gentle slopes
Refreshments: Green Dragon and Bell Inn, Brook; Sir Walter Tyrrell Inn, Canterton
Park: Rufus Stone car park between the A31 and Brook, near the western end of the M27

Coast to Coast on the Isle of Wight

Connecting tidal and fresh water nature reserves on the western side of this lovely island

1 From The Square in Yarmouth head towards the church and walk along St James Street to cross the A3054 into Mill Road. At the sharp left bend, follow the arrowed path ahead (signed Freshwater) towards the old tide mill. Ignore the footpath left, walk beside the mudflats and turn right along the old railway. Remain on this path for 1½ miles (2.4km) to the causeway at Freshwater.

2 Turn left, away from the river, and follow the lane to the B3399. Turn left and cross almost immediately into Manor Road. In a few paces bear left (Freshwater Way) and gently ascend across grassland towards Afton Down. Go straight at a junction beside the golf course, soon to follow the gravel track right to the clubhouse. Go through the gate, pass in front of the building and walk down the access track, keeping left, to the A3055. Turn right, downhill, into Freshwater Bay.

3 Walk past the car park and turn right into Coastguard Lane, opposite Albion Tavern. Keep ahead at the end, along a path skirting the edge of marsh and eventually reaching a road. Turn right, then, just before the river bridge, turn left into Afton Marshes Nature Reserve.

4 Cross the footbridge, bear right towards Yarmouth and join the nature trail, following the left-hand path beside the stream, through the reserve to the A3055. Turn left and almost immediately cross over to join footpath F61 along the old railway. In ½ mile, (800m) reach The Causeway and turn left, following the lane to Freshwater church and the Red Lion.

5 Take the waymarked path (Freshwater Way) between a cottage and the churchyard. Cross a stile and proceed along the farm road. At the farmyard entrance cross the double stile on the left and bear right along the field edge, skirting a barn to a stile. On reaching a track and the main entrance to Kings Manor Farm, cross the stile ahead beside double gates and follow a wide track to a gate and junction of paths.

6 Climb the stile to the right of the metal gate, pass through a copse to a stile and bear left, uphill, along the field edge. Enter the field on your left and keep to the path along the right-hand edge to a stile on the edge of woodland. Soon drop down through the wood to a track and turn left, following it to the A3054. Turn right along the pavement, back into Yarmouth.

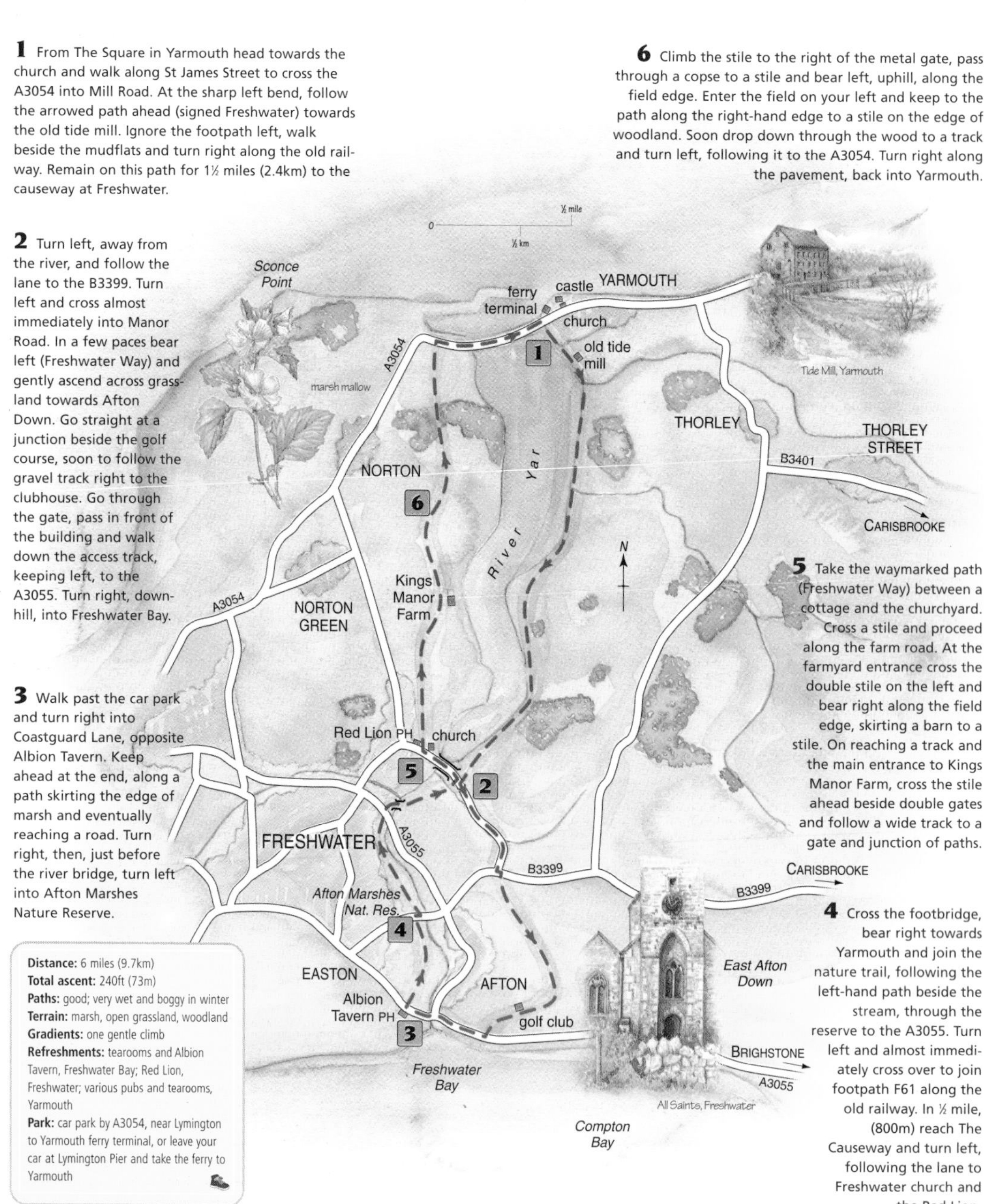

Distance: 6 miles (9.7km)
Total ascent: 240ft (73m)
Paths: good; very wet and boggy in winter
Terrain: marsh, open grassland, woodland
Gradients: one gentle climb
Refreshments: tearooms and Albion Tavern, Freshwater Bay; Red Lion, Freshwater; various pubs and tearooms, Yarmouth
Park: car park by A3054, near Lymington to Yarmouth ferry terminal, or leave your car at Lymington Pier and take the ferry to Yarmouth

Chobham Common – Last of the Surrey Heaths

The ever present gorse marks this heath apart from the sprawl of Surrey's commuterland

Distance: 7 miles (11.3km)
Total ascent: 245ft (75m)
Paths: mostly good; can become waterlogged after heavy rain
Terrain: heath, common, woodland, fields, several stretches of road
Gradients: gentle
Refreshments: Four Horseshoes and Cricketers Inn, Burrowhill
Park: Longcross car park, just off the B386, western end of Longcross village

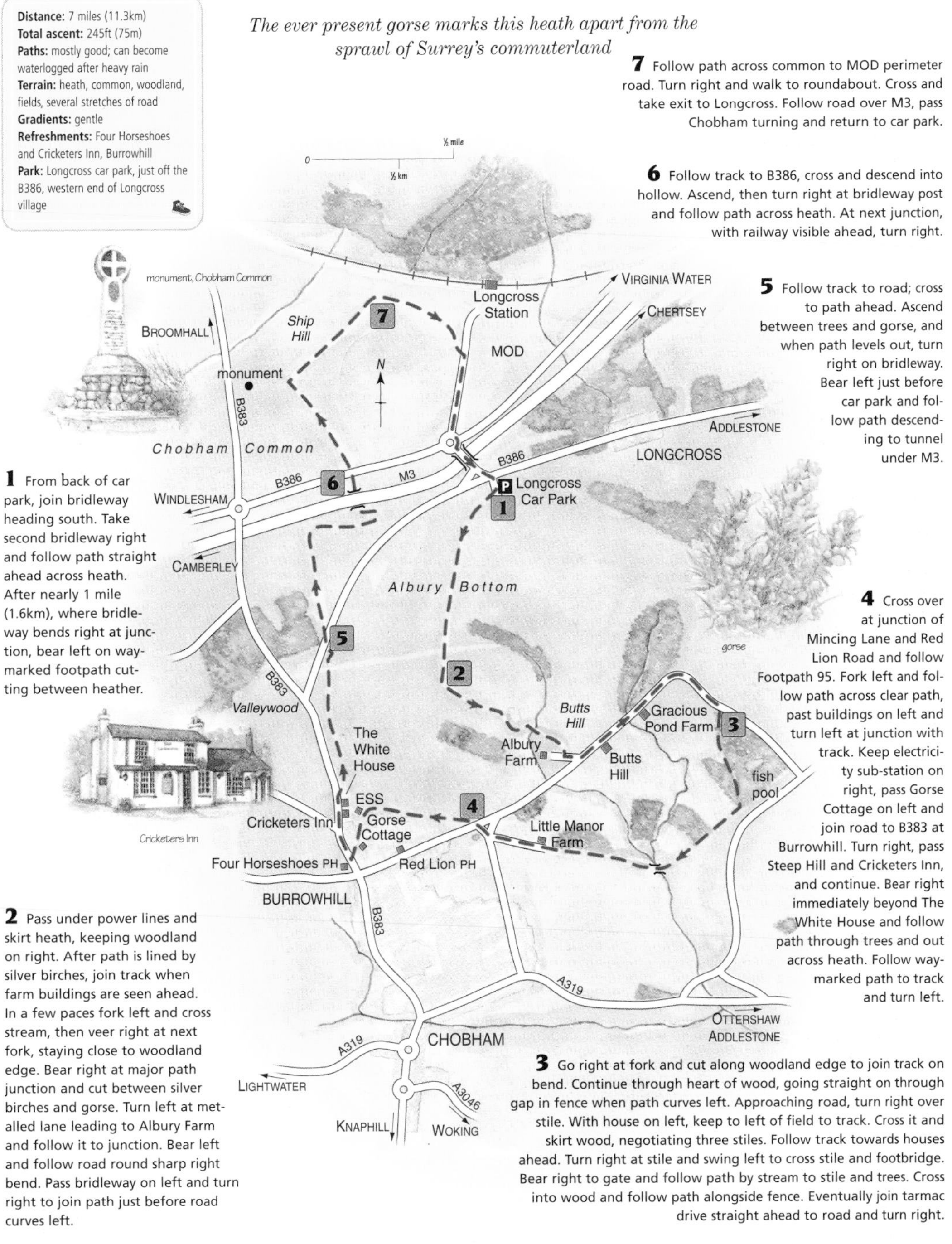

1 From back of car park, join bridleway heading south. Take second bridleway right and follow path straight ahead across heath. After nearly 1 mile (1.6km), where bridleway bends right at junction, bear left on waymarked footpath cutting between heather.

2 Pass under power lines and skirt heath, keeping woodland on right. After path is lined by silver birches, join track when farm buildings are seen ahead. In a few paces fork left and cross stream, then veer right at next fork, staying close to woodland edge. Bear right at major path junction and cut between silver birches and gorse. Turn left at metalled lane leading to Albury Farm and follow it to junction. Bear left and follow road round sharp right bend. Pass bridleway on left and turn right to join path just before road curves left.

3 Go right at fork and cut along woodland edge to join track on bend. Continue through heart of wood, going straight on through gap in fence when path curves left. Approaching road, turn right over stile. With house on left, keep to left of field to track. Cross it and skirt wood, negotiating three stiles. Follow track towards houses ahead. Turn right at stile and swing left to cross stile and footbridge. Bear right to gate and follow path by stream to stile and trees. Cross into wood and follow path alongside fence. Eventually join tarmac drive straight ahead to road and turn right.

4 Cross over at junction of Mincing Lane and Red Lion Road and follow Footpath 95. Fork left and follow path across clear path, past buildings on left and turn left at junction with track. Keep electricity sub-station on right, pass Gorse Cottage on left and join road to B383 at Burrowhill. Turn right, pass Steep Hill and Cricketers Inn, and continue. Bear right immediately beyond The White House and follow path through trees and out across heath. Follow waymarked path to track and turn left.

5 Follow track to road; cross to path ahead. Ascend between trees and gorse, and when path levels out, turn right on bridleway. Bear left just before car park and follow path descending to tunnel under M3.

6 Follow track to B386, cross and descend into hollow. Ascend, then turn right at bridleway post and follow path across heath. At next junction, with railway visible ahead, turn right.

7 Follow path across common to MOD perimeter road. Turn right and walk to roundabout. Cross and take exit to Longcross. Follow road over M3, pass Chobham turning and return to car park.

Riverbank Tales from the Thames at Cookham

This section of the majestic Thames inspired poets, artists and the author of 'The Wind in the Willows'

Distance: 8 miles (12.9km)
Total ascent: 316ft (96m)
Paths: mostly good; can get very wet and muddy
Terrain: riverbank, meadow, escarpment, woodland, fields
Gradients: one short steep section
Refreshments: various in Cookham; The Jolly Farmer at Cookham Dean
Park: Cookham Moor car park, west of Cookham

1 From car park walk across grass towards village. Ignore kissing gate left and follow Cookham High Street to junction with A4094. Turn left towards Wooburn and Bourne End, past Tarry Stone. Turn left through churchyard towards riverbank.

2 At Thames Path turn left, passing through two gates by sailing club. Continue upstream, crossing Marsh Meadow to kissing gate leading to Cock Marsh. Follow path by river, veering left under railway bridge.

3 With line of villas right, follow path back to riverbank. Pass through kissing gate and veer away from river at Ferry Cottage. Turn left at concrete drive and head towards Winter Hill. Follow track across field to pond. Pass through kissing gate to junction and turn right. Head diagonally up to gate and stile, then join road.

4 Turn right past Stonehouse Lane and Gibraltar Lane, following road above river. Shortly, veer half-right to path running parallel with road. Walk past several parking areas to path into woods. Turn right after several steps and follow drive to 'Rivendell' entrance. Bear immediately right of gate and follow woodland path. Veer right at fork and follow path to road. Cross and head up steep bank to seat on right. Join path just beyond seat and follow for about 100yards (91m) through Quarry Wood. Turn sharp left then immediate right fork, making for woodland corner by road.

5 Bear right into Grubwood Lane and pass houses. Turn left immediately beyond and follow path parallel to wide drive. Make for bottom of slope, then head up on path beside fence towards farm buildings. In field corner join woodland path to left. At green at Cookham Dean follow lane to war memorial. Turn right into Church Road.

6 Bear left immediately beyond church and just before Jolly Farmer Inn, then left at next footpath sign. Follow road to Huntsman's Cottage and York House as it becomes a green lane, to gate, and continue to road. Bear left to road junction. Cross to Bradcutts Lane and follow for about ½ mile (800m). Turn right at Hillgrove Farm and follow path to right, over concrete stile. Fork left to lane and cross over to footpath opposite.

7 Keep left of September Grange and follow path to field corner. Turn right past golf course sign, keeping fence and hedge on right. Cross fairways, aim left of corrugated barns and make for railway bridge ahead. Cross it and turn right to follow grassy path by fence and hedge. Join track and follow it to road. Turn left by drive to 'Fiveways' and follow path to kissing gate. Bear right and return to Cookham Moor car park, crossing footbridge over Fleet Ditch just before it.

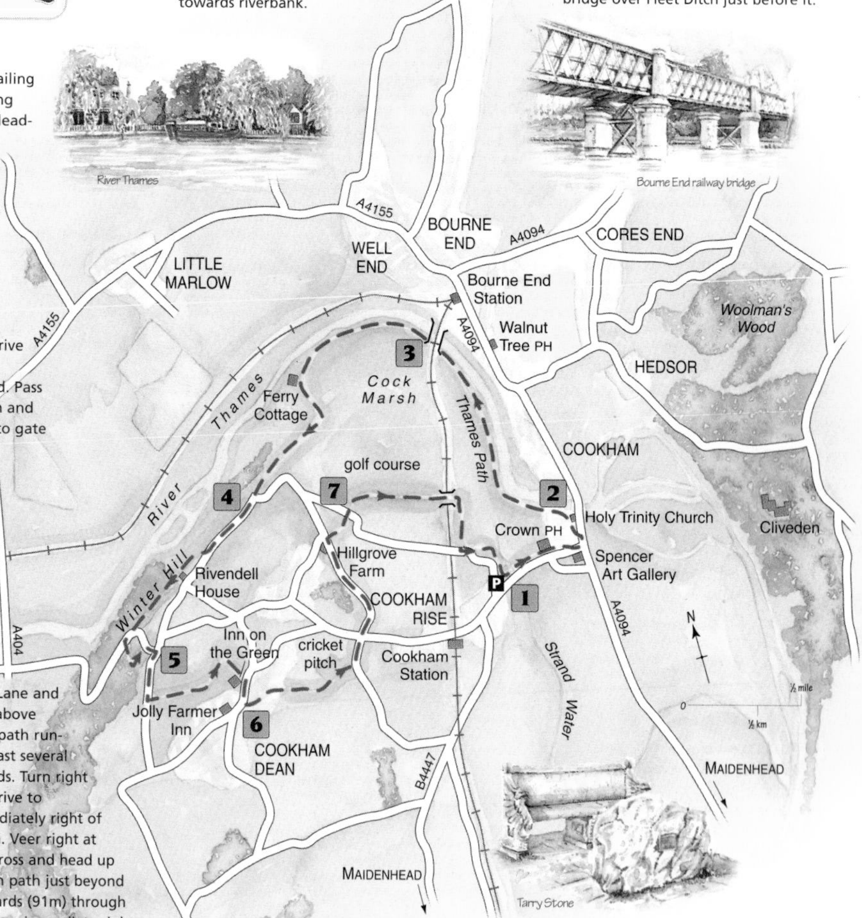

The Devil's Punch Bowl

A little bit of wilderness hides in the Surrey Hills

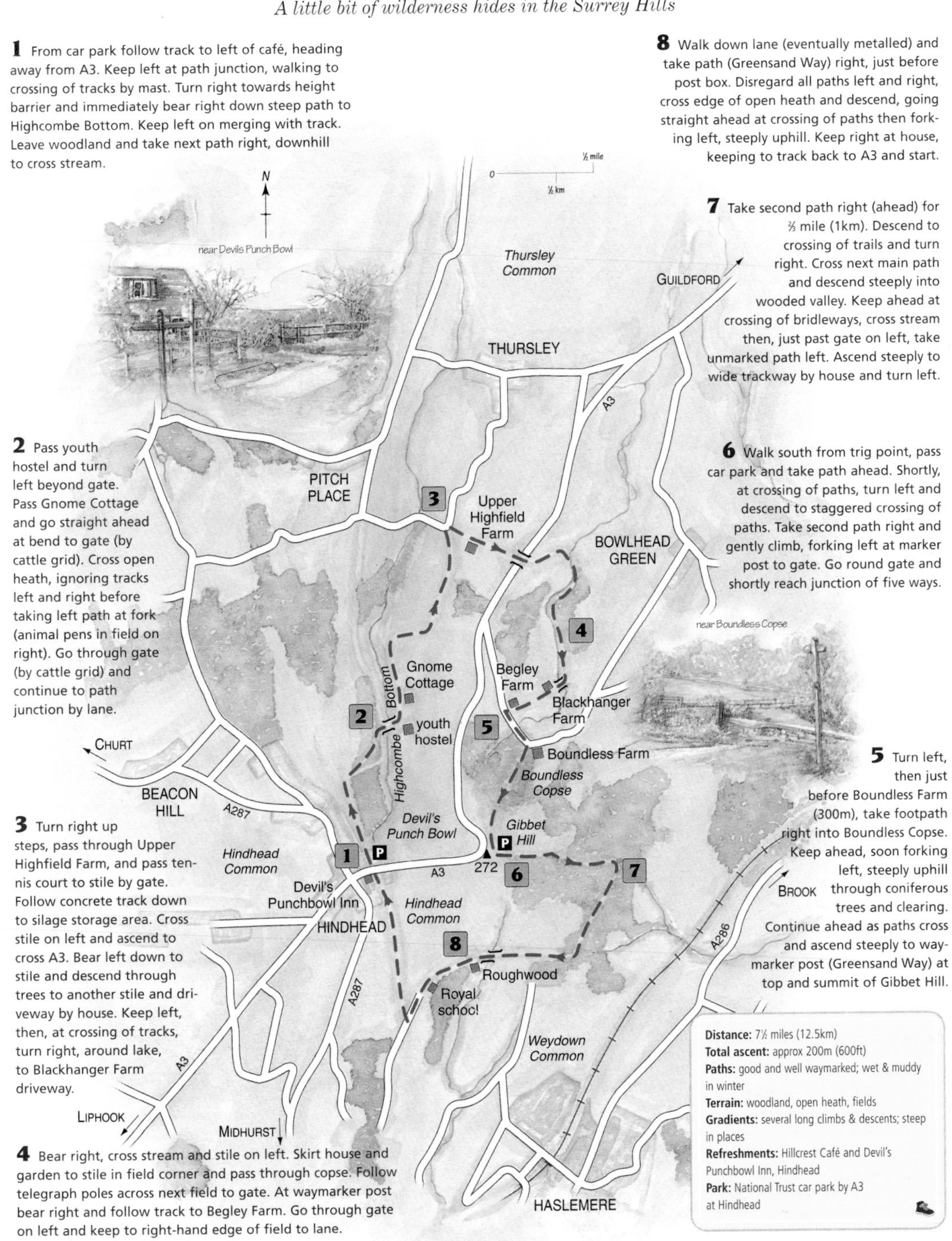

1 From car park follow track to left of café, heading away from A3. Keep left at path junction, walking to crossing of tracks by mast. Turn right towards height barrier and immediately bear right down steep path to Highcombe Bottom. Keep left on merging with track. Leave woodland and take next path right, downhill to cross stream.

2 Pass youth hostel and turn left beyond gate. Pass Gnome Cottage and go straight ahead at bend to gate (by cattle grid). Cross open heath, ignoring tracks left and right before taking left path at fork (animal pens in field on right). Go through gate (by cattle grid) and continue to path junction by lane.

3 Turn right up steps, pass through Upper Highfield Farm, and pass tennis court to stile by gate. Follow concrete track down to silage storage area. Cross stile on left and ascend to cross A3. Bear left down to stile and descend through trees to another stile and driveway by house. Keep left, then, at crossing of tracks, turn right, around lake, to Blackhanger Farm driveway.

4 Bear right, cross stream and stile on left. Skirt house and garden to stile in field corner and pass through copse. Follow telegraph poles across next field to gate. At waymarker post bear right and follow track to Begley Farm. Go through gate on left and keep to right-hand edge of field to lane.

5 Turn left, then just before Boundless Farm (300m), take footpath right into Boundless Copse. Keep ahead, soon forking left, steeply uphill through coniferous trees and clearing. Continue ahead as paths cross and ascend steeply to waymarker post (Greensand Way) at top and summit of Gibbet Hill.

6 Walk south from trig point, pass car park and take path ahead. Shortly, at crossing of paths, turn left and descend to staggered crossing of paths. Take second path right and gently climb, forking left at marker post to gate. Go round gate and shortly reach junction of five ways.

7 Take second path right (ahead) for ⅔ mile (1km). Descend to crossing of trails and turn right. Cross next main path and descend steeply into wooded valley. Keep ahead at crossing of bridleways, cross stream then, just past gate on left, take unmarked path left. Ascend steeply to wide trackway by house and turn left.

8 Walk down lane (eventually metalled) and take path (Greensand Way) right, just before post box. Disregard all paths left and right, cross edge of open heath and descend, going straight ahead at crossing of paths then forking left, steeply uphill. Keep right at house, keeping to track back to A3 and start.

Distance: 7½ miles (12.5km)
Total ascent: approx 200m (600ft)
Paths: good and well waymarked; wet & muddy in winter
Terrain: woodland, open heath, fields
Gradients: several long climbs & descents; steep in places
Refreshments: Hillcrest Café and Devil's Punchbowl Inn, Hindhead
Park: National Trust car park by A3 at Hindhead

Historic Routes across the Chilterns

Along the Ridgeway to Ivinghoe Beacon, then back through beechwoods, this is a trail steeped in history

Distance: 7½ miles (12km)
Total ascent: 1,100ft (335m)
Paths: good; can be muddy
Terrain: farmland, downland and woodland
Gradients: moderate, two steeper sections
Refreshments: two pubs and a shop in Aldbury
Park: in the centre of Aldbury, by the pond

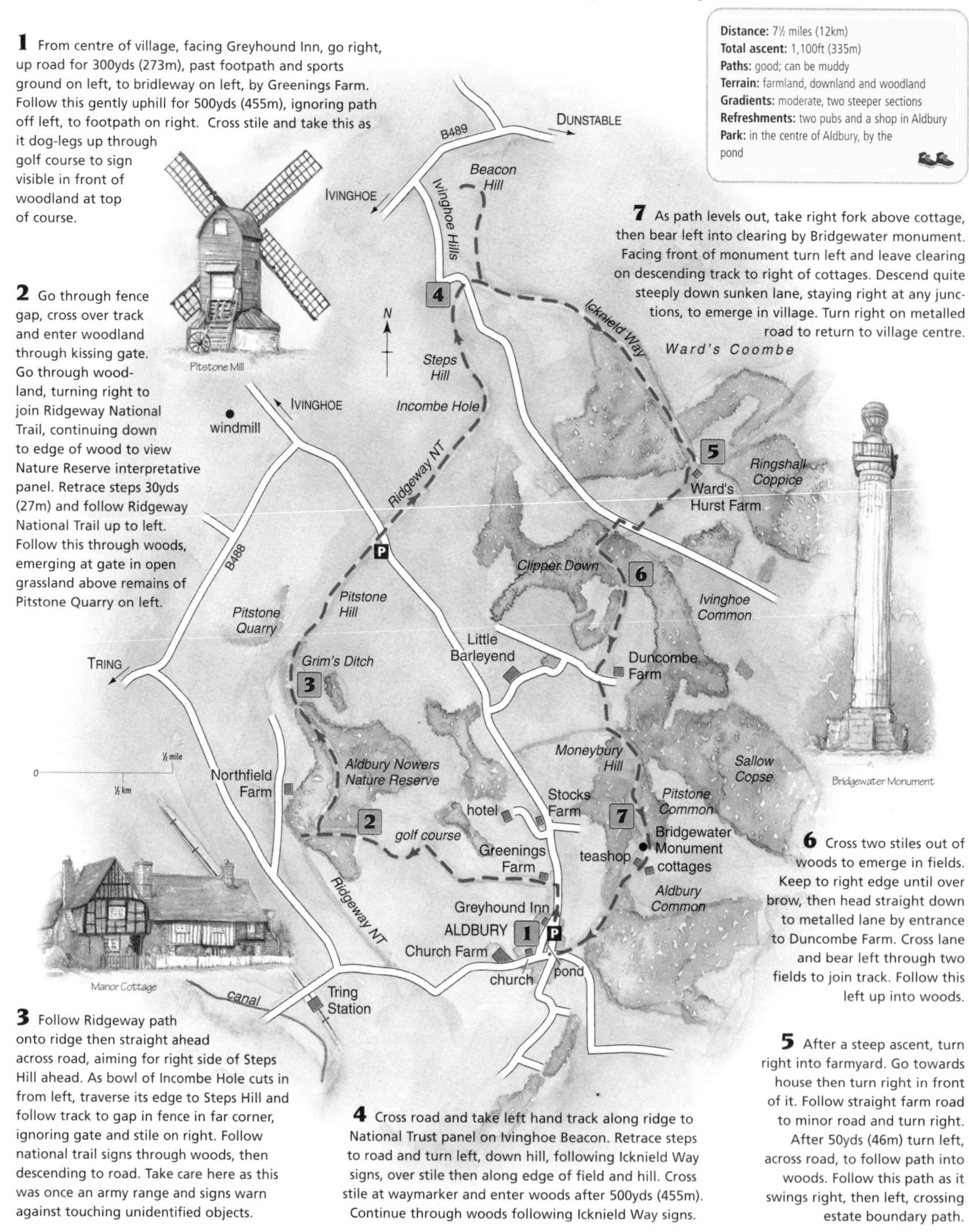

1 From centre of village, facing Greyhound Inn, go right, up road for 300yds (273m), past footpath and sports ground on left, to bridleway on left, by Greenings Farm. Follow this gently uphill for 500yds (455m), ignoring path off left, to footpath on right. Cross stile and take this as it dog-legs up through golf course to sign visible in front of woodland at top of course.

2 Go through fence gap, cross over track and enter woodland through kissing gate. Go through woodland, turning right to join Ridgeway National Trail, continuing down to edge of wood to view Nature Reserve interpretative panel. Retrace steps 30yds (27m) and follow Ridgeway National Trail up to left. Follow this through woods, emerging at gate in open grassland above remains of Pitstone Quarry on left.

3 Follow Ridgeway path onto ridge then straight ahead across road, aiming for right side of Steps Hill ahead. As bowl of Incombe Hole cuts in from left, traverse its edge to Steps Hill and follow track to gap in fence in far corner, ignoring gate and stile on right. Follow national trail signs through woods, then descending to road. Take care here as this was once an army range and signs warn against touching unidentified objects.

4 Cross road and take left hand track along ridge to National Trust panel on Ivinghoe Beacon. Retrace steps to road and turn left, down hill, following Icknield Way signs, over stile then along edge of field and hill. Cross stile at waymarker and enter woods after 500yds (455m). Continue through woods following Icknield Way signs.

5 After a steep ascent, turn right into farmyard. Go towards house then turn right in front of it. Follow straight farm road to minor road and turn right. After 50yds (46m) turn left, across road, to follow path into woods. Follow this path as it swings right, then left, crossing estate boundary path.

6 Cross two stiles out of woods to emerge in fields. Keep to right edge until over brow, then head straight down to metalled lane by entrance to Duncombe Farm. Cross lane and bear left through two fields to join track. Follow this left up into woods.

7 As path levels out, take right fork above cottage, then bear left into clearing by Bridgewater monument. Facing front of monument turn left and leave clearing on descending track to right of cottages. Descend quite steeply down sunken lane, staying right at any junctions, to emerge in village. Turn right on metalled road to return to village centre.

In London's East End

History unfolds, street after street, in this exploration of a lesser-known London

1 From the Tower Thistle Hotel, by Tower Bridge, turn right and walk up St Katharine's Way. Cross the road and take the right fork which is Mansell Street. Go under the subway and take exit 14 marked Middlesex Street (Petticoat Lane).

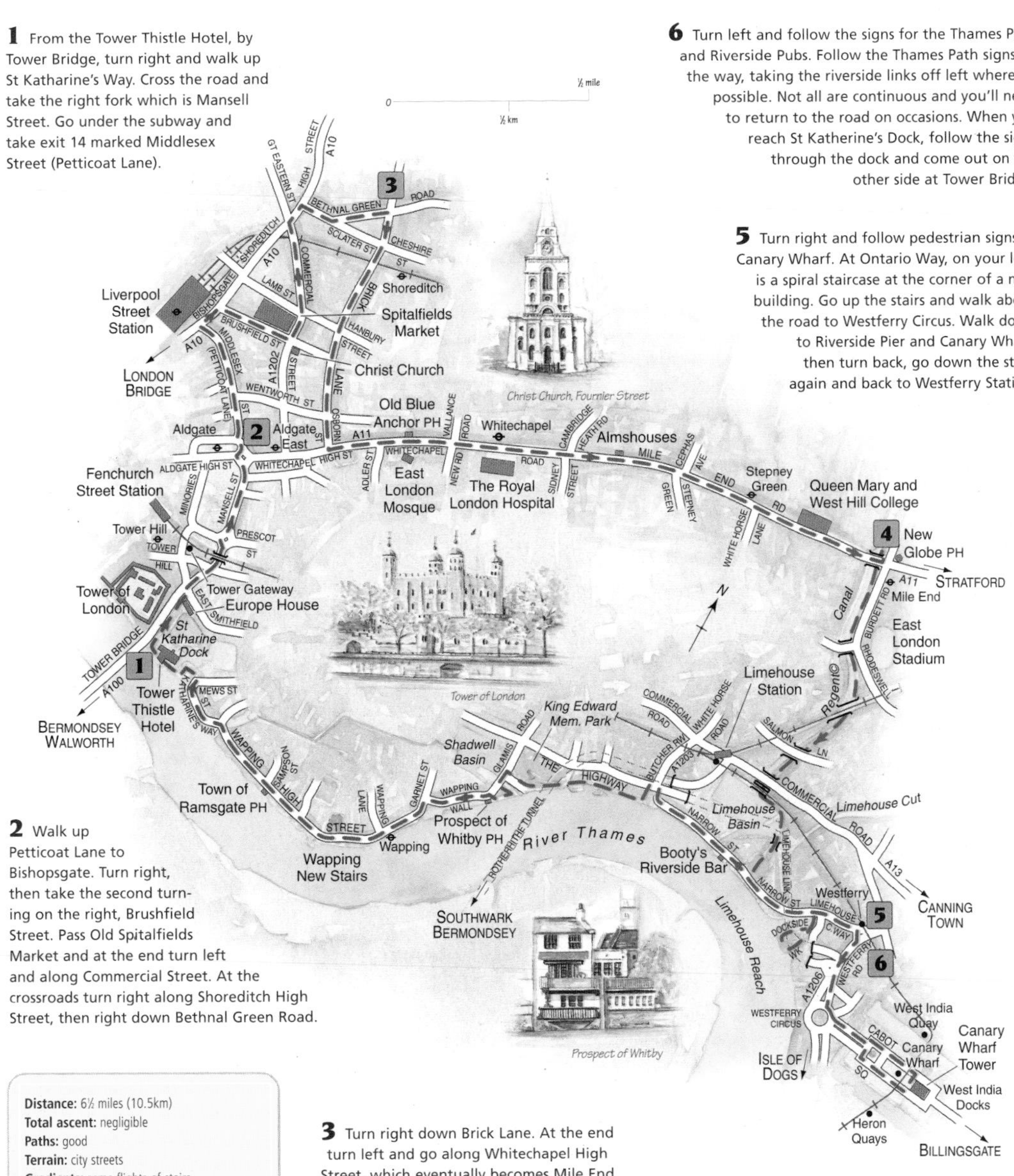

Christ Church, Fournier Street

Tower of London

Prospect of Whitby

2 Walk up Petticoat Lane to Bishopsgate. Turn right, then take the second turning on the right, Brushfield Street. Pass Old Spitalfields Market and at the end turn left and along Commercial Street. At the crossroads turn right along Shoreditch High Street, then right down Bethnal Green Road.

3 Turn right down Brick Lane. At the end turn left and go along Whitechapel High Street, which eventually becomes Mile End Road. Keep walking ahead until you reach the bridge over the Regent's Canal. Go over the bridge and immediately turn left. Take the steps down to the canal and walk down to the left.

4 Walk down to Limehouse Basin, under the Docklands Light Railway, then turn left. Go over a bridge, through a play area then turn left at the converted wharves and walk along Barleycorn Way and Limehouse Causeway to Westferry Station.

5 Turn right and follow pedestrian signs to Canary Wharf. At Ontario Way, on your left, is a spiral staircase at the corner of a new building. Go up the stairs and walk above the road to Westferry Circus. Walk down to Riverside Pier and Canary Wharf, then turn back, go down the steps again and back to Westferry Station.

6 Turn left and follow the signs for the Thames Path and Riverside Pubs. Follow the Thames Path signs all the way, taking the riverside links off left wherever possible. Not all are continuous and you'll need to return to the road on occasions. When you reach St Katharine's Dock, follow the signs through the dock and come out on the other side at Tower Bridge.

Distance: 6½ miles (10.5km)
Total ascent: negligible
Paths: good
Terrain: city streets
Gradients: some flights of stairs
Refreshments: pubs, cafés and restaurants all along route
Park: NCP St Katharine's Way car park, next to Tower Thistle Hotel, by Tower Bridge

Hethel Airfield and Norfolk's American Invasion

On the trail of American airmen in a tiny Norfolk village

Distance: 7 miles (11.2m)
Total ascent: 120ft (37m)
Paths: mostly good; can be muddy; some roads
Terrain: farmland and villages
Gradients: mainly flat; some gentle ascents
Refreshments: Bird in Hand, Wreningham
Park: on verge just past Hethel church, ¾ mile (1.2km) from B1113 at Bracon Ash

1 From lane by Hethel church continue to T-junction and turn right. Turn left to view air-raid shelters. Retrace steps to lane and T-junction.

2 Cross stile by gate on left and go diagonally across field towards left of White Cottage. Cross stile near pond in front of cottage, then bear left towards Hethel Thorn. Cross stile in corner then walk diagonally across field to stile in corner by trees. Walk with field left and trees right to track.

3 Turn right and follow track past farm buildings to lane. Turn right and, after 150yds (137m), take footpath left. Cross stile and continue through woods. At gate path crosses ditch to right. Cross another ditch and follow right-hand ditch past small pond to corner of wood.

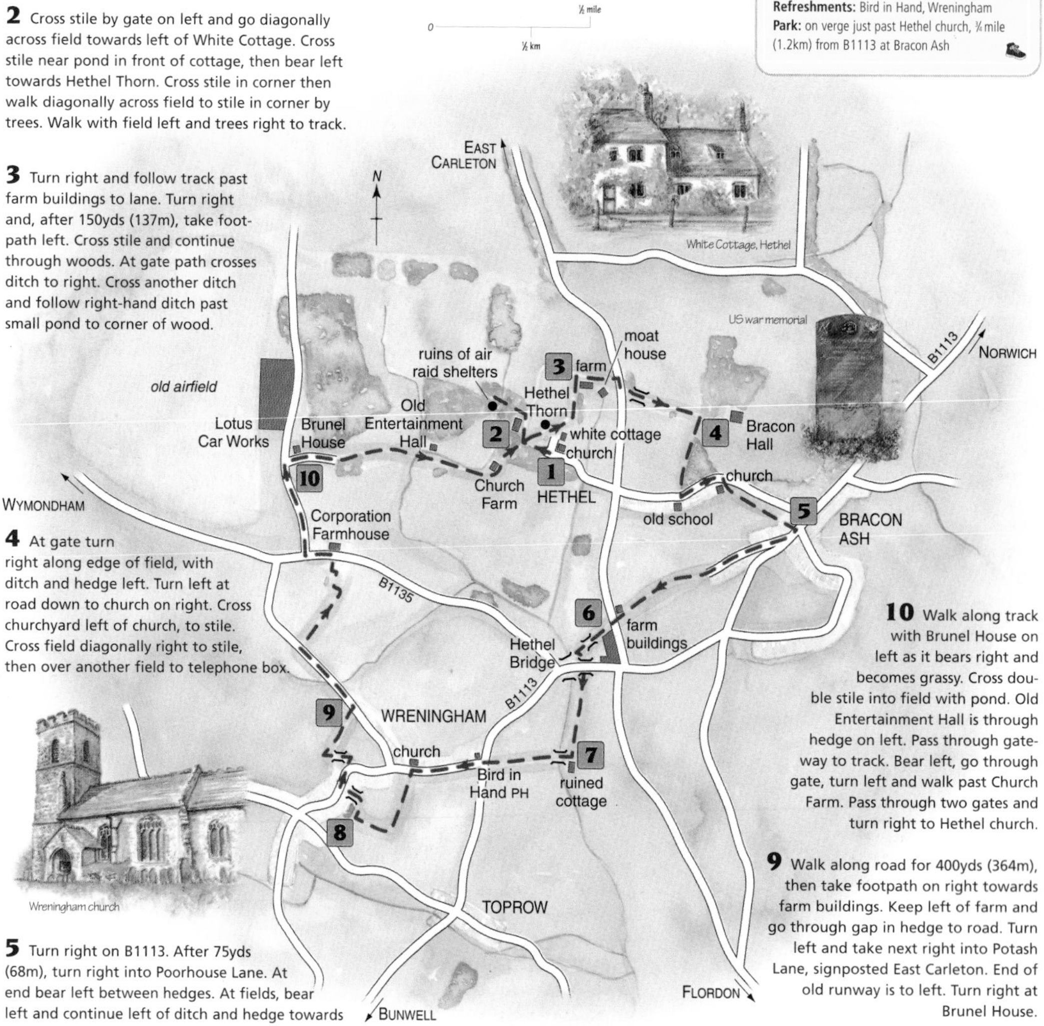

4 At gate turn right along edge of field, with ditch and hedge left. Turn left at road down to church on right. Cross churchyard left of church, to stile. Cross field diagonally right to stile, then over another field to telephone box.

5 Turn right on B1113. After 75yds (68m), turn right into Poorhouse Lane. At end bear left between hedges. At fields, bear left and continue left of ditch and hedge towards farm buildings. Cross lane to stile and path.

6 Continue by field edge to footbridge. Cross to next field and stile ahead. Cross to road, turn left then right, over stile to path under B1113. Continue with fence on left for 400yds (364m) to cottage. Bear right over footbridge.

7 Turn right, then immediately left with hedge and ditch left. Follow to road and cross to lane past Bird in Hand to Wreningham church. Take path opposite, along field edge to end. Turn right towards wood.

8 Don't cross stile, but turn right and after 60yds (55m) turn left over bridge. Take path to road and turn right. Where road bends right, take footpath left. After 50yds (46m) bear left over stile and bridge. Go right again, keeping ditch and hedge on right, to kissing-gate. Pass through and turn left on road.

9 Walk along road for 400yds (364m), then take footpath on right towards farm buildings. Keep left of farm and go through gap in hedge to road. Turn left and take next right into Potash Lane, signposted East Carleton. End of old runway is to left. Turn right at Brunel House.

10 Walk along track with Brunel House on left as it bears right and becomes grassy. Cross double stile into field with pond. Old Entertainment Hall is through hedge on left. Pass through gateway to track. Bear left, go through gate, turn left and walk past Church Farm. Pass through two gates and turn right to Hethel church.

The Huntingdon Home of Oliver Cromwell

On the banks of the Great Ouse in search of the Lord Protector

Distance: 8 miles (13km)
Total ascent: negligible
Paths: good, but very muddy after rain; flooding possible in winter
Terrain: meadows, riverside, some streets
Gradients: none
Refreshments: good choice in Huntingdon and Godmanchester; pubs at Hemingford Abbots and Houghton
Park: car park in Malthouse Close off Princess Street, opposite bus station

1 From Princess Street, follow Literary Walk to High Street and turn left to All Saints' Church, the Falcon Tavern and the Cromwell Museum. Continue past the church and turn left into George Street.

2 Go straight on at the traffic lights. When the road bends to the right, turn left along a footpath to Mill Common. Go diagonally left to a road and turn right, past Castle Hill, under the A14 and over a brook to join the Ouse Valley Way in Port Holme Meadow.

3 Walk straight across to a footbridge at Godmanchester Lock. Having crossed, turn left to reach Chinese Bridge. Cross into Godmanchester, leaving the Ouse Valley Way. Cross the B1043 to Cambridge Street, then left into Chadley Lane to St Mary's Church.

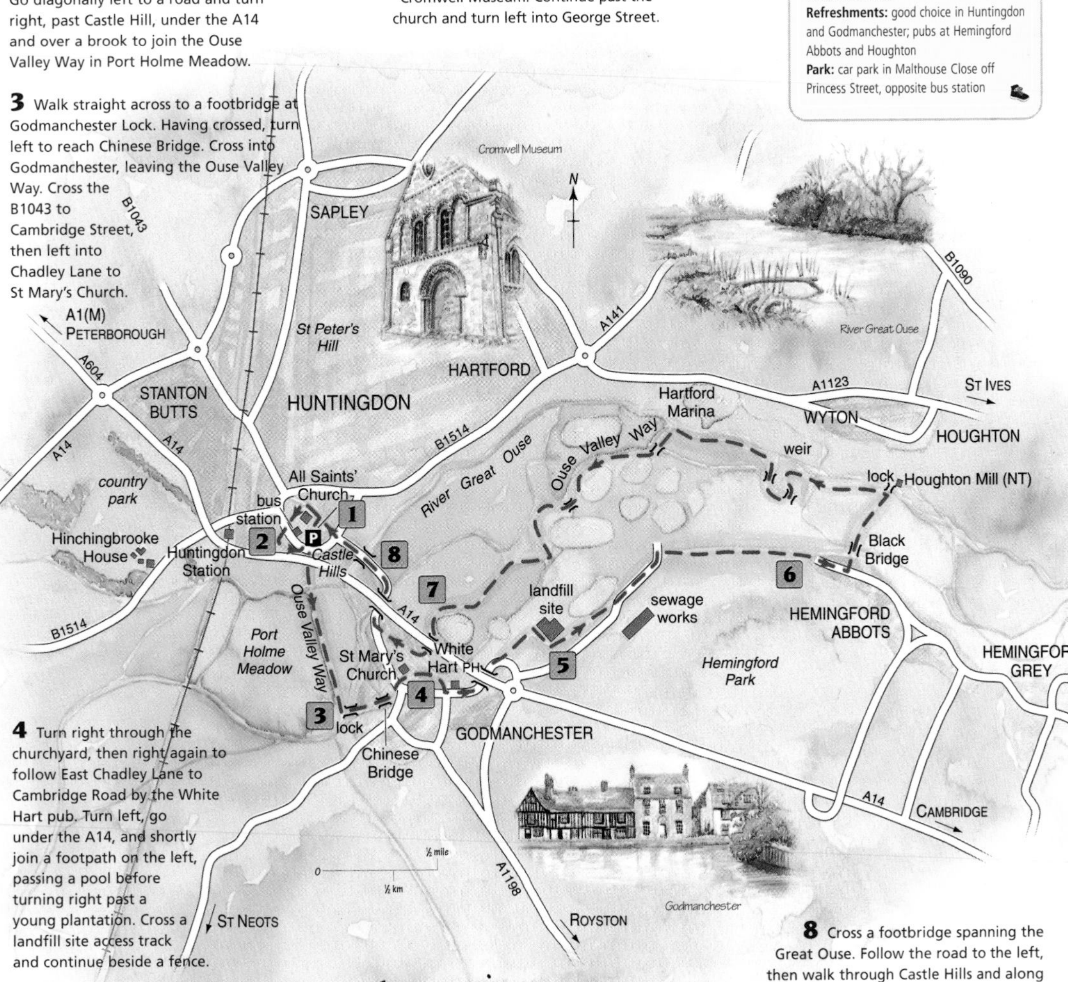

4 Turn right through the churchyard, then right again to follow East Chadley Lane to Cambridge Road by the White Hart pub. Turn left, go under the A14, and shortly join a footpath on the left, passing a pool before turning right past a young plantation. Cross a landfill site access track and continue beside a fence.

5 Ignore access to Cow Lane and carry straight on, climbing onto an embankment to walk along the top. At the far end descend to Cow Lane. Turn left, then join the second path on the right, a bridleway running beside a dismantled railway across a common.

6 After passing a pond, the bridleway veers slightly right to join Common Lane at Hemingford Abbots. Go straight on to reach Meadow Lane and turn left. Cross Black Bridge and Hemingford Meadow to Houghton Lock. Turn left beside the River Great Ouse, rejoining the Ouse Valley Way. Just follow the frequent waymarks now as the route explores the river, a tributary and flooded gravel pits.

7 Take an underpass beneath the A14 and head towards Godmanchester. Pass a housing estate to intercept a footpath/cycleway and turn right to the B1043. Turn right towards Huntingdon, crossing at the lights.

8 Cross a footbridge spanning the Great Ouse. Follow the road to the left, then walk through Castle Hills and along a passageway to Castle Hill. Proceed to Mill Common and turn right to Princess Street.

Grimes Graves and Brooding Breckland

The heathlands of central Norfolk hide a prehistoric flint mining site

Distance: 6½ miles (10km)
Total Ascent: 100ft (30m)
Paths: good; grassy tracks, metalled roads
Terrain: forest and heathland
Gradients: mainly flat, some gradual ascents
Refreshments: shop in Santon Downham
Park: Forestry Commission car park in Santon Downham, off B1107 between Brandon and Thetford

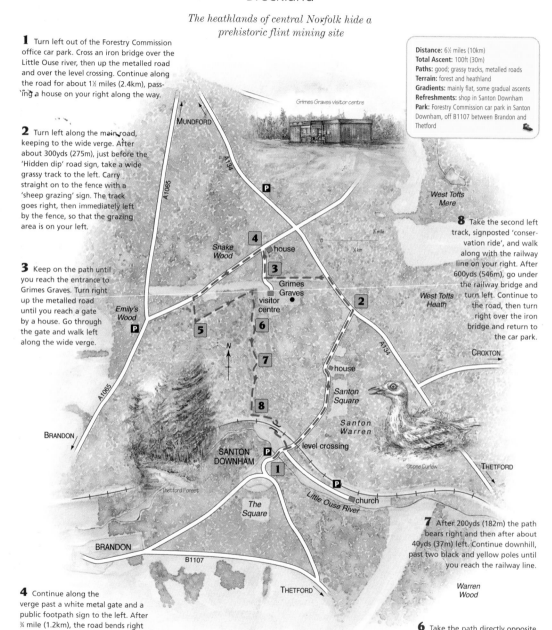

1 Turn left out of the Forestry Commission office car park. Cross an iron bridge over the Little Ouse river, then up the metalled road and over the level crossing. Continue along the road for about 1½ miles (2.4km), passing a house on your right along the way.

2 Turn left along the main road, keeping to the wide verge. After about 300yds (275m), just before the 'Hidden dip' road sign, take a wide grassy track to the left. Carry straight on to the fence with a 'sheep grazing' sign. The track goes right, then immediately left by the fence, so that the grazing area is on your left.

3 Keep on the path until you reach the entrance to Grimes Graves. Turn right up the metalled road until you reach a gate by a house. Go through the gate and walk left along the wide verge.

4 Continue along the verge past a white metal gate and a public footpath sign to the left. After ¾ mile (1.2km), the road bends right and there is another white gate on your left. Take the next immediate left along a wide grassy track. Follow this straight path until another wide track crosses it. Here, turn left to follow a yellow arrow waymark.

5 Go straight on past two more yellow arrows. At the next yellow marker, turn right. After about 550yds (500m), at a clearing, five paths converge.

6 Take the path directly opposite which bears only slightly to the left, not the one by the white signpost. After 300yds (275m), the path bears diagonally right and then, very shortly, to the left. Continue, following the yellow signs.

7 After 200yds (182m) the path bears right and then after about 40yds (37m) left. Continue downhill, past two black and yellow poles until you reach the railway line.

8 Take the second left track, signposted 'conservation ride', and walk along with the railway line on your right. After 600yds (546m), go under the railway bridge and turn left. Continue to the road, then turn right over the iron bridge and return to the car park.

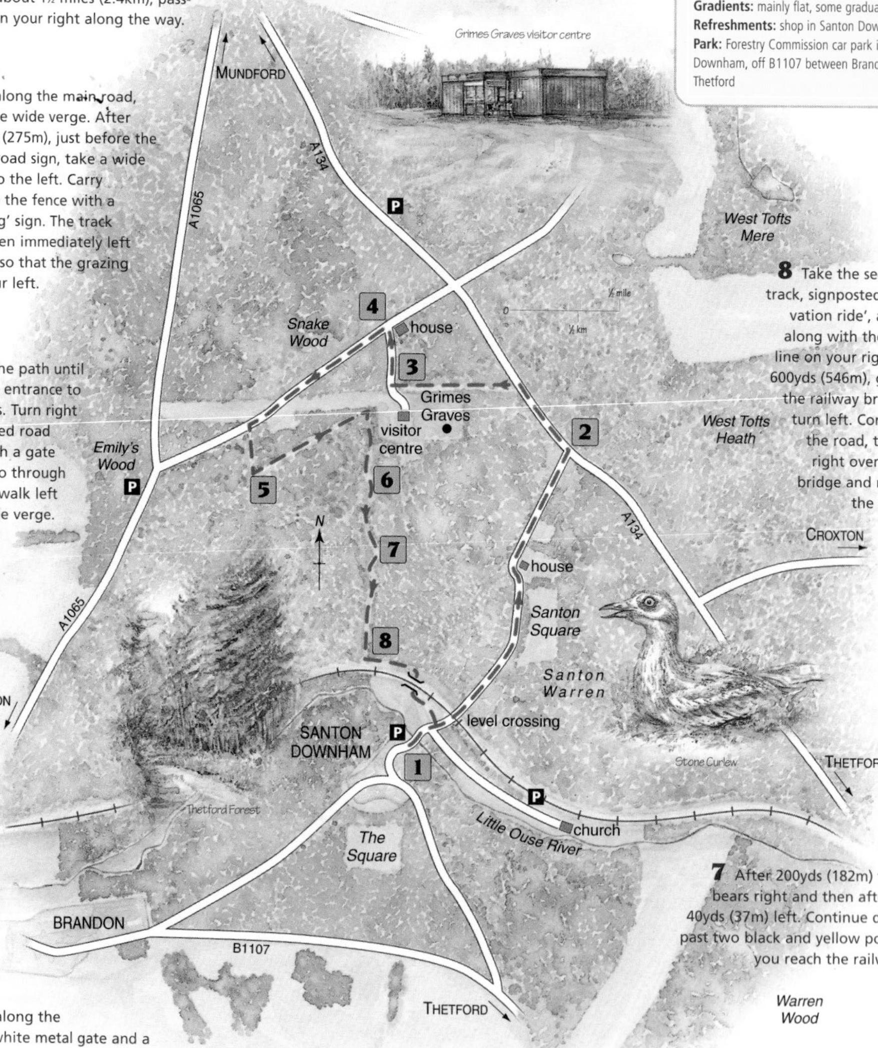

Central England

Often regarded as a vague term for an amorphous region, the Midlands have always been at the centre of the country's developing communications. The area was first criss-crossed by a series of Roman roads – indeed Watling Street and the Foss Way are still important cross-country thoroughfares. Canals converged on the big city of Birmingham while the town of Crewe grew at a fortuitous intersection of roads and railways. Ironbridge was where the Industrial Revolution started. Moving eastwards across country, signs of industry diminish and there are vast, rolling fields and prosperous farmlands.

Yet there are also a few wonderful pockets of wilderness and a surprising amount of historical interest and heritage to discover in the midst of urbanisation and extensive farming acreage. The Malverns offer a taste of wilderness in an essentially agricultural region, and the huddled range of the Shropshire Hills also rises abruptly from fertile plains. The real upland wilderness though, is the Dark Peak – more specifically, the grough-riven blanket bogs of the Kinder plateau. The gentler White Peak is no less spectacular, but the landforms are altogether different and much influenced by the underlying carboniferous limestone.

It's a landscape well fought over through the centuries. During the Wars of the Roses one of the largest armies ever assembled descended on Bosworth Field so that rival claims to the throne could be settled. The same thing happened at Naseby, only this time it was full-blown civil war. In World War II the Midlands suffered mightily – not for nothing is this region known as the Battlefield of England.

You can walk in Shakespeare's footsteps in rural Warwickshire, and, if literary themes are to your liking, D H Lawrence's old haunts can also be investigated in Nottinghamshire. A variation on the theme could take you to Malvern, where Edward Elgar found musical inspiration.

Best of the Rest

Dovedale Dovedale has been one of the most popular beauty spots in the Peak District for centuries – Izaak Walton came here to fish and Lord Byron compared it to Greece and Switzerland. Late spring is the best time to explore the valley of the Dove, when the wildflowers are at their best, either on a continuous walk along the river through lush meadows and woodland or on any of the circular walks starting from nearby villages such as Hartington and Biggin.

Stiperstones The last outpost of the Shropshire Hills is a mysterious spread of rocks over a pocket of sweeping moorland. So close to the Welsh border, this is a strange, unpopulated land, with peculiar Anglo-Welsh placenames and a wealth of tracks and bridleways to tempt the explorer on foot. The Stiperstones themselves can form the basis for a variety of fine circular walks from Pennerley.

Cannock Chase The Heart of England Way traverses the Country Park which protects this surprising pocket of heathland to the north of the West Midlands conurbation. Though its proximity to so many people makes the popular parts very crowded, there are still many oases of quiet to be discovered by the walker who is willing to look for them.

Monsal Trail The Peak District has an enviable network of relatively easy trails based around the former railway lines which criss-crossed its complex landscape. In Monsal Dale you can get a feel for how it must have been for passengers as the trail appears and reappears in this tight little wooded valley, much loved by photographers.

Birmingham canals It is a cliché to say that this major West Midlands city has more miles of canal than Venice, but the potential this offers the walker who wishes to explore the fascinating underbelly of a historic industrial landscape is not to be overlooked. Much of the network is waymarked and a pleasing variety of scenery can be encountered, from stately parkland to state-of-the-art new developments; still-pounding heavy industry to the haunted scars of former industrial giants.

Valley of Revolution

Coalbrookdale witnessed the birth of industry, but time has healed the scars

Distance: 5½ miles (8.8km)
Total ascent: 300ft (91m)
Paths: mostly good; riverside tracks are unsurfaced and can be muddy; steps
Terrain: roads and pavements, unsurfaced river track
Gradients: steep climb to top of ridge
Refreshments: several cafés and pubs in Ironbridge
Park: in long-stay car park beyond roundabout from visitor centre

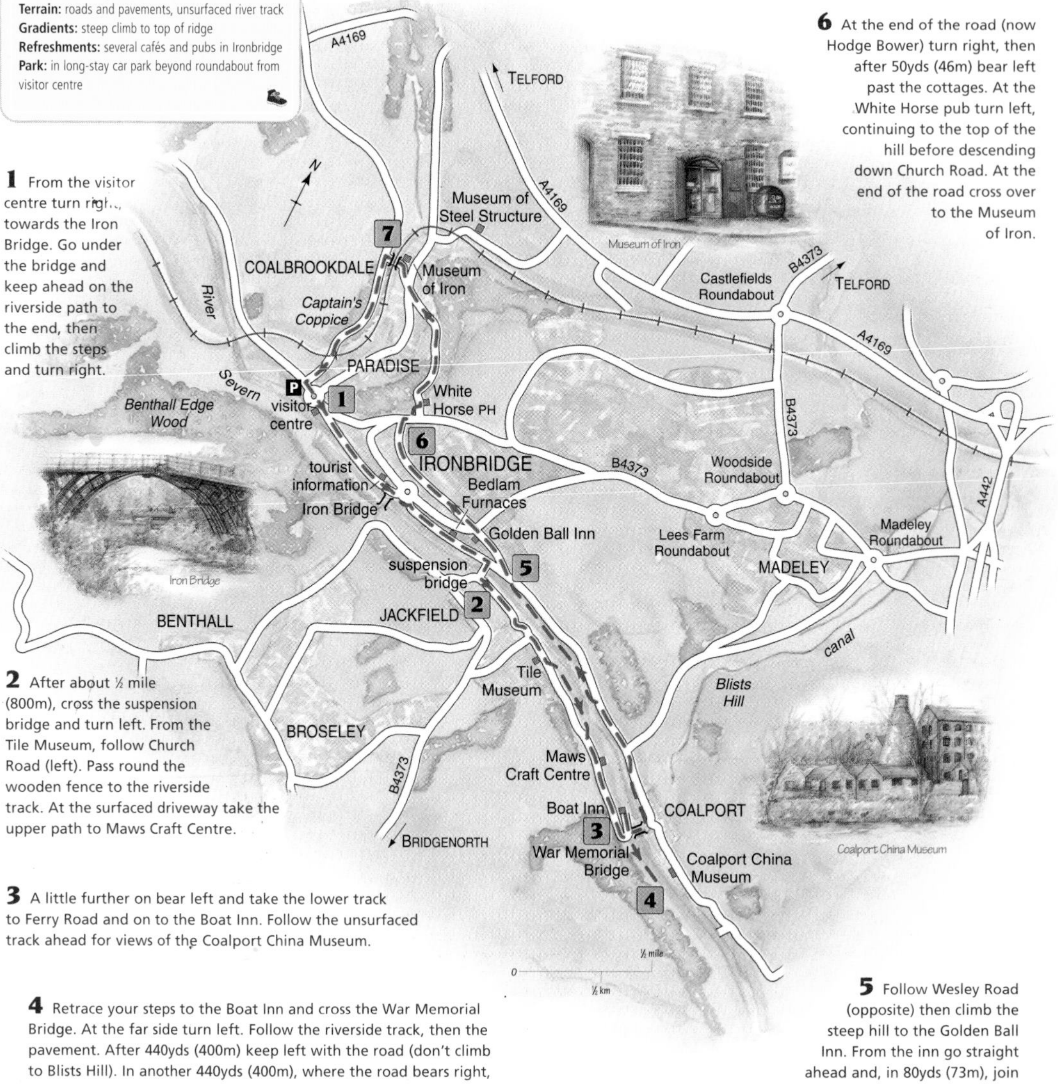

1 From the visitor centre turn right, towards the Iron Bridge. Go under the bridge and keep ahead on the riverside path to the end, then climb the steps and turn right.

2 After about ½ mile (800m), cross the suspension bridge and turn left. From the Tile Museum, follow Church Road (left). Pass round the wooden fence to the riverside track. At the surfaced driveway take the upper path to Maws Craft Centre.

3 A little further on bear left and take the lower track to Ferry Road and on to the Boat Inn. Follow the unsurfaced track ahead for views of the Coalport China Museum.

4 Retrace your steps to the Boat Inn and cross the War Memorial Bridge. At the far side turn left. Follow the riverside track, then the pavement. After 440yds (400m) keep left with the road (don't climb to Blists Hill). In another 440yds (400m), where the road bears right, branch left over a stile and along a meandering, wooded riverside path. Eventually a waymarker points to the right. Ascend a flight of narrow steps here to emerge at a junction with Wesley Road.

5 Follow Wesley Road (opposite) then climb the steep hill to the Golden Ball Inn. From the inn go straight ahead and, in 80yds (73m), join the pedestrian path with the railing. Cross the next road and take Belmont Road, ahead.

6 At the end of the road (now Hodge Bower) turn right, then after 50yds (46m) bear left past the cottages. At the White Horse pub turn left, continuing to the top of the hill before descending down Church Road. At the end of the road cross over to the Museum of Iron.

7 Facing the museum gates, turn left, following the road under the railway bridge. Immediately after the bridge turn left into Coach Road. At the end (now Station Road) turn left to return to the visitor centre.

Panorama from the Wrekin

A walk up Shropshire's most prominent landmark reveals enormous views

Distance: 5 miles (8km)
Total ascent: 820ft (250m)
Paths: good, but muddy in places after rain
Terrain: roads, woodland, fields and steep ridge
Gradients: gentle, except for final very steep climb to the summit
Refreshments: Huntsman pub, Little Wenlock
Park: lay-by at Forest Glen, on minor road between Wellington and Little Wenlock, near a reservoir

1 Walk to the nearby road junction and turn right, heading for Little Wenlock. Continue (with care as there is no footway) until the road makes a pronounced bend to the right, where you leave it by branching left onto a shady green lane.

2 The green lane rises through trees to a track junction close to a group of ruined buildings. Beyond, the track – an old route to the hamlet of Huntington – descends gently, but you must leave it only a few strides after the ruined buildings by turning right onto an initially indistinct path into a narrow belt of woodland.

3 The path meanders through the woodland but eventually reaches a more direct, and slightly raised, path parallel with the woodland edge.

4 Leave the woodland at a stile and cross the field to another stile, before a short stretch of farm track leads you out to a road. Turn right and go down the road until, just before it bends sharply right, you can leave it at a stile on the left, to enter more light woodland.

5 A woodland path guides you down to a farm track. Cross this to a stile opposite, leading to open pasture. Turn left along the field edge and, after crossing an intermediate stile, continue up the field to another stile, beyond which is a broad forest track.

6 Turn left and follow the track for about ½ mile (800m) along the wooded base of the Wrekin until, just as it begins to descend, the track forks. Here, branch right into trees onto a path that also descends, as it rounds the southwestern edge of the hill. Continue with the track to an obvious path junction.

7 Here, by a prominent yew tree, turn right and climb very steeply, finally breaking free of the tree cover as you approach a conspicuous rocky outcrop. The summit of the Wrekin rises just a short distance further on, and, on a clear day, is a good place to linger. A nearby toposcope identifies distant hills and features.

8 Continue across the summit ridge, soon descending through Heaven Gate and Hell Gate, and following a broad track as it curves past a semi-derelict cottage. After a little more descent, another bend, and a final fling with the woodland, the track ends directly opposite the start point.

Over the Long Mynd

Traversing the high moorland ridge above Church Stretton

Distance: 8¾ miles (14km)
Total ascent: 1,150ft (350m)
Paths: mostly clear and firm, some boggy areas and some parts muddy when wet
Terrain: extensive heather moorlands buttressed by steep hill slopes
Gradients: fairly steep early on but much gentler ascent to the top
Refreshments: various in Church Stretton; Ragleth Inn and Mynd House Hotel at Little Stretton
Park: car parks on Easthope Road in the middle of Church Stretton

1 From the car park leave town by walking along the Shrewsbury Road. Turn left into a road signposted for Carding Mill Valley and golf course. Fork right up a winding road at Trevor Hill, eventually turning left to reach the golf course and clubhouse.

2 Go through the gate to the right of the clubhouse marked 'Public Footpath to the Hills'. Turn right and walk alongside beeches, then turn left and follow marker posts up a valley and across the golf course. The path runs around the head of a valley and passes a shelter, then climbs a rise before heading off to the left. Keep following the marker posts, passing a black hut, until you overlook the Carding Mill Valley.

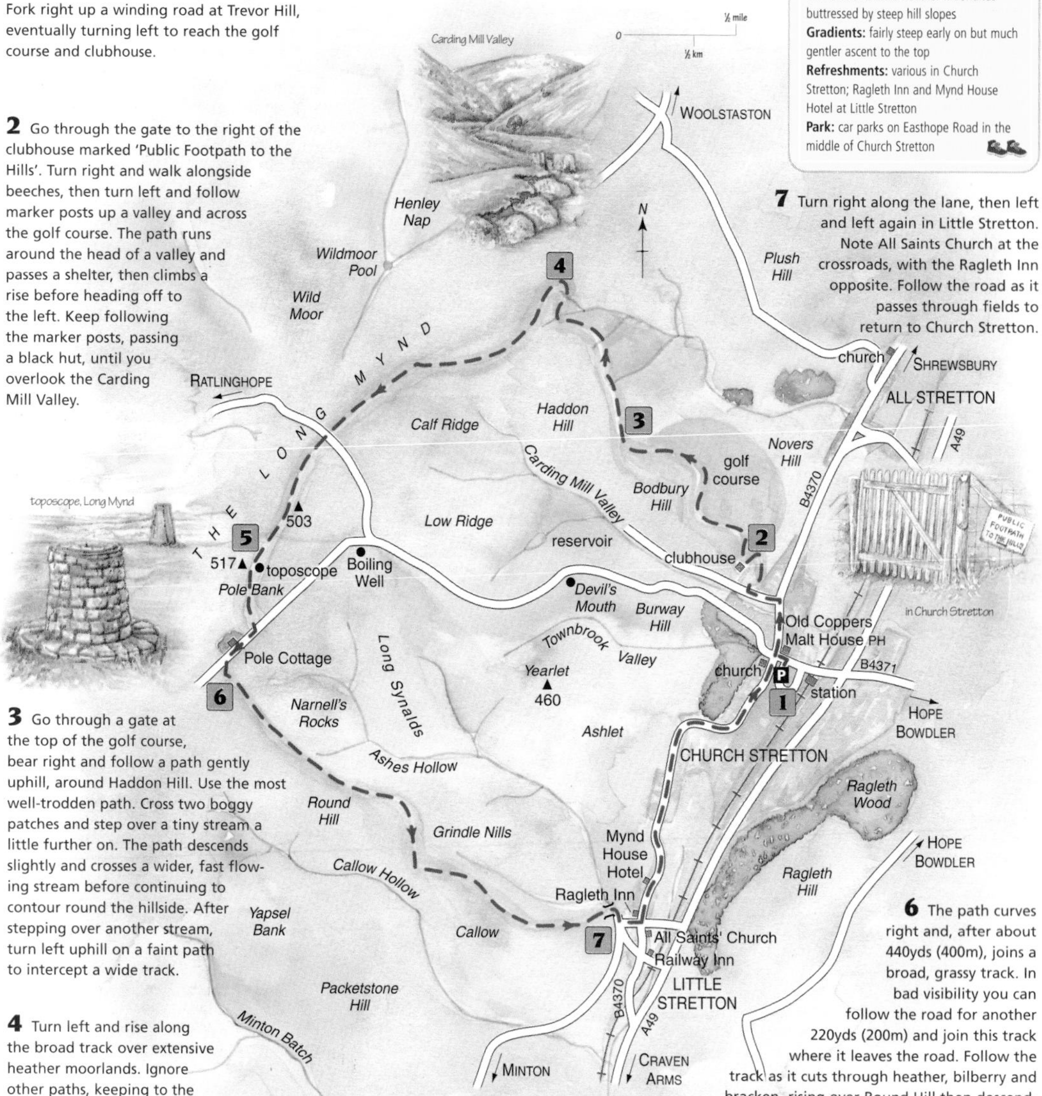

Carding Mill Valley

toposcope, Long Mynd

in Church Stretton

3 Go through a gate at the top of the golf course, bear right and follow a path gently uphill, around Haddon Hill. Use the most well-trodden path. Cross two boggy patches and step over a tiny stream a little further on. The path descends slightly and crosses a wider, fast flowing stream before continuing to contour round the hillside. After stepping over another stream, turn left uphill on a faint path to intercept a wide track.

4 Turn left and rise along the broad track over extensive heather moorlands. Ignore other paths, keeping to the broad track. At one junction there is a view down Carding Mill Valley to Church Stretton. Keep straight on, rising gently to reach a complex junction. Simply step to the right to follow a narrow track uphill.

5 The track leads finally to the top of the Long Mynd (1,696ft/517m). There is a trig point (small cement pillar) and a toposcope. Snowdon is named in the view, 63 miles (101km) away. Walk straight on down to a narrow road and turn right. After passing Pole Cottage (a black hut surrounded by trees) take a grassy path on the left.

6 The path curves right and, after about 440yds (400m), joins a broad, grassy track. In bad visibility you can follow the road for another 220yds (200m) and join this track where it leaves the road. Follow the track as it cuts through heather, bilberry and bracken, rising over Round Hill then descending to a saddle. The path rises to the right, then goes round a steep slope to reach another saddle. The gentle gradient eventually gives way to a steep descent to a gate by a stream. Ford the stream and cross a footbridge to reach a lane.

7 Turn right along the lane, then left and left again in Little Stretton. Note All Saints Church at the crossroads, with the Ragleth Inn opposite. Follow the road as it passes through fields to return to Church Stretton.

On Elgar's Malverns

The town and shapely string of distinctive hills inspired one of Britain's greatest composers

1 From the car park go through the red gates towards the pool's entrance, but bear right to walk beside the building. Bear left around the back of the pool, then turn right across the footbridge over the pond. Follow the path through Priory Park, bearing left in front of the theatres building to reach a prominent lamp. Here, turn right to leave the park, bearing left, then right up a lane.

2 When the lane reaches Grange Road, turn left to a T-junction with Abbey Road.

3 Turn right along Abbey Road, passing the Abbey Hotel and going through the arch of the Abbey Gatehouse. Opposite the post office, bear left up the steps and turn right along Worcester Road. Just after The Unicorn, turn left up St Ann's Road. Go up the rising road, keeping straight ahead through the trees to reach a 'Turning Place Only' sign on the right. Here turn sharply back right on a path which rises through trees and rhododendrons.

4 Ignore a crossing path, continuing to join a wider path (from left) and following it to Ivy Scar Rocks, the largest Malvern rock outcrop. Immediately beyond the outcrop, bear left up a steep, narrow path, zig-zagging through gorse, broom and bracken.

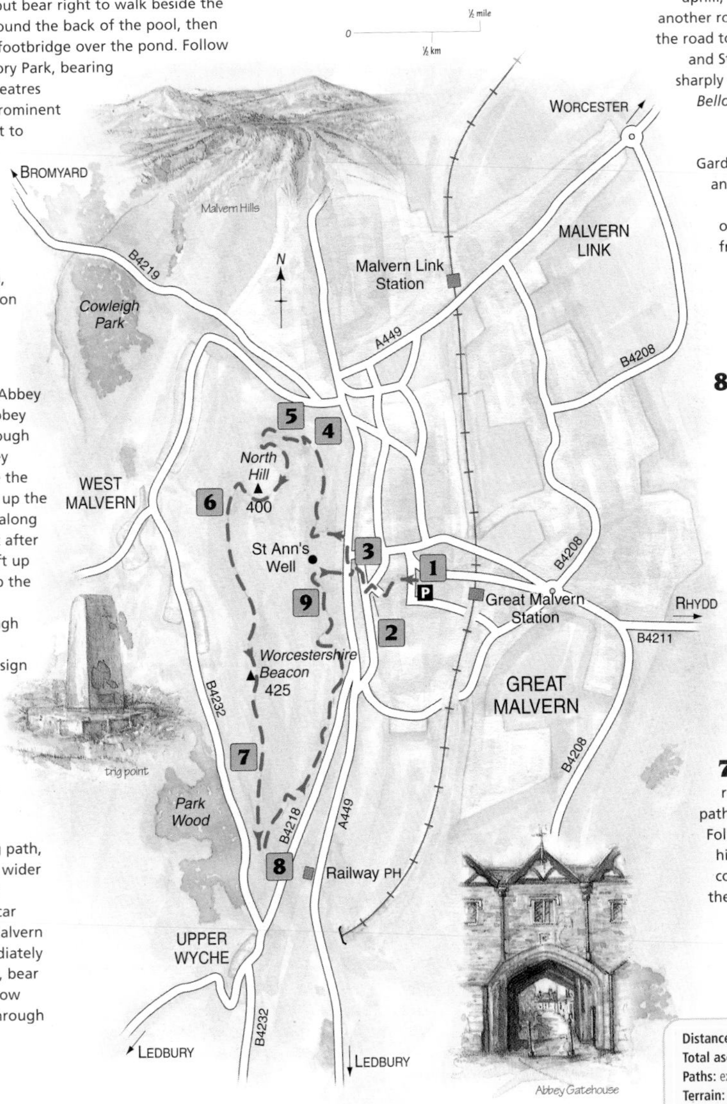

5 At a T-junction with a wider path (Lady Howard de Walden Drive), turn right, soon reaching a seat. Turn left up a steep, but obvious, grassy path. Bear right at a junction, continuing to the top of North Hill with its splendid views.

6 Go downhill towards Table Hill ahead, bearing left at the col between the peaks and following a grassy path down to rejoin de Walden Drive. Turn right and follow the track towards Worcestershire Beacon, prominent ahead. At a panorama dial, bear right off the path for a steep short-cut to the summit.

7 Go downhill along the ridge top to reach a wide path at the base of a hillock. Follow the path around the hillock (on left) and past a covered reservoir, to reach the Gold Mine, a cylindrical stone signpost.

8 Turn sharply left along a path between trees. Just after the reservoir railings begin, fork left along a narrow, rising, grassy path passing above a quarry to the right, then zig-zagging to the quarry base. Continue ahead, with the quarry to the right, for a few paces, then turn left down a wide path.

9 Just as you reach a road, bear left, uphill, along a narrow path to another road. Bear left, following the road to signs for Foley Terrace and St Ann's Road. Soon turn sharply right along the drive to *Bello Squardo*. Go down the steps to the left of the gateway to Rose Bank Gardens. Continue to a road and bear left across it to a road down to the post office. Retrace your steps from point 3 to return to the start.

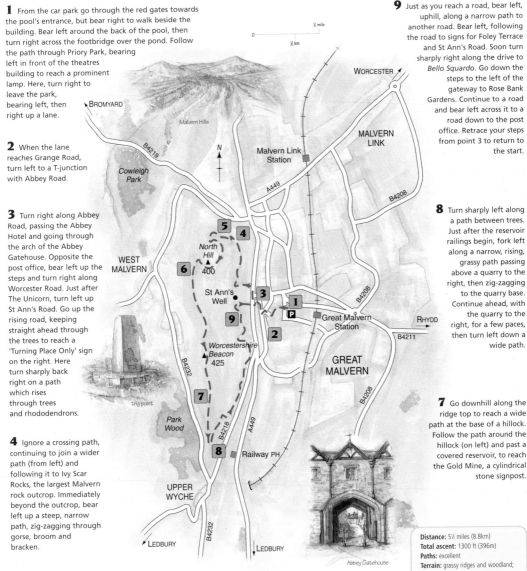

Distance: 5½ miles (8.8km)
Total ascent: 1300 ft (396m)
Paths: excellent
Terrain: grassy ridges and woodland; town walking at start and finish
Gradients: mostly gradual, but steep on ascent of North Hill
Refreshments: lots in Great Malvern
Park: car park opposite Splash swimming pool, Priory Road, Great Malvern

WALK 44

Border Lines – on Offa's Dyke

A walk along England's border with Wales reveals much more than the great Saxon boundary marker

1 Across the road from the Chirk Bank post office follow the canal towpath back towards Chirk, crossing the aqueduct to a tunnel at the end of it. A footpath now climbs to the Glyn Ceiriog road.

2 Turn left down the road for 100yds (91m) to a house named Pen-y-Waen, then follow a waymarked footpath on the right, across the cutting of the old Glyn Valley Tramway. Walk through woodland, returning to the road just short of Pont-Faen (bridge).

3 Cross the bridge and turn right along the lane. After 150yds (137m), near a telephone box, go over a stile into fields. The path follows the south banks of the Ceiriog. Take the left fork on entering Woodland Trust land and climb through Pentre Wood to a country lane. turn right and follow the lane for 300yds (274m) to The Old School.

Distance: 5¾ miles (9.3km)
Total ascent: 900ft (274m)
Paths: waymarked but faint; field paths muddy after rain
Terrain: fields, country lanes, woodland and canal towpath
Gradients: gradual
Refreshments: hot take-away snacks at Chirk Bank Post Office and the Bridge Inn
Park: by Chirk Bank Post Office, in Chirk Bank, on English side of border near Chirk, between Oswestry and Llangollen

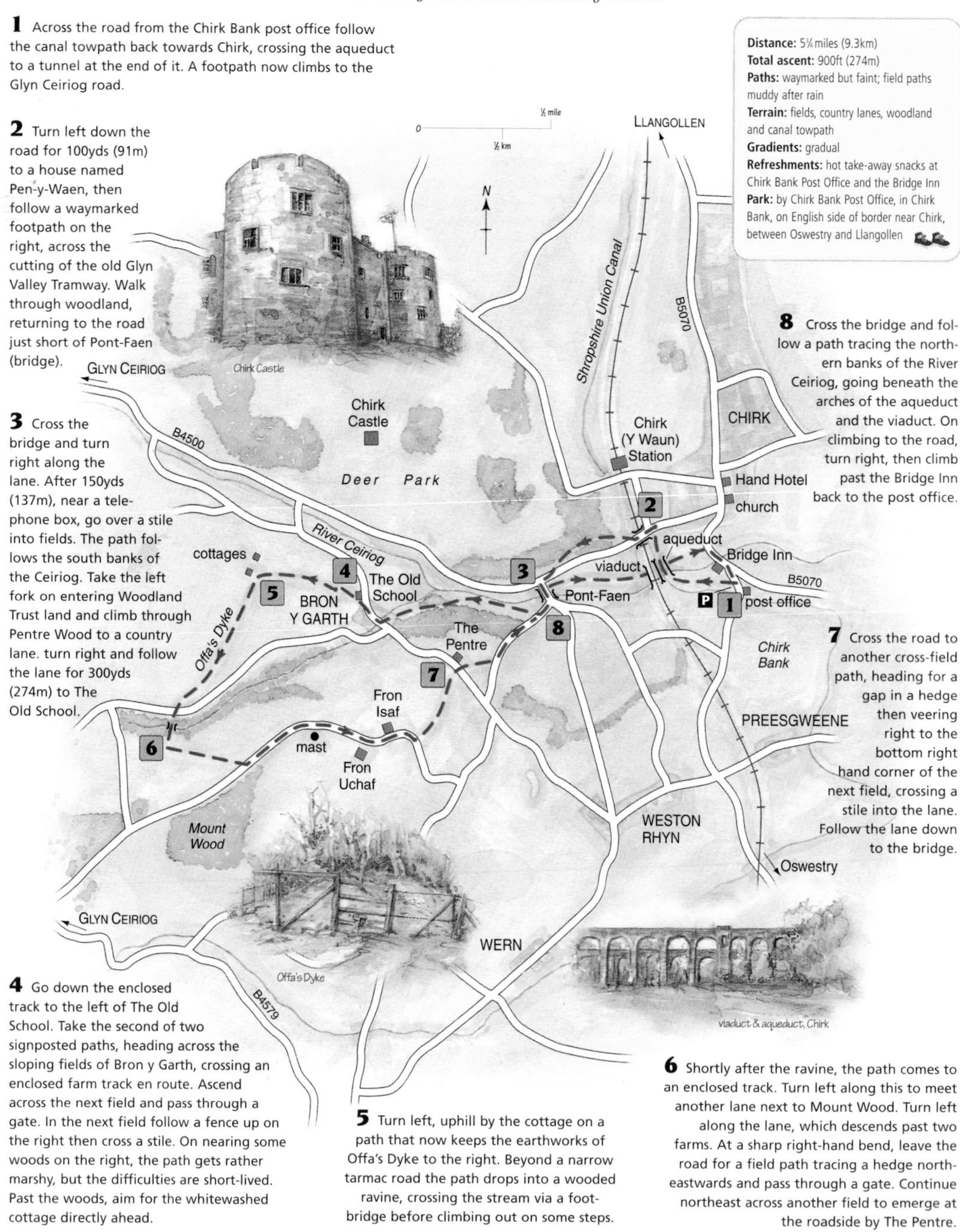

8 Cross the bridge and follow a path tracing the northern banks of the River Ceiriog, going beneath the arches of the aqueduct and the viaduct. On climbing to the road, turn right, then climb past the Bridge Inn back to the post office.

7 Cross the road to another cross-field path, heading for a gap in a hedge then veering right to the bottom right hand corner of the next field, crossing a stile into the lane. Follow the lane down to the bridge.

4 Go down the enclosed track to the left of The Old School. Take the second of two signposted paths, heading across the sloping fields of Bron y Garth, crossing an enclosed farm track en route. Ascend across the next field and pass through a gate. In the next field follow a fence up on the right then cross a stile. On nearing some woods on the right, the path gets rather marshy, but the difficulties are short-lived. Past the woods, aim for the whitewashed cottage directly ahead.

5 Turn left, uphill by the cottage on a path that now keeps the earthworks of Offa's Dyke to the right. Beyond a narrow tarmac road the path drops into a wooded ravine, crossing the stream via a footbridge before climbing out on some steps.

6 Shortly after the ravine, the path comes to an enclosed track. Turn left along this to meet another lane next to Mount Wood. Turn left along the lane, which descends past two farms. At a sharp right-hand bend, leave the road for a field path tracing a hedge northeastwards and pass through a gate. Continue northeast across another field to emerge at the roadside by The Pentre.

The Goyt Valley

A circuit in one of the Peak District's most famously conserved valleys

1 Follow the nature trail signs leading up into the forest. Soon after entering the trees join a broad path and turn right, following and eventually crossing a stream. At a sharp bend and path junction, turn right to arrive at the partly reconstructed ruins of Errwood Hall.

2 Left of the Hall ruins, up waymarked steps, continue on the woodland walk as it leads off into the trees, past some gateposts and the remains of estate workers' cottages on the edge of open country.

3 Turn right by the cottages, down to some steps which lead to a footbridge and a crossroads of paths, where you turn left, going up through the sparse trees to contour below wooded Foxlow Edge. Beyond the trees a short detour takes you to a circular shrine, erected in 1889 by the Grimshawes in memory of their childrens' governess.

4 Climb up the steps from the shrine, back on the main path which leads up to the road ahead, which is known as The Street. This was a packhorse route from Buxton to the west. Turn uphill on the road to its summit, known as Pym's Chair, after John Pym, the 17th-century Puritan leader.

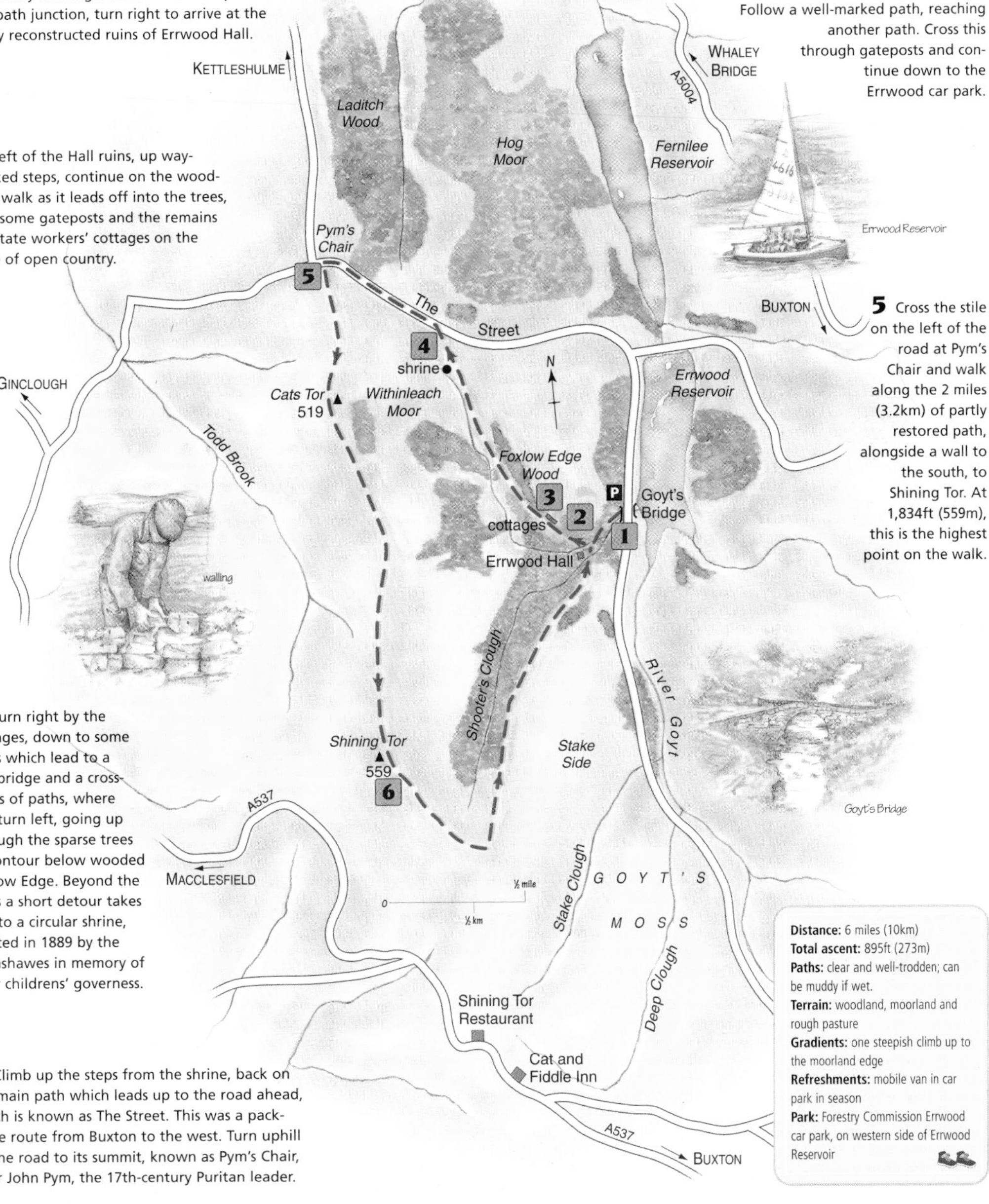

5 Cross the stile on the left of the road at Pym's Chair and walk along the 2 miles (3.2km) of partly restored path, alongside a wall to the south, to Shining Tor. At 1,834ft (559m), this is the highest point on the walk.

6 From the summit, which is reached by crossing a ladder stile, drop down to a stile from which a broad green track heads left above Shooter's Clough (to the left), contouring gently down. Follow a well-marked path, reaching another path. Cross this through gateposts and continue down to the Errwood car park.

Distance: 6 miles (10km)
Total ascent: 895ft (273m)
Paths: clear and well-trodden; can be muddy if wet.
Terrain: woodland, moorland and rough pasture
Gradients: one steepish climb up to the moorland edge
Refreshments: mobile van in car park in season
Park: Forestry Commission Errwood car park, on western side of Errwood Reservoir

The Wonders of the Peak at Castleton

Early tourists were filled with awe at the sights around this Derbyshire village

Distance: 5 miles (8km)
Total ascent: 1,035ft (315m)
Paths: can be muddy if wet; ridge mostly paved
Terrain: rocky start then easy going on ridge and through fields
Gradients: one steep, 1,000ft (305m) ascent to the Mam Tor ridge
Refreshments: restaurants, pubs and cafes in Castleton, picnic tables at Mam Nick
Park: main car park, Castleton

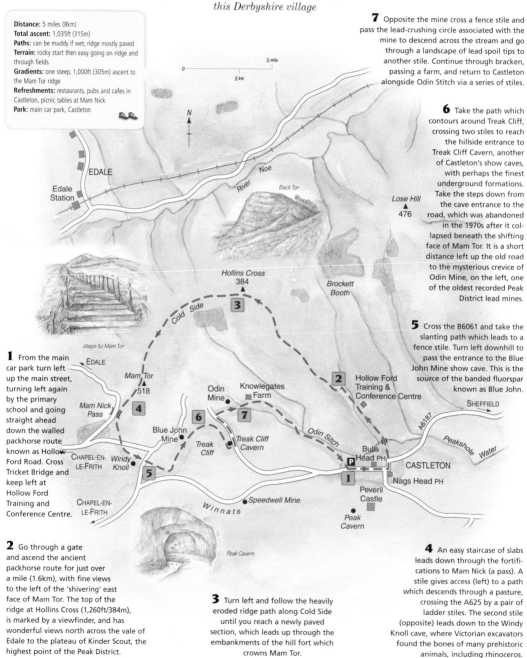

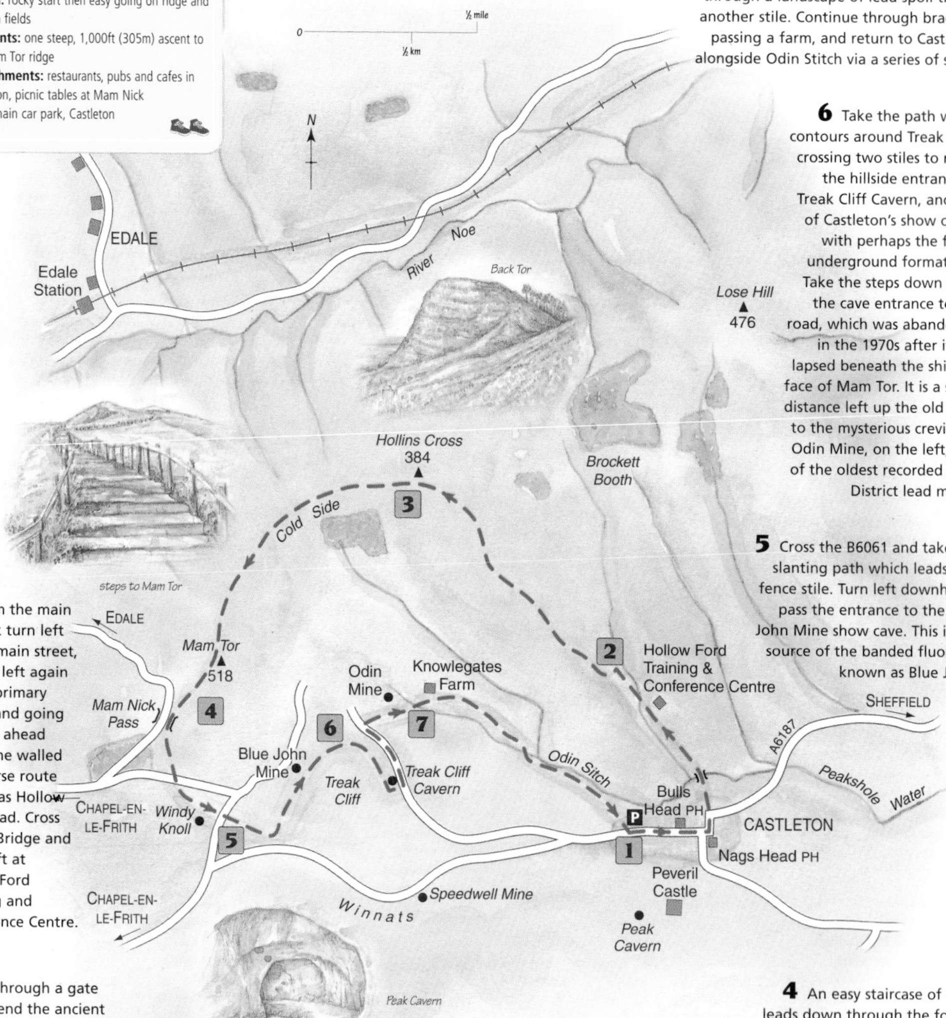

1 From the main car park turn left up the main street, turning left again by the primary school and going straight ahead down the walled packhorse route known as Hollow Ford Road. Cross Tricket Bridge and keep left at Hollow Ford Training and Conference Centre.

2 Go through a gate and ascend the ancient packhorse route for just over a mile (1.6km), with fine views to the left of the 'shivering' east face of Mam Tor. The top of the ridge at Hollins Cross (1,260ft/384m), is marked by a viewfinder, and has wonderful views north across the vale of Edale to the plateau of Kinder Scout, the highest point of the Peak District.

3 Turn left and follow the heavily eroded ridge path along Cold Side until you reach a newly paved section, which leads up through the embankments of the hill fort which crowns Mam Tor.

4 An easy staircase of slabs leads down through the fortifications to Mam Nick (a pass). A stile gives access (left) to a path which descends through a pasture, crossing the A625 by a pair of ladder stiles. The second stile (opposite) leads down to the Windy Knoll cave, where Victorian excavators found the bones of many prehistoric animals, including rhinoceros.

5 Cross the B6061 and take the slanting path which leads to a fence stile. Turn left downhill to pass the entrance to the Blue John Mine show cave. This is the source of the banded fluorspar known as Blue John.

6 Take the path which contours around Treak Cliff, crossing two stiles to reach the hillside entrance to Treak Cliff Cavern, another of Castleton's show caves, with perhaps the finest underground formations. Take the steps down from the cave entrance to the road, which was abandoned in the 1970s after it collapsed beneath the shifting face of Mam Tor. It is a short distance left up the old road to the mysterious crevice of Odin Mine, on the left, one of the oldest recorded Peak District lead mines.

7 Opposite the mine cross a fence stile and pass the lead-crushing circle associated with the mine to descend across the stream and go through a landscape of lead spoil tips to another stile. Continue through bracken, passing a farm, and return to Castleton alongside Odin Stitch via a series of stiles.

Lud's Church and the Green Knight

Legends haunt the strange rock shapes and hollows along and beyond The Roaches

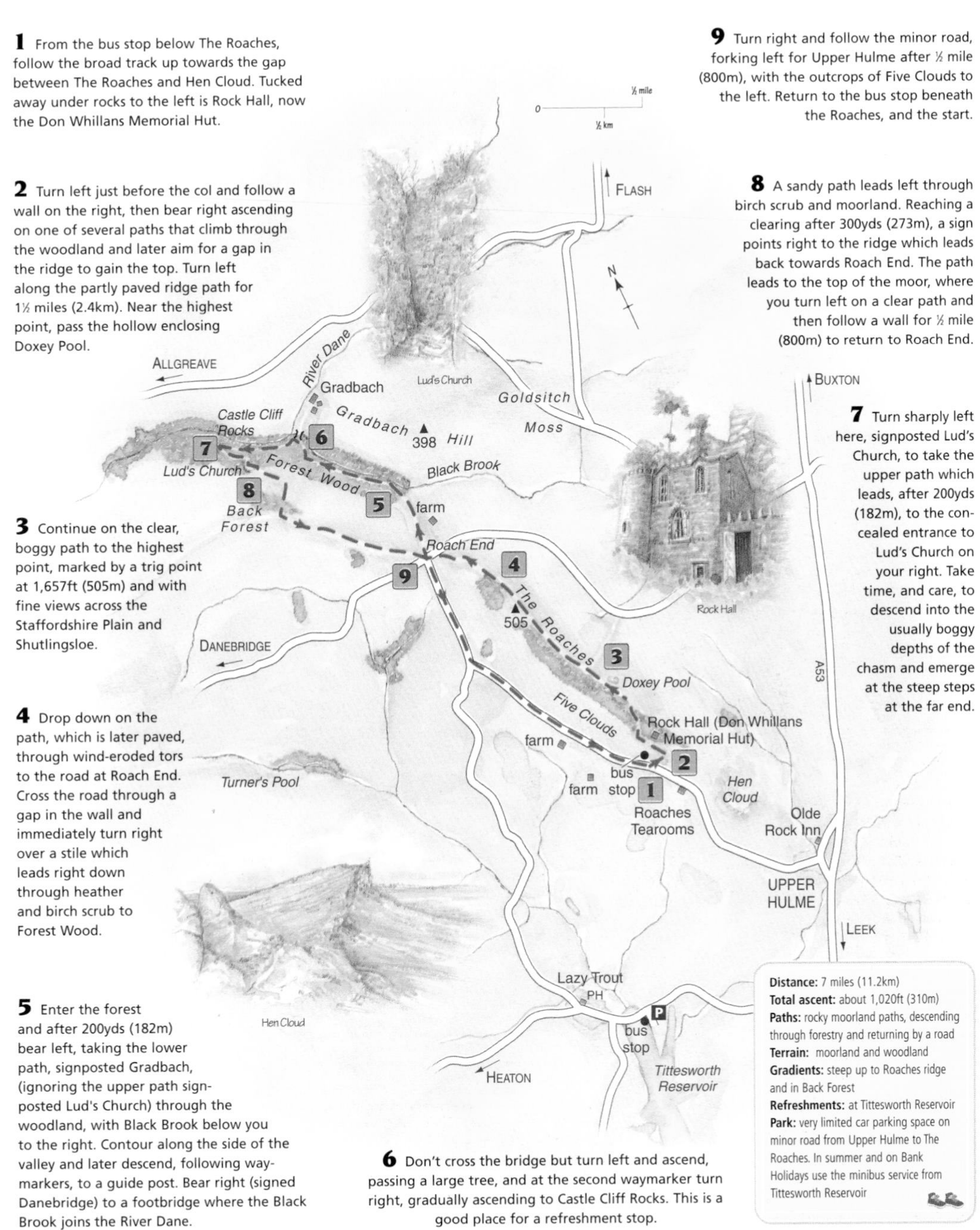

1 From the bus stop below The Roaches, follow the broad track up towards the gap between The Roaches and Hen Cloud. Tucked away under rocks to the left is Rock Hall, now the Don Whillans Memorial Hut.

2 Turn left just before the col and follow a wall on the right, then bear right ascending on one of several paths that climb through the woodland and later aim for a gap in the ridge to gain the top. Turn left along the partly paved ridge path for 1½ miles (2.4km). Near the highest point, pass the hollow enclosing Doxey Pool.

3 Continue on the clear, boggy path to the highest point, marked by a trig point at 1,657ft (505m) and with fine views across the Staffordshire Plain and Shutlingsloe.

4 Drop down on the path, which is later paved, through wind-eroded tors to the road at Roach End. Cross the road through a gap in the wall and immediately turn right over a stile which leads right down through heather and birch scrub to Forest Wood.

5 Enter the forest and after 200yds (182m) bear left, taking the lower path, signposted Gradbach, (ignoring the upper path signposted Lud's Church) through the woodland, with Black Brook below you to the right. Contour along the side of the valley and later descend, following waymarkers, to a guide post. Bear right (signed Danebridge) to a footbridge where the Black Brook joins the River Dane.

6 Don't cross the bridge but turn left and ascend, passing a large tree, and at the second waymarker turn right, gradually ascending to Castle Cliff Rocks. This is a good place for a refreshment stop.

7 Turn sharply left here, signposted Lud's Church, to take the upper path which leads, after 200yds (182m), to the concealed entrance to Lud's Church on your right. Take time, and care, to descend into the usually boggy depths of the chasm and emerge at the steep steps at the far end.

8 A sandy path leads left through birch scrub and moorland. Reaching a clearing after 300yds (273m), a sign points right to the ridge which leads back towards Roach End. The path leads to the top of the moor, where you turn left on a clear path and then follow a wall for ½ mile (800m) to return to Roach End.

9 Turn right and follow the minor road, forking left for Upper Hulme after ½ mile (800m), with the outcrops of Five Clouds to the left. Return to the bus stop beneath the Roaches, and the start.

Distance: 7 miles (11.2km)
Total ascent: about 1,020ft (310m)
Paths: rocky moorland paths, descending through forestry and returning by a road
Terrain: moorland and woodland
Gradients: steep up to Roaches ridge and in Back Forest
Refreshments: at Tittesworth Reservoir
Park: very limited car parking space on minor road from Upper Hulme to The Roaches. In summer and on Bank Holidays use the minibus service from Tittesworth Reservoir

A Walk in the Dark Peak

Up to the bleak Kinder Plateau, where the Pennine hills first assert their mountain credentials

Distance: 6½ miles (10.5km)
Total ascent: 1,100 feet (335m)
Paths: mainly unsurfaced, some very rough; some short road sections
Terrain: fields, peat moorlands
Gradients: very steep in parts (do the walk in reverse for a more gradual ascent)
Refreshments: Ramblers Inn, Old Nag's Head, Edale
Park: Edale car park, signed off A625

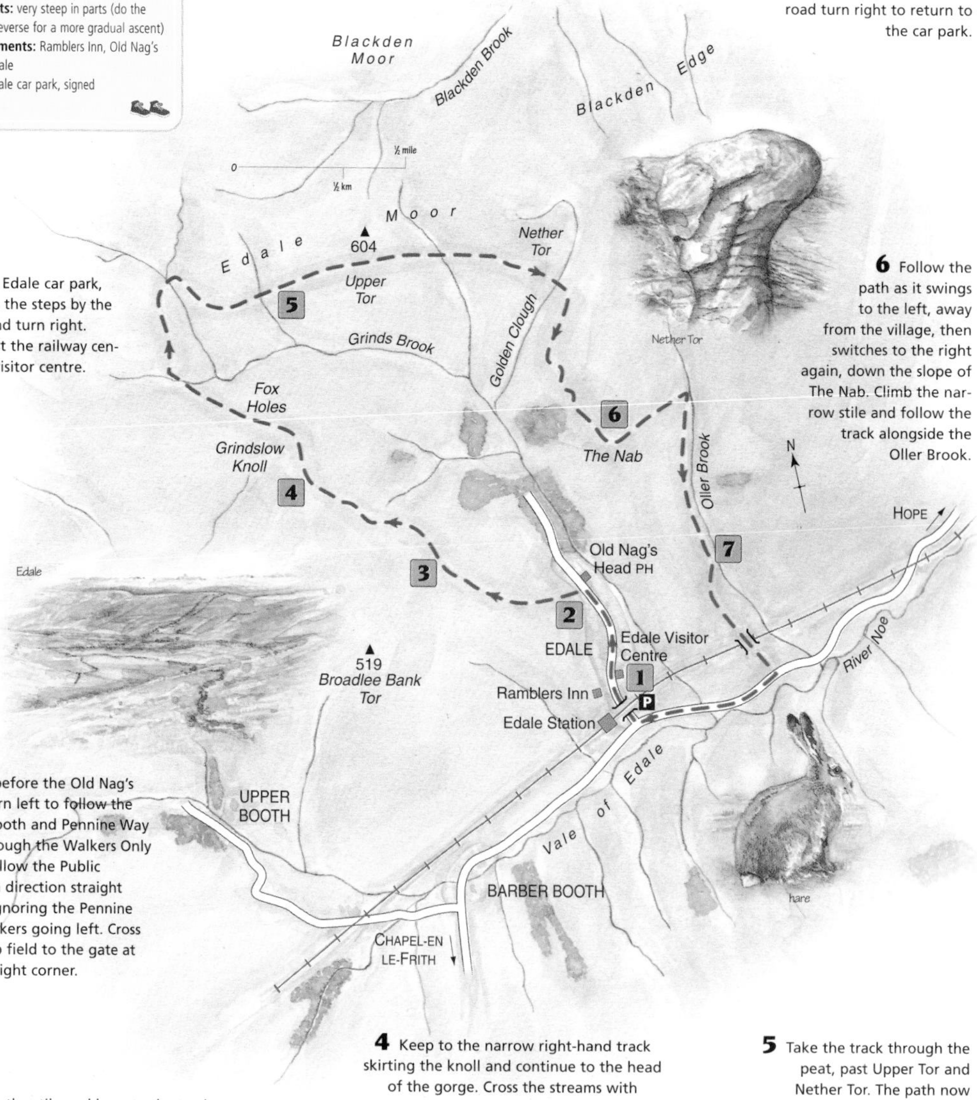

1 From Edale car park, go down the steps by the toilets and turn right. Walk past the railway centre and visitor centre.

2 Just before the Old Nag's Head, turn left to follow the Upper Booth and Pennine Way sign (through the Walkers Only gate). Follow the Public Footpath direction straight ahead, ignoring the Pennine Way markers going left. Cross the steep field to the gate at the top right corner.

3 Climb the stile and keep to the track. Climb on, continuing between the cairns. The upper reaches here are very steep and rocky, and should be climbed only if you have some experience and have sturdy footwear.

4 Keep to the narrow right-hand track skirting the knoll and continue to the head of the gorge. Cross the streams with extreme care. Turn right and head south, following the path alongside the stream you have just crossed, back along the other side of the gorge.

5 Take the track through the peat, past Upper Tor and Nether Tor. The path now begins its descent, and Edale appears in the valley below. After crossing Golden Clough, take the path right and keep right on a well-defined path.

6 Follow the path as it swings to the left, away from the village, then switches to the right again, down the slope of The Nab. Climb the narrow stile and follow the track alongside the Oller Brook.

7 At Ollerbrook Farm go through the narrow stile and continue along the path ahead. Cross the railway bridge and at the road turn right to return to the car park.

Eyam – Village of the Damned

A fascinating walk around the village which sacrificed itself to save its neighbours from the plague

Distance: 5½ miles (9km)
Total ascent: 632 feet (193m)
Paths: mostly good; some parts narrow, rocky
Terrain: village roads, fields, woods, unsurfaced tracks
Gradients: very steep in parts
Refreshments: tea rooms and pubs in Eyam
Park: car park opposite Eyam Museum, Hawkshill Road, Eyam (west of Chesterfield, off A623)

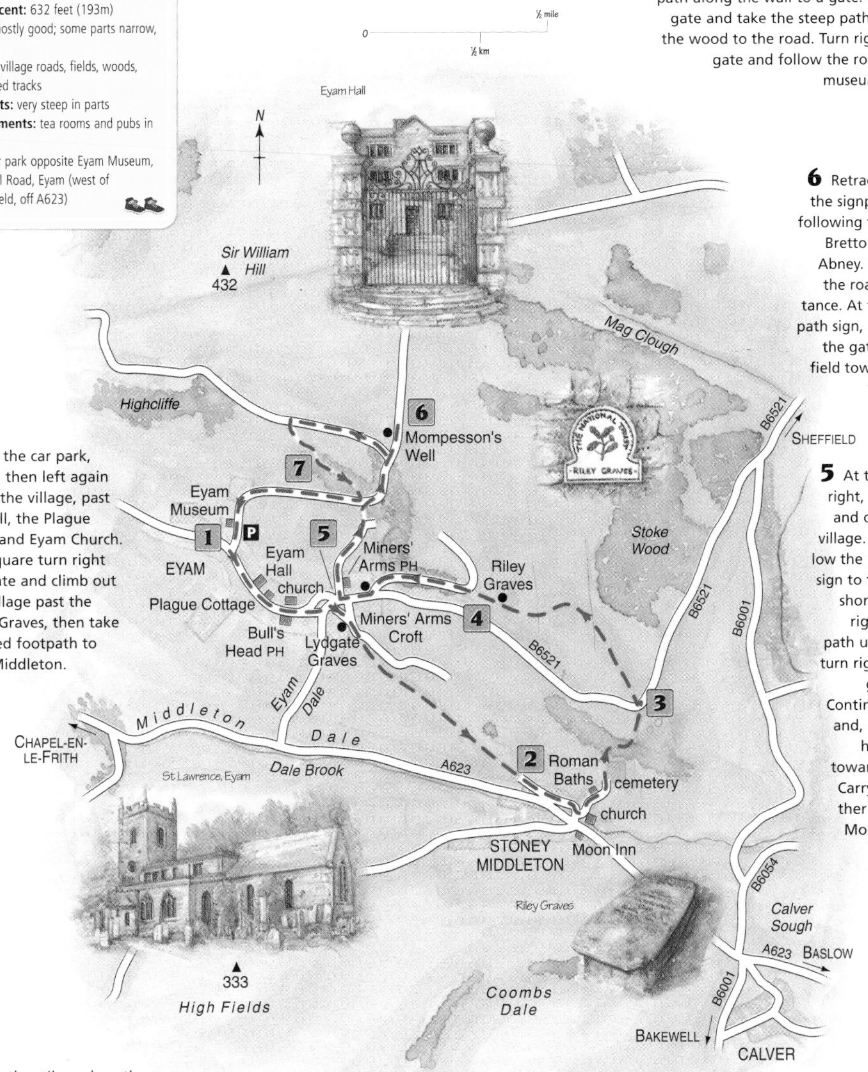

1 From the car park, turn left, then left again through the village, past Eyam Hall, the Plague Cottage and Eyam Church. At the square turn right up Lydgate and climb out of the village past the Lydgate Graves, then take the signed footpath to Stoney Middleton.

2 Climb the stile and continue along a single track road into Stoney Middleton, bearing left as you join the next road. Just before the stream, turn left towards the church. Follow the road past the Roman Baths and continue up the steep track that climbs out of the village past the cemetery.

3 At the top of the track, turn left, cross the road and pass through the narrow entrance by a gate. Follow the track alongside the stone wall. At the top corner of the field, by a trough, go through the gate ahead and continue climbing around to the right. At the top of a steep climb, turn left onto a farm track.

4 Beyond Riley Graves, continue ahead as you join the single track road that leads downhill through the trees. At the bottom, continue ahead into Eyam.

5 At the square, turn right, up Water Lane, and climb out of the village. At the top, follow the public footpath sign to the left. After a short distance, bear right onto a steep path up the field, and turn right through the gate at the top. Continue up the road and, at the signpost, head straight on towards Grindleford. Carry on a little further until you reach Mompesson's Well.

6 Retrace your steps to the signpost. Turn right, following the direction to Bretton, Hucklow and Abney. Continue along the road for some distance. At the public footpath sign, go left through the gate and cross the field towards the wood.

7 At the edge of the wood, follow the footpath along the wall to a gate. Go through the gate and take the steep path down through the wood to the road. Turn right through the gate and follow the road down to the museum and car park.

Packhorse Trails across the Peak

In the footsteps of the Jaggers, whose packhorses carried goods over the moors before the industrial revolution

Distance: 5 miles (8km)
Total ascent: 206ft (63m)
Paths: generally good but sometimes indistinct
Terrain: moorland and woodland
Gradients: one slight climb to White Edge Moor
Refreshments: Longshaw Lodge cafe (seasonal), Fox House Inn or Grouse Inn
Park: Longshaw Estate National Trust car park off A625 Sheffield to Hathersage road, near Fox House Inn

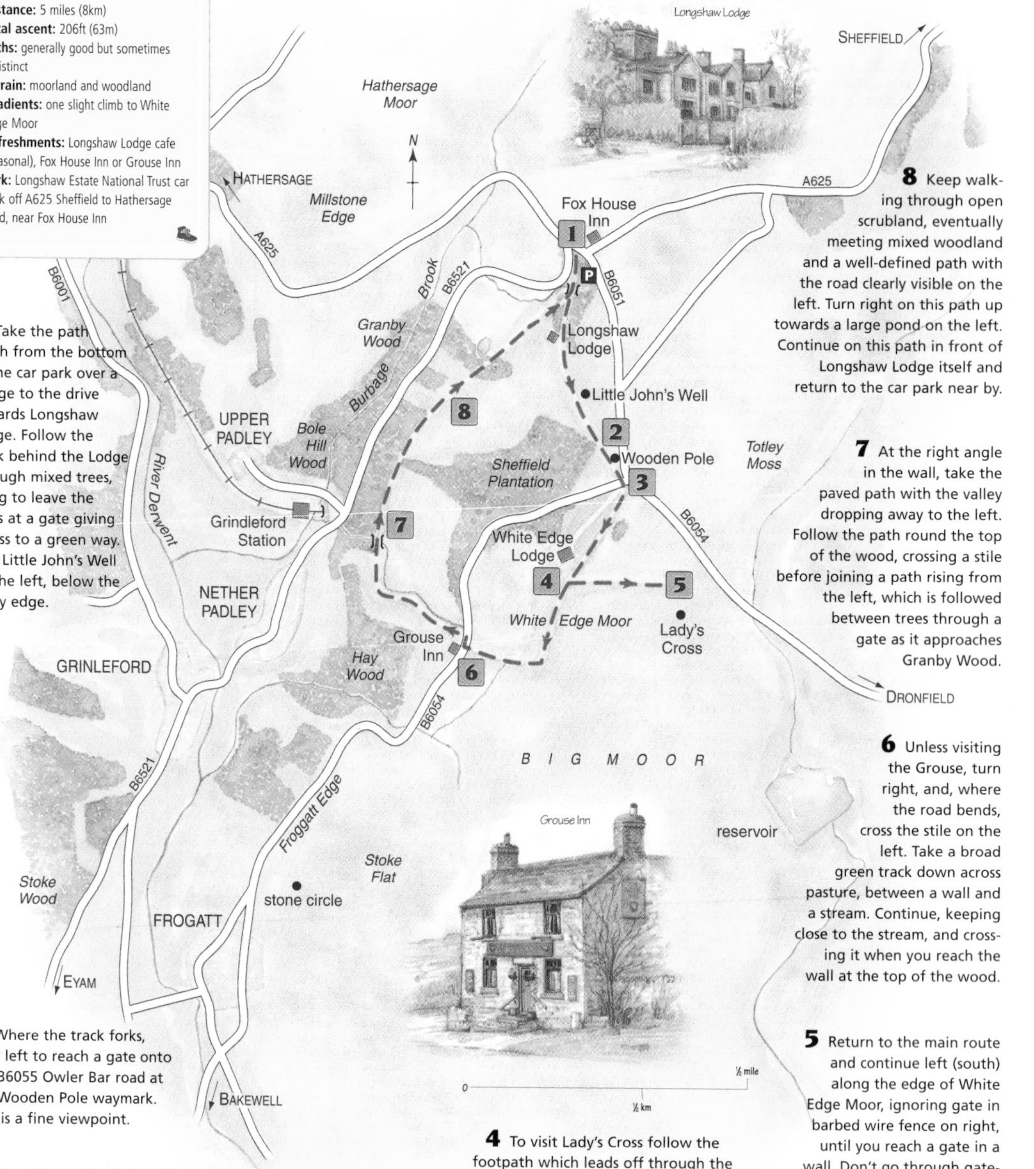

1 Take the path south from the bottom of the car park over a bridge to the drive towards Longshaw Lodge. Follow the track behind the Lodge through mixed trees, rising to leave the trees at a gate giving access to a green way. Pass Little John's Well on the left, below the rocky edge.

2 Where the track forks, bear left to reach a gate onto the B6055 Owler Bar road at the Wooden Pole waymark. This is a fine viewpoint.

3 Cross the road and at an Open Country access sign, cross the stile and follow the fence towards the brow of White Edge Moor. Do not follow track on the right to White Edge Lodge. Pass above two small, windswept plantations, with White Edge Lodge beneath you to the right. The way rises to the highest point of the walk, at 1,273ft (388m).

4 To visit Lady's Cross follow the footpath which leads off through the heather to the left. Lady's Cross is soon seen 50yds (46m) to the right of the path. First mentioned in a document dated 1263, it was a guide cross on the Hope–Chesterfield and Sheffield–Tideswell routes.

5 Return to the main route and continue left (south) along the edge of White Edge Moor, ignoring gate in barbed wire fence on right, until you reach a gate in a wall. Don't go through gateway but take the path sharp right dropping down through the heather to a bridleway, which you join and follow to reach the B6054 near the Grouse Inn.

6 Unless visiting the Grouse, turn right, and, where the road bends, cross the stile on the left. Take a broad green track down across pasture, between a wall and a stream. Continue, keeping close to the stream, and crossing it when you reach the wall at the top of the wood.

7 At the right angle in the wall, take the paved path with the valley dropping away to the left. Follow the path round the top of the wood, crossing a stile before joining a path rising from the left, which is followed between trees through a gate as it approaches Granby Wood.

8 Keep walking through open scrubland, eventually meeting mixed woodland and a well-defined path with the road clearly visible on the left. Turn right on this path up towards a large pond on the left. Continue on this path in front of Longshaw Lodge itself and return to the car park near by.

WALK 51

Land of Legend, Lair of Outlaws

Robin Hood is believed to have roamed this lasting part of the great Sherwood Forest

1 From the visitor centre cafe, follow the waymarked path to Major Oak (not the path which goes through the complex and out the other side).

2 Go around the oak, following the path signed 'Visitor Centre 20 minutes', but turn almost immediately left onto the minor track.

3 After about 1 mile (1.6km), at a barrier and crossroads, turn left (before the Public Bridleway signs) on to a wide, straight route of red shingle. The path reaches the A6075 and swings right. Keep on the red path alongside the main road until it emerges on to it and you can cross safely. Take the tarmac path through the woods on the opposite side.

4 Beyond Archway House, cross the River Maun. Go under the railway bridge and turn right before the second bridge. Pass under another railway bridge (with signalbox) and follow this path to the end for a view of King John's Palace.

5 Retrace your steps to the river. Just beyond the bridge, turn right onto the waymarked track on the riverbank.

6 Continue to the Edwinstowe playing fields. Take the lower track (signed Public Bridleway) along the edge of the fields into the village.

7 Walk through the housing estate and along Sixth Avenue. Follow the road round to the left and turn right into Fourth Avenue. At the end, turn left and continue to the traffic lights; cross to St Mary's Church.

8 Leave the church by the Church Street gate (with steps, right). Continue up Church Street, out of the village. A footpath leads back to the visitor centre from the Sherwood Forest Country Park sign on the left.

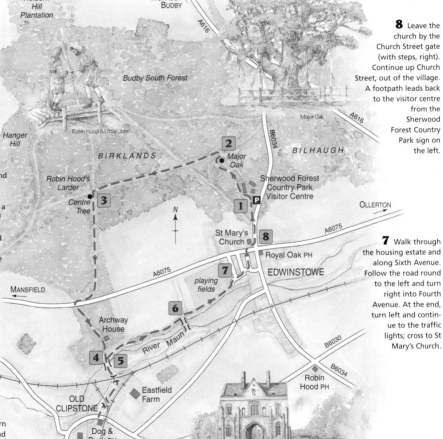

Distance: 5½ miles (8.8km)
Total ascent: negligible
Paths: good; may be muddy
Terrain: woodlands and fields
Gradients: none
Refreshments: various in Edwinstowe; The Forest Table at visitor centre
Park: Sherwood Forest Country Park visitor centre, on B6034, north of Edwinstowe

DH Lawrence's Nottinghamshire

Tracing the characters and places of Lawrence's once controversial writing in Eastwood and its surrounding countryside

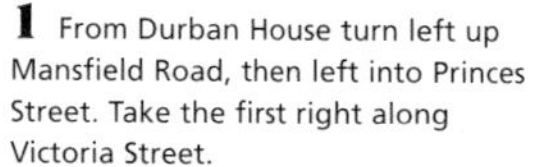

1 From Durban House turn left up Mansfield Road, then left into Princes Street. Take the first right along Victoria Street.

2 Turn left onto Nottingham Road. Opposite the war memorial turn left up Walker Street and follow it round. Take the third right onto Lynncroft. At the end turn left onto Dovecote Road and continue into Moorgreen.

3 At the Horse & Groom pub turn right, then first left up New Road.

4 Follow New Road (tarmacked) for about 1¼ miles (2km) before turning left at the public footpath sign to Hucknall, Annesley and Underwood. The track swings left, running parallel with the M1, passing a sign for the footbridge over the motorway. Eventually it leads you into the woods. At the next junction turn right to continue alongside the motorway.

5 At the next junction, follow the Public Footpath sign ahead to the edge of the wood, then turn left. After descending the hill, at the surfaced track, turn left to the site of Felley Mill Farm.

6 Cross the stream by the little concrete bridge and enter the woods on the right. Take the track which runs parallel with the stream, leading eventually to a wider track (with a wooden fence). Moorgreen Reservoir will come into view on the right. Eventually this track leads onto a tarmac road, emerging at Beauvale Lodge.

7 Turn left towards Moorgreen (B600). Turn right at the entrance to Collier's Wood and take the left-hand path back into Eastwood.

8 At the exit, turn left (Engine Lane); this long road eventually becomes Greenhills Road and leads back to Durban House.

Distance: 8¼ miles (13km)
Total ascent: 230ft (70m)
Paths: mostly good. Some shallow steps; one stile; some tracks narrow and unsurfaced, and can be muddy, especially in woods
Terrain: urban, woodland, fields
Gradients: gradual
Refreshments: Restaurant in Durban House; cafés in Eastwood; Horse & Groom pub in Moorgreen
Park: at Durban House, Mansfield Road, Eastwood

The Battle of Bosworth Field

The dramatic scene of Richard III's death is brought alive by this walk through the Bosworth battlefield

1 From the car park entrance, turn right to cross the canal bridge; go down the steps (right) and follow the Ashby Canal footpath, straight ahead.

8 Just before the visitor centre, turn right and take the path signed to the Marsh and Sutton Cheney Wharf. This leads across the field, through the woods and along the canal to the car park.

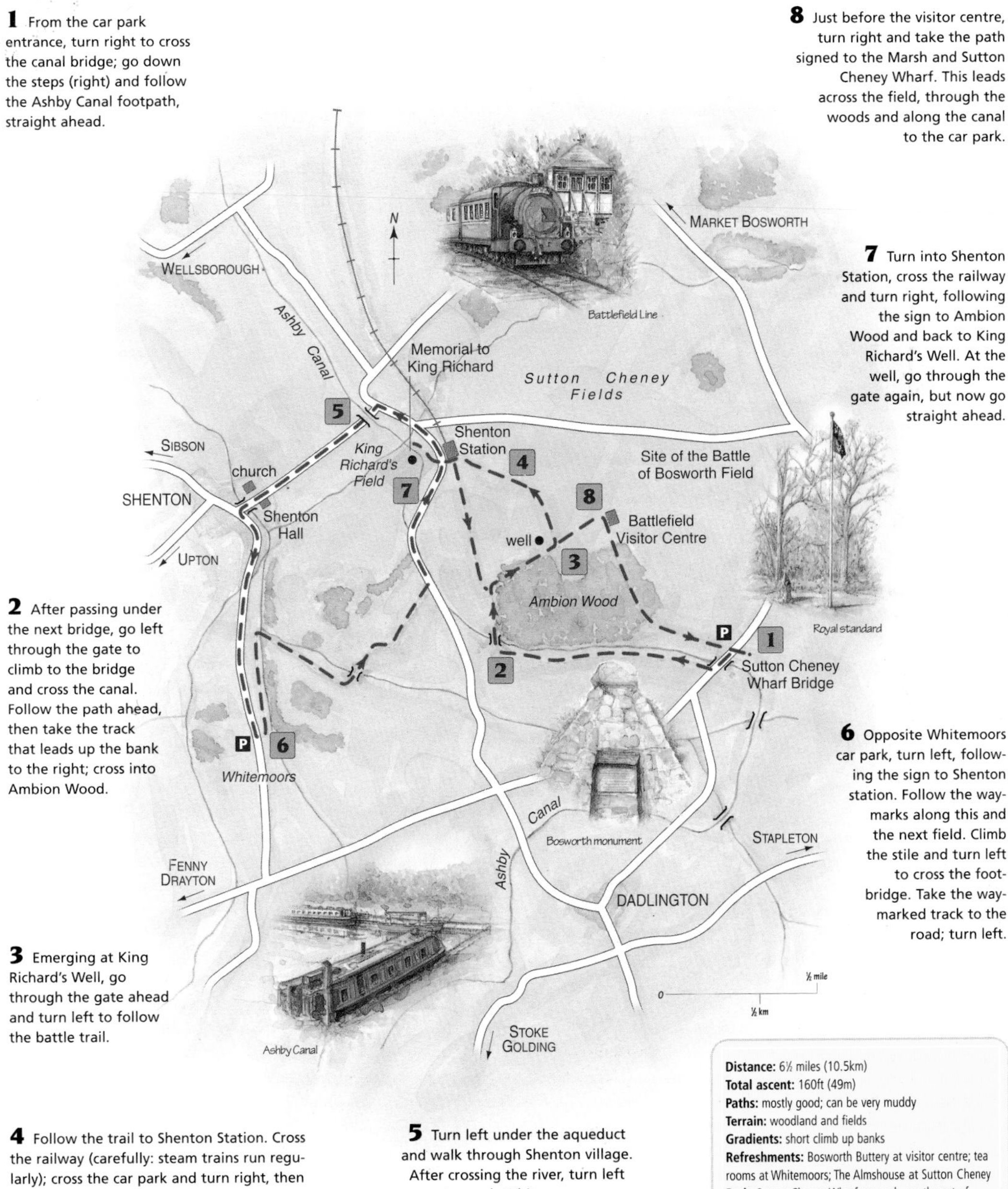

7 Turn into Shenton Station, cross the railway and turn right, following the sign to Ambion Wood and back to King Richard's Well. At the well, go through the gate again, but now go straight ahead.

2 After passing under the next bridge, go left through the gate to climb to the bridge and cross the canal. Follow the path ahead, then take the track that leads up the bank to the right; cross into Ambion Wood.

6 Opposite Whitemoors car park, turn left, following the sign to Shenton station. Follow the waymarks along this and the next field. Climb the stile and turn left to cross the footbridge. Take the waymarked track to the road; turn left.

3 Emerging at King Richard's Well, go through the gate ahead and turn left to follow the battle trail.

4 Follow the trail to Shenton Station. Cross the railway (carefully: steam trains run regularly); cross the car park and turn right, then left onto the waymarked trail to King Richard's Field. Return to the road and continue towards Shenton.

5 Turn left under the aqueduct and walk through Shenton village. After crossing the river, turn left towards Whitemoors.

Distance: 6½ miles (10.5km)
Total ascent: 160ft (49m)
Paths: mostly good; can be very muddy
Terrain: woodland and fields
Gradients: short climb up banks
Refreshments: Bosworth Buttery at visitor centre; tea rooms at Whitemoors; The Almshouse at Sutton Cheney
Park: Sutton Cheney Wharf car park, southwest of Sutton Cheney along Wharf Lane

A Woodland Walk in Charnwood Forest

A Leicestershire country park preserves many fascinating pockets of a vanishing landscape

Distance: 5 miles (8km)
Total ascent: 655ft (200m)
Paths: firm paths on Beacon Hill but can be muddy around Broombriggs
Terrain: woodland, heathland, fields and farmland
Gradients: gradual
Refreshments: a variety of pubs and restaurants at Woodhouse Eaves
Park: Broombriggs car park on B591 Beacon Road above Woodhouse Eaves

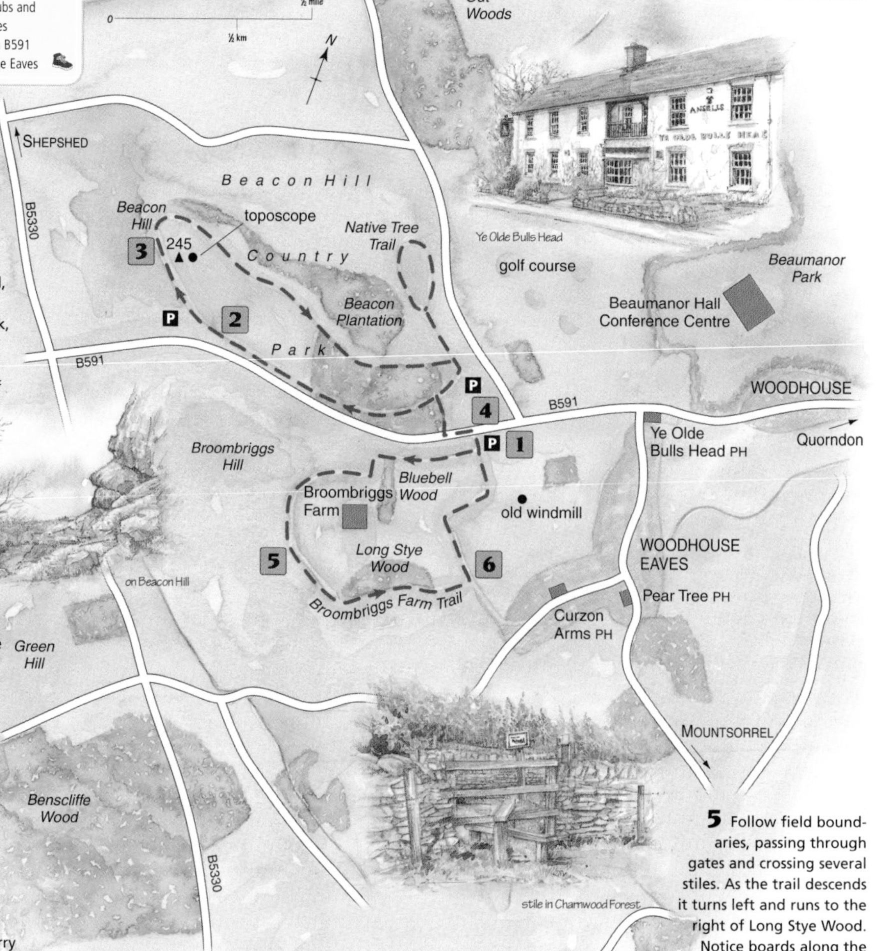

1 From the car park, cross Beacon Road, walk uphill a few paces and turn right into Beacon Hill Country Park. A woodland path climbs up to join a broad, clear path. Turn left on this path, passing tall oak, beech and birch trees. Open heath is reached, which is being cleared of bracken and scrub.

on Beacon Hill

2 Keep straight on, climbing gradually, while off to the left is a car park with toilets. To the right is the bare summit of Beacon Hill. Climb over grass and rocks to reach a trig point and an old AA toposcope.

3 Continue along the path, curving right as it descends. Banks of bilberry precede denser woods. When a gateway and car park are reached at the bottom, detour left to look at the Native Tree Collection, returning to the car park later. To continue the walk, exit from the car park near the toilets and follow a path uphill signposted for Broombriggs. Cross the road to return to the Broombriggs car park.

4 Broombriggs Farm Trail is marked with yellow rectangles, with separate paths for walkers and horseriders. Cross a stile and walk up through fields, parallel to Beacon Road, to enter Bluebell Wood. When the farm access road is reached, turn left, then turn right to pick up the next section of the trail. A broad, grassy strip has been fenced off and this climbs above the Hall Field to reach the Trust Field. This is the highest part of the farm and there are good views westwards.

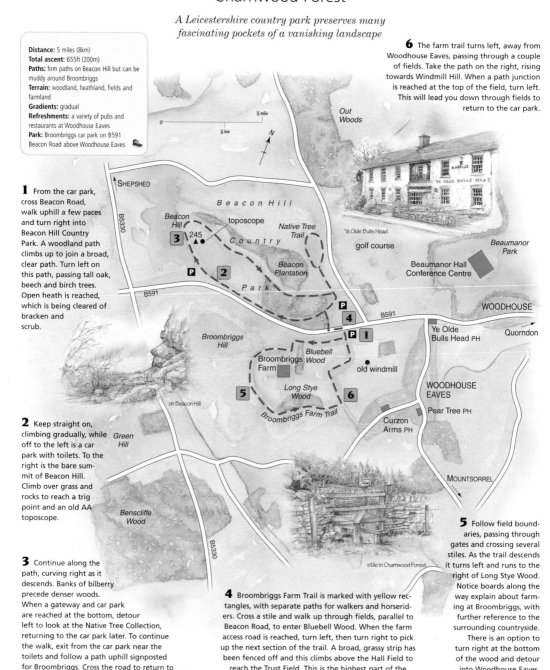

stile in Charnwood Forest

5 Follow field boundaries, passing through gates and crossing several stiles. As the trail descends it turns left and runs to the right of Long Stye Wood. Notice boards along the way explain about farming at Broombriggs, with further reference to the surrounding countryside. There is an option to turn right at the bottom of the wood and detour into Woodhouse Eaves, if desired.

Ye Olde Bulls Head

6 The farm trail turns left, away from Woodhouse Eaves, passing through a couple of fields. Take the path on the right, rising towards Windmill Hill. When a path junction is reached at the top of the field, turn left. This will lead you down through fields to return to the car park.

The New Model Army at Naseby

Across the battle site where Cromwell led his soldiers to change the course of British history

1 From the car park, walk into Naseby village to All Saints' Church and the Fitzgerald Arms. Follow the road signposted Sibbertoft, leaving the village and heading downhill. Turn right and follow a minor road, rising over a busy main road, crossing over Mill Hill and several gentle humps.

2 On the left is a stone monument, overlooking the countryside; an information board sketches out the salient points of the battle. You are now standing in Parliament's front line, facing the King's men on Dust Hill opposite.

3 Continue along the minor road, rising over Dust Hill, so that you can turn around and see things from the Royalists' point of view. When a road junction is reached, Sibbertoft is signposted to the left.

4 A bridleway is signposted at a gateway just to the left of the junction. If the fields have just been ploughed, then note that the signpost points exactly to the crucial gap in a hedge giving access to the next field. At that point, a gateway can be seen leading onto the next road. Turn left to walk into Sibbertoft.

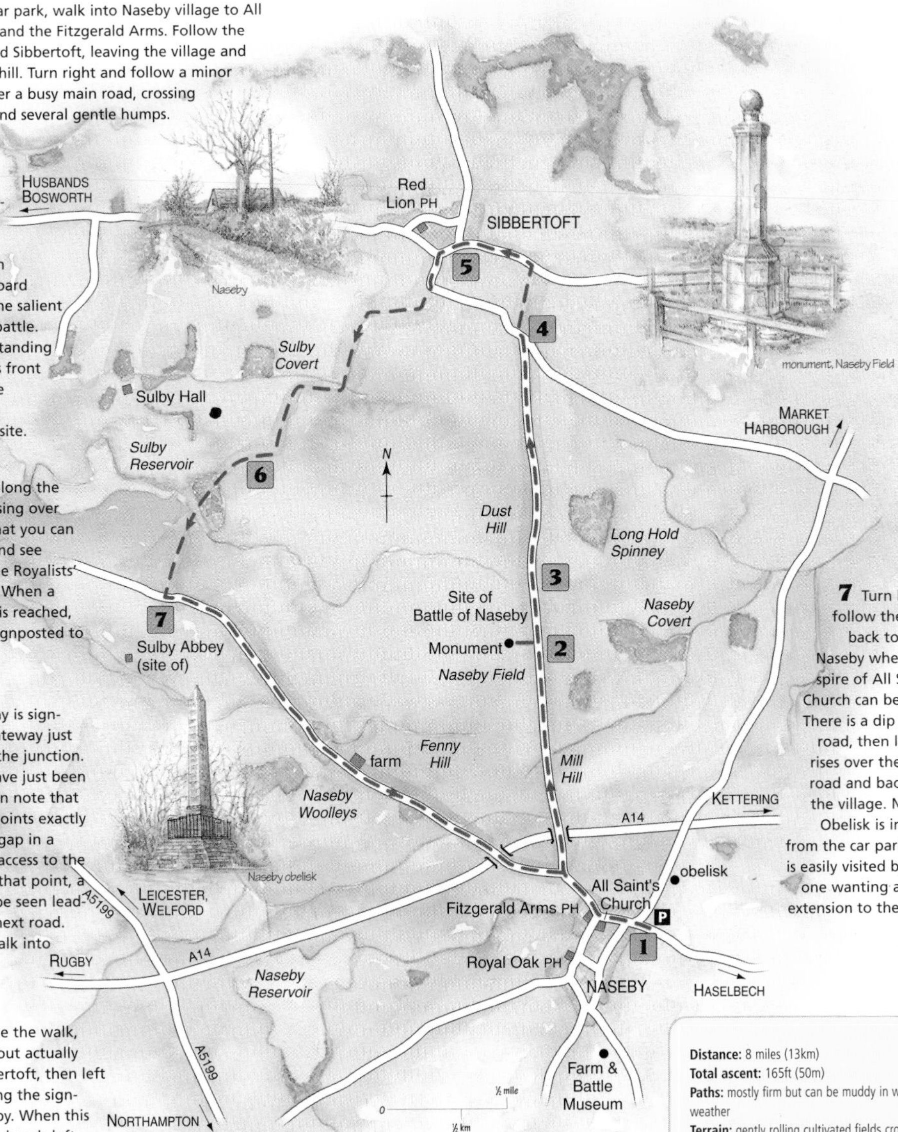

5 To continue the walk, turn left without actually entering Sibbertoft, then left again following the signpost for Naseby. When this road suddenly bends left, walk straight on along another signposted bridleway, and turn right to follow a track past a brick building. The track runs alongside hedgerows bounding fields, so it twists left and right as it proceeds. When a junction of tracks is reached, turn right.

6 The track loses its firm surface and can be muddy. When a gate is reached on the left, go through it, then head off to the right to find a small gate leading into a woodland. There is a muddy track through the wood. When the track leaves the wood, it rises to a quiet minor road.

7 Turn left to follow the road back towards Naseby where the spire of All Saints' Church can be seen. There is a dip in the road, then later it rises over the main road and back into the village. Naseby Obelisk is in sight from the car park, and is easily visited by anyone wanting a short extension to the walk.

Naseby

monument, Naseby Field

Naseby obelisk

Distance: 8 miles (13km)
Total ascent: 165ft (50m)
Paths: mostly firm but can be muddy in wet weather
Terrain: gently rolling cultivated fields crossed by roads and paths
Gradients: very gradual
Refreshments: Royal Oak and Fitzgeralds Arms, Naseby; Red Lion, Sibbertoft.
Park: Recreation Ground on the Haselbech road in Naseby

The Edge of the Wolds

Rising from the flatlands, the Lincolnshire Wolds at Snipe Dales conceal a rich variety of wildlife

Distance: 5 miles (8km)
Total Ascent: 170 feet (51m)
Paths: mostly unsurfaced; can be very waterlogged and muddy
Terrain: woodland, grassland, fields, village streets
Gradients: gradual
Refreshments: none
Park: Snipe Dales Country Park car park, west of Lusby on B1195

1 Follow Forest Trail (green fir tree symbol) and Snipe Dales Round (red square symbol) signs to right of main noticeboard at bottom of car park. Route emerges from trees at flight of steps. Continue downhill to footbridge across stream with pond to left. Cross bridge and follow Snipe Dales Round right along hardcore path, now also part of Bolingbroke Way (signposted).

2 After about ½ mile (800m), path reaches another pond. Follow Bolingbroke Way right, skirting pond and crossing stile. Turn immediately right up around edge of field. At top, turn left to follow field boundary to end of field. Climb stile and carry on alongside Winceby Beck (left) to minor road.

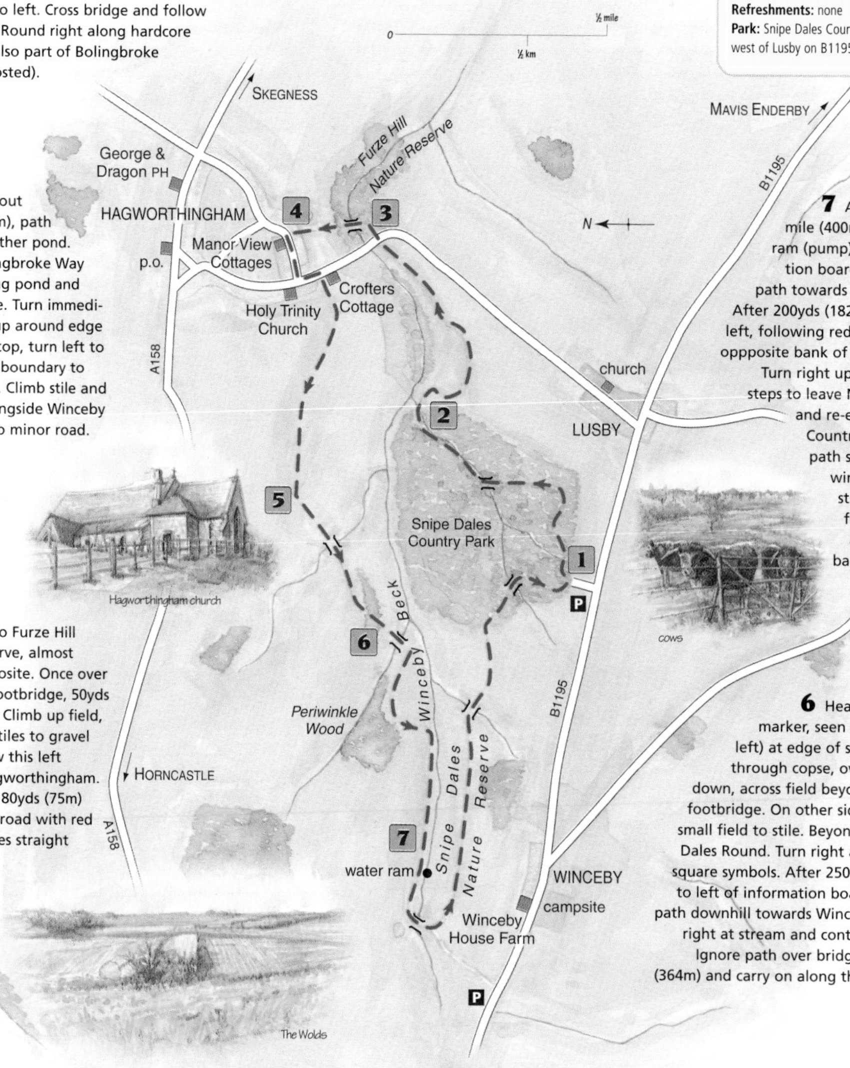

Hagworthingham church

3 Cross into Furze Hill Nature Reserve, almost directly opposite. Once over stile, cross footbridge, 50yds (46m) away. Climb up field, over three stiles to gravel drive. Follow this left towards Hagworthingham. After about 80yds (75m) drive meets road with red brick cottages straight ahead.

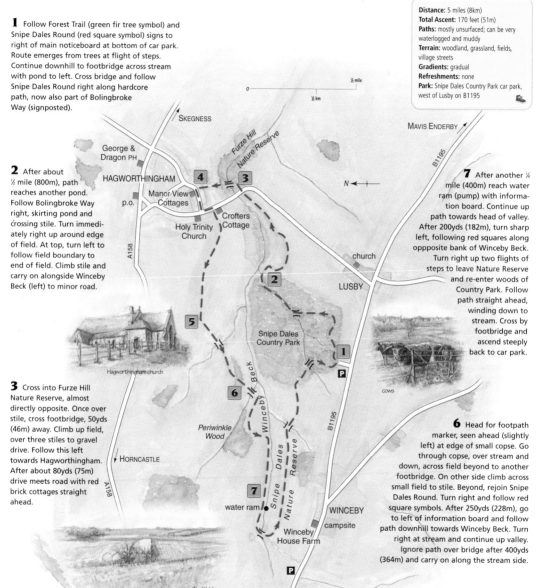

The Wolds

4 Turn left and follow road through edge of village to road back to Lusby. Turn left and head out of village for 100yds (91m), where stile leads to footpath to right of Crofters Cottage. Follow narrow, green belt between two houses to another stile, then go straight ahead across several fields.

5 Path heads down after third field turning, first sharply right, then left, before entering an open field. Cross footbridge at far edge of field and continue straight ahead to stile. Cross this and another stile, heading straight ahead then bearing left to top of rise in field.

6 Head for footpath marker, seen ahead (slightly left) at edge of small copse. Go through copse, over stream and down, across field beyond to another footbridge. On other side climb across small field to stile. Beyond, rejoin Snipe Dales Round. Turn right and follow red square symbols. After 250yds (228m), go to left of information board and follow path downhill towards Winceby Beck. Turn right at stream and continue up valley. Ignore path over bridge after 400yds (364m) and carry on along the stream side.

cows

7 After another ¼ mile (400m) reach water ram (pump) with information board. Continue up path towards head of valley. After 200yds (182m), turn sharp left, following red squares along oppposite bank of Winceby Beck. Turn right up two flights of steps to leave Nature Reserve and re-enter woods of Country Park. Follow path straight ahead, winding down to stream. Cross by footbridge and ascend steeply back to car park.

0 ½ mile ½ km
SKEGNESS
MAVIS ENDERBY
George & Dragon PH
HAGWORTHINGHAM
Furze Hill Nature Reserve
Manor View Cottages
p.o.
Crofters Cottage
Holy Trinity Church
A158
B1195
N
church
LUSBY
Snipe Dales Country Park
Winceby Beck
Periwinkle Wood
HORNCASTLE
Snipe Dales Nature Reserve
water ram
Winceby House Farm
WINCEBY
campsite

Huge Skyscapes above the Wash

The wind and tide add drama to an otherwise empty landscape

1 From parking space follow path signed Freiston Shore Marsh, passing through metal gate and crossing up and over inner sea bank. Follow path to left (Prison road signed right), then curve right almost immediately to go straight on towards outer sea bank. About ½ mile (800m) further on, just before pumping station, go right through 2 metal gates and onto outer sea bank. Follow bank to left.

2 After 2 miles (3.2km) turn right by another pumping station, leaving outer sea wall, to follow path alongside drainage ditch for ¼ mile (400m) to inner sea bank. Ignore private farm road parallel to bank and climb stile onto inner sea bank, following it right for 1½ miles (2.4km), passing several pill boxes and crossing 3 stiles.

3 At another brick pumping station and red stone tablet in middle of bank, turn left down track leading away from pumping station, with wide drainage ditch on right.

4 In ½ mile (800m) continue down track 150yds (136m) beyond farm buildings on left to third, much older sea bank. As track cuts through bank, climb stile to left onto bank and go along crest. Natural avenue of trees marks route, crossing tracks as they cut through it. Eventually, after ¾ mile (1.2km), route springs out from trees into open land. Follow bank to farm visible in Benington Sea End, about ½ mile (800m) ahead.

5 Stick to overgrown path as it passes buildings for short distance to road by pond on right. Turn right onto road, then almost immediately left as bank continues. Walk on road, with crest of bank to right. When road swings right, bisecting bank, clamber through woodland to left. Avenue of trees along top of bank persists, with arrows carved in some trees at intervals. After ¾ mile (1.2km), path takes sharp left turn and heads almost directly back towards second pumping station. However, after 120yds (109m) turn sharply right to continue in former direction for another ¾ mile (1.2km).

6 Bank emerges onto minor road opposite white house called Chimnies. Path continues to right of house, then into open ground with farmland below bank right and left. Inner bank clearly visible to left. In distance, right, the Stump of Boston's St Botolph's Church can be seen on a clear day.

7 Follow bank for 1 mile (1.6km) before route turns sharp left, then straight ahead to emerge onto another minor road. Turn right and walk towards distant houses. At T-junction turn left back towards parking area.

Distance: 8 miles (12.9km)
Total ascent: negligible
Paths: generally clear; some may be overgrown and muddy
Terrain: sea banks overlooking sea marshes and farmland
Gradients: some short steps up banks
Refreshments: none
Park: by the telephone kiosk in Freiston Shore

Northern England

Bounded east and west by the North Sea and the Irish Sea respectively, and along its northern frontier by the Anglo-Scottish border, the north of England possesses landscapes that are breathtakingly beautiful, exciting, wild and desolate. Here there are rugged heights, delectable dales, invigorating coastal margins, windswept moorlands, rivers, lakes, forests, towns, villages, folklore, wildlife, history, intrigue and mystery in great abundance.

Down the centre of the region, the Pennines form the geological 'backbone of England'. The Dales, of course, are renowned for their outstanding natural beauty and dramatic scenery, as at Malham Cove, a favourite with walkers, rock climbers and botanists alike. Above lies a spread of limestone pavement, one of Britain's rarest habitats. Apart from the fascinating shapes of the rock formations, the special interest of limestone pavement lies in its plant life, which includes 18 rare or scarce species, and in its record of glacial and post-glacial history.

Rare and beautiful too, are the landscapes of Cumbria and the North York Moors, the coast and the quiet folds of Northumberland and Durham.

That this landscape is an important part of our national heritage is demonstrated by the designation in this region of four national parks, six Areas of Outstanding Natural Beauty, 41 national nature reserves, and innumerable Sites of Special Scientific Interest.

At the northern edge stands Hadrian's Wall, the greatest extant example of Roman determination in Britain. Everywhere is at peace now but, long after the Romans had gone, the lands of the north were a violent and troubled place, where rustlers, outlaws and gangsters from both sides terrorised the Anglo-Scottish border, and spawned the building of fortified castles and strongholds.

Elsewhere, mystery surrounds the tales of witchcraft and stone circles, while the joys of wilderness walking lead you into the rolling fells of the Forest of Bowland. Literary associations are woven through the fabric of the north, with the Lake Poets, Lewis Carroll, and the Brontë sisters featuring here.

Best of the Rest

Wharfedale Most visited of the Yorkshire Dales, Wharfedale never fails to captivate with its rich and varied scenery. Away from the honeypots of Bolton Abbey and Grassington there is a wide choice of excellent footpaths across liberating open moorlands. On the moors between Grassington and nearby Hebden extensive remains of lead-mining remind you that life was once much harder for Dales folk.

North York Moors The Cleveland Way follows the escarpment of the Hambleton and Cleveland Hills before turning south again to follow the coastline to Scarborough. The best parts of the inland, moorland section can be found above Osmotherley, with enormous views across the Vale of York and north towards County Durham the reward for comparatively little effort.

Cheviots In the last hills in England deep valleys incise the huge rounded grasslands, making for excellent, remote, but quite straightforward walking. Around Ingram particularly, permissive paths have been linked up to make a series of walks which epitomise the Cheviot landscape of mountain sheepwalks and ancient settlement remains.

Howgills Like the Cheviots, the Howgills are rounded grassy mountains, cut by deep valleys leading to their remote heart. However, they cover a much smaller area, in the 'no-man's land' between the Yorkshire Dales and the Lake District, and all their exhilarating high ridges can be traversed in a few days of good walking. A favourite is the ascent of the Calf via Winder from Sedbergh, returning by Cautley Spout.

Keswick The rewards for escaping the seemingly endless outdoor clothing shops in the self-styled capital of the northern Lakes are many. Perhaps the best-loved getaway into this magnificent walkers' landscape is to the south of the town, up to the inspirationally-sited stone circle at Castlerigg, then on to the breathtaking viewpoint on Walla Crag. Choose an early spring morning with mist in the valley for the ultimate Lakeland view.

Garrigill The valley of the River South Tyne hides away in the North Pennines Area of Outstanding Natural Beauty. Amidst the high moorlands and below the shadow of Cross Fell, miners and farmers eked out a living from this hostile environment. Their legacy is a fine network of footpaths and bridleways across delightful meadows and high pasture, connecting hamlets and villages like Garrigill with the upland mining areas.

A Poet's View of the Buttermere Valley

The poet Coleridge stepped this way across a tranquil Lakeland scene

1 From the Bridge Hotel walk down to the left of the Fish Hotel, then through a gate, signposted to Scale Force and Scale Bridge. Go over a bridge, through a gate and turn right.

2 In ¼ mile (400m), after crossing a stream via a footbridge, take the path to the left which runs along the base of a rocky slope with occasional cairns. Eventually reach a gap in a wall. Descend to cross a footbridge. Scale Force waterfall is on your left.

3 Ascend for a few paces, then turn right, downhill, on a bank with a stream on your right. At the confluence with another stream, cross a footbridge then turn right. Later the path veers away from the stream towards the shore, then left alongside the lake.

4 Towards the end of the lake the track divides. Take the right-hand path through the gate and follow the water's edge. Go ahead at next gate and, just past a broken-down wall, turn left to pass a ruin, then aim for a group of pine trees by the shore. Pass through a kissing gate and then along a wall to a pumping station. Continue along the shore to cross a footbridge over a river. Later turn right over two bridges. Continue on shore path through Lanthwaite Woods and later past a boat house, then along by the lake. The path leads over several stiles and small bridges until it bears left at a wall.

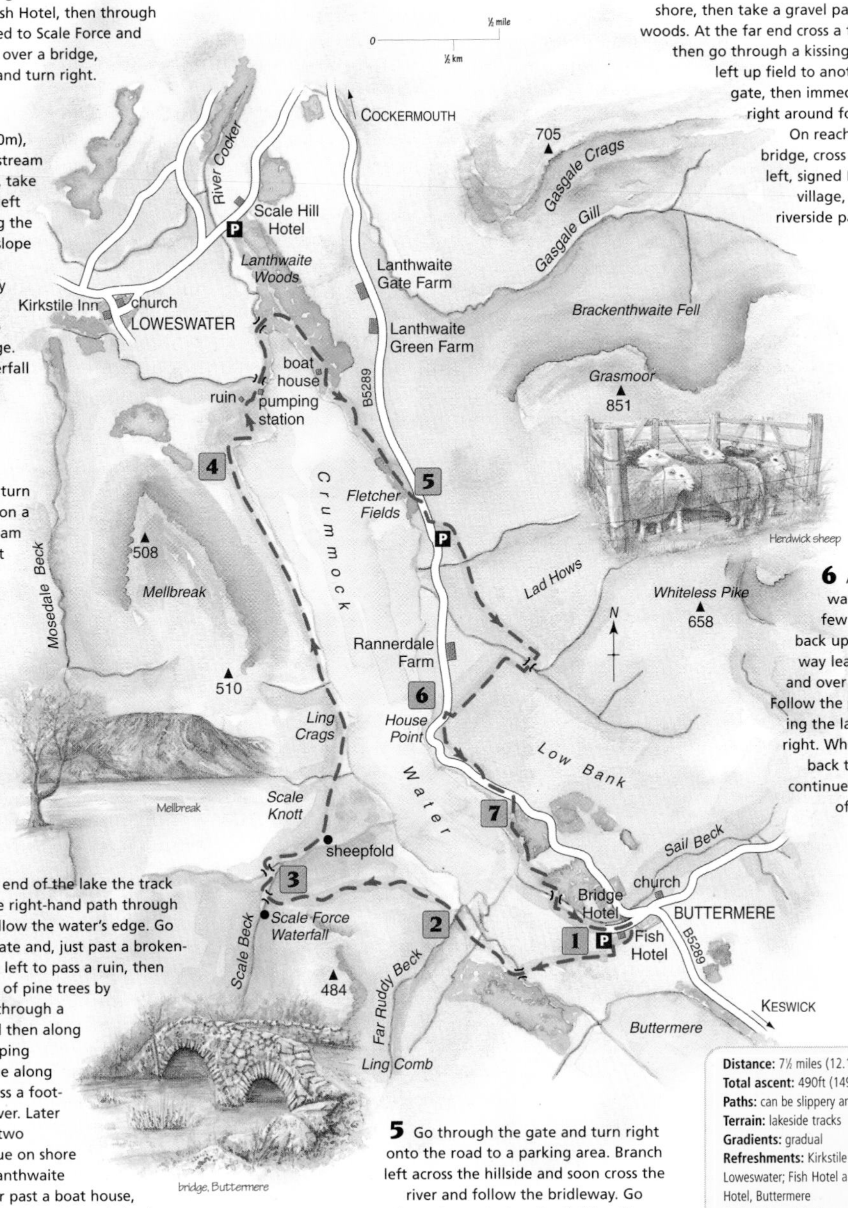

5 Go through the gate and turn right onto the road to a parking area. Branch left across the hillside and soon cross the river and follow the bridleway. Go through a gate, to a footbridge. Cross over, then turn right to double-back and go down hill.

6 At the road walk left for a few paces then back up the bridleway leading uphill and over a shoulder. Follow the path, keeping the lake on your right. When it comes back to the road, continue to a group of pine trees.

7 Pass through a kissing gate and follow the shore, then take a gravel path through woods. At the far end cross a footbridge, then go through a kissing gate. Turn left up field to another kissing gate, then immediately turn right around foot of crag. On reaching a footbridge, cross it and turn left, signed Buttermere village, and follow riverside path back to car park.

Herdwick sheep

Mellbreak

bridge, Buttermere

Distance: 7½ miles (12.1km)
Total ascent: 490ft (149m)
Paths: can be slippery and boggy
Terrain: lakeside tracks
Gradients: gradual
Refreshments: Kirkstile Inn, Loweswater; Fish Hotel and Bridge Hotel, Buttermere
Park: National Park car park near Bridge Hotel, Buttermere

Claife Heights and the Victorian View of Windermere

The Victorians tried to 'improve' the beauty of this lake and moorland walk with romantic architecture

1 Turn left (north) out of car park and follow the lakeside for 2 miles (3.2km). The metalled lane soon becomes an unmade track through woodland.

2 As the track approaches Belle Grange turn left just before the house up a steep and stony bridleway, signposted to Letterbarrow and Near Sawrey. Ignoring a path to the left, continue on uphill (signposted to Hawkshead) until the path levels out and reaches a broad bridleway at a complex intersection.

3 Cross the bridleway and follow path (signed to Sawrey via Tarns) that bears slightly to the left. Cross another intersection, still following the signs to Sawrey, up a steep and stony path. This soon joins a broader track that passes through a gate and stile to reach the open moorland on Claife Heights.

4 Follow faint path down towards the nearest tarn, where the route becomes much clearer. Follow trackway as it swings to left below an old stone dam, passes through a wooden gate and dips down to Moss Eccles Tarn. Continue on the track as it drops down from the moor, splashes through a little stream and runs between stone walls.

5 Where the track forks to Near and Far Sawrey bear left through a gate and follow bridleway down to join a metalled lane into Far Sawrey. Turn left along the village street to the Sawrey Hotel.

6 Just beyond the hotel car park bear left up a track signposted to ferry. The footpath skirts the gardens of a private house, then drops towards the lake beside a high stone wall. Continue on across a driveway, down a path through overhanging rhododendrons, to the road.

7 Turn left down the hill, then cross the road onto footpath separated from the traffic by a wall. Follow path downhill and across the road, through woodland to a car park.

8 At far end of this car park, take footpath into woods and up steps to Claife Station. At top of steps turn right along the terrace walk, which drops down to the road. Turn left, then bear immediately left along a narrow lane to return to car park.

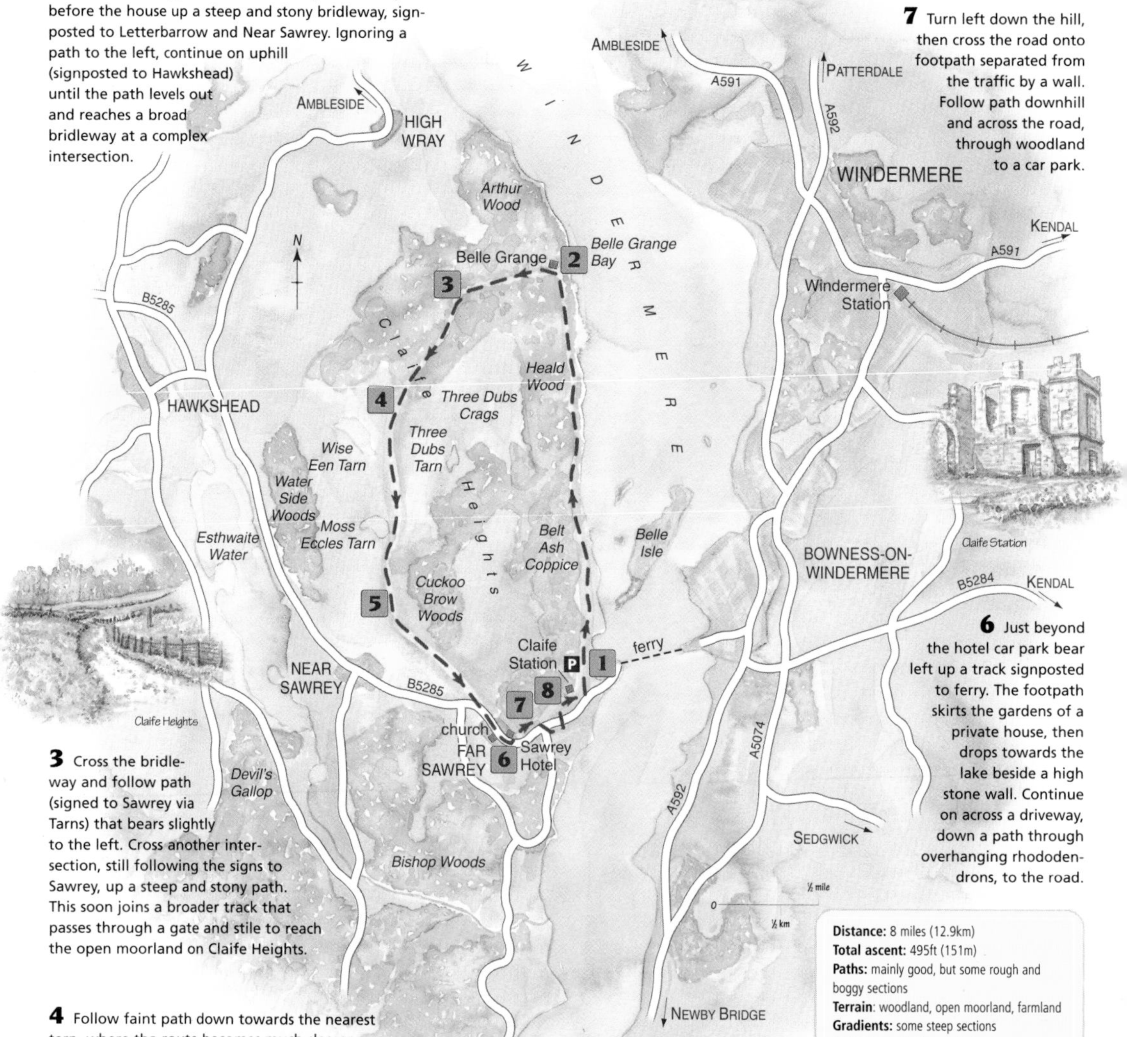

Distance: 8 miles (12.9km)
Total ascent: 495ft (151m)
Paths: mainly good, but some rough and boggy sections
Terrain: woodland, open moorland, farmland
Gradients: some steep sections
Refreshments: Sawrey Hotel
Park: Harrow Slack National Trust car park, off the B5285 on the west shore of Windermere, 200yds (182m) along the lakeside lane northwest of Bowness Ferry

The Contrasts of Upper Eskdale

From a lowland vale to England's highest mountains, following the River Esk into the remote heart of Lakeland

1 Begin from a roadside parking area at the foot of Hardknott Pass, and descend to follow the access to Brotherilkeld Farm (right, by the telephone box). As you near the farm, branch left on a path parallel with the River Esk. Ignore a footbridge and continue up-river.

2 Beyond a gate follow a broad track crossing rough pasture. This leads past a series of delightful waterfalls, and ultimately arrives at Lingcove Bridge, directly below the crags of Throstle Garth.

3 Cross the bridge and climb left, still alongside, but well above, the river. Two pronounced rises follow before the path reaches Scar Lathing, where the river makes a distinct bend westwards. Cross an inflowing stream, and bear left to pass beneath Scar Lathing, beyond which lies the bleak arena of Great Moss, spread below the soaring heights of Sca Fell and the lower cliffs of Cam Spout Crag.

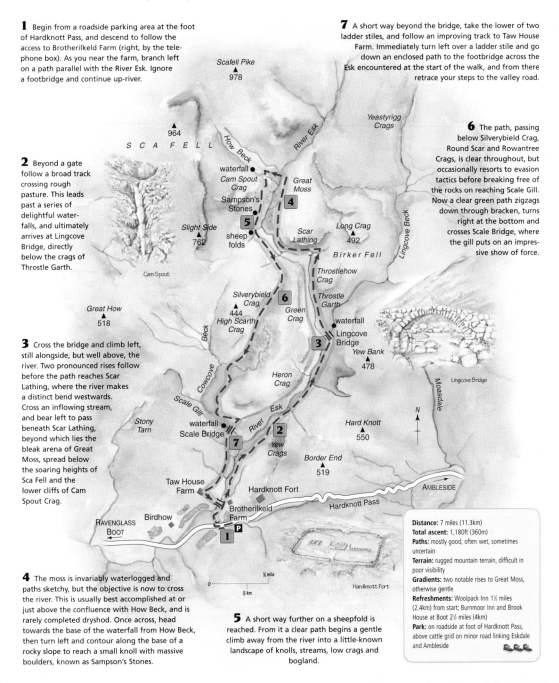

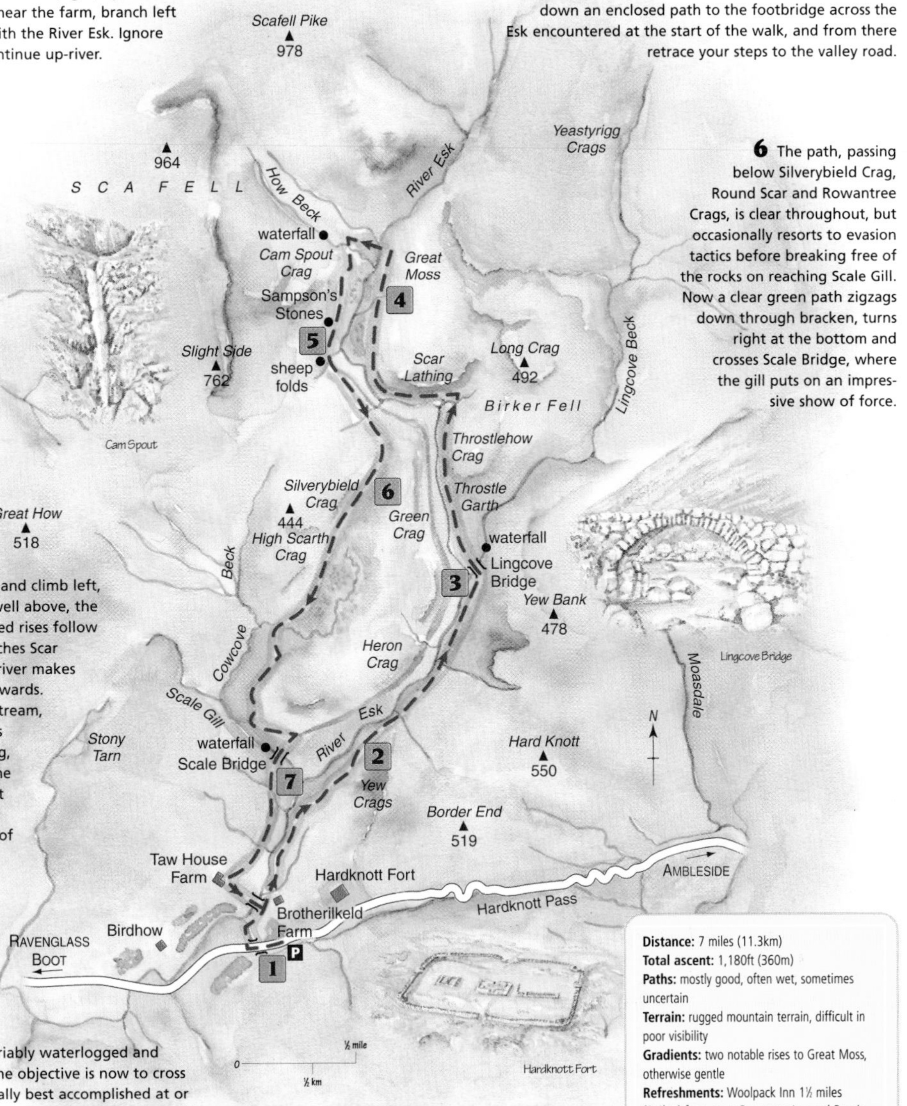

4 The moss is invariably waterlogged and paths sketchy, but the objective is now to cross the river. This is usually best accomplished at or just above the confluence with How Beck, and is rarely completed dryshod. Once across, head towards the base of the waterfall from How Beck, then turn left and contour along the base of a rocky slope to reach a small knoll with massive boulders, known as Sampson's Stones.

5 A short way further on a sheepfold is reached. From it a clear path begins a gentle climb away from the river into a little-known landscape of knolls, streams, low crags and bogland.

6 The path, passing below Silverybield Crag, Round Scar and Rowantree Crags, is clear throughout, but occasionally resorts to evasion tactics before breaking free of the rocks on reaching Scale Gill. Now a clear green path zigzags down through bracken, turns right at the bottom and crosses Scale Bridge, where the gill puts on an impressive show of force.

7 A short way beyond the bridge, take the lower of two ladder stiles, and follow an improving track to Taw House Farm. Immediately turn left over a ladder stile and go down an enclosed path to the footbridge across the Esk encountered at the start of the walk, and from there retrace your steps to the valley road.

Distance: 7 miles (11.3km)
Total ascent: 1,180ft (360m)
Paths: mostly good, often wet, sometimes uncertain
Terrain: rugged mountain terrain, difficult in poor visibility
Gradients: two notable rises to Great Moss, otherwise gentle
Refreshments: Woolpack Inn 1½ miles (2.4km) from start; Burnmoor Inn and Brook House at Boot 2½ miles (4km)
Park: on roadside at foot of Hardknott Pass, above cattle grid on minor road linking Eskdale and Ambleside

Swindale and the Eastern Fells

Exploring forgotten valleys on the Lake District's eastern fringe

1 Leave Keld on a moorland road to Tailbert Farm. At Tailbert, abandon the road for a track across the hillside, later descending through bracken and gorse into Swindale. Cross a ford or a nearby bridge. Turn left, follow the minor road to Swindale Head Farm and go through gates onto a bridleway signed Mosedale.

2 After a final building on the left, branch left through glacial moraine, and climb through the rocky outcrops of Selside Pike. Cross open moorland to a fence at Swine Gill. Go through a gate and continue to a dilapidated building and a collapsed wall nearby.

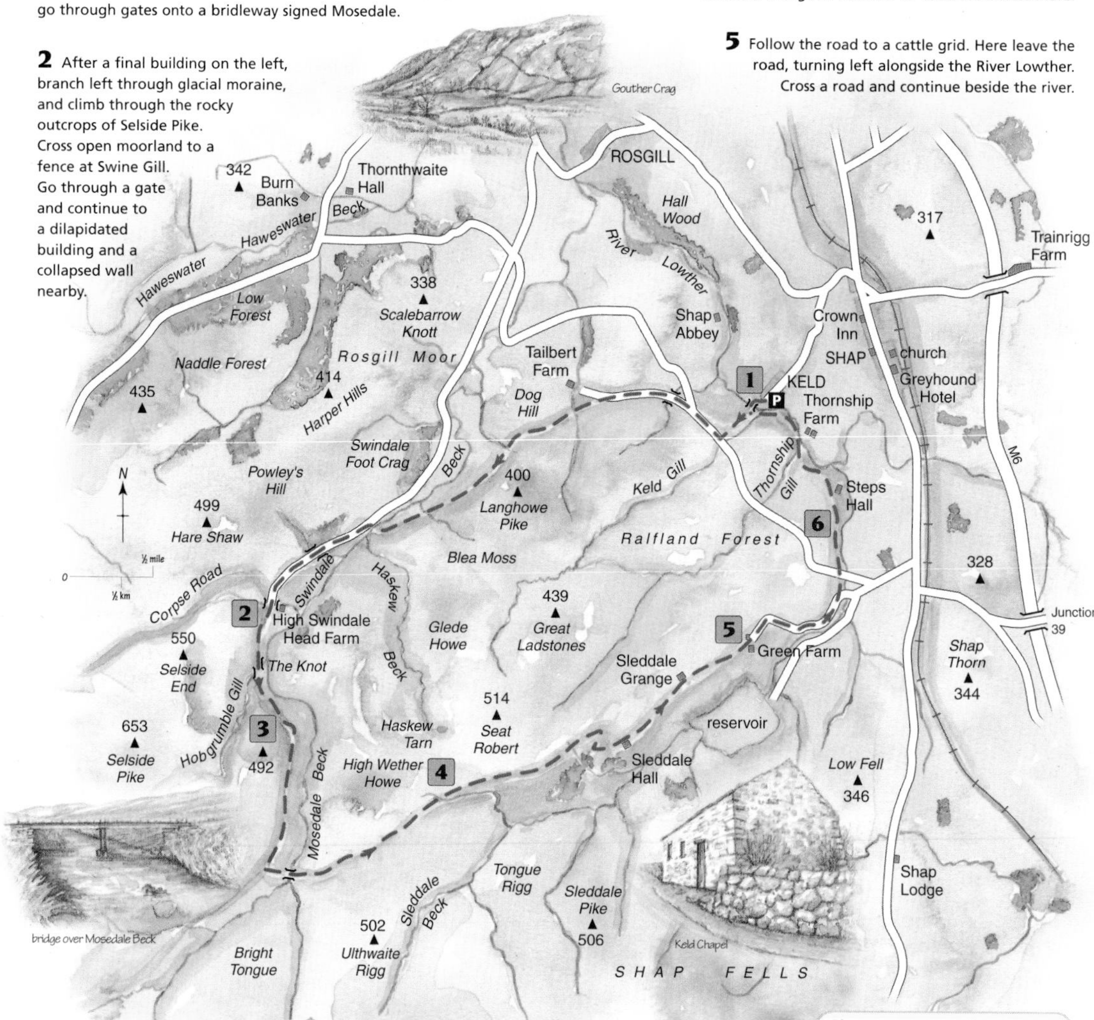

3 Keep on until a bridge spanning Mosedale Beck comes into view. Stay on the path to a vehicle track cutting down to the bridge. On the other side ascend one of the tracks which climb onto a broad grassy ridge, rising to a fence and gate. Beyond, a grassy track climbs further. When this forks, branch right.

4 After a steady climb the path descends into Wet Sleddale. After the second ladder stile leave the main track and turn down zigzags to Sleddale Hall. Here go down to a lower track, through a gate beside a barn and forward to Sleddale Grange. Beyond this follow a rough-surfaced road to Green Farm.

5 Follow the road to a cattle grid. Here leave the road, turning left alongside the River Lowther. Cross a road and continue beside the river.

6 When the river makes a pronounced bend to the right, move away from it to a wall. Go past Steps Hall, following a rough track towards Thornship Farm. Opposite the farm continue alongside the river to reach Keld once more.

Distance: 10½ miles (17km)
Total ascent: 1,115ft (340m)
Paths: generally good, but variable and wet in Mosedale
Terrain: moorland and cultivated valleys
Gradients: mostly gentle; one steep ascent
Refreshment: Shap; Keld (seasonal)
Park: Keld, on minor road west of A6 at Shap

High Pike – the Last Lakeland Hill

The Cumbrian Mountains end at a lonely viewpoint high above the Solway Plain

Distance: 6 miles (9.7km)
Total ascent: 1,560ft (476m)
Paths: mostly clear, but not advised in poor visibility; one short trackless section
Terrain: mainly high mountain moorland
Gradients: steep start but otherwise moderate
Refreshments: Mill Inn at Mungrisdale; pubs at Hesket Newmarket and Caldbeck
Park: roadside parking on Caldbeck Common, at site of Carrock End Mine, 1 mile north of Mosedale

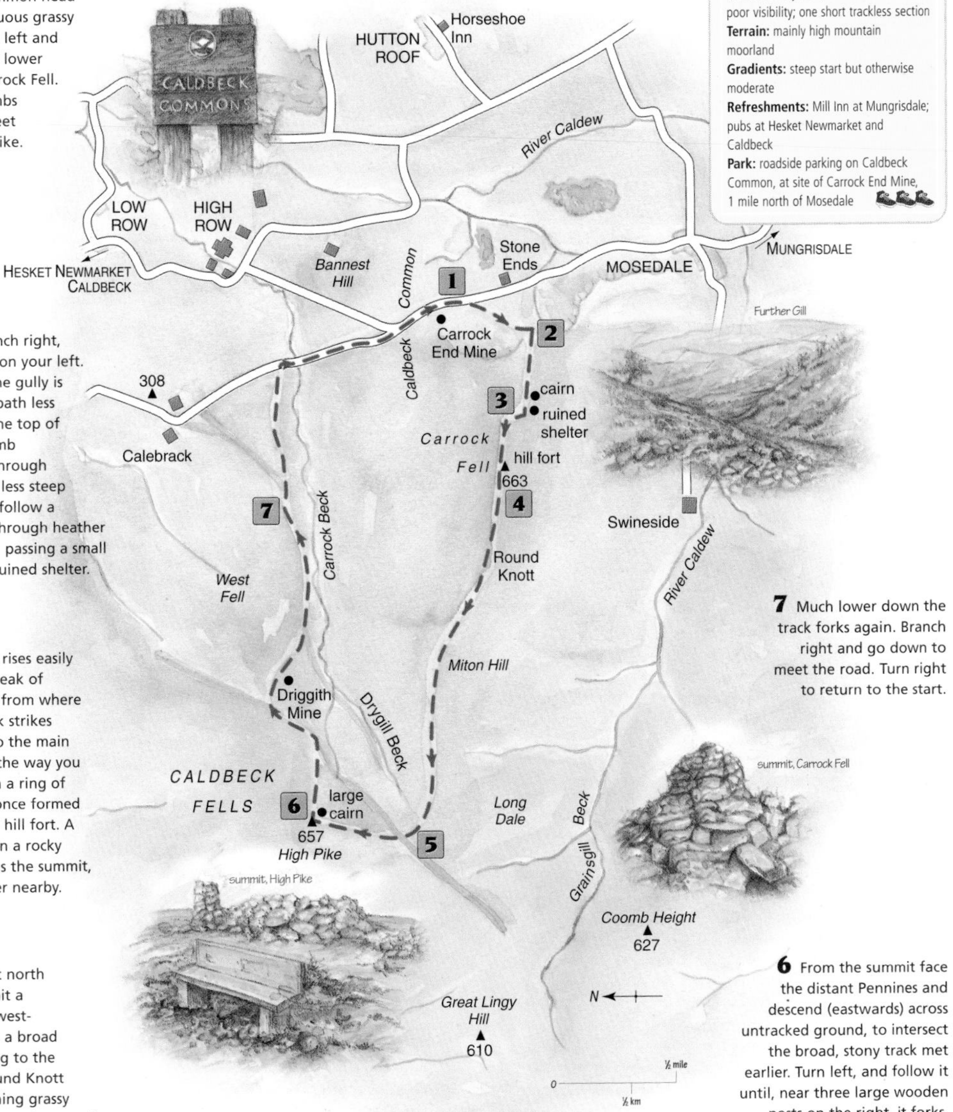

1 From the site of the old Carrock End Mine on Caldbeck Common head for a conspicuous grassy path slanting left and up across the lower slopes of Carrock Fell. The path climbs steeply to meet Further Gill Sike.

2 Here branch right, with the gill on your left. Higher up, the gully is dry and the path less distinct. At the top of the gully, climb straight on through heather to a less steep section, and follow a green path through heather and bracken, passing a small cairn and a ruined shelter.

3 The path rises easily to the east peak of Carrock Fell, from where a broad track strikes westwards to the main summit. On the way you pass through a ring of stones that once formed a substantial hill fort. A large cairn on a rocky plinth crowns the summit, with a shelter nearby.

4 From just north of the summit a path heads westwards across a broad ridge, passing to the north of Round Knott before reaching grassy Miton Hill. From here, walk northwest on a broad grassy track, passing Red Gate, an obvious cross-track, which offers a quick escape route northwards if necessary.

5 As you approach High Pike the path curves northwards to pass the top of Drygill Beck, a steep-sided ravine, beyond which it ascends easy grassy slopes to the summit, on the way crossing a broad stony track.

6 From the summit face the distant Pennines and descend (eastwards) across untracked ground, to intersect the broad, stony track met earlier. Turn left, and follow it until, near three large wooden posts on the right, it forks. Branch right, until you reach the top of a narrow gully. Bear right again, alongside the gully and soon cross it to pursue an old mining track above Carrock Beck.

7 Much lower down the track forks again. Branch right and go down to meet the road. Turn right to return to the start.

Long Meg and Lacy's Caves

A spectacular stone circle and intriguing Gothic caverns are linked by a walk in the verdant Eden Valley

Distance: 6 miles (9.7km)
Total ascent: 230ft (70m)
Paths: mainly good, but some muddy sections
Terrain: fields, woodland and riverside
Gradients: slight; one short steep section
Refreshments: The Watermill, Little Salkeld (Mon, Tue, Wed; seasonal)
Park: beside small village green in Little Salkeld, 1½ miles (2.4km) north of Langwathby and the A686 Penrith-Alston road. Turn left off road to Glassonby at sharp right bend

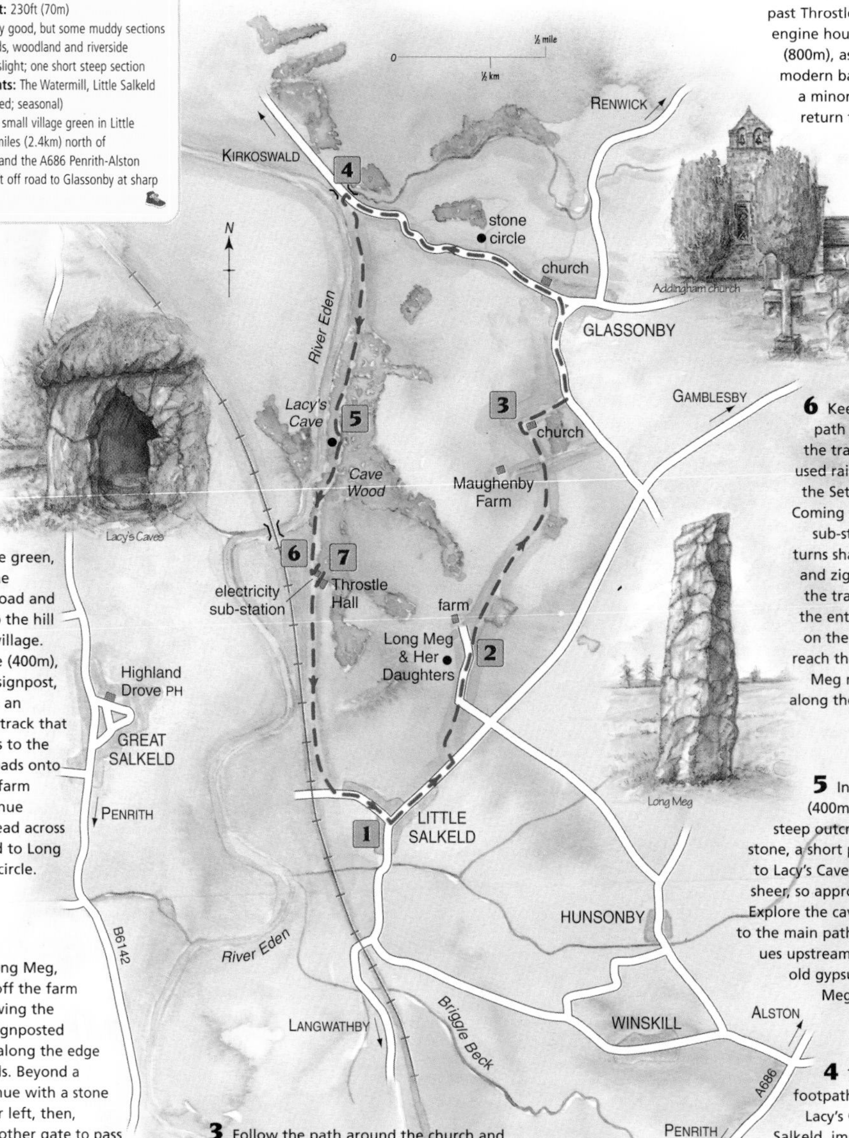

1 From the green, return to the Glassonby road and bear left up the hill out of the village. After ¼ mile (400m), opposite a signpost, turn left up an unsurfaced track that soon swings to the right and leads onto a metalled farm road. Continue straight ahead across a cattle grid to Long Meg stone circle.

2 From Long Meg, bear right off the farm road, following the footpath, signposted Glassonby, along the edge of two fields. Beyond a gate, continue with a stone wall to your left, then, through another gate to pass a small plantation on your right. The path now runs beside stone walls, through fields that can be very muddy, and crosses a farm lane to reach Addingham church.

3 Follow the path around the church and out onto a lane that runs down to the road. Turn left, towards Glassonby, keeping left at the village green to follow the road signposted to Kirkoswald. The road winds downhill for 1 mile (1.6km) to a bridge across a stream, with a lay-by to the left.

4 Turn left up the footpath, signposted to Lacy's Caves and Little Salkeld, immediately bearing to the left to make a short ascent up the wooded hillside. At the top of the slope, cross a stile and, bearing slightly to the right, follow the field edge above the river. Keep along the path as it descends gently to the riverbank and runs upstream, later through woodland.

5 In another ¼ mile (400m), just beyond a steep outcrop of red sandstone, a short path right leads to Lacy's Caves (the drops are sheer, so approach with care). Explore the caves, then return to the main path, which continues upstream by the ruins of old gypsum works. Long Meg viaduct is seen to the right.

6 Keep on along the path as it runs along the track bed of a disused railway parallel to the Settle-Carlisle line. Coming to an electricity sub-station, the path turns sharply to the left and zigzags up behind the transformers, past the entrance to a farm on the left. When you reach the gates of Long Meg mine, turn right along the surfaced lane.

7 Follow the concrete lane past Throstle Hall, a former engine house. After ½ mile (800m), as you come to a modern barn, bear left at a minor intersection to return to Little Salkeld village green.

Cross Fell – the Pennine Giant

Rising up above the Vale of Eden, the Pennines' highest hill is a wild and spectacular vantage point

1 In Kirkland head up the road alongside Kirkland Beck. Beyond the last buildings a walled track heads out onto rough upland pastures, eventually looping north to skirt High Cap above Ardale Beck.

2 The gradient, nowhere unduly steep, is eased by a few bends. Within sight of the summit plateau, and not far from a bothy, the ascending track bears sharply left. Here leave it to strike eastwards on a cairned and grassy path, crossing the watershed and passing around the northern scree slopes of Cross Fell to locate the Pennine Way.

3 A waymarker indicates the line of the Pennine Way, initially wet underfoot and clear enough to follow. It soon dries out, and a few large cairns guide you to the summit shelter-cairn and trig pillar.

4 In poor visibility the surest way down is to retreat. Otherwise, press on across the summit plateau, aiming for the distant summit of Great Dun Fell and its conspicuous masts and radar station. Near the edge of the Cross Fell plateau large cairns mark the way down to Tees Head.

5 From Tees Head a cairned path, not obvious, and narrow in places, leaves the Pennine Way and heads southwest across bouldery terrain to a cairn on the edge of Wildboar Scar. If you can't locate the line of cairns leaving Tees Head, drop beneath the downfall of scree and boulders and skirt along its lower edge until cairns appear in the far distance, and head for them.

6 Wildboar Scar is simply an abrupt escarpment of boulders and grass, and has a much clearer path. Ahead lies the dome of Grumply Hill, with the path keeping north of it to join a tributary of Crowdundle Beck.

7 Onwards a broad green path descends easily through bracken to a sheepfold and across a tract of rough ground to Wythwaite Farm. At the farm turn right through gates, and follow a broad track back to Kirkland.

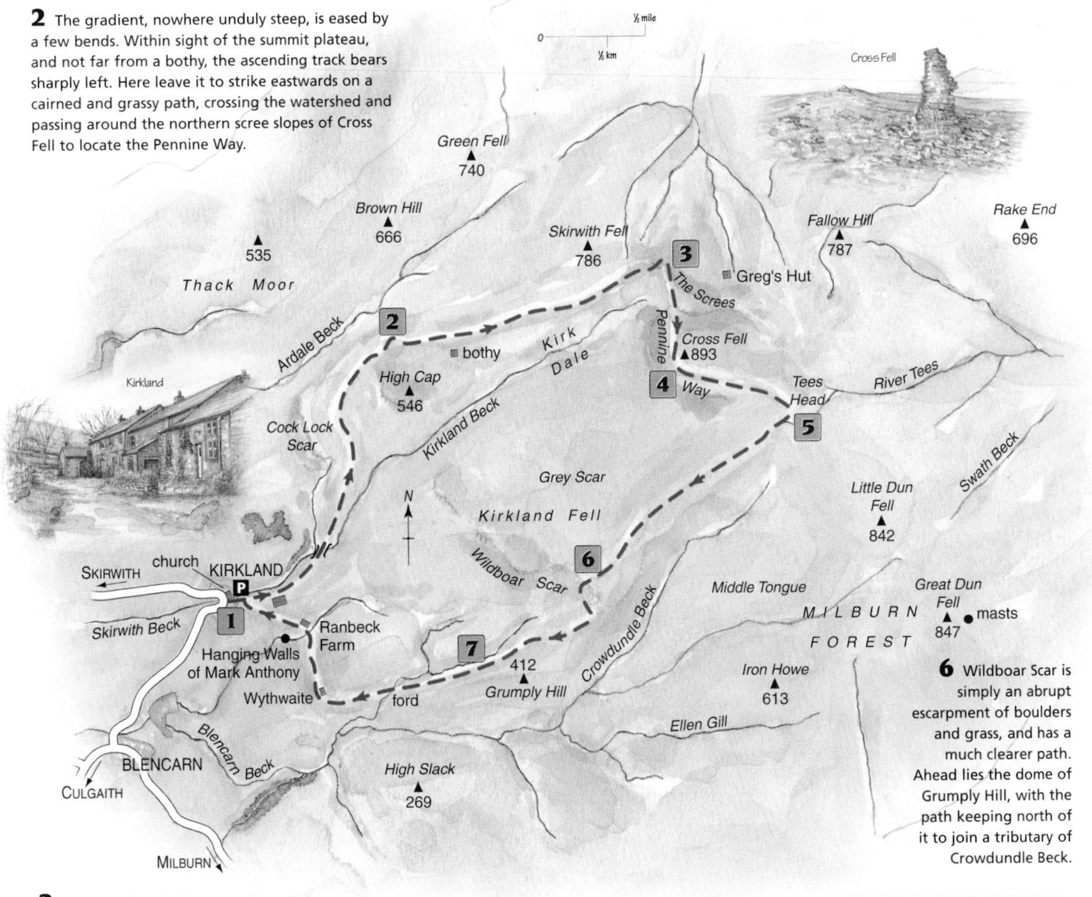

Distance: 9 miles (14.5km)
Total ascent: 2,265ft (690m)
Paths: good on ascent, thereafter sketchy
Terrain: high mountain plateau
Gradients: moderate
Refreshment: none nearby
Park: alongside river, opposite church in Kirkland, 5 miles (8km) east of A686 in Langwathby
Note: this route requires good navigational skills and should not be attempted in poor visibility

Up Gunnerside Gill with Swaledale Miners

A fine ramble up through classic Dales scenery reveals a landscape shaped by the search for lead

1 From the bridge in the centre of Gunnerside take the track on the eastern side up the beck, beginning opposite the Kings Head. After 100yds (91m), at a white gate, take stone steps to the right, then a walled path, emerging into open fields. The path descends to the beck as the valley broadens out. Cross a side beck on a tiny bridge, take two gap-stiles, close together, and follow a wall. Beyond two little gates you reach the beck again, and the first evidence of lead ore processing.

2 Pass two ore-dressing floors, one each side of the beck, and the entrance to a mining tunnel, known as a 'level'. Continue on the riverside path, following the yellow arrows, then go uphill, away from the beck. Cross a stile in the fence before going through a gap-stile in a wall. The path climbs gradually, as the valley becomes steeper-sided. Keep a wall to your left as the path levels out into the principal mining area.

3 Soon the Bunton mining complex comes into view. Pass through it and leave on a stony path uphill, with huge hushes on all sides. After 100yds (91m) uphill, fork left, downhill.

4 Approach Blakethwaite Smelting Mill, on a cramped site where Gunnerside Beck meets Blind Beck. Take a small bridge made from a slab of stone. Behind the mill the flue (mostly collapsed) rises steeply uphill. From the mill, the return path is clear, following a well-defined path gradually climbing up the west flank of Gunnerside Gill.

5 Cross another hush on a stone parapet; soon the southern end of Gunnerside Gill comes into view. Follow the track as it becomes stonier, makes a hairpin turn to cross Botcher Gill and joins a more substantial track.

6 Follow this track to the left, through a gate and past a little waterfall in Botcher Gill, before making a gentle descent. Across the valley the landscape changes back to a more familiar one of farms, walls and barns. When the track makes a long right turn, go left on a grassy path, by a small cairn.

7 Keep left (the track soon becomes more distinct), heading for the roofs of Gunnerside that soon appear. The path gradually becomes clearer and leads you downhill. Go through a little wooden gate and back into the village.

Distance: 6 miles (10km)
Total ascent: 660ft (201m)
Paths: good
Terrain: steep-sided Pennine valley
Gradients: gradual
Refreshments: Kings Head, Gunnerside
Park: opposite Kings Head, Gunnerside, on B6270 between Reeth and Kirkby Stephen

WALK 66

The Edge of an Empire on Hadrian's Wall

Walking on the wall which, for a while, marked the northern limits of the Roman Empire

Distance: 6 miles (9.6 km)
Total ascent: 560ft (171m)
Paths: mostly good but can get boggy
Terrain: fields, open country
Gradients: gradual
Refreshments: Haltwhistle town centre
Park: by Haltwhistle Railway Station

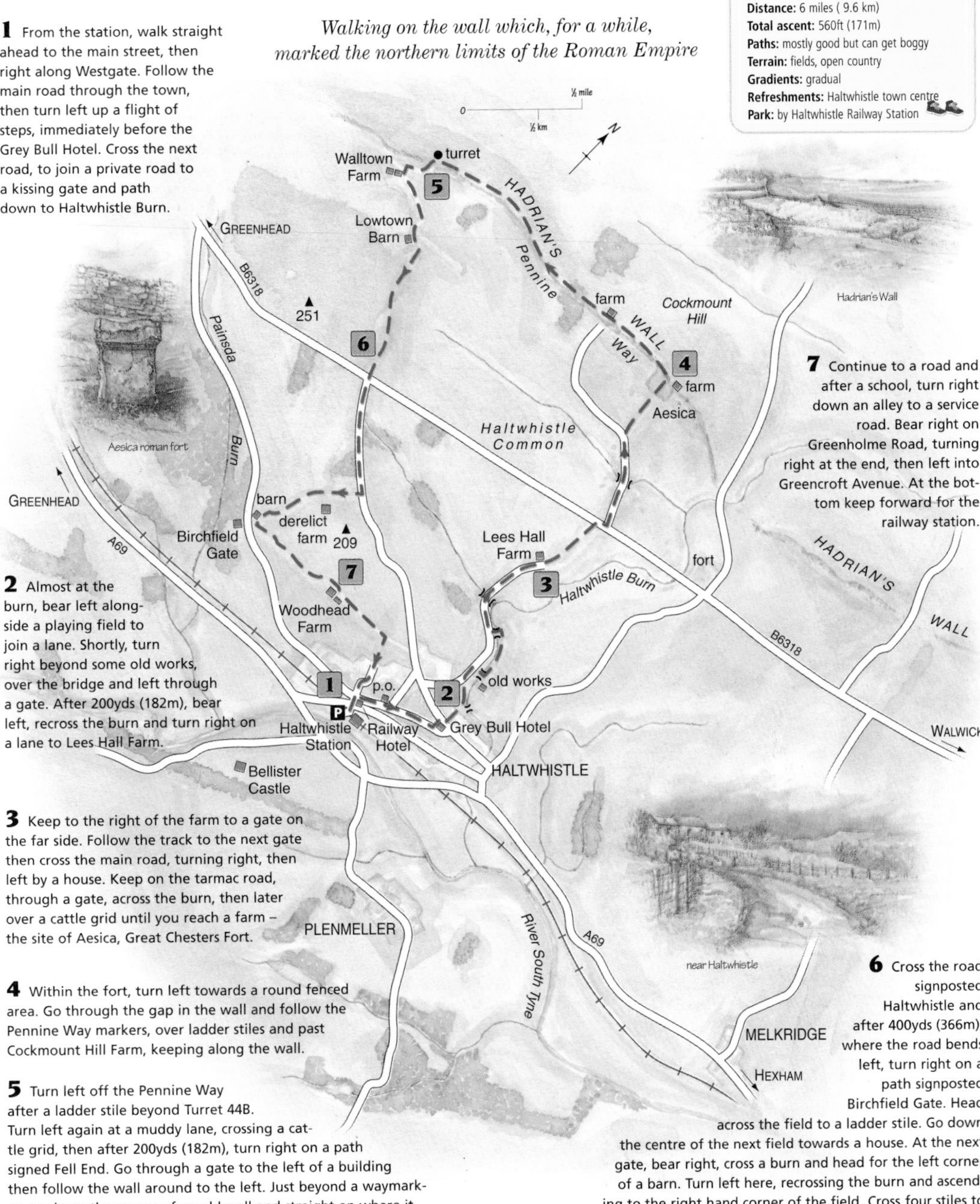

1 From the station, walk straight ahead to the main street, then right along Westgate. Follow the main road through the town, then turn left up a flight of steps, immediately before the Grey Bull Hotel. Cross the next road, to join a private road to a kissing gate and path down to Haltwhistle Burn.

2 Almost at the burn, bear left alongside a playing field to join a lane. Shortly, turn right beyond some old works, over the bridge and left through a gate. After 200yds (182m), bear left, recross the burn and turn right on a lane to Lees Hall Farm.

3 Keep to the right of the farm to a gate on the far side. Follow the track to the next gate then cross the main road, turning right, then left by a house. Keep on the tarmac road, through a gate, across the burn, then later over a cattle grid until you reach a farm – the site of Aesica, Great Chesters Fort.

4 Within the fort, turn left towards a round fenced area. Go through the gap in the wall and follow the Pennine Way markers, over ladder stiles and past Cockmount Hill Farm, keeping along the wall.

5 Turn left off the Pennine Way after a ladder stile beyond Turret 44B. Turn left again at a muddy lane, crossing a cattle grid, then after 200yds (182m), turn right on a path signed Fell End. Go through a gate to the left of a building then follow the wall around to the left. Just beyond a waymarker, go down the course of an old wall and straight on where it ends to the far side of the field. Pass through a gate then bear left to ascend to the lowest gap in the ridge ahead. Near the top, pass through a gate and cross the next field to a stile at the main road.

6 Cross the road signposted Haltwhistle and after 400yds (366m), where the road bends left, turn right on a path signposted Birchfield Gate. Head across the field to a ladder stile. Go down the centre of the next field towards a house. At the next gate, bear right, cross a burn and head for the left corner of a barn. Turn left here, recrossing the burn and ascending to the right hand corner of the field. Cross four stiles to a field on the left. Continue, to the left of Woodhead Farm, through two more gates and keep ahead, crossing a stile in the right hand corner of the field.

7 Continue to a road and after a school, turn right down an alley to a service road. Bear right on Greenholme Road, turning right at the end, then left into Greencroft Avenue. At the bottom keep forward for the railway station.

Flodden's Bloody Field

Scotland invaded England for the 'auld alliance' and the flower of its nobility was slaughtered in this Cheviot pastureland

Distance: 6 miles (9.6km)
Total ascent: 500ft (152m)
Paths: good; mostly minor roads and fields
Terrain: undulating pastureland
Gradients: gradual
Park: monument car park, Branxton

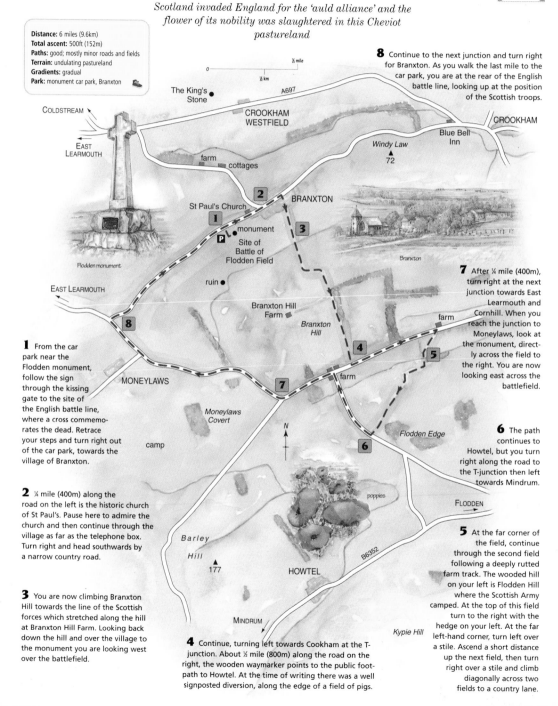

The King's Stone
A697
COLDSTREAM
EAST LEARMOUTH
CROOKHAM WESTFIELD
CROOKHAM
Blue Bell Inn
Windy Law
72
farm
cottages
BRANXTON
St Paul's Church
monument
Site of Battle of Flodden Field
Flodden monument
Branxton
ruin
EAST LEARMOUTH
Branxton Hill Farm
Branxton Hill
farm
MONEYLAWS
farm
Moneylaws Covert
camp
N
Flodden Edge
poppies
FLODDEN
Barley Hill
177
HOWTEL
B6352
MINDRUM
Kypie Hill

1 From the car park near the Flodden monument, follow the sign through the kissing gate to the site of the English battle line, where a cross commemorates the dead. Retrace your steps and turn right out of the car park, towards the village of Branxton.

2 ¼ mile (400m) along the road on the left is the historic church of St Paul's. Pause here to admire the church and then continue through the village as far as the telephone box. Turn right and head southwards by a narrow country road.

3 You are now climbing Branxton Hill towards the line of the Scottish forces which stretched along the hill at Branxton Hill Farm. Looking back down the hill and over the village to the monument you are looking west over the battlefield.

4 Continue, turning left towards Cookham at the T-junction. About ½ mile (800m) along the road on the right, the wooden waymarker points to the public footpath to Howtel. At the time of writing there was a well signposted diversion, along the edge of a field of pigs.

5 At the far corner of the field, continue through the second field following a deeply rutted farm track. The wooded hill on your left is Flodden Hill where the Scottish Army camped. At the top of this field turn to the right with the hedge on your left. At the far left-hand corner, turn left over a stile. Ascend a short distance up the next field, then turn right over a stile and climb diagonally across two fields to a country lane.

6 The path continues to Howtel, but you turn right along the road to the T-junction then left towards Mindrum.

7 After ¼ mile (400m), turn right at the next junction towards East Learmouth and Cornhill. When you reach the junction to Moneylaws, look at the monument, directly across the field to the right. You are now looking east across the battlefield.

8 Continue to the next junction and turn right for Branxton. As you walk the last mile to the car park, you are at the rear of the English battle line, looking up at the position of the Scottish troops.

WALK 68

Berwick's Bulwark against the Scots

The streets, ramparts and surrounding countryside of this historic border town make for a splendid circular walk

Distance: 5 miles (8km)
Total ascent: 100ft (30m)
Paths: undefined in places; can be muddy
Terrain: fields, town
Gradients: some steps
Refreshments: plenty in town
Park: the Maltings car park, Berwick upon Tweed

1 From the Maltings car park go left, down the hill. At the bottom, cross the road, then keep ahead over Berwick Old Bridge. Once over, turn right. At corner of Blakewell Road take path to the right, beside the river.

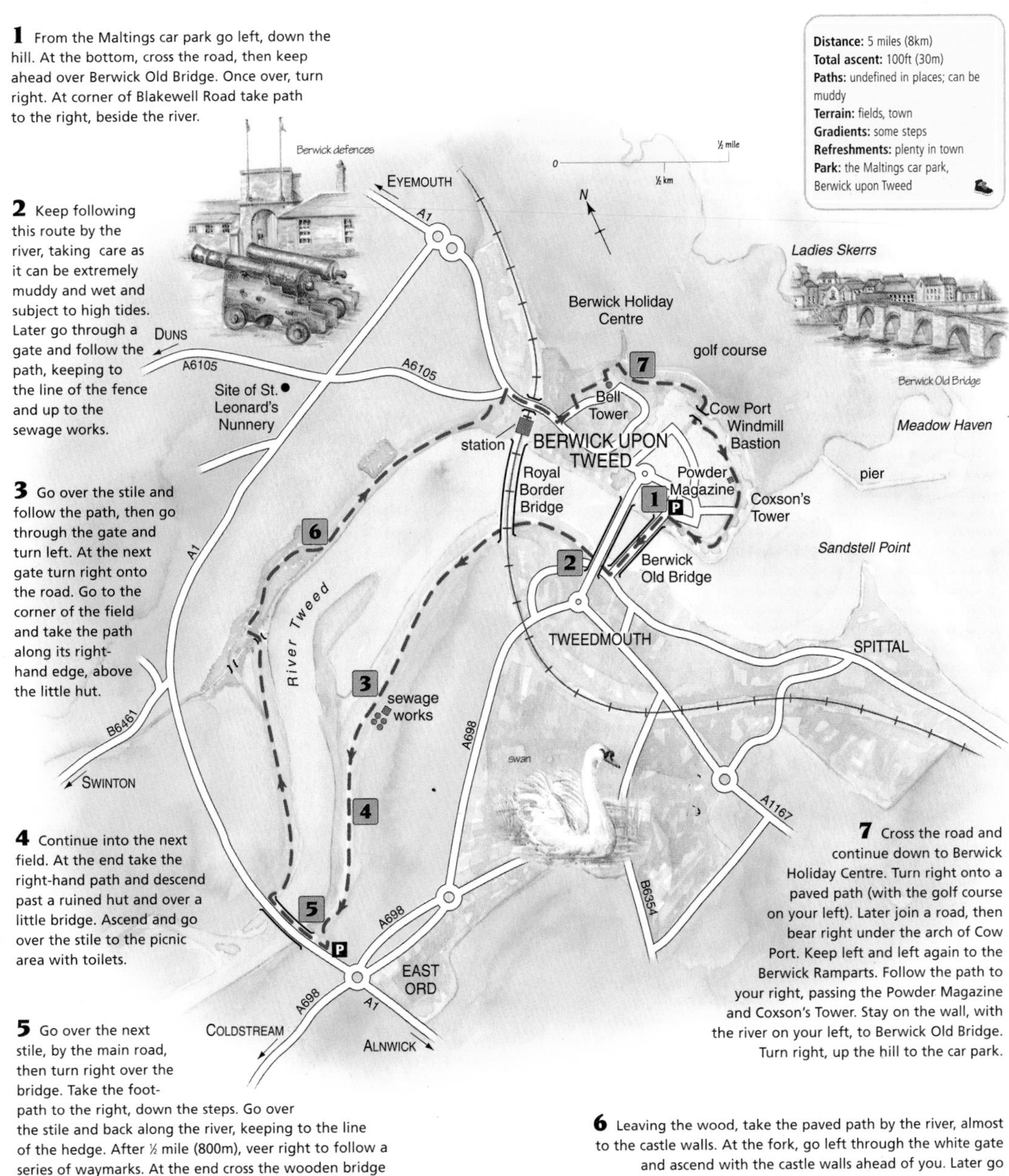

2 Keep following this route by the river, taking care as it can be extremely muddy and wet and subject to high tides. Later go through a gate and follow the path, keeping to the line of the fence and up to the sewage works.

3 Go over the stile and follow the path, then go through the gate and turn left. At the next gate turn right onto the road. Go to the corner of the field and take the path along its right-hand edge, above the little hut.

4 Continue into the next field. At the end take the right-hand path and descend past a ruined hut and over a little bridge. Ascend and go over the stile to the picnic area with toilets.

5 Go over the next stile, by the main road, then turn right over the bridge. Take the footpath to the right, down the steps. Go over the stile and back along the river, keeping to the line of the hedge. After ½ mile (800m), veer right to follow a series of waymarks. At the end cross the wooden bridge then a ladder stile and ascend through woodland. At the top of the wood turn right along a woodland path. (If the tide is in, stay with the hedge on your left to cross the stone bridge and turn right into the woodland.)

6 Leaving the wood, take the paved path by the river, almost to the castle walls. At the fork, go left through the white gate and ascend with the castle walls ahead of you. Later go through another gate and cross a small park. At the main road turn right, go over the bridge, cross the road, then go left along High Greens. In 200yds (182m) turn left into Bell Tower Place then, at a school, keep right to the Bell Tower.

7 Cross the road and continue down to Berwick Holiday Centre. Turn right onto a paved path (with the golf course on your left). Later join a road, then bear right under the arch of Cow Port. Keep left and left again to the Berwick Ramparts. Follow the path to your right, passing the Powder Magazine and Coxson's Tower. Stay on the wall, with the river on your left, to Berwick Old Bridge. Turn right, up the hill to the car park.

In the Hole of Horcum

Exploring this spectacular dip in the moorland plateau of the North York Moors

Distance: 8½ miles (13.7km)
Paths: good tracks and woodland paths; often muddy
Total ascent: 1,015ft (309m)
Terrain: moorland ridges and wooded valleys
Gradients: moderate; some steep sections
Refreshments: Levisham, or caravan in car park
Park: car park on the A169, 12 miles (19.2km) north of Pickering and 3 miles (4.8km) north of Lockton

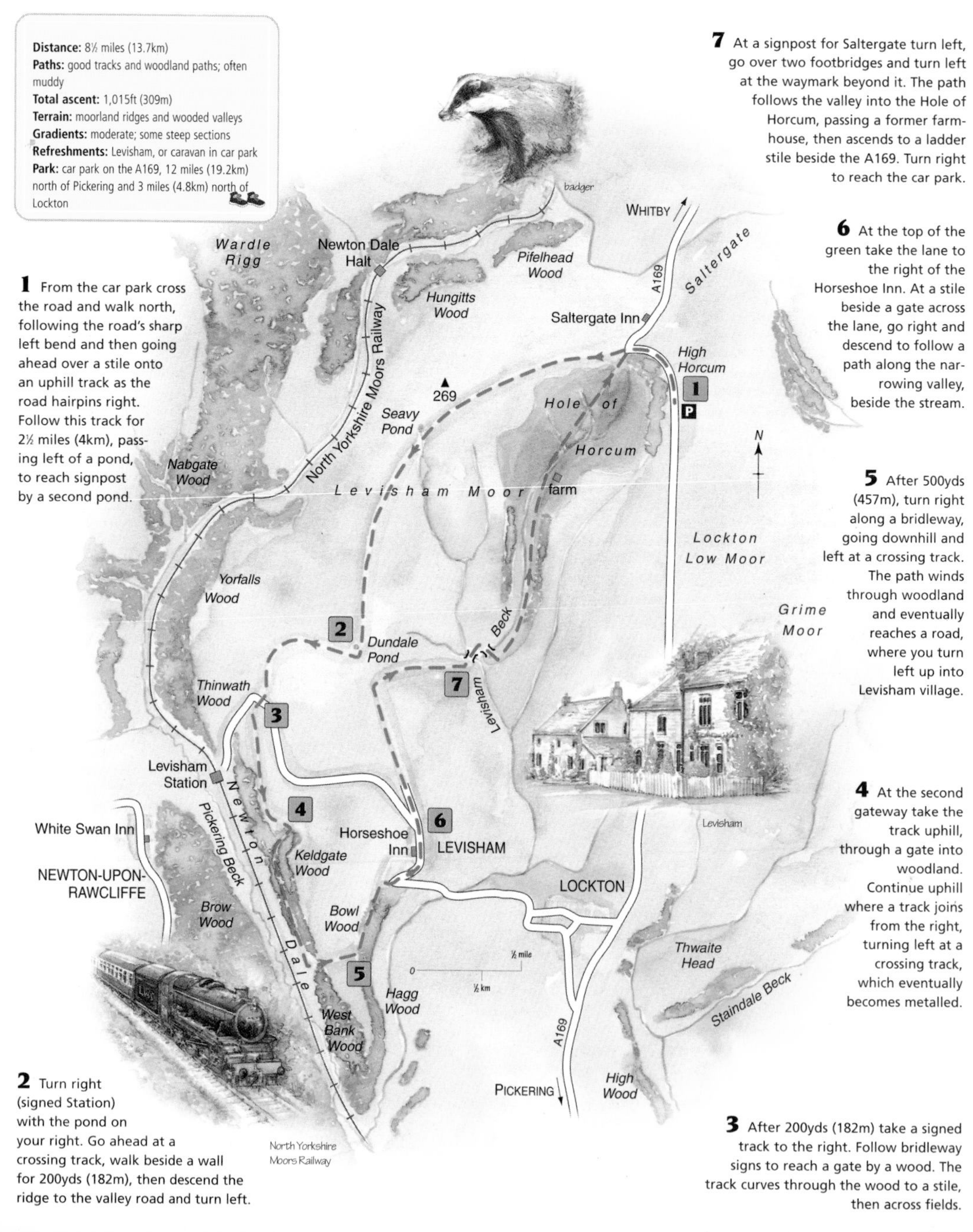

1 From the car park cross the road and walk north, following the road's sharp left bend and then going ahead over a stile onto an uphill track as the road hairpins right. Follow this track for 2½ miles (4km), passing left of a pond, to reach signpost by a second pond.

2 Turn right (signed Station) with the pond on your right. Go ahead at a crossing track, walk beside a wall for 200yds (182m), then descend the ridge to the valley road and turn left.

3 After 200yds (182m) take a signed track to the right. Follow bridleway signs to reach a gate by a wood. The track curves through the wood to a stile, then across fields.

4 At the second gateway take the track uphill, through a gate into woodland. Continue uphill where a track joins from the right, turning left at a crossing track, which eventually becomes metalled.

5 After 500yds (457m), turn right along a bridleway, going downhill and left at a crossing track. The path winds through woodland and eventually reaches a road, where you turn left up into Levisham village.

6 At the top of the green take the lane to the right of the Horseshoe Inn. At a stile beside a gate across the lane, go right and descend to follow a path along the narrowing valley, beside the stream.

7 At a signpost for Saltergate turn left, go over two footbridges and turn left at the waymark beyond it. The path follows the valley into the Hole of Horcum, passing a former farmhouse, then ascends to a ladder stile beside the A169. Turn right to reach the car park.

High and Deep on Yorkshire's Coast

From the soaring cliffs above pretty Staithes to the hidden depths of Boulby Mine, this walk shows the contrasts of the North Yorkshire coast

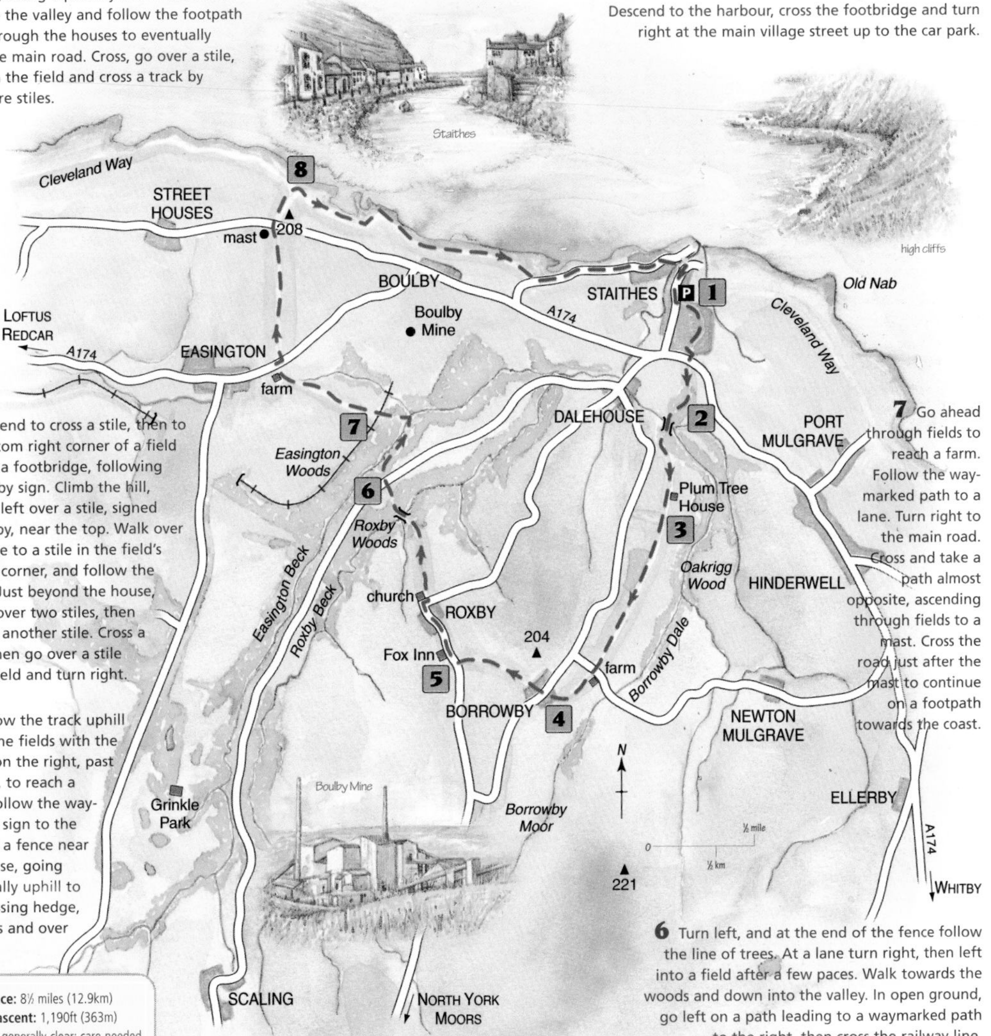

1 From the top of the car park walk left, past garages, along a path by allotments. Turn right up the valley and follow the footpath signs through the houses to eventually meet the main road. Cross, go over a stile, through the field and cross a track by two more stiles.

2 Descend to cross a stile, then to the bottom right corner of a field to cross a footbridge, following the Roxby sign. Climb the hill, veering left over a stile, signed Borrowby, near the top. Walk over the ridge to a stile in the field's top left corner, and follow the hedge. Just beyond the house, go left over two stiles, then right to another stile. Cross a track, then go over a stile into a field and turn right.

3 Follow the track uphill across the fields with the hedge on the right, past a wood, to reach a farm. Follow the way-marked sign to the right of a fence near the house, going diagonally uphill to the crossing hedge, up steps and over a stile.

4 Cross the field, going right of the barn, and over a stile to a road. Turn left, and just before the houses on the right, take a signed path up steps and over a stile. Cross three stiles, and as the hedge bends left, go diagonally across the fields to meet a lane.

5 Turn right, downhill, and go past the church to turn left down a signed track. Follow it beside woodland to the corner of a field. Go left over a stile into woodland. Follow waymarkers to cross a footbridge. Turn left, uphill, and left again where paths fork, ascending to a stile.

6 Turn left, and at the end of the fence follow the line of trees. At a lane turn right, then left into a field after a few paces. Walk towards the woods and down into the valley. In open ground, go left on a path leading to a waymarked path to the right, then cross the railway line.

7 Go ahead through fields to reach a farm. Follow the way-marked path to a lane. Turn right to the main road. Cross and take a path almost opposite, ascending through fields to a mast. Cross the road just after the mast to continue on a footpath towards the coast.

8 At a crossing track (the Cleveland Way), turn right and follow it to Staithes, following signs to Cowbar. Descend to the harbour, cross the footbridge and turn right at the main village street up to the car park.

Distance: 8½ miles (12.9km)
Total ascent: 1,190ft (363m)
Paths: generally clear; care needed in woodland and along cliff tops; often muddy
Terrain: farmland woods and cliffs
Gradients: some steep sections
Refreshments: Staithes
Park: Staithes village car park, off A174

Down the Ripon Rabbit Hole with Lewis Carroll

A walk connecting Ripon with the parkland of Studley Royal – scenery which inspired Lewis Carroll

1 Leave Ripon market square by Kirkgate (near the Unicorn Hotel), and continue along to visit the cathedral and its Lewis Carroll links. Leave by the north door, near the Mothers' Union Chapel, and turn left, following the road as it curves left.

2 At the traffic lights turn left up Allhallowgate and, at the T-junction at the top, go right along North Street. 300yds (273m) on, turn left up Coltsgate Hill, continuing past the College and turning right in to Kirkby Road.

3 Walk up the hill, turning left into Lark Lane beyond the post box. At the bottom, turn right, then first left into Bishopton Road. Where the road bends left, go straight ahead down a track, then over a stile on the left. At a stone stile by the bridge turn right and walk beside the road.

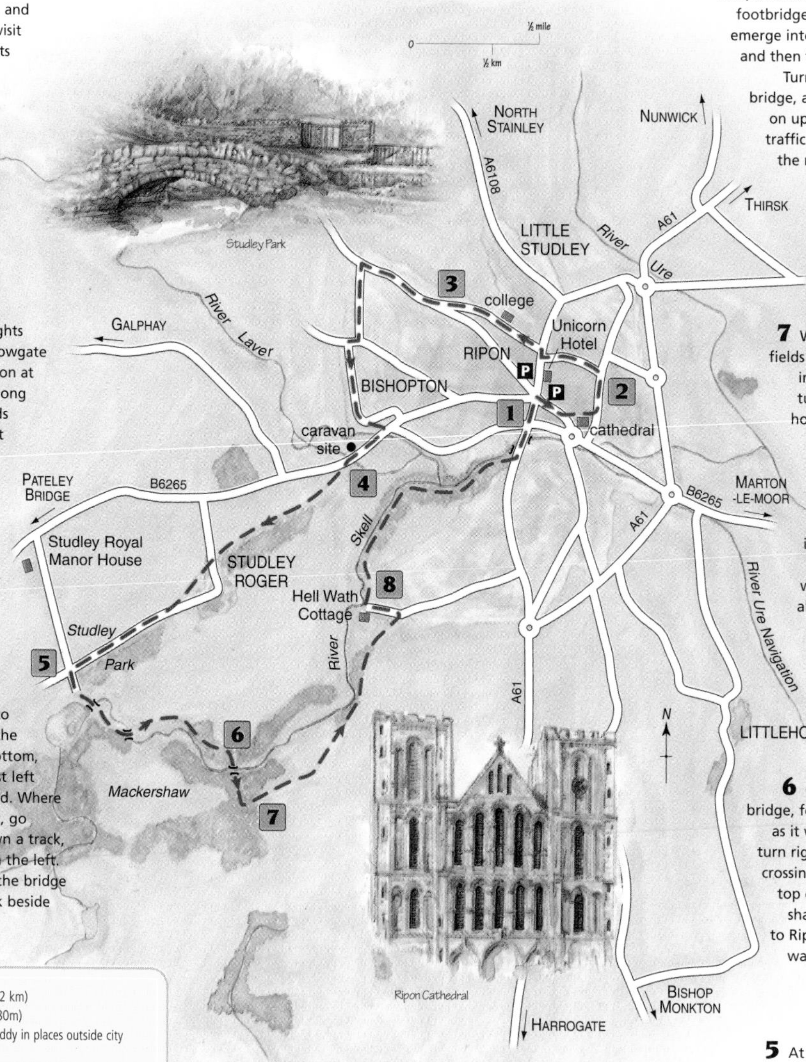

4 Where the road bends right by the caravan site, go through a kissing gate on the left and follow the footpath across the fields to Studley Roger. Cross the village street and go straight ahead, through two gates, to emerge into Studley Park, eventually turning right along the main drive.

5 At the crossroads turn left towards the lake, and leave the metalled road to walk round the left end of the lake, over the dam and left, following the path over five stone bridges. Go through the gate in the wall, and walk along to a footbridge.

6 Cross the footbridge, follow the path as it winds left, and turn right, uphill, at a crossing track. At the top of the hill turn sharp left, signed to Ripon, to reach a waymarked gate.

7 Walk across the fields to a handgate into a lane, and turn left. As the houses begin, go left for 100yds (91m) along the lane to Hell Wath Cottage, turning right along a signed path where the metalled road ends.

8 Follow the path beside the river, down steps and past a footbridge, eventually to emerge into a minor road and then the main road. Turn left, over the bridge, and go straight on up the hill at the traffic lights, back to the market square.

Studley Park

Ripon Cathedral

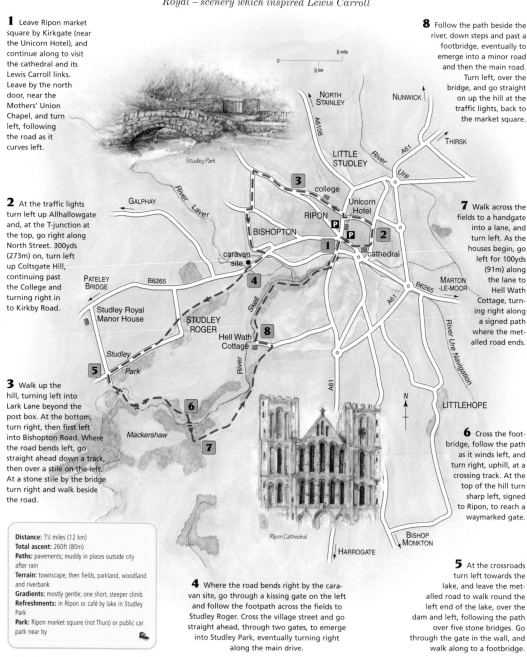

Distance: 7½ miles (12 km)
Total ascent: 260ft (80m)
Paths: pavements; muddy in places outside city after rain
Terrain: townscape, then fields, parkland, woodland and riverbank
Gradients: mostly gentle; one short, steeper climb
Refreshments: in Ripon or café by lake in Studley Park
Park: Ripon market square (not Thurs) or public car park near by

Wartime Remains on Spurn Point

Exploring the wartime remains on this remote, curling finger of land in the Mouth of the Humber

Distance: 8½ miles (13.5km)
Total ascent: negligible
Paths: well-signed and mostly good;muddy in places; some road walking. Obey any diversions resulting from storm damage
Terrain: sand-dunes and grassland
Gradients: none
Refreshments: seasonal at Spurn Point
Park: car park, Kilnsea (east of the village, just beyond the crossroads)

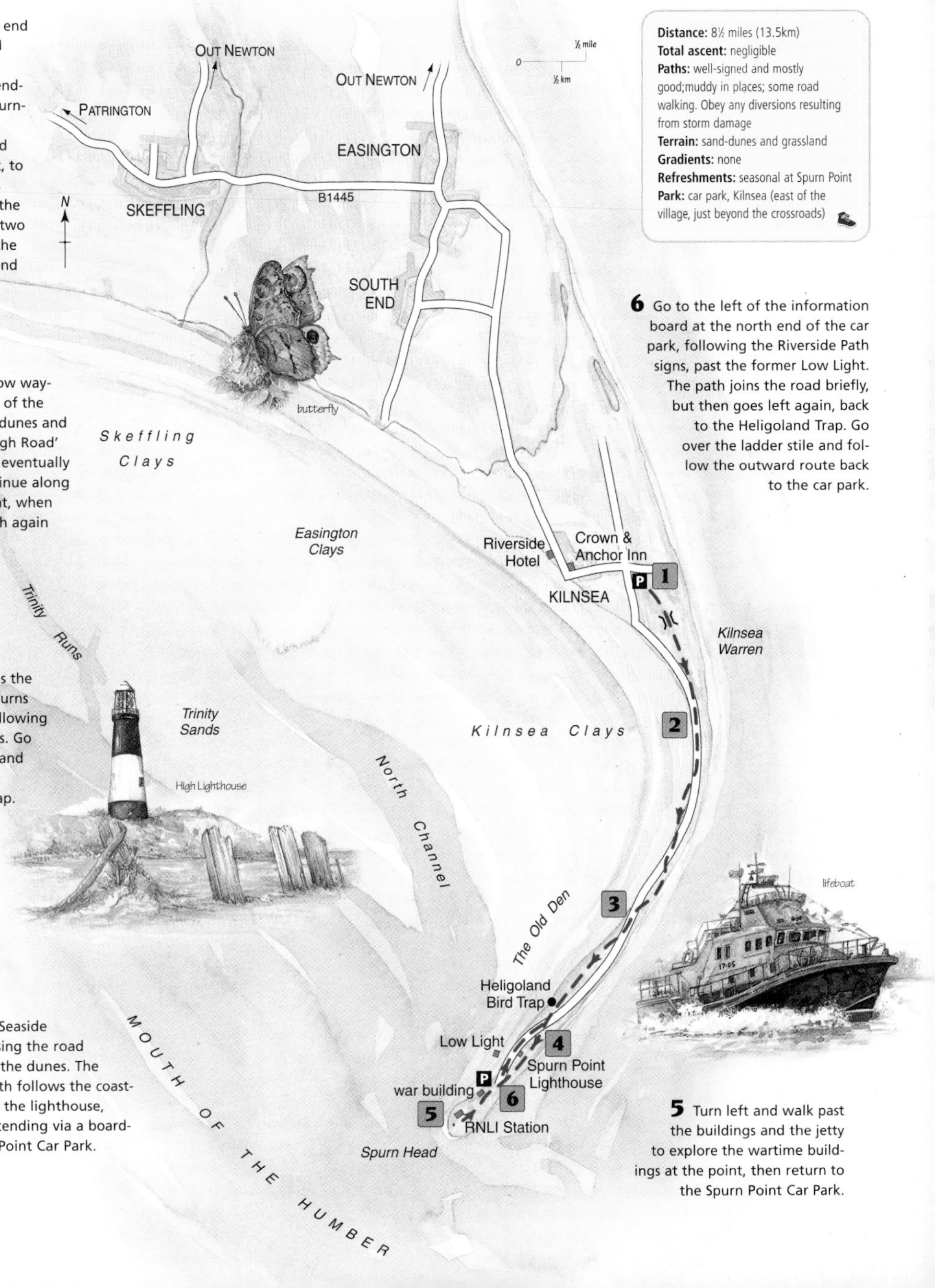

1 Walk to the far end of the car park and follow the Spurn Footpath sign, ascending the bank and turning right. Cross a bridge and stile and turn left then right, to follow waymarkers along the edge of the cliff. After passing two bird hides, follow the path right to descend beside bungalows towards the road.

2 Follow the yellow waymarkers to the left of the road, through the dunes and past the 'No Through Road' sign. The path will eventually join the road; continue along it until it veers right, when the signed footpath again goes to the left.

3 The path rejoins the road briefly, then turns off to the right, following the telegraph poles. Go over a ladder stile and towards the Heligoland Bird Trap. Go over another ladder stile to reach a signpost.

4 Follow the Seaside Path sign, crossing the road and ascending the dunes. The waymarked path follows the coastline and passes the lighthouse, eventually descending via a boardwalk to Spurn Point Car Park.

5 Turn left and walk past the buildings and the jetty to explore the wartime buildings at the point, then return to the Spurn Point Car Park.

6 Go to the left of the information board at the north end of the car park, following the Riverside Path signs, past the former Low Light. The path joins the road briefly, but then goes left again, back to the Heligoland Trap. Go over the ladder stile and follow the outward route back to the car park.

Limestone Landscapes around Malham

Above the spectacular face of Malham Cove lies a less-visited world of classic limestone scenery

Distance: 5 miles (8km)
Total ascent: 985ft (300m)
Paths: good; some steep, stepped sections
Terrain: limestone landscape and upland pasture
Gradients: mostly easy, apart from steps up side of cove
Refreshments: pubs and cafés, Malham
Park: car park by visitor centre, Malham

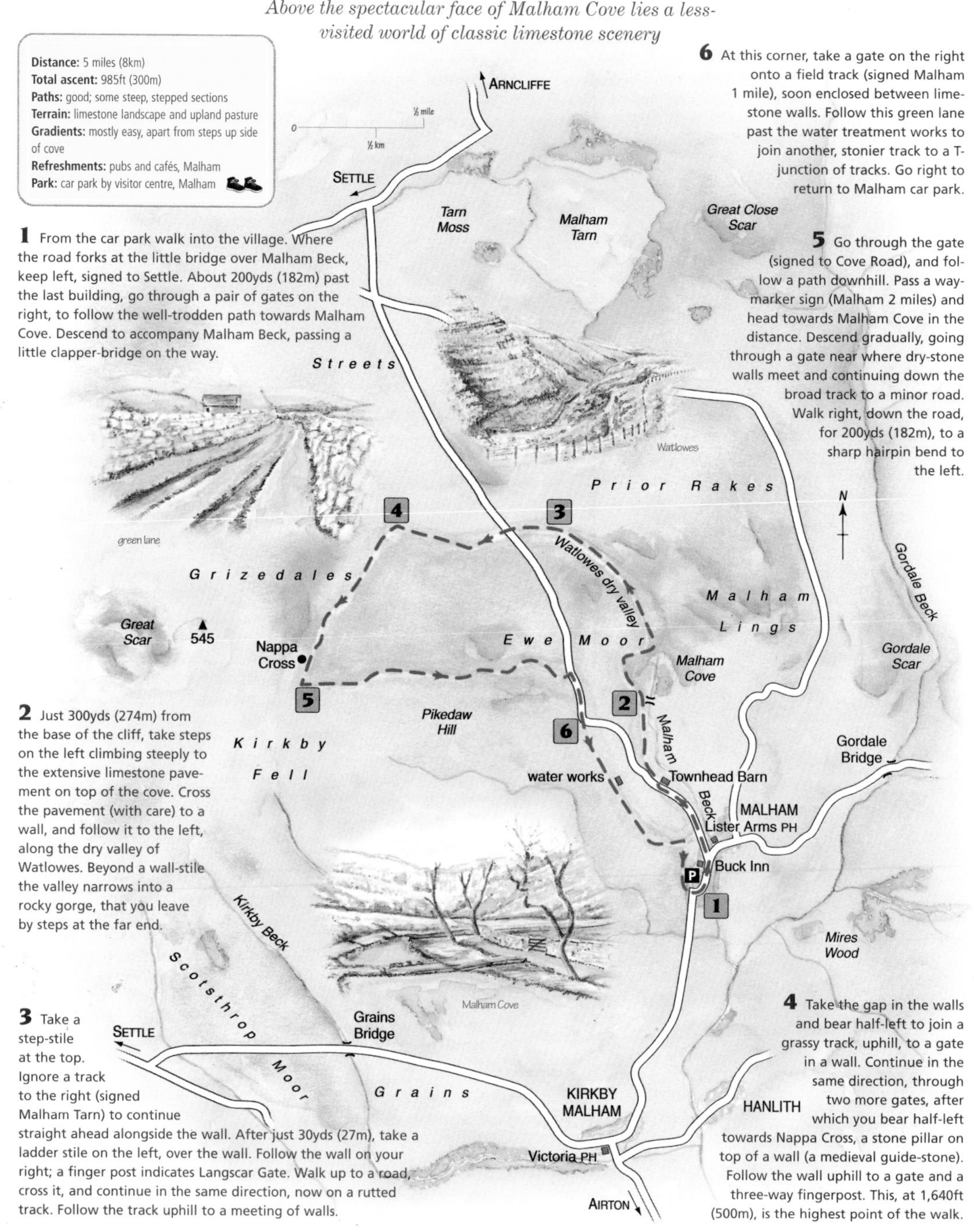

1 From the car park walk into the village. Where the road forks at the little bridge over Malham Beck, keep left, signed to Settle. About 200yds (182m) past the last building, go through a pair of gates on the right, to follow the well-trodden path towards Malham Cove. Descend to accompany Malham Beck, passing a little clapper-bridge on the way.

2 Just 300yds (274m) from the base of the cliff, take steps on the left climbing steeply to the extensive limestone pavement on top of the cove. Cross the pavement (with care) to a wall, and follow it to the left, along the dry valley of Watlowes. Beyond a wall-stile the valley narrows into a rocky gorge, that you leave by steps at the far end.

3 Take a step-stile at the top. Ignore a track to the right (signed Malham Tarn) to continue straight ahead alongside the wall. After just 30yds (27m), take a ladder stile on the left, over the wall. Follow the wall on your right; a finger post indicates Langscar Gate. Walk up to a road, cross it, and continue in the same direction, now on a rutted track. Follow the track uphill to a meeting of walls.

4 Take the gap in the walls and bear half-left to join a grassy track, uphill, to a gate in a wall. Continue in the same direction, through two more gates, after which you bear half-left towards Nappa Cross, a stone pillar on top of a wall (a medieval guide-stone). Follow the wall uphill to a gate and a three-way fingerpost. This, at 1,640ft (500m), is the highest point of the walk.

5 Go through the gate (signed to Cove Road), and follow a path downhill. Pass a waymarker sign (Malham 2 miles) and head towards Malham Cove in the distance. Descend gradually, going through a gate near where dry-stone walls meet and continuing down the broad track to a minor road. Walk right, down the road, for 200yds (182m), to a sharp hairpin bend to the left.

6 At this corner, take a gate on the right onto a field track (signed Malham 1 mile), soon enclosed between limestone walls. Follow this green lane past the water treatment works to join another, stonier track to a T-junction of tracks. Go right to return to Malham car park.

Haworth and the Brontë Moors

The moors above the Brontë's West Yorkshire home were a source of both inspiration and solace in their briefly flourishing lives

1 From the car park, go through gate posts opposite the museum and turn right. The lane soon becomes a paved field path that leads to the Haworth-Stanbury road. Walk left along the road and, after about 80yds (75m), take a left fork, signed to Penistone Hill. Continue along this quiet road to a T-junction.

2 Take the track straight ahead, soon signed Brontë Way and Top Withins, gradually descending to South Dean Beck where, within a few paces of the stone bridge, you'll find the Brontë Waterfall and Brontë Seat (a stone that resembles a chair). Cross the bridge and climb steeply uphill to a 3-way sign.

3 Keep left, uphill, on a paved path signed to Top Withins. The path soon levels out to accompany a dry-stone wall. Cross a stile and then keep left. Cross a tiny beck on stepping stones; a steep uphill climb brings you to a waymarker by a ruined building. A short detour of 200yds (182m), left, uphill, is needed if you want to investigate the lonely ruins of Top Withins.

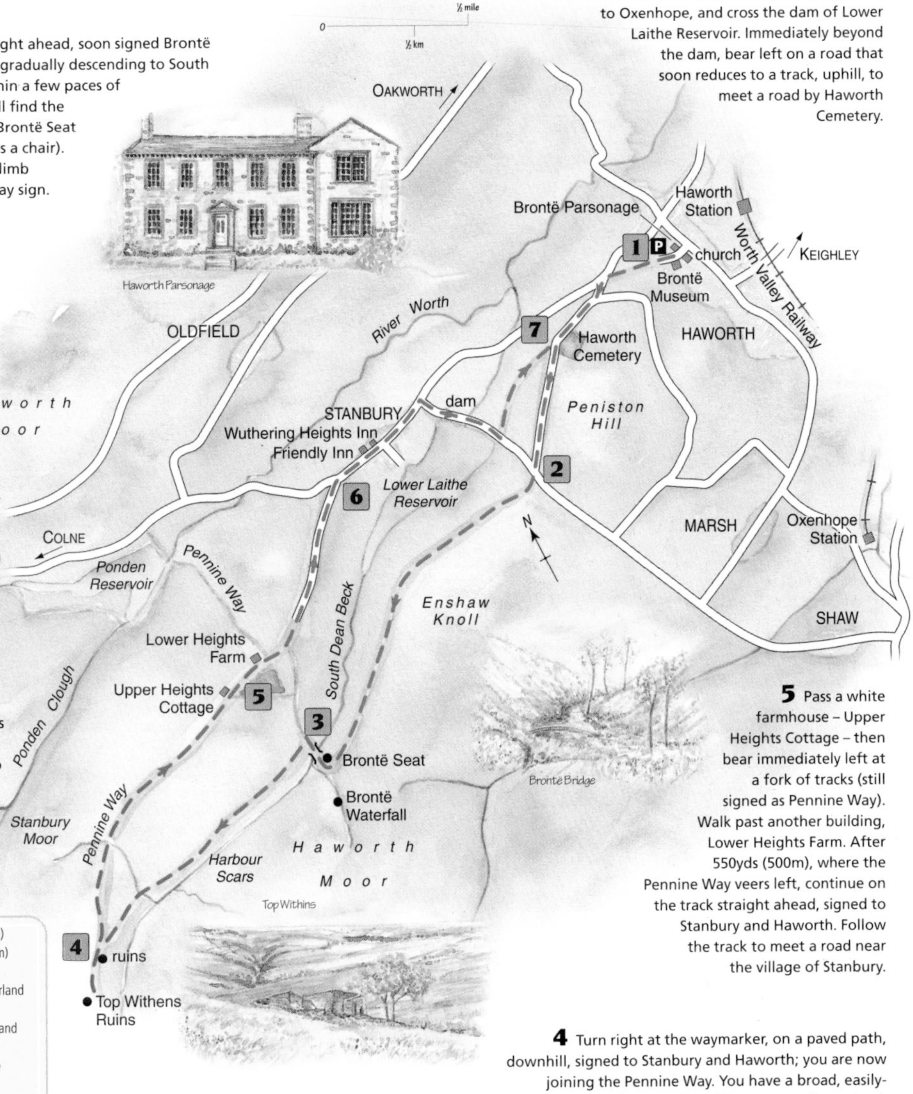

4 Turn right at the waymarker, on a paved path, downhill, signed to Stanbury and Haworth; you are now joining the Pennine Way. You have a broad, easily-followed track across the wide expanse of moorland.

5 Pass a white farmhouse – Upper Heights Cottage – then bear immediately left at a fork of tracks (still signed as Pennine Way). Walk past another building, Lower Heights Farm. After 550yds (500m), where the Pennine Way veers left, continue on the track straight ahead, signed to Stanbury and Haworth. Follow the track to meet a road near the village of Stanbury.

6 Bear right along the road through Stanbury, then take the first road on the right, signed to Oxenhope, and cross the dam of Lower Laithe Reservoir. Immediately beyond the dam, bear left on a road that soon reduces to a track, uphill, to meet a road by Haworth Cemetery.

7 From here you retrace your outward route: walk left along the road, soon taking a stile on the right, to follow the paved field path back into Haworth.

Distance: 7½ miles (12km)
Total ascent: 575ft (175m)
Paths: well-defined
Terrain: mostly open moorland
Gradients: gradual
Refreshments: Stanbury and Haworth
Park: car park near Brontë Parsonage, Haworth

Slaidburn and the Forest of Bowland

Exploring the great tract of moorland which opens out between the Yorkshire Dales and the Lancashire Plain

Distance: 11 miles (17.7km)
Total ascent: 985ft (300m)
Paths: good meadow paths, moorland roads and tracks.
Terrain: wild, open moors and hillsides, with steep stream valleys
Gradients: several longish gradual climbs, and one or two short sharp ones
Refreshments: Hark to Bounty Inn, Slaidburn; village shop, Dunsop Bridge
Park: public car park on edge of Slaidburn, 9 miles (15km) north of Clitheroe on the B6478
Note: not recommended in poor visibility

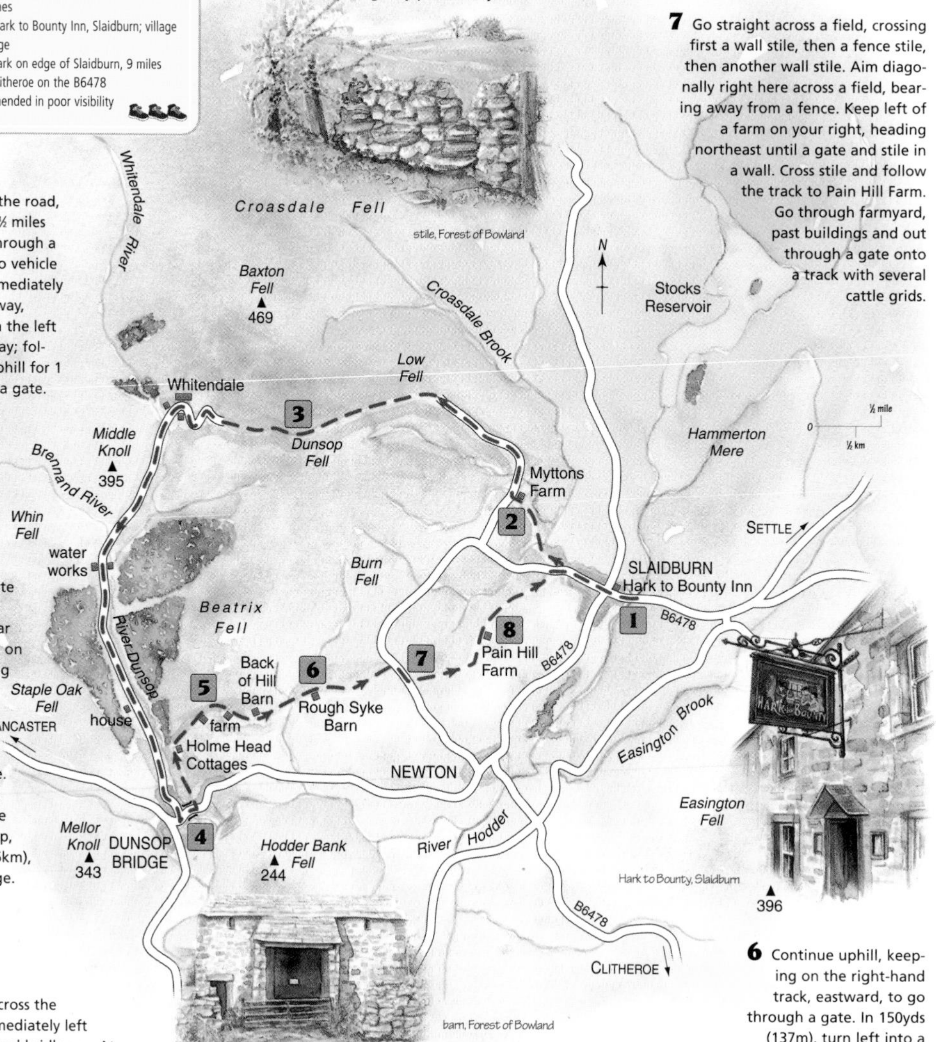

1 Walk into the village to the Hark to Bounty Inn. From the inn turn right. Past the health centre, turn right ('Wood House' sign) on a path by Croasdale Brook, then through meadows. At a T-junction, go right down the grassy path to Myttons Farm.

2 Turn left to the road, then right for 1½ miles (2.4km) to go through a gate marked 'No vehicle access'. Turn immediately left up a bridleway, where a wall on the left soon swings away; follow the track uphill for 1 mile (1.6km) to a gate.

3 From this gate at the top of Dunsop Fell, bear diagonally right on a path, following yellow-topped marker posts for 1¼ miles (2km) down into Whitendale. Turn left on the road here beside the River Dunsop, for 3½ miles (5.6km), to Dunsop Bridge.

4 Turn left to cross the bridge then immediately left again up a marked bridleway. At Holme Head Cottages go through a gate (blue and yellow arrows) .In 20yds (18m), turn right to climb steps up a steep bank. Cross a wall stile and follow telegraph poles to Beatrix.

5 At Beatrix turn left along the road. Pass houses, and take the track to Back of Hill Barn. Follow arrow waymarks down to the valley bottom, cross the stream and climb the track to Rough Syke Barn.

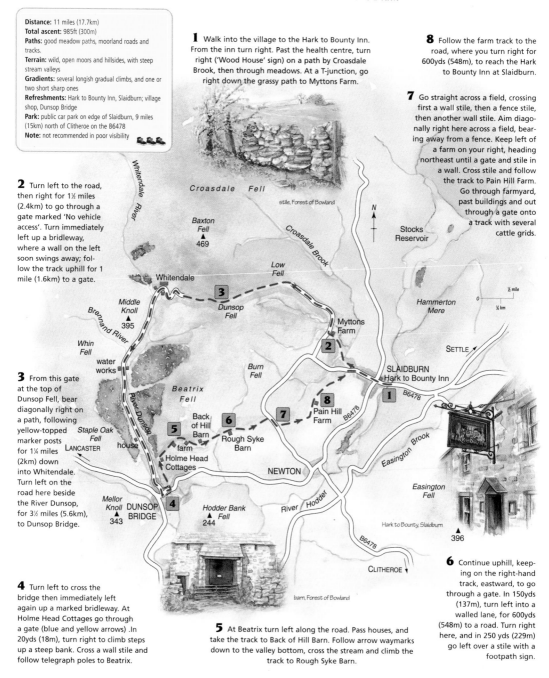

6 Continue uphill, keeping on the right-hand track, eastward, to go through a gate. In 150yds (137m), turn left into a walled lane, for 600yds (548m) to a road. Turn right here, and in 250 yds (229m) go left over a stile with a footpath sign.

7 Go straight across a field, crossing first a wall stile, then a fence stile, then another wall stile. Aim diagonally right here across a field, bearing away from a fence. Keep left of a farm on your right, heading northeast until a gate and stile in a wall. Cross stile and follow the track to Pain Hill Farm. Go through farmyard, past buildings and out through a gate onto a track with several cattle grids.

8 Follow the farm track to the road, where you turn right for 600yds (548m), to reach the Hark to Bounty Inn at Slaidburn.

Cloth and Canal-folk in Calderdale

Explore Calderdale's charming tangle of lanes and bridleways between working villages

1 From the crossroads in the centre of Hebden Bridge go down Holme Street to the Rochdale Canal and walk right, along the towpath. After about 1 mile (1.6km) you come to a broadening of the canal, next to a mill and lock; immediately before the next bridge over the canal, go right to meet the A646.

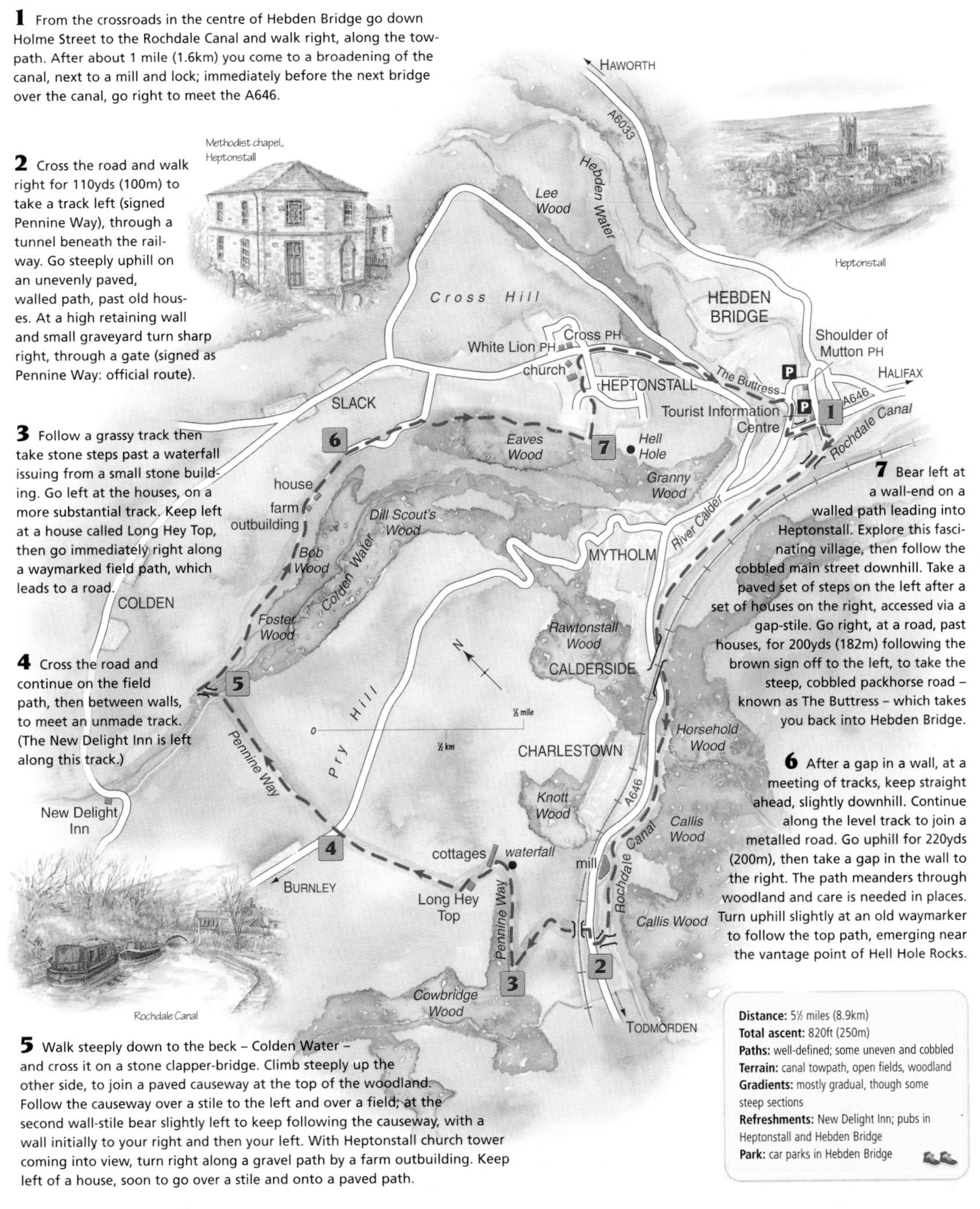

2 Cross the road and walk right for 110yds (100m) to take a track left (signed Pennine Way), through a tunnel beneath the railway. Go steeply uphill on an unevenly paved, walled path, past old houses. At a high retaining wall and small graveyard turn sharp right, through a gate (signed as Pennine Way: official route).

3 Follow a grassy track then take stone steps past a waterfall issuing from a small stone building. Go left at the houses, on a more substantial track. Keep left at a house called Long Hey Top, then go immediately right along a waymarked field path, which leads to a road.

4 Cross the road and continue on the field path, then between walls, to meet an unmade track. (The New Delight Inn is left along this track.)

5 Walk steeply down to the beck – Colden Water – and cross it on a stone clapper-bridge. Climb steeply up the other side, to join a paved causeway at the top of the woodland. Follow the causeway over a stile to the left and over a field; at the second wall-stile bear slightly left to keep following the causeway, with a wall initially to your right and then your left. With Heptonstall church tower coming into view, turn right along a gravel path by a farm outbuilding. Keep left of a house, soon to go over a stile and onto a paved path.

6 After a gap in a wall, at a meeting of tracks, keep straight ahead, slightly downhill. Continue along the level track to join a metalled road. Go uphill for 220yds (200m), then take a gap in the wall to the right. The path meanders through woodland and care is needed in places. Turn uphill slightly at an old waymarker to follow the top path, emerging near the vantage point of Hell Hole Rocks.

7 Bear left at a wall-end on a walled path leading into Heptonstall. Explore this fascinating village, then follow the cobbled main street downhill. Take a paved set of steps on the left after a set of houses on the right, accessed via a gap-stile. Go right, at a road, past houses, for 200yds (182m) following the brown sign off to the left, to take the steep, cobbled packhorse road – known as The Buttress – which takes you back into Hebden Bridge.

Distance: 5½ miles (8.9km)
Total ascent: 820ft (250m)
Paths: well-defined; some uneven and cobbled
Terrain: canal towpath, open fields, woodland
Gradients: mostly gradual, though some steep sections
Refreshments: New Delight Inn; pubs in Heptonstall and Hebden Bridge
Park: car parks in Hebden Bridge

The Witches of Pendle Hill

A walk up this prominent Lancashire hill reveals a landscape where witches were once thought a problem

Distance: 5½ miles (9km)
Total ascent: 1,310 feet (400m)
Paths: clear, but not obvious in poor visibility; muddy in places
Terrain: mountain and upland pasture
Gradients: one steep ascent and a lesser climb through a plantation
Refreshments: pubs, restaurant and refreshments in Barley
Park: car park in Barley, north of Burnley, off A6068

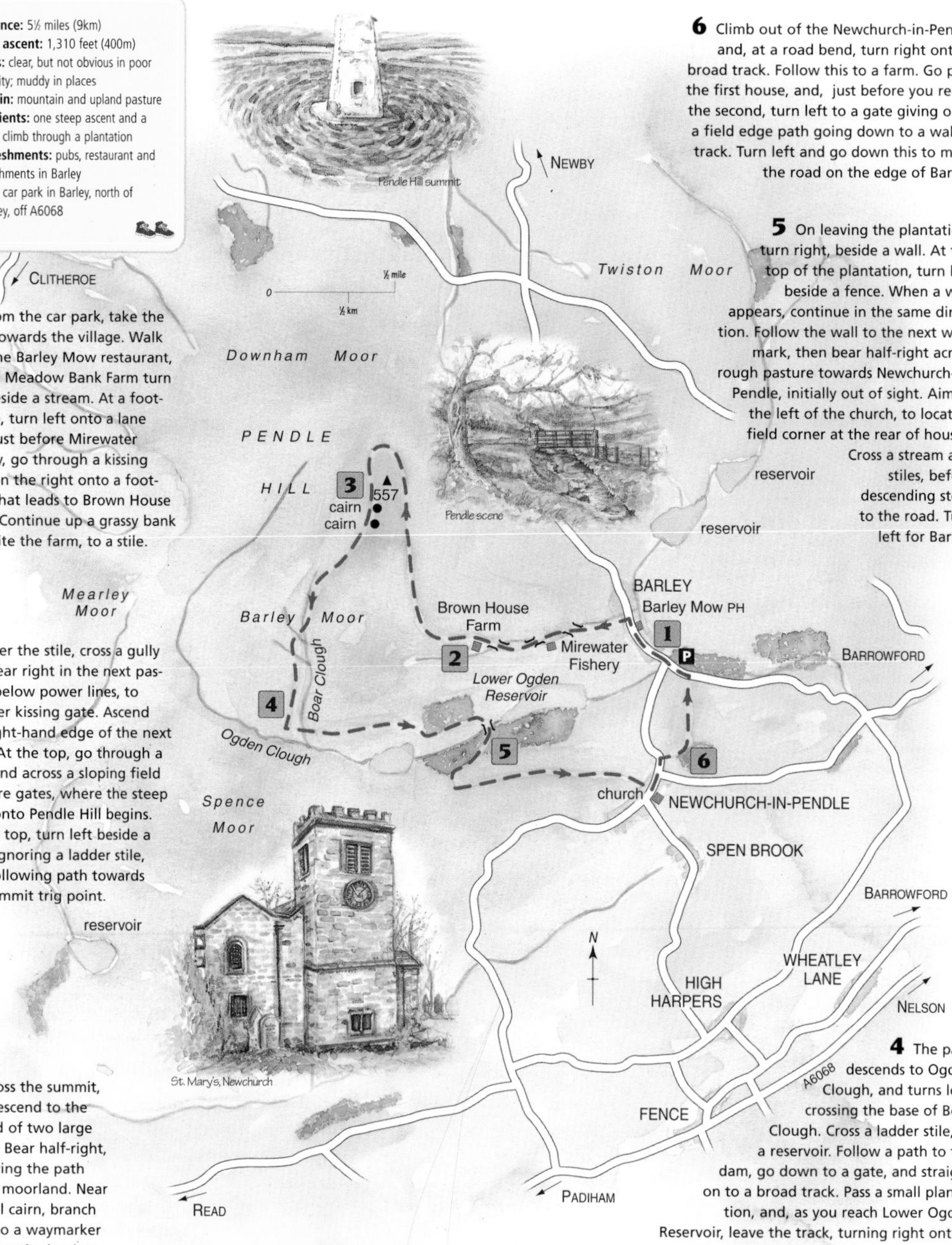

1 From the car park, take the path towards the village. Walk past the Barley Mow restaurant, and at Meadow Bank Farm turn left beside a stream. At a footbridge, turn left onto a lane and, just before Mirewater Fishery, go through a kissing gate on the right onto a footpath that leads to Brown House Farm. Continue up a grassy bank opposite the farm, to a stile.

2 Over the stile, cross a gully and bear right in the next pasture, below power lines, to another kissing gate. Ascend the right-hand edge of the next field. At the top, go through a gate and across a sloping field to more gates, where the steep path onto Pendle Hill begins. At the top, turn left beside a wall, ignoring a ladder stile, and following path towards the summit trig point.

3 Cross the summit, and descend to the second of two large cairns. Bear half-right, following the path across moorland. Near a small cairn, branch right to a waymarker pole, continuing into Boar Clough.

4 The path descends to Ogden Clough, and turns left, crossing the base of Boar Clough. Cross a ladder stile, to a reservoir. Follow a path to the dam, go down to a gate, and straight on to a broad track. Pass a small plantation, and, as you reach Lower Ogden Reservoir, leave the track, turning right onto a path, soon descending left down steps to a footbridge. Beyond, you climb into a plantation.

5 On leaving the plantation, turn right, beside a wall. At the top of the plantation, turn left beside a fence. When a wall appears, continue in the same direction. Follow the wall to the next waymark, then bear half-right across rough pasture towards Newchurch-in-Pendle, initially out of sight. Aim to the left of the church, to locate a field corner at the rear of houses. Cross a stream and stiles, before descending steps to the road. Turn left for Barley.

6 Climb out of the Newchurch-in-Pendle and, at a road bend, turn right onto a broad track. Follow this to a farm. Go past the first house, and, just before you reach the second, turn left to a gate giving onto a field edge path going down to a walled track. Turn left and go down this to meet the road on the edge of Barley.

Pendle Hill summit

Pendle scene

St. Mary's, Newchurch

Saltaire's Model Streets and the Five Rise

Titus Salt built his vision of an industrial village beside the engineering triumph of the Leeds-Liverpool Canal

Distance: 8½ miles (13.7km)
Total ascent: 430ft (131m)
Paths: generally clear and well-signed; boggy in places
Terrain: canal bank, woodland and open moorland
Gradients: some steep sections
Refreshments: Saltaire, Bingley, Shipley Glen
Park: at Hirst Wood, 1 mile (1.6km) along Hirst Lane from A650 Saltaire roundabout

1 Cross the canal by the swing bridge, turn left onto the canal towpath and follow the canal for 2 miles (3.2km) to Five Rise Locks.

2 At the locks' summit turn right over the metal bridge and walk up the road, bending right alongside the stone wall. Just before a road joins from the right, turn left up a narrow metalled lane between two walls.

3 Follow this path, with a stream on your right, uphill, crossing two roads and passing through a small housing estate, to reach the hilltop on Lady Lane, where you turn right.

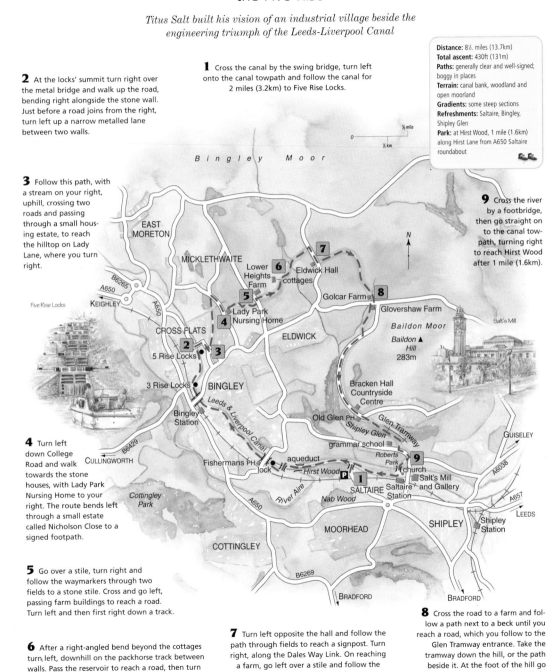

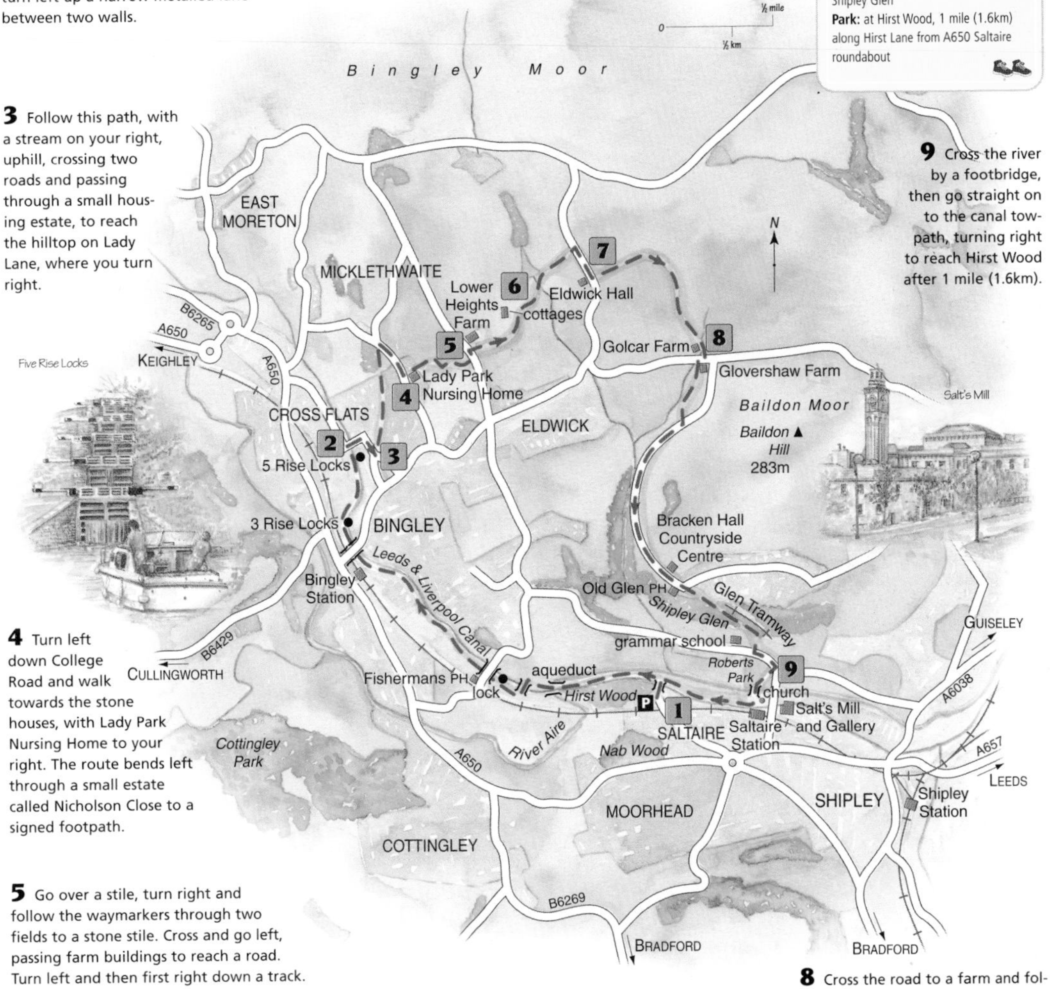

4 Turn left down College Road and walk towards the stone houses, with Lady Park Nursing Home to your right. The route bends left through a small estate called Nicholson Close to a signed footpath.

5 Go over a stile, turn right and follow the waymarkers through two fields to a stone stile. Cross and go left, passing farm buildings to reach a road. Turn left and then first right down a track.

6 After a right-angled bend beyond the cottages turn left, downhill on the packhorse track between walls. Pass the reservoir to reach a road, then turn right to reach Eldwick Hall on your right.

7 Turn left opposite the hall and follow the path through fields to reach a signpost. Turn right, along the Dales Way Link. On reaching a farm, go left over a stile and follow the farm drive to the road.

8 Cross the road to a farm and follow a path next to a beck until you reach a road, which you follow to the Glen Tramway entrance. Take the tramway down the hill, or the path beside it. At the foot of the hill go straight ahead through Roberts Park.

9 Cross the river by a footbridge, then go straight on to the canal towpath, turning right to reach Hirst Wood after 1 mile (1.6km).

WALK 79

High Pennine Byways over Blackstone Edge

A beautifully preserved section of ancient road leads over the moors between Yorkshire and Lancashire

1 From station take underpass beneath railway. Walk left, along tow-path, crossing canal at first set of locks, to follow path that emerges onto Ealees Road. Continue straight ahead on metalled track, passing a mill and Old Mill Cottage. As track curves right, take steps on your left and follow path uphill. Bear left, immediately before farm at top, to walk up a wooded valley. Cross footbridge; when path levels out, you see a canal drain. Don't cross it, but follow it to the left, to Owlet Hall.

6 Keep to lakeside road before going right, past visitor centre. At far end of car park join metalled path. Cross footbridge and follow stream to bigger track. Go left here and retrace your earlier steps, keeping straight ahead on path to canal, and back along towpath into Littleborough.

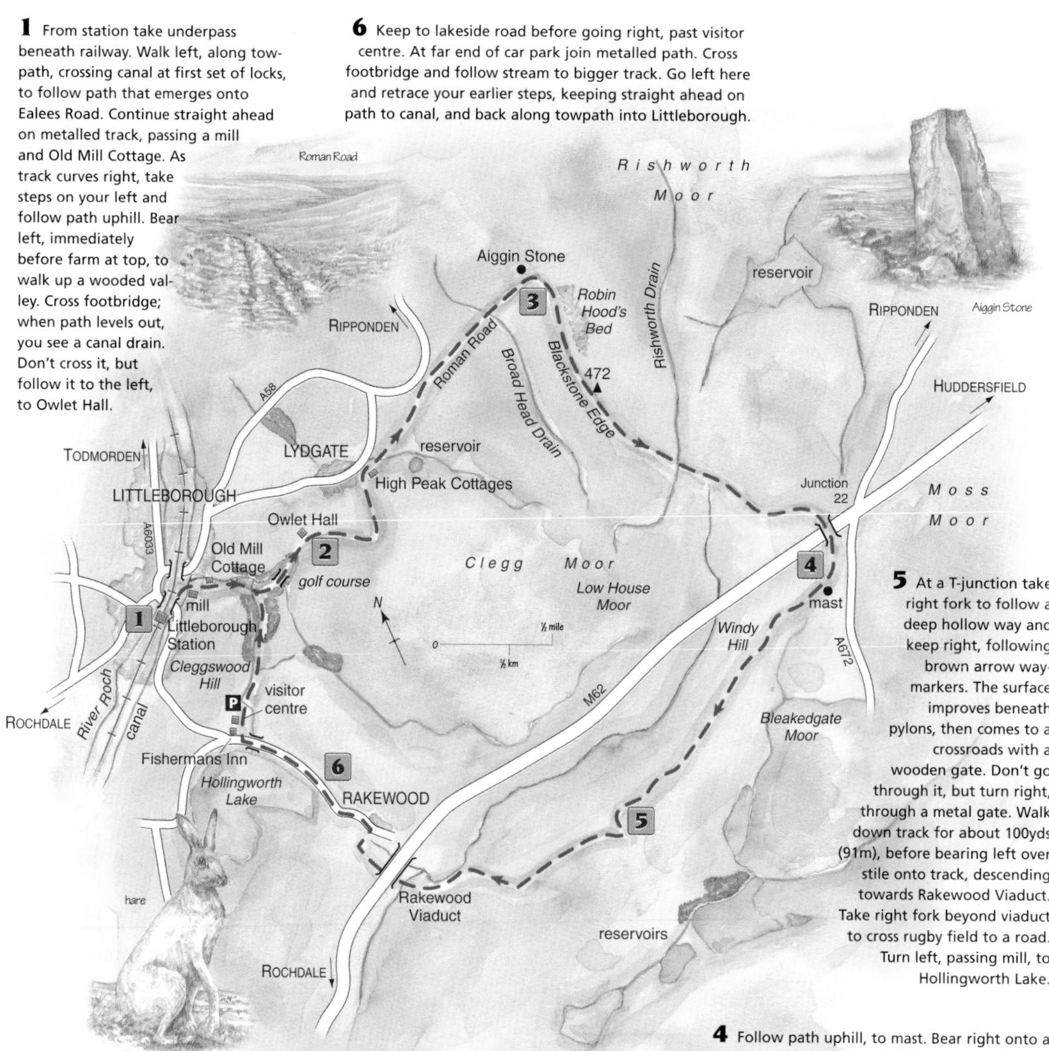

5 At a T-junction take right fork to follow a deep hollow way and keep right, following brown arrow way-markers. The surface improves beneath pylons, then comes to a crossroads with a wooden gate. Don't go through it, but turn right, through a metal gate. Walk down track for about 100yds (91m), before bearing left over stile onto track, descending towards Rakewood Viaduct. Take right fork beyond viaduct to cross rugby field to a road. Turn left, passing mill, to Hollingworth Lake.

4 Follow path uphill, to mast. Bear right onto a track, then, at far end of the mast's perimeter fence, bear half-left on rutted track, downhill. Go through a wall-gap, then by a wall over Windy Hill. Eventually it becomes a walled track or hollow way.

3 Go right from the stone, through a gate, to join the Pennine Way. Small cairns mark the path along Blackstone Edge. Past a trig point (the highest point of the walk), follow a sandy track (aim for mast in the middle distance), bearing left to cross the M62 on a footbridge.

2 Go through wooden gates and around front of house to join a field path, and follow a wall on your left with a golf course right. Go left along a stony track, keeping left past a farm, then turning left on bridleway to Blackstone Edge Road by High Peak Cottages. Turn right on path directly in front of cottages, continuing on a field path with a wall on right. At farm track go right for a few paces, then head left, up the hill on obvious path. Soon you are on the famous 'Roman Road' to the Aiggin Stone, a medieval waymarker.

Distance: 9 miles (14.5km)
Total ascent: 1,148ft (350m)
Paths: mostly well-defined; may be boggy after rain
Terrain: mostly open moorland; best not attempted in bad weather or poor visibility
Gradients: mostly gradual
Refreshments: Littleborough
Park: Littleborough railway station

Wales

This is a most beautiful and varied country, one where there is still resistance to cultural change and a strong desire to retain an identity quite uninfluenced by external forces. Here in Wales are craggy heights, rock-strewn, heather-clad hillsides, barren moors, bright green valleys, silver rivers, mountain lakes, rocky, storm-tossed coastlines and sublime golden beaches. And over it all lies a complex mantle of history and mystery.

Much of walkers' North Wales is contained within the Snowdonia National Park, from time immemorial known to its inhabitants as Eryri, the 'Place of Eagles'. The popularity of Snowdon, the Carneddau, the Glyderau, the Rhinogs and the other mountains of Eryri has scarcely abated since the first recorded ascent of Snowdon in 1639 by botanist Thomas Johnson.

The eastern moorlands of Denbighshire flow westwards to the great natural barrier that is the River Conwy below the eastern fringes of the Carneddau. North and west, the isle of Anglesey, the 'Mother of Wales', and the delectable Lleyn Peninsula boast renowned landscapes to make your heart ache and your spirit rejoice.

A hundred years after the Domesday Book, Archbishop Baldwin of Canterbury began his mission to preach the Crusades in Wales in the quiet heartlands of Mid-Wales, at New Radnor, part of the great hunting Forest of Radnor.

Further south, the Rhinogs are rugged and rough, and certain to exact perspiration by the bucketful, as they no doubt did when traders first constructed their route through Cwm Bychan.

In the south, the borderland Black Mountains (Mynyddoedd Duon) are a paradise for walkers who revel in long, lofty ridges separated by valleys of quiet calm. To the west rise the distinctive, flat-topped summits of the Brecon Beacons, another Black Mountain (Mynydd Du) and the Fforest Fawr, names that speak of wilderness and desolation, and all contained within the Brecon Beacons National Park. The further west you go, the greater the feeling of isolation, but never in an over-powering way, for here the seclusion works as a panacea for workaday ills.

Best of the Rest

The Monmouthshire and Brecon Canal The only canal through a national park, the Monmouthshire and Brecon Canal offers easy walking amidst spectacular scenery. The ridges of the Brecon Beacons loom above, but the way along the towpath remains completely level, all the way into the centre of Brecon itself.

The Valleys The harsh edges of South Wales' industrial heartlands were always softened by the proximity of steeply wooded hillsides and liberating open moorlands. Now the industry has departed and the walker can return to the valleys, making good use of disused railway lines and the network of paths and tracks that kept workers and materials moving throughout the Industrial Revolution. The head of the Rhondda valley is particularly worth exploring.

Mid-Wales To the south of Strata Florida Abbey the wilds of Mid-Wales are often overlooked by walkers aiming for the mountains of Snowdonia or the high hills of the Brecon Beacons. And yet here is a landscape of intricate upland valleys, not at all spoiled by its forestation or reservoir developments. In fact it is these corporate utility invaders which have opened up the place for walkers, with car parks and nature trails. The serene upper reaches of the Afon Tywi, in particular, support a fine network of paths and trails for the walker in search of solitude.

Gower The beautiful sweeps of sand which characterise the handful of beaches on the Gower Peninsula attract thousands of holidaymakers in the summer months. Less well known is the fine stretch of cliff path which connects them – as dramatic as anything in Cornwall or Pembrokeshire. If you have a few days, the coast can be walked as a continuous path, otherwise extensive inland links allow each section to be done as a circular walk.

Betws-y-coed In the shadow of the great mountain mass of the Carneddau in Snowdonia a series of pretty valleys spreads like fingers to that of the much larger Afon Conwy. The environment here, though remote and sometimes inhospitable, has been much utilised, by early farmers, miners, reservoir-builders and foresters. The resulting landscape, around Llyn Crafnant and Llyn Geirionydd is a delightful tangle of lanes and paths amid small lakes, intriguingly overgrown old workings and ancient hill farms.

Breidden Hills – the Gateway to Wales

Long famed for their extensive views, the Breidden Hills hint at the great mountains beyond

1 From car park, walk up lane directly opposite Breidden Hotel. Ignore footpath left and follow lane towards Middleton Quarry. Fork right at junction, soon turning left on path uphill through gorse and bracken. Keep climbing through all path junctions to ridge at the top. Turn right on wide track to Middletown Hill.

2 Walk along ridge to summit then down to saddle. Descend left to lane and turn right. Pass Belleisle Farm and carry on to track on left, taking you past another farm, into pastureland. Maintain direction through first field, then follow left-hand hedge to woods. Cross stream and follow waymarked bridleway rising through woods. It crosses a flinty forestry road then continues to climb up to Rodneys Pillar, taking two left forks along the way. Beyond stile in fence, path traverses open hillside to another stile preceding steep climb to Rodney's Pillar.

3 From the summit, head along ridge (southwest) to edge of wood, then turn sharp left to double-back down hillside and through sparse woodland to open area.

4 Go through gate and follow grassy bridleway to cross forestry track before climbing through conifers of New Pieces. At junction, ignore grassy track descending southwest, but double-back left uphill to vehicle turning circle. Descend (southwest) to forest edge. Go through gate and past cottage to farm track leading to narrow lane. Turn right for ¾ mile (1.2km).

5 Turn left along drive at Bescot to stile, beyond which path traverses afforested western slopes of Moel y Golfa.

6 Signpost marks diversion of steep path to top of Moel y Golfa. Tired walkers can continue on lower path, tracing woodland edge to meet hill route, close to Middletown. Waymarked, winding hill route climbs through woods and up crags to summit monument. From here, narrow path continues along crest to gate at edge of woods. Turn right and follow zigzagging path down towards Middletown.

7 At signpost by fence corner, near lower edge of wood, turn right. Two routes meet up by stile at edge of wood. Turn sharp left if you have just descended from higher route. Another stile leads to field. Turn left along its edge, past pig enclosure to farm track. Turn right to road, a little way out of Middletown, and follow it left, back into village.

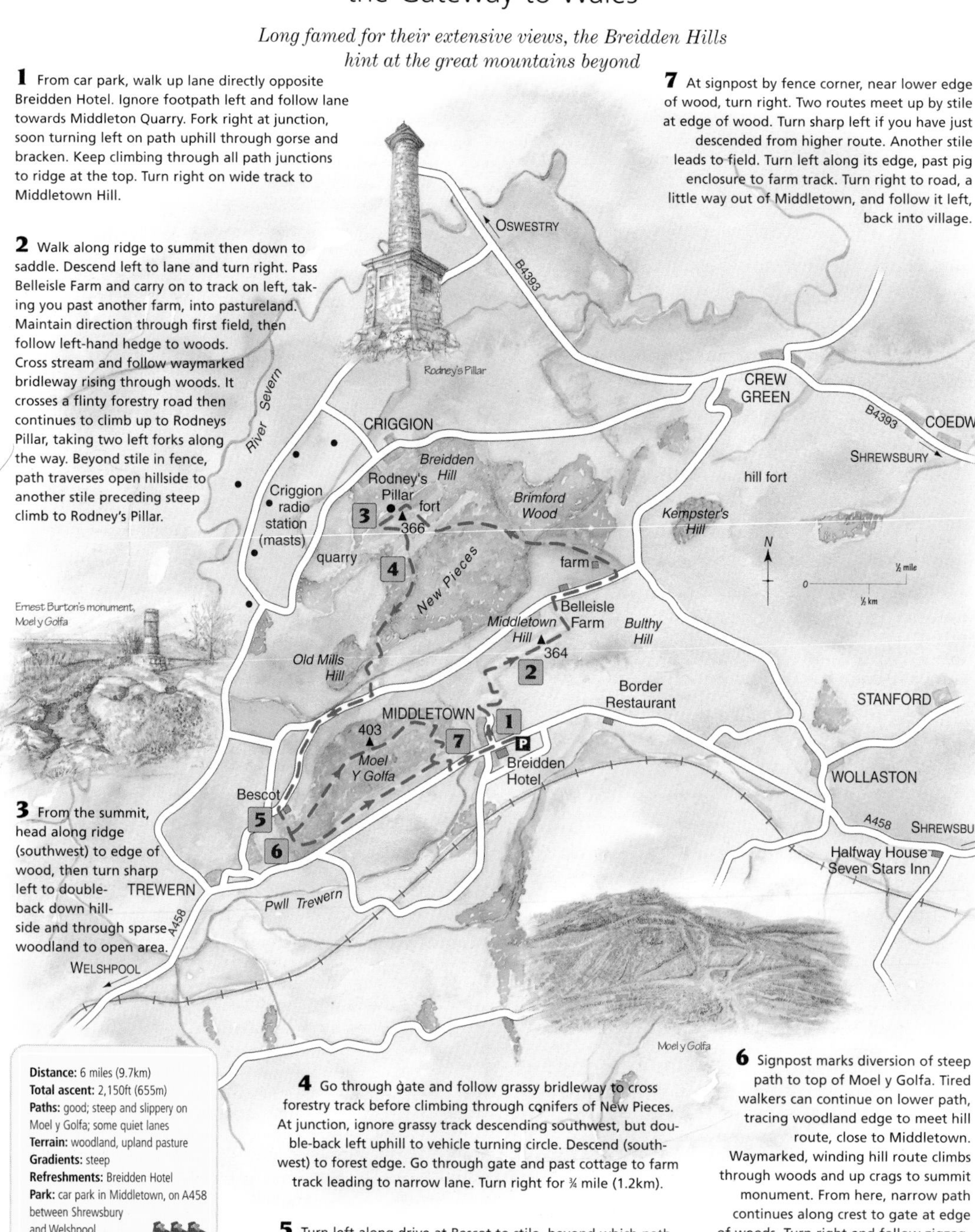

Distance: 6 miles (9.7km)
Total ascent: 2,150ft (655m)
Paths: good; steep and slippery on Moel y Golfa; some quiet lanes
Terrain: woodland, upland pasture
Gradients: steep
Refreshments: Breidden Hotel
Park: car park in Middletown, on A458 between Shrewsbury and Welshpool

Monmouthshire's White Castle

The gentle Monmouthshire countryside hides a grim castle with a dark past

1 From the Hostry Inn turn right down the lane. In 300yds (275m), on a left bend, keep ahead to St Teilo's Church.

2 Walk down the stone steps from the west end of the graveyard and take the signed footpath between a wire fence and the churchyard wall. Go through a kissing gate and over a field to the B4233. Across the road is the moated site of Hen Cwrt, the Old Court.

3 Turn left along the B4233. In 90yds (82m) turn right over a stile, and follow Offa's Dyke Path signs across five fields to a farm track at Great Treadam. Turn left to the road, and right for 150yds (137m), to turn right into a lane.

4 Follow the lane northwards for ¾ mile (1.2km) to a road by a large white house. Keep forward for 250yds (229m) to White Castle.

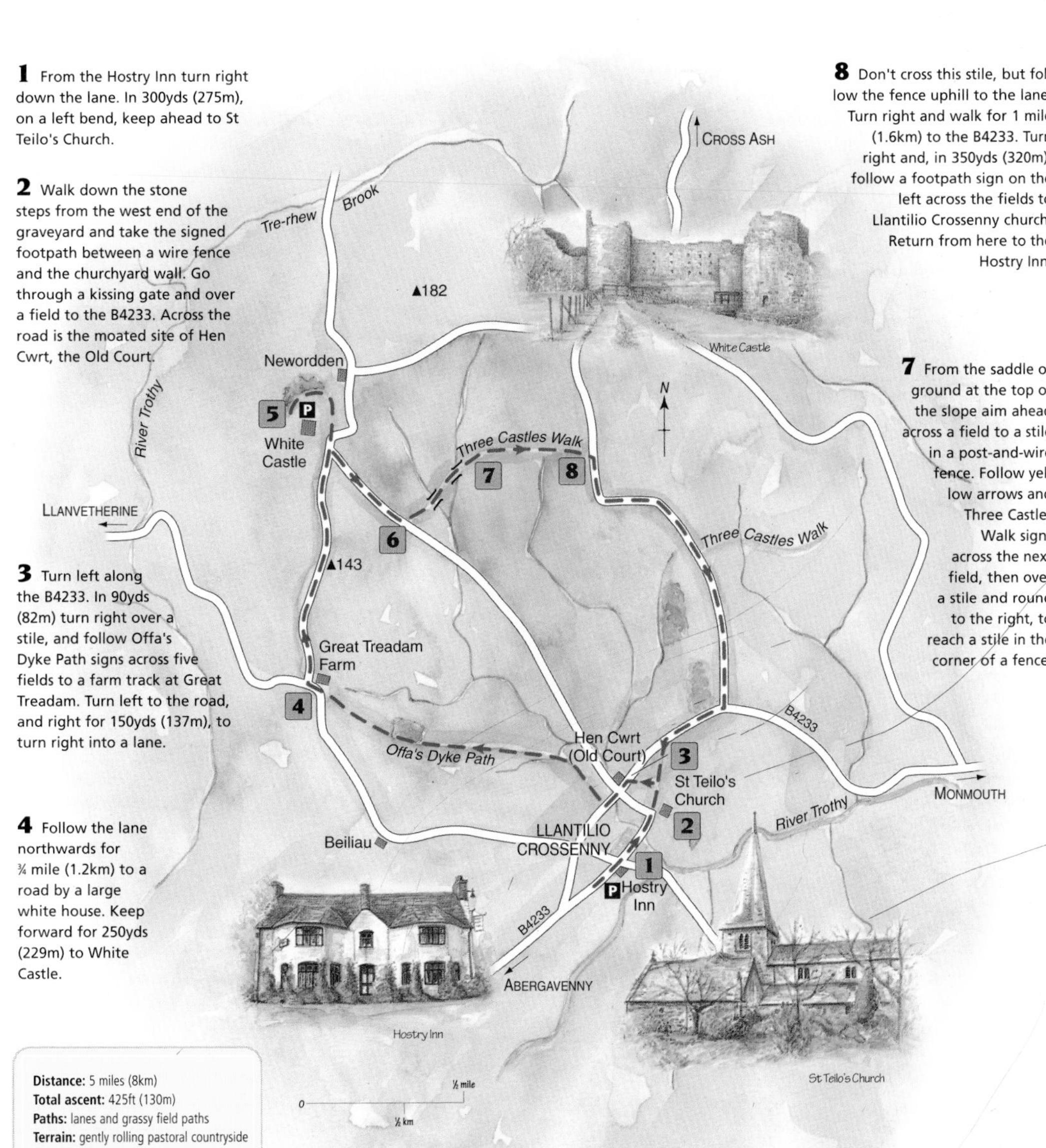

Distance: 5 miles (8km)
Total ascent: 425ft (130m)
Paths: lanes and grassy field paths
Terrain: gently rolling pastoral countryside
Gradients: one short, steep ascent
Refreshments: Hostry Inn, Llantilio Crossenny
Park: by Hostry Inn, Llantilio Crossenny, signposted from the B4233, 8 miles (12.9km) west of Monmouth

5 From White Castle entrance kiosk retrace your steps to the head of the lane from Treadam but bear left here, downhill, on the road. In 450yds (412m) turn left up the steps at a Three Castles Walk sign, over a stile into a field.

6 Continue across three fields and down to cross a stream by a footbridge. Head diagonally left across the next field and, in 200yds (182m), bear right over a stream. Follow the hedge ahead, diagonally left up the slope.

7 From the saddle of ground at the top of the slope aim ahead across a field to a stile in a post-and-wire fence. Follow yellow arrows and Three Castles Walk signs across the next field, then over a stile and round to the right, to reach a stile in the corner of a fence.

8 Don't cross this stile, but follow the fence uphill to the lane. Turn right and walk for 1 mile (1.6km) to the B4233. Turn right and, in 350yds (320m), follow a footpath sign on the left across the fields to Llantilio Crossenny church. Return from here to the Hostry Inn.

Eric Gill in the Black Mountains

In this high valley in theBlack Mountains, the artist and sculptor Eric Gill settled into an eccentric lifestyle with his extended family

1 Take the lane between the chapel and the telephone box, climbing the hill. After 800 yards (730m), by a sign to the youth hostel, go right through a gate, down the track, over the river and up to a second gate.

2 Turn left before the gate and walk ahead with the hedge to your right. Cross two more fields to go over a stream and pass through a metal gate. Follow the wall on the left as it curves opposite a stone ruin.

3 Walk down the hill through the trees, crossing the stream, going through a metal gate. Continue downhill, with the stream recrossing your path, to go over a foot-bridge. Walk uphill to meet the lane at a stile to the left of a farm building.

4 Turn right and walk up the lane for ¾ mile (1.2km) to the cattle grid. Immediately, turn sharp left along the hillside. The path follows the hill's contours, keeping beside or parallel with a ruined stone wall.

5 The path curves around the hillside, giving fine valley views. Eventually you will see two white houses on the opposite hillside. The larger, on the left, is The Monastery, Eric Gill's home from 1924 to 1928.

6 When the path reaches the lane, turn left down the hill, go over a ford and pass The Monastery back to the village.

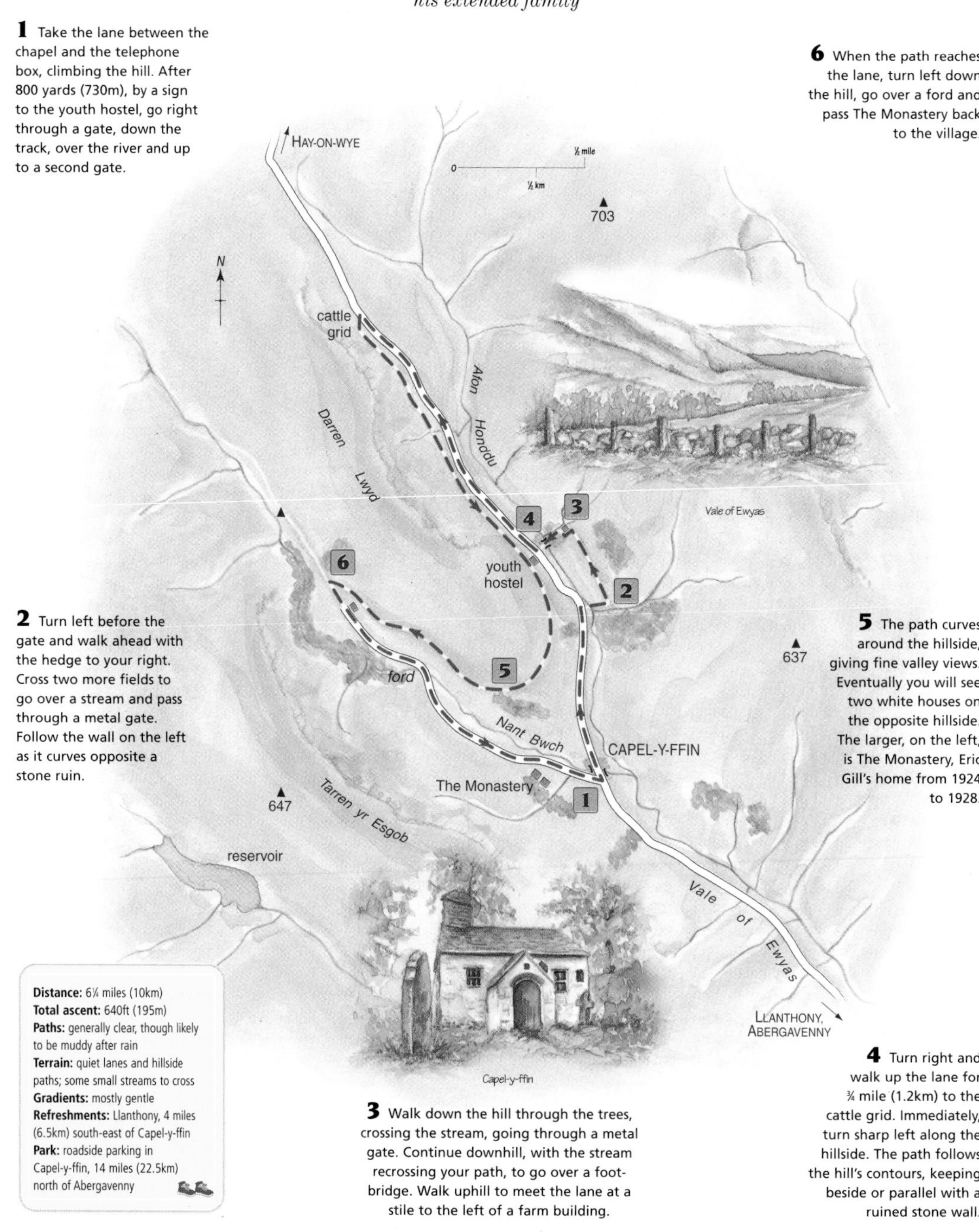

Capel-y-ffin

Distance: 6¼ miles (10km)
Total ascent: 640ft (195m)
Paths: generally clear, though likely to be muddy after rain
Terrain: quiet lanes and hillside paths; some small streams to cross
Gradients: mostly gentle
Refreshments: Llanthony, 4 miles (6.5km) south-east of Capel-y-ffin
Park: roadside parking in Capel-y-ffin, 14 miles (22.5km) north of Abergavenny

WALK 83

Raglan's Civil War Fortress

During the Civil War Charles I retreated to this imposing castle in the beautiful Welsh Marches

Distance: 5 miles (8km)
Total ascent: 250ft (76m)
Paths: good; can be muddy after rain
Terrain: fields, enclosed bridleway
Gradients: few ascents and very gradual
Refreshments: various in Raglan
Park: Castle Street, Raglan or by Raglan Castle

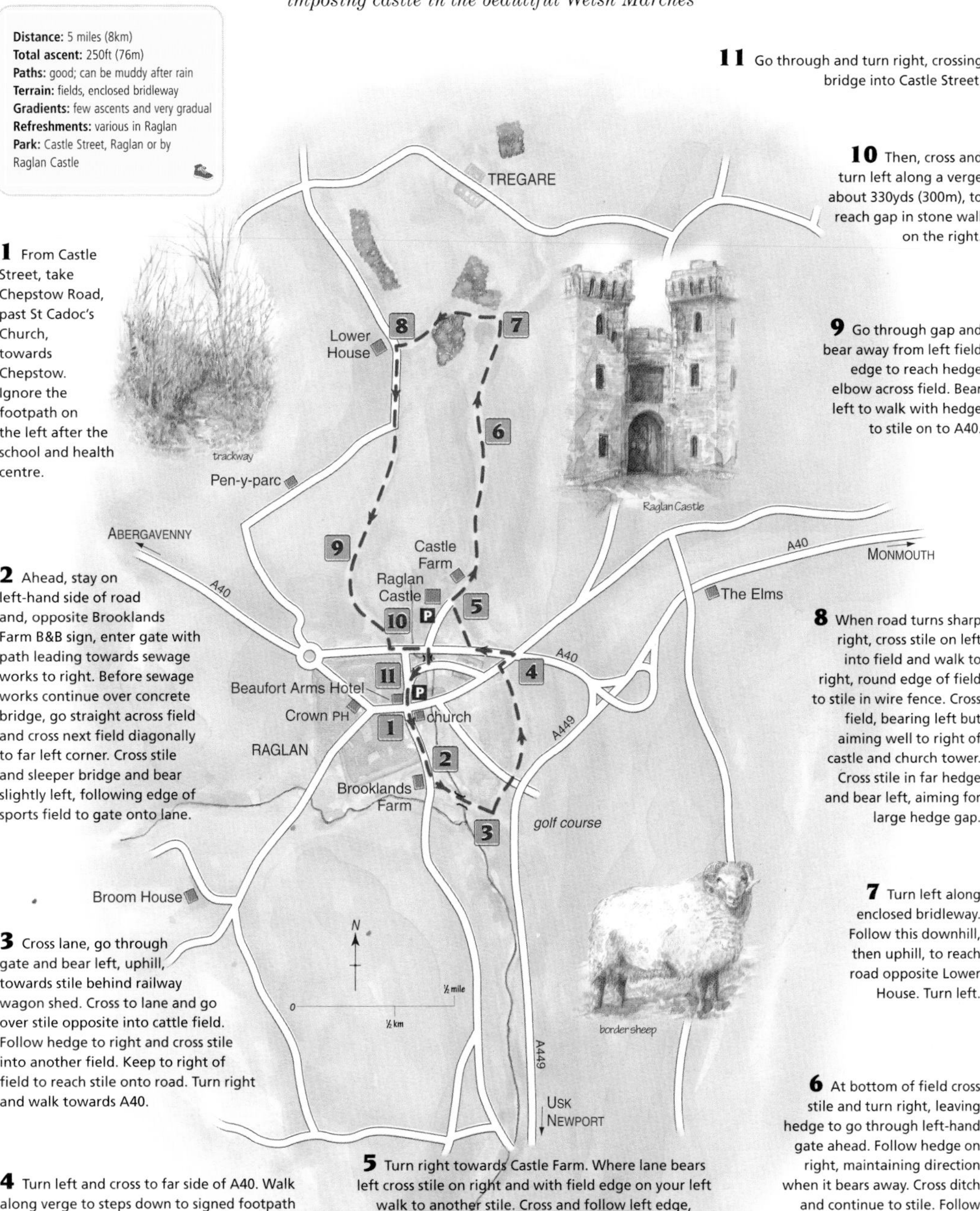

1 From Castle Street, take Chepstow Road, past St Cadoc's Church, towards Chepstow. Ignore the footpath on the left after the school and health centre.

2 Ahead, stay on left-hand side of road and, opposite Brooklands Farm B&B sign, enter gate with path leading towards sewage works to right. Before sewage works continue over concrete bridge, go straight across field and cross next field diagonally to far left corner. Cross stile and sleeper bridge and bear slightly left, following edge of sports field to gate onto lane.

3 Cross lane, go through gate and bear left, uphill, towards stile behind railway wagon shed. Cross to lane and go over stile opposite into cattle field. Follow hedge to right and cross stile into another field. Keep to right of field to reach stile onto road. Turn right and walk towards A40.

4 Turn left and cross to far side of A40. Walk along verge to steps down to signed footpath and stile into field. Cross field uphill to reach gate onto lane leading to Raglan Castle car park.

5 Turn right towards Castle Farm. Where lane bears left cross stile on right and with field edge on your left walk to another stile. Cross and follow left edge, crossing stile in it and bearing right to stile. Cross and turn left through gate. Cross track, go over stile and turn half-right across field beyond, passing small hillock.

6 At bottom of field cross stile and turn right, leaving hedge to go through left-hand gate ahead. Follow hedge on right, maintaining direction when it bears away. Cross ditch and continue to stile. Follow hedge on right, crossing stile over it and turn left uphill. Where field widens, turn left to cross stile.

7 Turn left along enclosed bridleway. Follow this downhill, then uphill, to reach road opposite Lower House. Turn left.

8 When road turns sharp right, cross stile on left into field and walk to right, round edge of field to stile in wire fence. Cross field, bearing left but aiming well to right of castle and church tower. Cross stile in far hedge and bear left, aiming for large hedge gap.

9 Go through gap and bear away from left field edge to reach hedge elbow across field. Bear left to walk with hedge to stile on to A40.

10 Then, cross and turn left along a verge about 330yds (300m), to reach gap in stone wall on the right.

11 Go through and turn right, crossing bridge into Castle Street.

A Fairy Lake and the Black Mountain

A fine mountain walk in the backwaters of the Brecon Beacons National Park

1 From the car park at Blaenau, follow the stony reservoir supply track by the Sawdde stream up to the shores of Llyn y Fan Fach, taking the right fork just before the reservoir.

2 Swing right (westwards) on a grassy path up easy slopes to the ridge. The path arcs round towards the tiered cliffs that rise from behind the lakeshore. Follow the edge high above the lake to the cairn on Picws Du. The path then drops steeply to a pass overlooking both the Twrch and Sychlwch streams.

3 After fording the Twrch, carry straight on as the edge path goes off to the left, climbing east across rough moor to the trig point and wind shelter that top Fan Brycheiniog.

4 Turn left (north), following the edge of the eastern cliffs to Fan Foel, where a cairn is surrounded by a circular pattern of stones. Continue north from the top to locate the good path that descends down the nose of the hill.

5 Where the ground levels out – a place marked by some rocks on the left – leave the path and head 11 o'clock left (northwest) down the pathless (except for sheep tracks) grassy ridge with the rounded hill, Bryn Mawr, ahead and in the mid-distance. A faint path develops and descends to a meeting of paths at the head of Sychnant stream.

6 Turn left on a path descending above the north banks of the stream. The path comes down the sides of Bryn Mawr, towards a bridge conveying the outward track across the stream. It then swings right to avoid some squat cliffs. Look out for a little path on the left which makes the final descent to the car park at Blaenau.

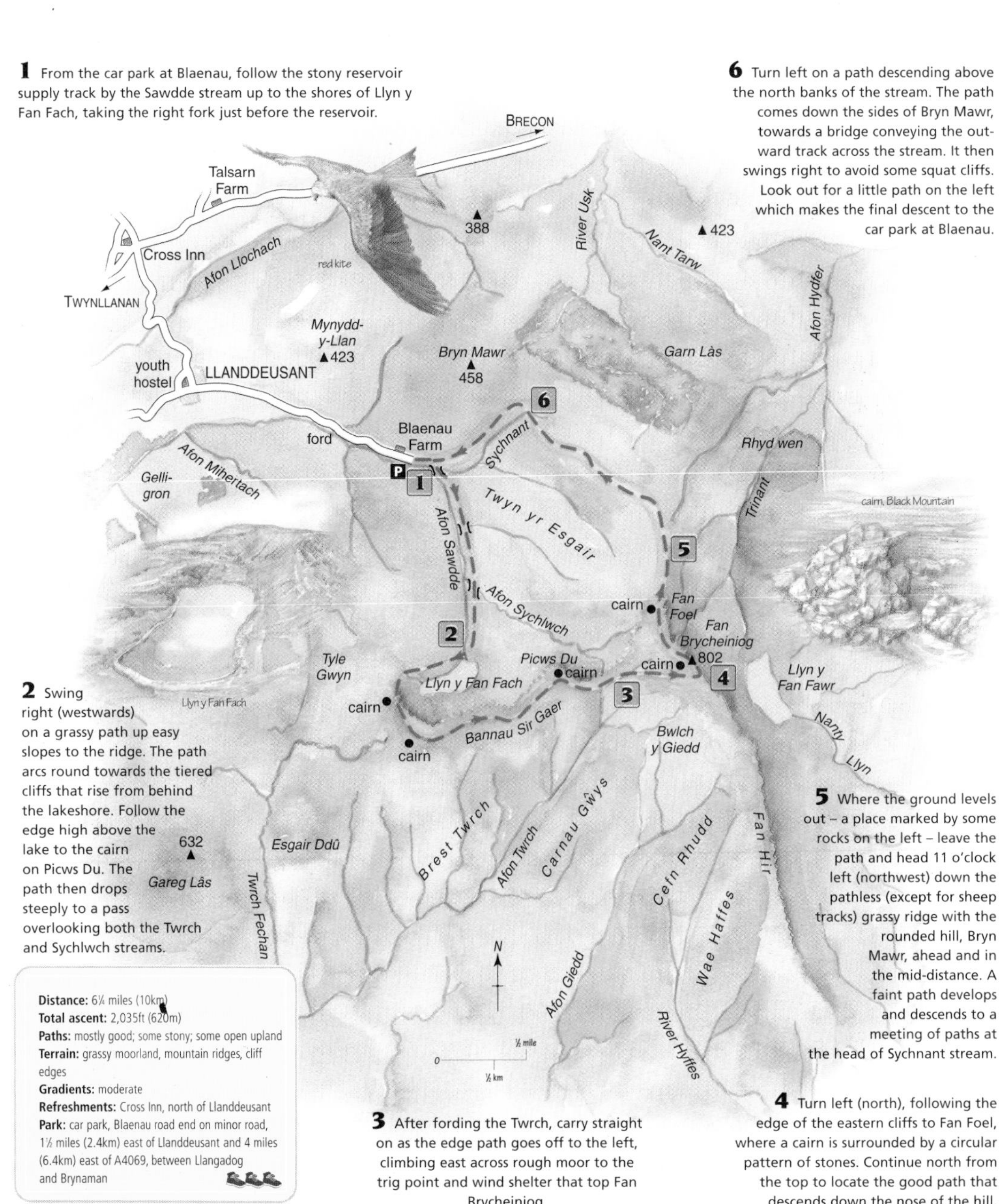

Distance: 6¼ miles (10km)
Total ascent: 2,035ft (620m)
Paths: mostly good; some stony; some open upland
Terrain: grassy moorland, mountain ridges, cliff edges
Gradients: moderate
Refreshments: Cross Inn, north of Llanddeusant
Park: car park, Blaenau road end on minor road, 1½ miles (2.4km) east of Llanddeusant and 4 miles (6.4km) east of A4069, between Llangadog and Brynaman

Dale – a Pembroke Peninsula

At the entrance to Milford Haven, the Dale Peninsula has always played a strategic role in maritime history

1 From the National Trust car park return to the road and go left where the road bends right towards Dale. Turn left to follow a concrete track which bears left to a stile beside a gate. Cross this, turn right and take another stile to reach the coast path.

2 Go left to walk with the sea on your right (leaving the islands of Skokholm and Skomer behind you). Follow the coast path to the road as it approaches St Ann's Head.

3 Go right along the road to pass the old High Lighthouse on your right, then turn left through a gate and turn right immediately to take a signposted path towards the Low Lighthouse. Turn sharply left, as signposted, to follow the coast path towards Mill Bay, still walking with the sea on your right.

4 Descend steps to cross a footbridge and climb up the other side. Continue with the sea on your right around West Blockhouse Point (with it's three transit marks – navigational aids). Follow the coast path around Watwick Point (where there is a single transit mark), cross a footbridge above Castle Beach and climb to join a road on Dale Point.

5 Turn left to follow the road downhill into Dale. Ignore a turning on your left and reach the Griffin Inn. Take a footpath on your left immediately after the pub and just before a boathouse. This leads to a road. Cross this and go ahead over a stile beside a gate and turn right to cross a stone stile and reach another road.

6 Go left along the road to pass St James' Church on your left. When the road turns left, leave it by going straight ahead on a track which passes Dale Castle on your right. When this track bends left, take the signposted footpath ahead to Westdale Bay.

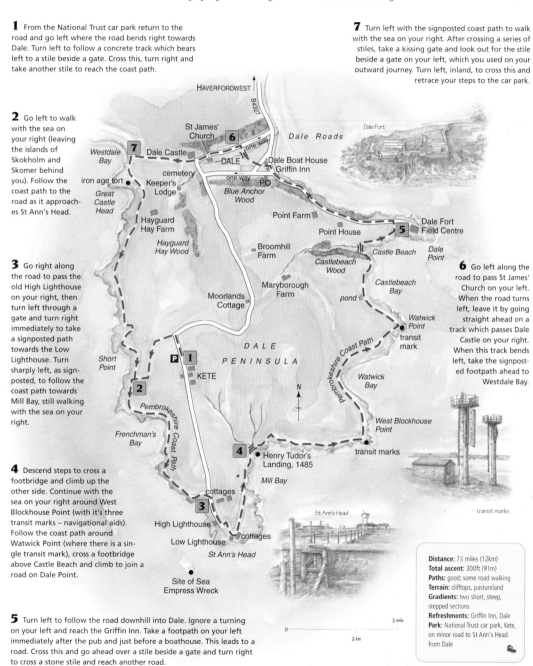

7 Turn left with the signposted coast path to walk with the sea on your right. After crossing a series of stiles, take a kissing gate and look out for the stile beside a gate on your left, which you used on your outward journey. Turn left, inland, to cross this and retrace your steps to the car park.

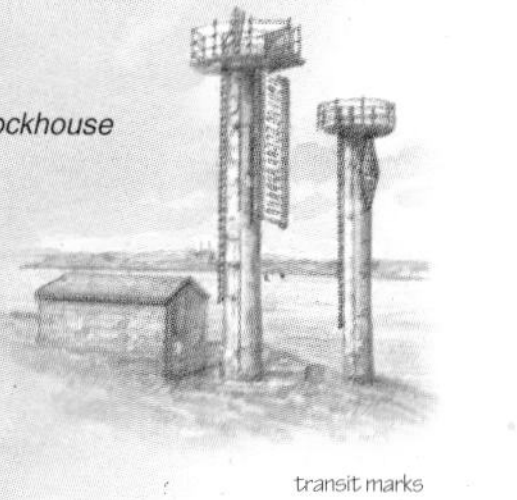

Distance: 7½ miles (12km)
Total ascent: 300ft (91m)
Paths: good; some road walking
Terrain: clifftops, pastureland
Gradients: two short, steep, stepped sections
Refreshments: Griffin Inn, Dale
Park: National Trust car park, Kete, on minor road to St Ann's Head from Dale

Strumble Head and the French Invasion

A memorial stone on this spectacular coastal walk marks the point where a Napoleonic army invaded Britain

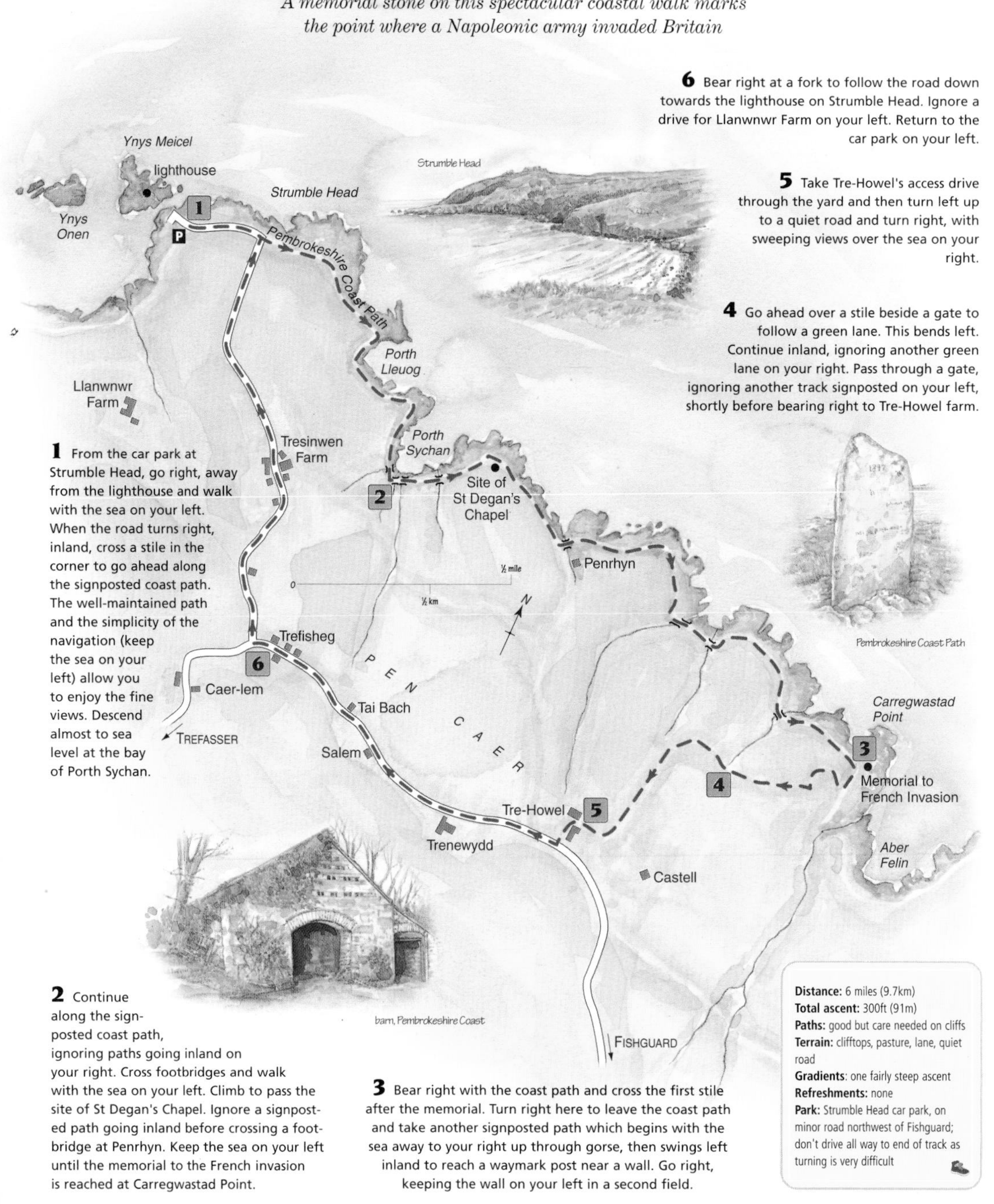

barn, Pembrokeshire Coast

1 From the car park at Strumble Head, go right, away from the lighthouse and walk with the sea on your left. When the road turns right, inland, cross a stile in the corner to go ahead along the signposted coast path. The well-maintained path and the simplicity of the navigation (keep the sea on your left) allow you to enjoy the fine views. Descend almost to sea level at the bay of Porth Sychan.

2 Continue along the signposted coast path, ignoring paths going inland on your right. Cross footbridges and walk with the sea on your left. Climb to pass the site of St Degan's Chapel. Ignore a signposted path going inland before crossing a footbridge at Penrhyn. Keep the sea on your left until the memorial to the French invasion is reached at Carregwastad Point.

3 Bear right with the coast path and cross the first stile after the memorial. Turn right here to leave the coast path and take another signposted path which begins with the sea away to your right up through gorse, then swings left inland to reach a waymark post near a wall. Go right, keeping the wall on your left in a second field.

4 Go ahead over a stile beside a gate to follow a green lane. This bends left. Continue inland, ignoring another green lane on your right. Pass through a gate, ignoring another track signposted on your left, shortly before bearing right to Tre-Howel farm.

5 Take Tre-Howel's access drive through the yard and then turn left up to a quiet road and turn right, with sweeping views over the sea on your right.

6 Bear right at a fork to follow the road down towards the lighthouse on Strumble Head. Ignore a drive for Llanwnwr Farm on your left. Return to the car park on your left.

Distance: 6 miles (9.7km)
Total ascent: 300ft (91m)
Paths: good but care needed on cliffs
Terrain: clifftops, pasture, lane, quiet road
Gradients: one fairly steep ascent
Refreshments: none
Park: Strumble Head car park, on minor road northwest of Fishguard; don't drive all way to end of track as turning is very difficult

Abbey in the Wilderness

In the heart of Wales, Strata Florida Abbey was an important oasis amidst wild but beautiful uplands

Distance: 5½ miles (9km)
Total ascent: 500 ft (152m)
Paths: mainly obvious paths and lanes
Terrain: fields, country lanes and forestry
Gradients: gradual
Refreshments: Red Lion and Black Lion, Pontrhydfendigaid
Park: along main street or in lay-by at southern entrance to village, Pontrhydfendigaid

1 From lay-by at south end of village, continue south along road towards Tregaron, going gently uphill to stile and ancient wooden footpath sign on left.

2 Cross stile and follow track beyond towards caravans. Go on to caravan site road and bear left, between vans. As road bears right, bear left past last caravan to stile in corner.

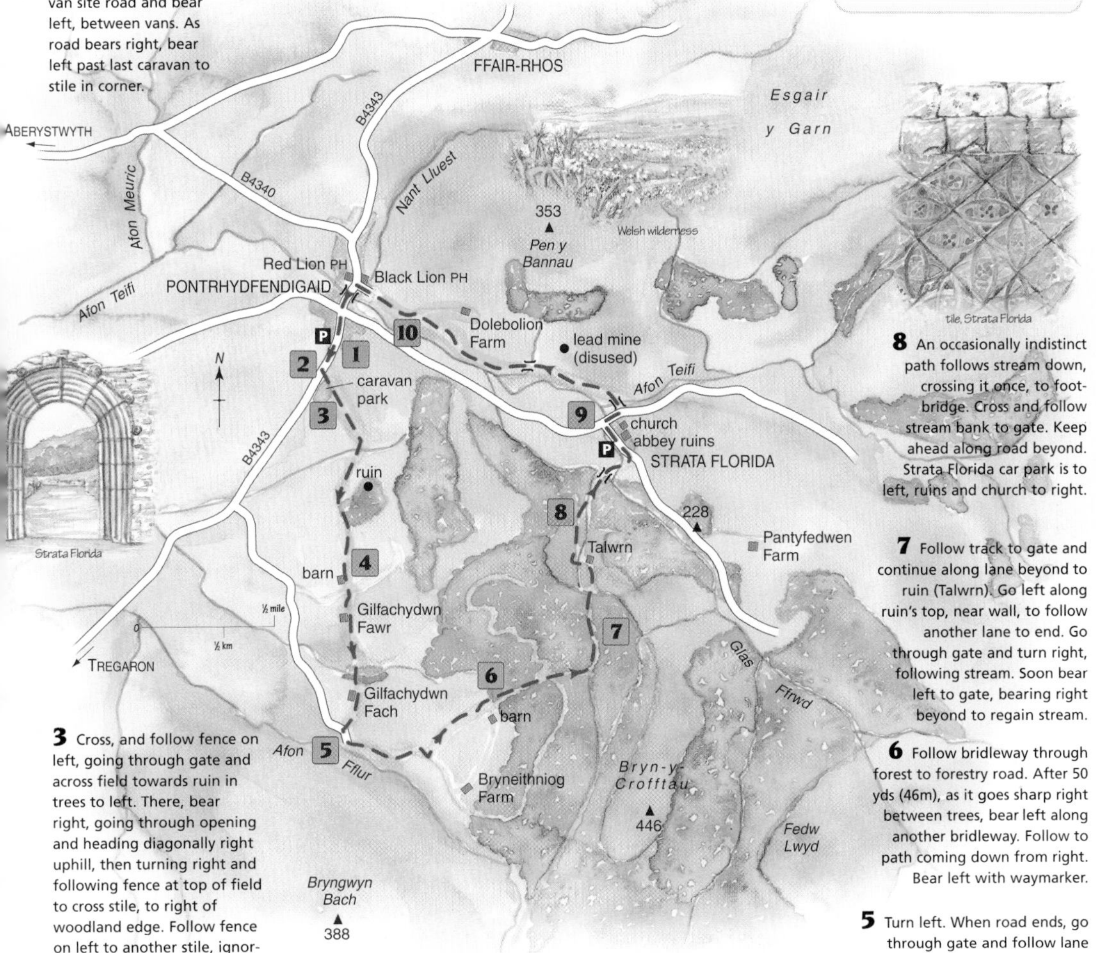

3 Cross, and follow fence on left, going through gate and across field towards ruin in trees to left. There, bear right, going through opening and heading diagonally right uphill, then turning right and following fence at top of field to cross stile, to right of woodland edge. Follow fence on left to another stile, ignoring gate, then go diagonally right across field to reach gate in top right corner. Go through and turn left immediately through another gate. Go diagonally right towards barn.

4 Go through gate beside barn and along farm lane opposite. Beyond first farm, lane degenerates to track, but remains obvious. Beyond farmyard keep to left of hut and take lower, right-hand track into trees. Ford stream, go through gate and follow track uphill to second farm. Go through gate and ahead along farm lane to road.

5 Turn left. When road ends, go through gate and follow lane beyond. As farm comes into view about ¼ mile (400m) ahead, take lane coming in from left, following it uphill. Approaching barn, go through gate on left and turn right along fence to gate into forest.

6 Follow bridleway through forest to forestry road. After 50 yds (46m), as it goes sharp right between trees, bear left along another bridleway. Follow to path coming down from right. Bear left with waymarker.

7 Follow track to gate and continue along lane beyond to ruin (Talwrn). Go left along ruin's top, near wall, to follow another lane to end. Go through gate and turn right, following stream. Soon bear left to gate, bearing right beyond to regain stream.

8 An occasionally indistinct path follows stream down, crossing it once, to footbridge. Cross and follow stream bank to gate. Keep ahead along road beyond. Strata Florida car park is to left, ruins and church to right.

9 As road turns sharp left, go right past telephone box and, soon, cross waymarked stile on left. Cross footbridge and bear left towards waymarked stile by gate. The path now follows Afon Teifi (left) all the way to Pontrhydfendigaid, with occasional waymarkers, stiles and gates.

10 At farm lane bear left to road. Turn left, crossing hump-backed bridge and passing road, on left, for Strata Florida, to return to start.

Welsh wilderness

tile, Strata Florida

Strata Florida

Sarn Helen – the Roman Highway through Wales

A stretch of Roman Road leads to the legendary burial place of a great Welsh bard

1 Start at the Wildfowler Inn in Tre'r-ddôl. On the village street, face the pub, go right, past the garage, shop and café, to join the A487. Turn right towards Machynlleth, and, after passing the last house, turn right through a wooden gate into a forestry plantation. Climb with an attractive, narrow, path.

2 Bear left when the path forks. Ignore paths descending from your right. Go ahead across clear-felled hillside. The path becomes a firm track before reaching a lane. Go right uphill, passing a number of houses and, eventually, farm buildings at Cefngweiriog.

3 Reach the junction with Sarn Helen, coming as a track through a gate on your left. Turn right to walk along this quiet lane. Follow this section of Sarn Helen for over 1 mile (1.6km), ignoring a lane descending on your right. Cross a bridge over the Afon Clettwr and climb towards Gwar-cwm-uchaf farm. Turn left before you reach it, onto a rising track and ignore all branching paths.

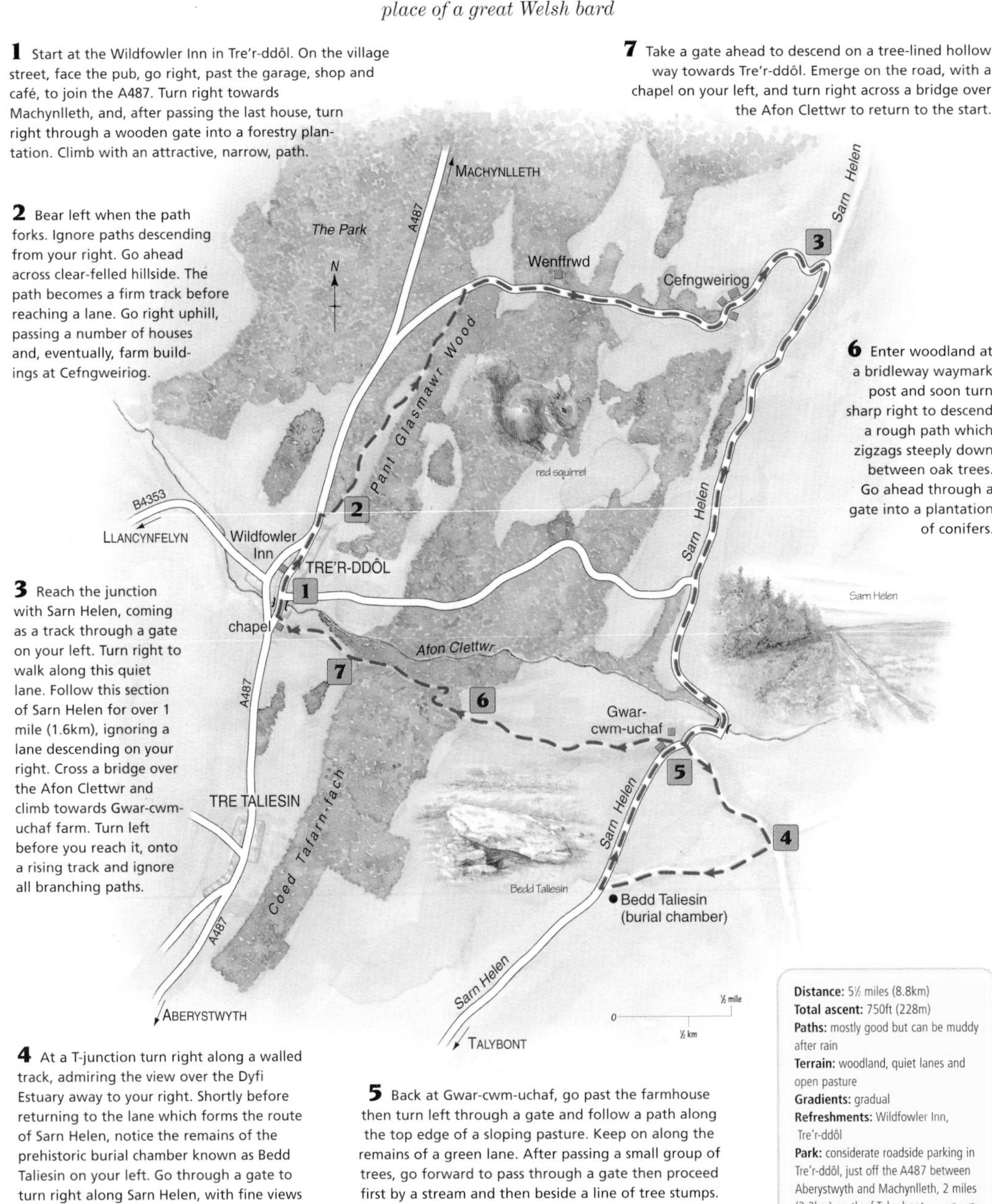

4 At a T-junction turn right along a walled track, admiring the view over the Dyfi Estuary away to your right. Shortly before returning to the lane which forms the route of Sarn Helen, notice the remains of the prehistoric burial chamber known as Bedd Taliesin on your left. Go through a gate to turn right along Sarn Helen, with fine views towards Aberdyfi over the stone wall on your left.

5 Back at Gwar-cwm-uchaf, go past the farmhouse then turn left through a gate and follow a path along the top edge of a sloping pasture. Keep on along the remains of a green lane. After passing a small group of trees, go forward to pass through a gate then proceed first by a stream and then beside a line of tree stumps. Keep on in the same direction along a hedged section and then along a rutted path.

6 Enter woodland at a bridleway waymark post and soon turn sharp right to descend a rough path which zigzags steeply down between oak trees. Go ahead through a gate into a plantation of conifers.

7 Take a gate ahead to descend on a tree-lined hollow way towards Tre'r-ddôl. Emerge on the road, with a chapel on your left, and turn right across a bridge over the Afon Clettwr to return to the start.

Distance: 5½ miles (8.8km)
Total ascent: 750ft (228m)
Paths: mostly good but can be muddy after rain
Terrain: woodland, quiet lanes and open pasture
Gradients: gradual
Refreshments: Wildfowler Inn, Tre'r-ddôl
Park: considerate roadside parking in Tre'r-ddôl, just off the A487 between Aberystwyth and Machynlleth, 2 miles (3.2km) north of Tal-y-bont

WALK 89

Cadair Idris – the Mountain Nature Reserve

A challenging mountain walk around the bowl of Cwm Cau in the Cadair Idris National Nature Reserve

Distance: 5½ miles (8.8km)
Total Ascent: 2,950ft (899m)
Paths: good; some rough; stream crossing difficult after heavy rain
Terrain: rocky, mountainous
Gradients: steep; occasionally very steep
Refreshments: none
Park: Minffordd car park at junction of A487 and B4405

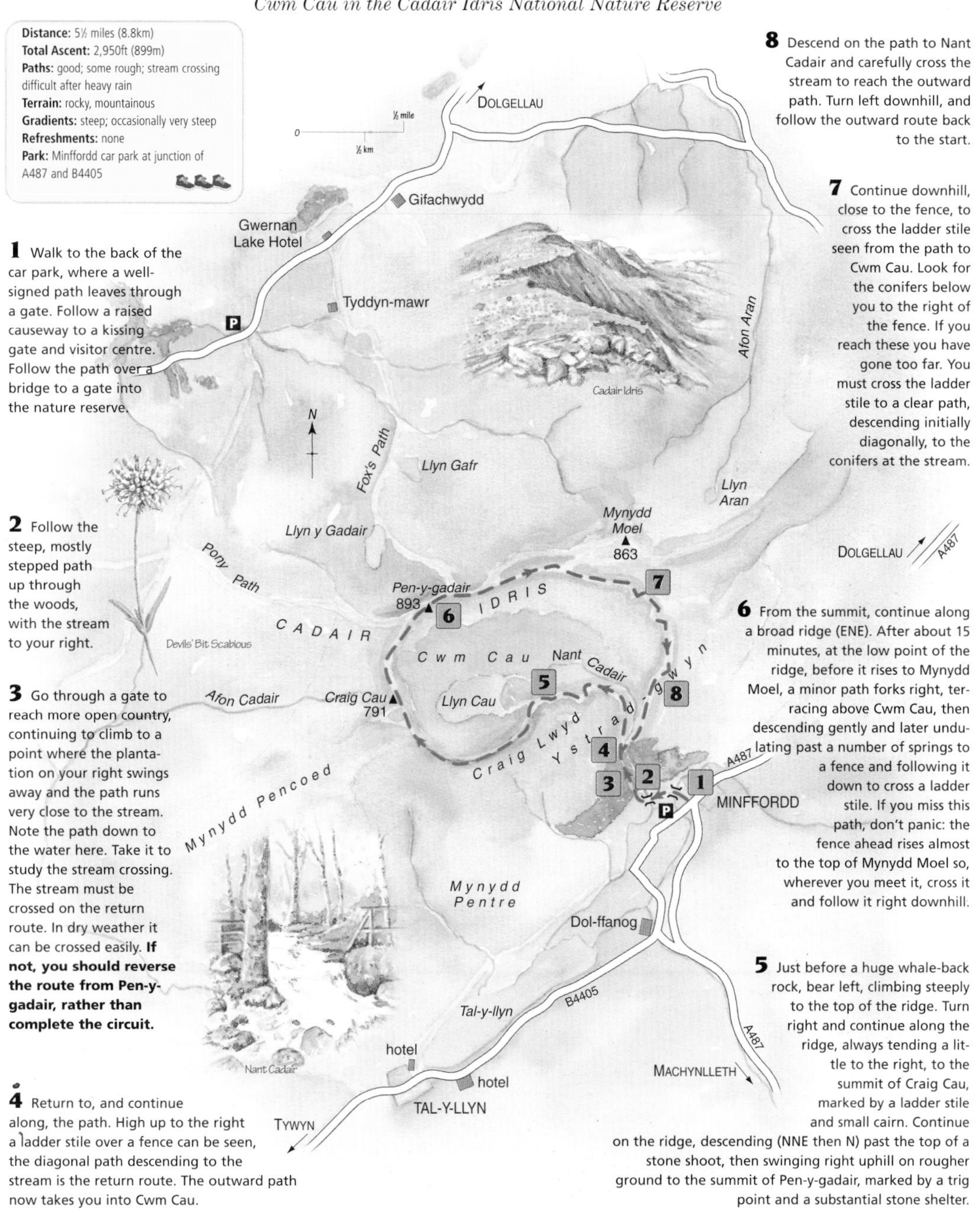

1 Walk to the back of the car park, where a well-signed path leaves through a gate. Follow a raised causeway to a kissing gate and visitor centre. Follow the path over a bridge to a gate into the nature reserve.

2 Follow the steep, mostly stepped path up through the woods, with the stream to your right.

3 Go through a gate to reach more open country, continuing to climb to a point where the plantation on your right swings away and the path runs very close to the stream. Note the path down to the water here. Take it to study the stream crossing. The stream must be crossed on the return route. In dry weather it can be crossed easily. **If not, you should reverse the route from Pen-y-gadair, rather than complete the circuit.**

4 Return to, and continue along, the path. High up to the right a ladder stile over a fence can be seen, the diagonal path descending to the stream is the return route. The outward path now takes you into Cwm Cau.

5 Just before a huge whale-back rock, bear left, climbing steeply to the top of the ridge. Turn right and continue along the ridge, always tending a little to the right, to the summit of Craig Cau, marked by a ladder stile and small cairn. Continue on the ridge, descending (NNE then N) past the top of a stone shoot, then swinging right uphill on rougher ground to the summit of Pen-y-gadair, marked by a trig point and a substantial stone shelter.

6 From the summit, continue along a broad ridge (ENE). After about 15 minutes, at the low point of the ridge, before it rises to Mynydd Moel, a minor path forks right, terracing above Cwm Cau, then descending gently and later undulating past a number of springs to a fence and following it down to cross a ladder stile. If you miss this path, don't panic: the fence ahead rises almost to the top of Mynydd Moel so, wherever you meet it, cross it and follow it right downhill.

7 Continue downhill, close to the fence, to cross the ladder stile seen from the path to Cwm Cau. Look for the conifers below you to the right of the fence. If you reach these you have gone too far. You must cross the ladder stile to a clear path, descending initially diagonally, to the conifers at the stream.

8 Descend on the path to Nant Cadair and carefully cross the stream to reach the outward path. Turn left downhill, and follow the outward route back to the start.

WALK 90

On the Roman Steps through the Rhinogs

This ancient pathway through the heart of the Rhinog hills was one of many trade routes across the mountains

1 Leave the car park through the gate at its top end and turn right. Cross the causeway over the stream, then a ladder stile, following the path rising through a wood.

Distance: 4½ miles (7.2km)
Total ascent: 1,150 ft (350m)
Paths: excellent as far as the path to Llyn Du, rugged or poor thereafter
Terrain: heather clad and rocky mountains
Gradients: gradual, then steep and difficult
Refreshments: none
Park: car park at Llyn Cwm Bychan at end of minor road, 5 miles east of A496 in Harlech

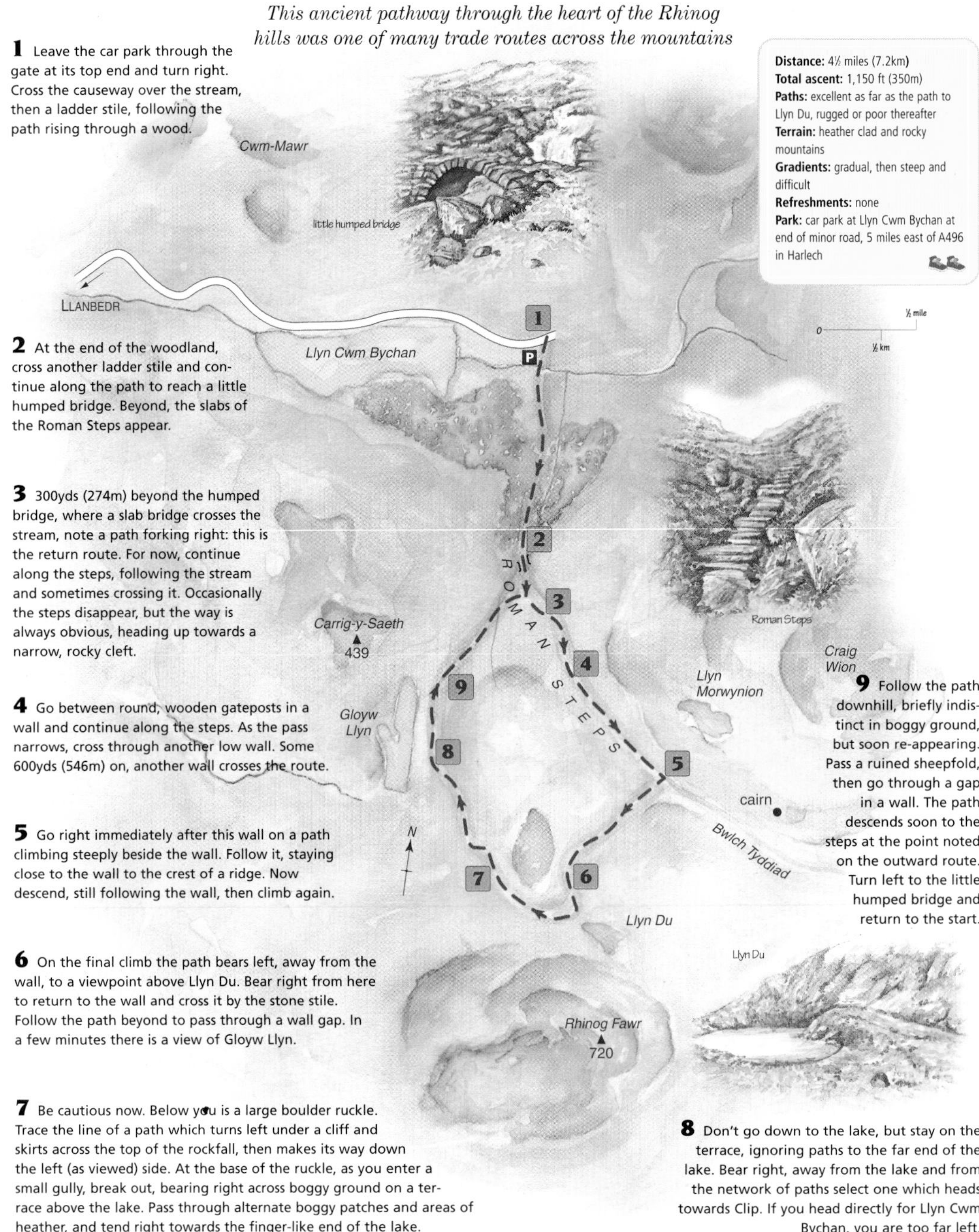

2 At the end of the woodland, cross another ladder stile and continue along the path to reach a little humped bridge. Beyond, the slabs of the Roman Steps appear.

3 300yds (274m) beyond the humped bridge, where a slab bridge crosses the stream, note a path forking right: this is the return route. For now, continue along the steps, following the stream and sometimes crossing it. Occasionally the steps disappear, but the way is always obvious, heading up towards a narrow, rocky cleft.

4 Go between round, wooden gateposts in a wall and continue along the steps. As the pass narrows, cross through another low wall. Some 600yds (546m) on, another wall crosses the route.

5 Go right immediately after this wall on a path climbing steeply beside the wall. Follow it, staying close to the wall to the crest of a ridge. Now descend, still following the wall, then climb again.

6 On the final climb the path bears left, away from the wall, to a viewpoint above Llyn Du. Bear right from here to return to the wall and cross it by the stone stile. Follow the path beyond to pass through a wall gap. In a few minutes there is a view of Gloyw Llyn.

7 Be cautious now. Below you is a large boulder ruckle. Trace the line of a path which turns left under a cliff and skirts across the top of the rockfall, then makes its way down the left (as viewed) side. At the base of the ruckle, as you enter a small gully, break out, bearing right across boggy ground on a terrace above the lake. Pass through alternate boggy patches and areas of heather, and tend right towards the finger-like end of the lake.

8 Don't go down to the lake, but stay on the terrace, ignoring paths to the far end of the lake. Bear right, away from the lake and from the network of paths select one which heads towards Clip. If you head directly for Llyn Cwm Bychan, you are too far left.

9 Follow the path downhill, briefly indistinct in boggy ground, but soon re-appearing. Pass a ruined sheepfold, then go through a gap in a wall. The path descends soon to the steps at the point noted on the outward route. Turn left to the little humped bridge and return to the start.

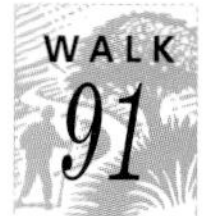

Mary Jones in the Dysynni Valley

In the footsteps of a remarkable woman, whose exploits were commemorated by Victorian missionaries

Distance: 6¼ miles (10km)
Total ascent: 330ft (100m)
Paths: clear tracks and quiet lanes; muddy stretch between Tyn-y-ddôl and Pen-y-meini
Terrain: hillside pasture and valley floor
Gradients: gentle
Refreshments: at Abergynolwyn, south of Llanfihangel-y-pennant
Park: opposite the church in Llanfihangel-y-pennant

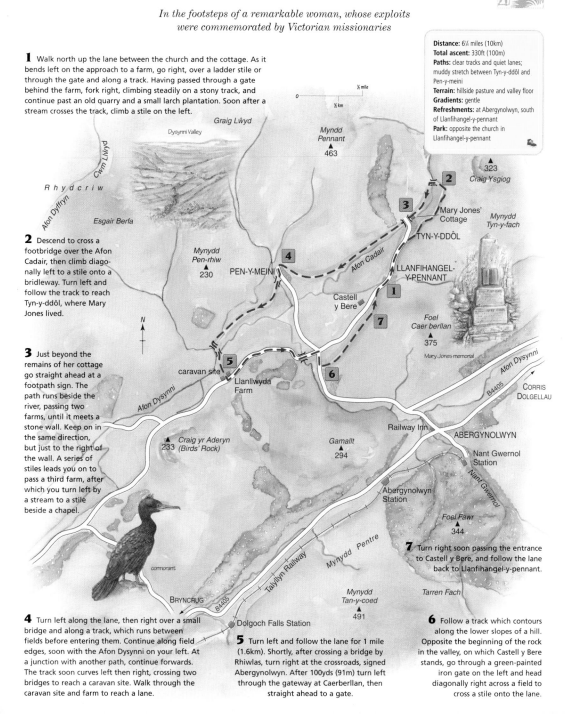

1 Walk north up the lane between the church and the cottage. As it bends left on the approach to a farm, go right, over a ladder stile or through the gate and along a track. Having passed through a gate behind the farm, fork right, climbing steadily on a stony track, and continue past an old quarry and a small larch plantation. Soon after a stream crosses the track, climb a stile on the left.

2 Descend to cross a footbridge over the Afon Cadair, then climb diagonally left to a stile onto a bridleway. Turn left and follow the track to reach Tyn-y-ddôl, where Mary Jones lived.

3 Just beyond the remains of her cottage go straight ahead at a footpath sign. The path runs beside the river, passing two farms, until it meets a stone wall. Keep on in the same direction, but just to the right of the wall. A series of stiles leads you on to pass a third farm, after which you turn left by a stream to a stile beside a chapel.

4 Turn left along the lane, then right over a small bridge and along a track, which runs between fields before entering them. Continue along field edges, soon with the Afon Dysynni on your left. At a junction with another path, continue forwards. The track soon curves left then right, crossing two bridges to reach a caravan site. Walk through the caravan site and farm to reach a lane.

5 Turn left and follow the lane for 1 mile (1.6km). Shortly, after crossing a bridge by Rhiwlas, turn right at the crossroads, signed Abergynolwyn. After 100yds (91m) turn left through the gateway at Caerberllan, then straight ahead to a gate.

6 Follow a track which contours along the lower slopes of a hill. Opposite the beginning of the rock in the valley, on which Castell y Bere stands, go through a green-painted iron gate on the left and head diagonally right across a field to cross a stile onto the lane.

7 Turn right soon passing the entrance to Castell y Bere, and follow the lane back to Llanfihangel-y-pennant.

Rhaeadr Ddu – the Black Waterfall

Deep forests cloak a lovely waterfall, where poets and writers found inspiration

1 From car park, follow main road left (south) for a few paces to black corrugated village hall and turn right between hall and river on gated lane. Climb gradually upstream with river away to left. Ignore drive to Ty-cerig on right.

2 About 200yds (182m) beyond drive, where lane bends right, look for waymark post in woodland ahead. Go to it and bear left along waymarked path towards footbridge over river. Just before footbridge, keep to path which leads directly to viewpoint of waterfall upstream from bridge. See lines of poetry carved on rock then retrace route a few paces and cross footbridge.

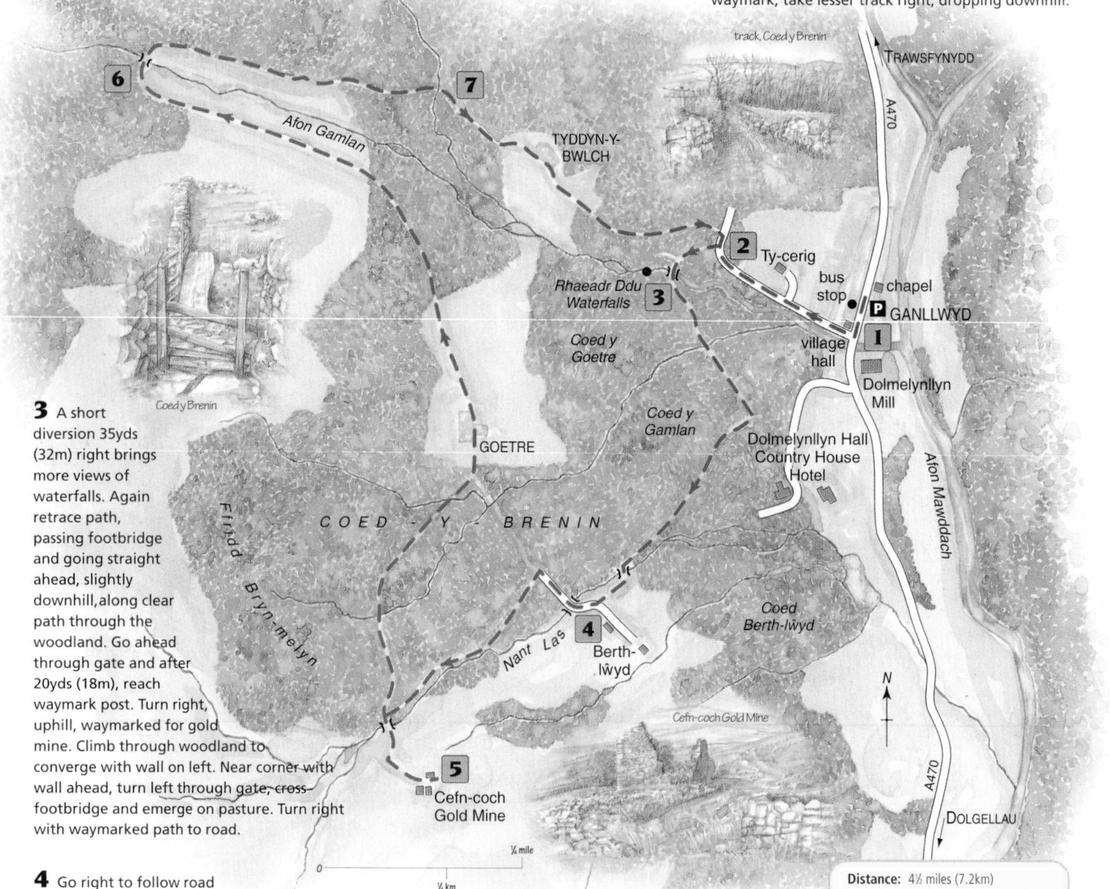

3 A short diversion 35yds (32m) right brings more views of waterfalls. Again retrace path, passing footbridge and going straight ahead, slightly downhill, along clear path through the woodland. Go ahead through gate and after 20yds (18m), reach waymark post. Turn right, uphill, waymarked for gold mine. Climb through woodland to converge with wall on left. Near corner with wall ahead, turn left through gate, cross footbridge and emerge on pasture. Turn right with waymarked path to road.

4 Go right to follow road across bridge and gate to re-enter woodland. After 80yds (73m), turn left along track between trees. Again converge with stream on left and ignore tracks on right. Turn left through narrow gap in wall, over collapsible stile and footbridge. Climb with paved way to ruins of Cefn-coch Gold Mine.

5 Retrace steps and cross footbridge and collapsible stile again. Go 35yds (32m) downhill on outward approach route to track junction and take track going ahead (ignoring track bearing left uphill and track used to reach here on right). Follow downhill to major track and go left through gate to pass buildings of Goetre. Continue along firm track through open space and back into forest. Then, back into open country, track rises to converge with river (Afon Gamlan) on right.

6 At track junction, turn right to follow track across river. Take track on right and, ignoring tracks through forest on left, bear right at two forks, keeping alongside river. At mountain bike waymark, take lesser track right, dropping downhill.

7 As track swings left, go ahead through small gate and descend with walled path. Pass buildings of Tyddyn-y-bwlch and through gate into woodland and, in 20yds (18m), after second gate, bear right at fork. Drop down to lane, go right (downhill) and follow it back to village and car park in Ganllwyd.

Distance: 4½ miles (7.2km)
Total ascent: 600ft (189m)
Paths: good
Terrain: oak woodland, conifer forest, pasture, quiet road
Gradients: some gradual climbs
Refreshments: none
Park: National Trust car park on eastern side of A470 in Ganllwyd, 5 miles (8km) north of Dolgellau

WALK 93

Pilgrims and Mysteries on Lleyn's Peninsula

A coastal walk through a landscape dominated by rituals

1 From car park, return to road junction and turn left, without crossing either bridge. Bear left uphill, ignoring turnings to right. When level with entrance to Dwyros camping site on right, turn left down signposted path. Pass houses and cross footbridge over Afon Saint to enter National Trust land.

6 On right is gate, stile and National Trust pillar, with track dropping down to Porth Meudwy valley. This is short cut described earlier. Continue past Cwrt (left) and go right at successive road junctions to retrace steps into Aberdaron, passing Dwyros on left.

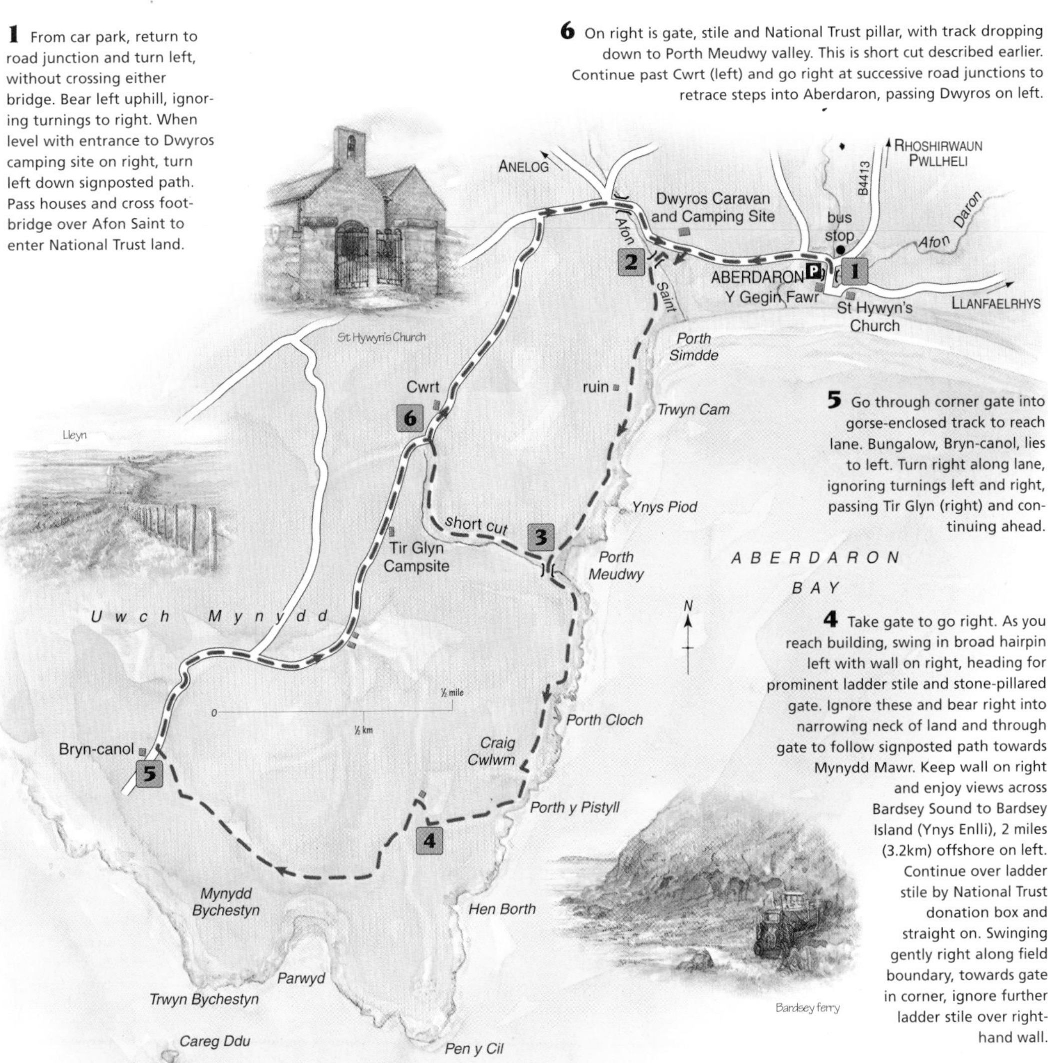

5 Go through corner gate into gorse-enclosed track to reach lane. Bungalow, Bryn-canol, lies to left. Turn right along lane, ignoring turnings left and right, passing Tir Glyn (right) and continuing ahead.

4 Take gate to go right. As you reach building, swing in broad hairpin left with wall on right, heading for prominent ladder stile and stone-pillared gate. Ignore these and bear right into narrowing neck of land and through gate to follow signposted path towards Mynydd Mawr. Keep wall on right and enjoy views across Bardsey Sound to Bardsey Island (Ynys Enlli), 2 miles (3.2km) offshore on left. Continue over ladder stile by National Trust donation box and straight on. Swinging gently right along field boundary, towards gate in corner, ignore further ladder stile over right-hand wall.

2 Follow coast path, keeping sea on left and ignoring path descending to beach at Porth Simdde. Continue past ruin (right) and through kissing-gate to log seat, then another kissing-gate before descending steps to inlet of Porth Meudwy. Track right offers short cut from here to stage 6 (near Cwrt). If you use this, keep to main track in valley bottom, ignoring side tracks.

3 Going ahead with signposted coast path, cross footbridge and climb steps up to stile. Ignore further stile, immediately on right skyline. Resume clifftop walk, keeping sea on left, passing Porth Cloch, then rising to pass Craig Cwlwm with its summit pond. Descend awkward outcrop to disused quarry. Ignore path and stile leading inland and continue on coast path, descending initially for 15 minutes to Porth y Pistyll. At its inland point, fork right, keeping to right-hand edge of field as you climb to gate in top right-hand corner.

Distance: 5½ miles (8.8km)
Total ascent: 350ft (107m)
Paths: good; some roads
Terrain: clifftop, pastureland
Gradients: some steep, stepped sections
Refreshments: many places in Aberdaron
Park: car park in Aberdaron, on B4413 16 miles (25.6km) west of Pwllheli

WALK 94

Quarrymen's Trails around Blaenau Ffestiniog

A fascinating mountain walk amidst the ruins of a once-thriving slate industry

Distance: 6 miles (9.7km)
Total ascent: 1,275ft (389m)
Paths: rough
Terrain: old quarry workings, rough moorland and bouldery mountainside
Gradients: fairly steep in places
Refreshments: café at power station visitor centre
Park: car park on minor road to power station visitor centre, Tanygrisiau, north of A496 between Blaenau Ffestiniog and Maentwrog

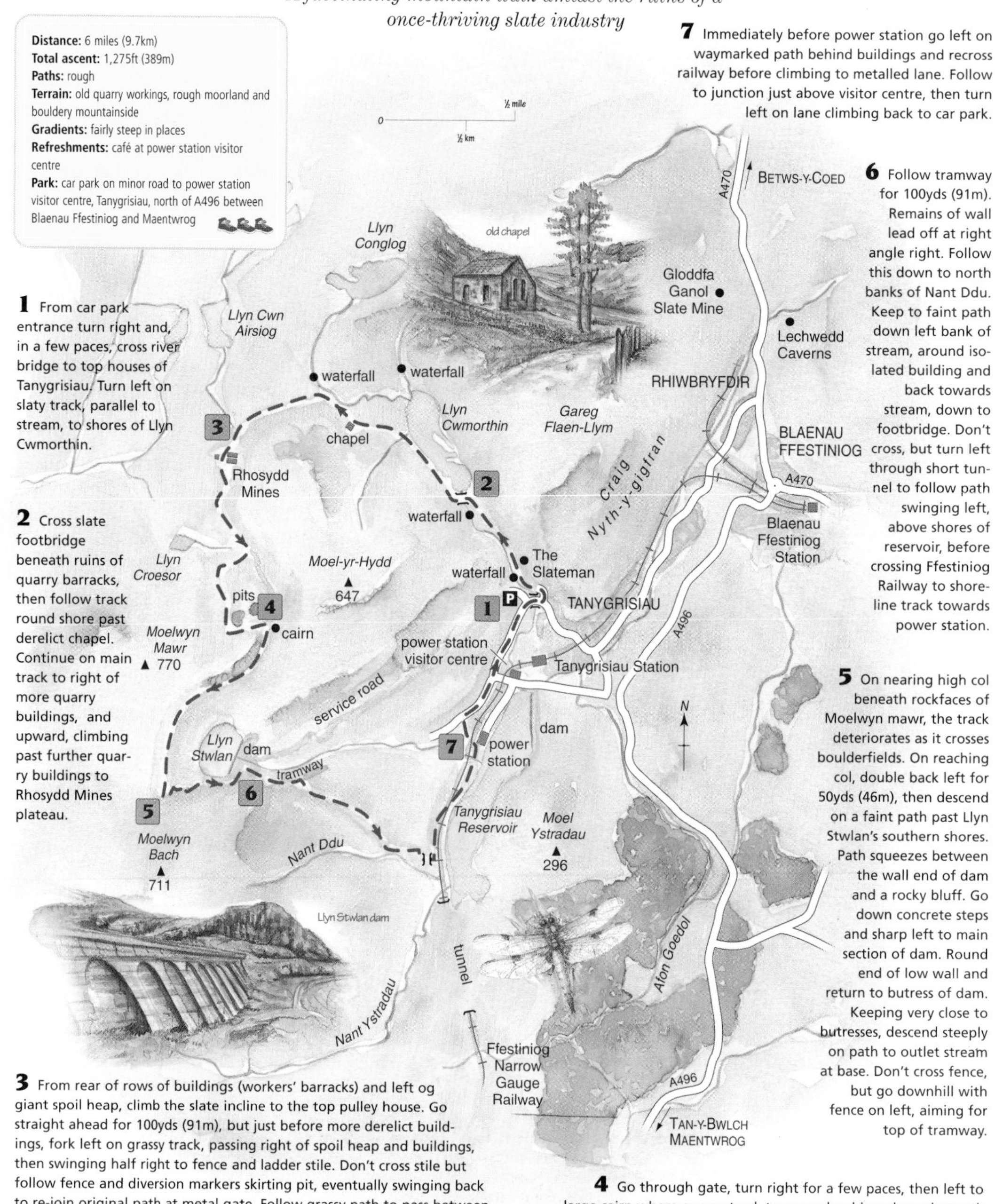

1 From car park entrance turn right and, in a few paces, cross river bridge to top houses of Tanygrisiau. Turn left on slaty track, parallel to stream, to shores of Llyn Cwmorthin.

2 Cross slate footbridge beneath ruins of quarry barracks, then follow track round shore past derelict chapel. Continue on main track to right of more quarry buildings, and upward, climbing past further quarry buildings to Rhosydd Mines plateau.

3 From rear of rows of buildings (workers' barracks) and left og giant spoil heap, climb the slate incline to the top pulley house. Go straight ahead for 100yds (91m), but just before more derelict buildings, fork left on grassy track, passing right of spoil heap and buildings, then swinging half right to fence and ladder stile. Don't cross stile but follow fence and diversion markers skirting pit, eventually swinging back to re-join original path at metal gate. Follow grassy path to pass between Moel-yr-Hydd and Moelwyn Mawr.

4 Go through gate, turn right for a few paces, then left to large cairn where quarry track traverses bouldery slopes beneath cliffs of Cragysgafn and high above Llyn Stwlan.

5 On nearing high col beneath rockfaces of Moelwyn mawr, the track deteriorates as it crosses boulderfields. On reaching col, double back left for 50yds (46m), then descend on a faint path past Llyn Stwlan's southern shores. Path squeezes between the wall end of dam and a rocky bluff. Go down concrete steps and sharp left to main section of dam. Round end of low wall and return to butress of dam. Keeping very close to butresses, descend steeply on path to outlet stream at base. Don't cross fence, but go downhill with fence on left, aiming for top of tramway.

6 Follow tramway for 100yds (91m). Remains of wall lead off at right angle right. Follow this down to north banks of Nant Ddu. Keep to faint path down left bank of stream, around isolated building and back towards stream, down to footbridge. Don't cross, but turn left through short tunnel to follow path swinging left, above shores of reservoir, before crossing Ffestiniog Railway to shoreline track towards power station.

7 Immediately before power station go left on waymarked path behind buildings and recross railway before climbing to metalled lane. Follow to junction just above visitor centre, then turn left on lane climbing back to car park.

WALK 95

Groves and Graves in Anglesey

Peaceful lowland Anglesey is home to a wealth of prehistoric landmarks

Distance: 8¼ miles (13.3km)
Total ascent: 280ft (85m)
Paths: mostly clear tracks and field paths; often muddy
Terrain: undulating farmland, with some woodland
Gradients: slight
Refreshments: Plas Coch or Brynsiencyn
Park: at the end of the Moel-y-don peninsula, south of the A4080

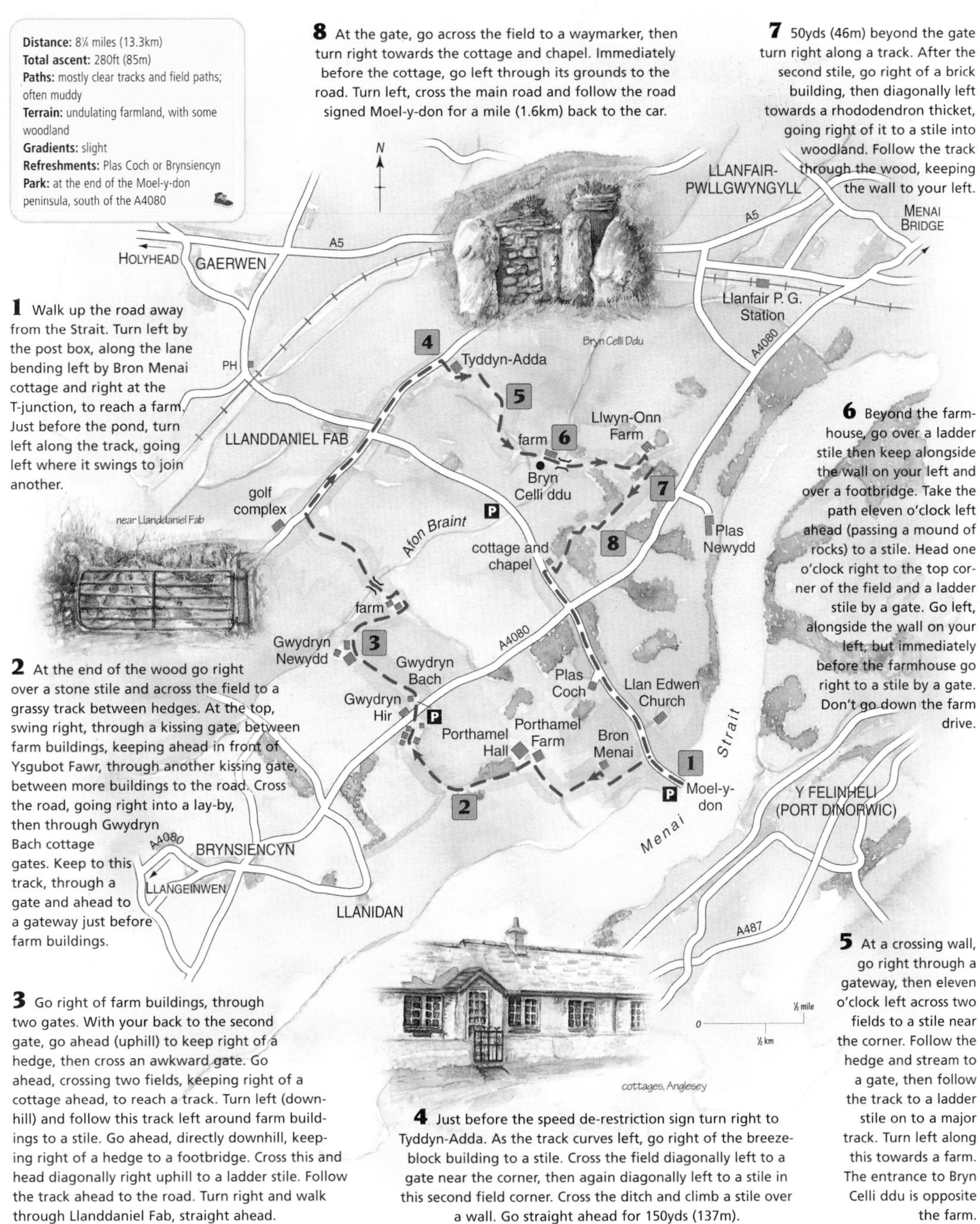

1 Walk up the road away from the Strait. Turn left by the post box, along the lane bending left by Bron Menai cottage and right at the T-junction, to reach a farm. Just before the pond, turn left along the track, going left where it swings to join another.

2 At the end of the wood go right over a stone stile and across the field to a grassy track between hedges. At the top, swing right, through a kissing gate, between farm buildings, keeping ahead in front of Ysgubot Fawr, through another kissing gate, between more buildings to the road. Cross the road, going right into a lay-by, then through Gwydryn Bach cottage gates. Keep to this track, through a gate and ahead to a gateway just before farm buildings.

3 Go right of farm buildings, through two gates. With your back to the second gate, go ahead (uphill) to keep right of a hedge, then cross an awkward gate. Go ahead, crossing two fields, keeping right of a cottage ahead, to reach a track. Turn left (downhill) and follow this track left around farm buildings to a stile. Go ahead, directly downhill, keeping right of a hedge to a footbridge. Cross this and head diagonally right uphill to a ladder stile. Follow the track ahead to the road. Turn right and walk through Llanddaniel Fab, straight ahead.

4 Just before the speed de-restriction sign turn right to Tyddyn-Adda. As the track curves left, go right of the breeze-block building to a stile. Cross the field diagonally left to a gate near the corner, then again diagonally left to a stile in this second field corner. Cross the ditch and climb a stile over a wall. Go straight ahead for 150yds (137m).

5 At a crossing wall, go right through a gateway, then eleven o'clock left across two fields to a stile near the corner. Follow the hedge and stream to a gate, then follow the track to a ladder stile on to a major track. Turn left along this towards a farm. The entrance to Bryn Celli ddu is opposite the farm.

6 Beyond the farmhouse, go over a ladder stile then keep alongside the wall on your left and over a footbridge. Take the path eleven o'clock left ahead (passing a mound of rocks) to a stile. Head one o'clock right to the top corner of the field and a ladder stile by a gate. Go left, alongside the wall on your left, but immediately before the farmhouse go right to a stile by a gate. Don't go down the farm drive.

7 50yds (46m) beyond the gate turn right along a track. After the second stile, go right of a brick building, then diagonally left towards a rhododendron thicket, going right of it to a stile into woodland. Follow the track through the wood, keeping the wall to your left.

8 At the gate, go across the field to a waymarker, then turn right towards the cottage and chapel. Immediately before the cottage, go left through its grounds to the road. Turn left, cross the main road and follow the road signed Moel-y-don for a mile (1.6km) back to the car.

Watkin Path and the Heart of Snowdonia

Gentle walking in the heart of the Snowdon range, with a challenging option for greater views

1 From car park follow road towards Beddgelert for 50yds (46m), then cross to reach signed path. Cross cattle grid and follow tarmac lane away from main road, with river on right and woodland on left.

2 Leave tarmac lane at footpath sign, bearing left through gate on rough track, with wall on left and rhododendrons on right. Go ahead through gate and follow track curving right to reach kissing-gate, shortly after obvious incline up and down hillside.

3 Kissing-gate allows access to Snowdon National Nature Reserve. Within reserve track runs close to river. Cross bridge of massive sleepers over river and continue past ruined copper mines, and tall cypress tree looking distinctly out of place. Ahead now is bulky flat-topped rock outcrop of Gladstone Rock.

4 Beyond rock track continues into Cwm Llan, eventually bearing right by old slate quarry buildings to offer superb view of Snowdon, to left, and Lliwedd, to right, with Bwlch y Saethau and Bwlch Ciliau between them. This walk terminates here and it is interesting to explore the old quarry buildings carefully.

5 As this is the walk's furthest point, it's now simple to reverse route back to start.

6 A fine, but arduous, extension follows rough path to right, just 70yds (64m) after recrossing sleeper bridge. Follow this diagonal path up to tramway track and turn right. Follow level tramway to where stream is crossed by slate slab bridge, with waterfall down to right. Just before crossing bridge, turn left off tramway and follow stream upwards. Path is very faint and intermittent. Where in doubt, head a little left of low point on ridge ahead, skirting bowl below and then swinging right, directly to pass of Bwlch-Cwm-Llan.

7 At pass, just before gap in wall, turn left and follow wall, using ladder stile to cross it and then keep wall on left, even when it drops slightly before rising again to ladder stile. Don't cross stile, but turn sharp right to follow stony track to summit of Yr Aran.

8 To descend, retrace path to ladder stile, cross it and follow to left of wall. Descent flattens, before low point of ridge. Carefully turn left and descend steeply heading cross-country, northeast. Aim just a little right of prominent waterfall in valley below, so as to avoid cliffs of Clogwyn Brith. When tramway is reached, a short detour right visits ruins of drumhouse at top of incline. Don't be tempted to climb down incline. Instead, return along tramway and descend to regain Watkin Path. Turn right and reverse route back to start.

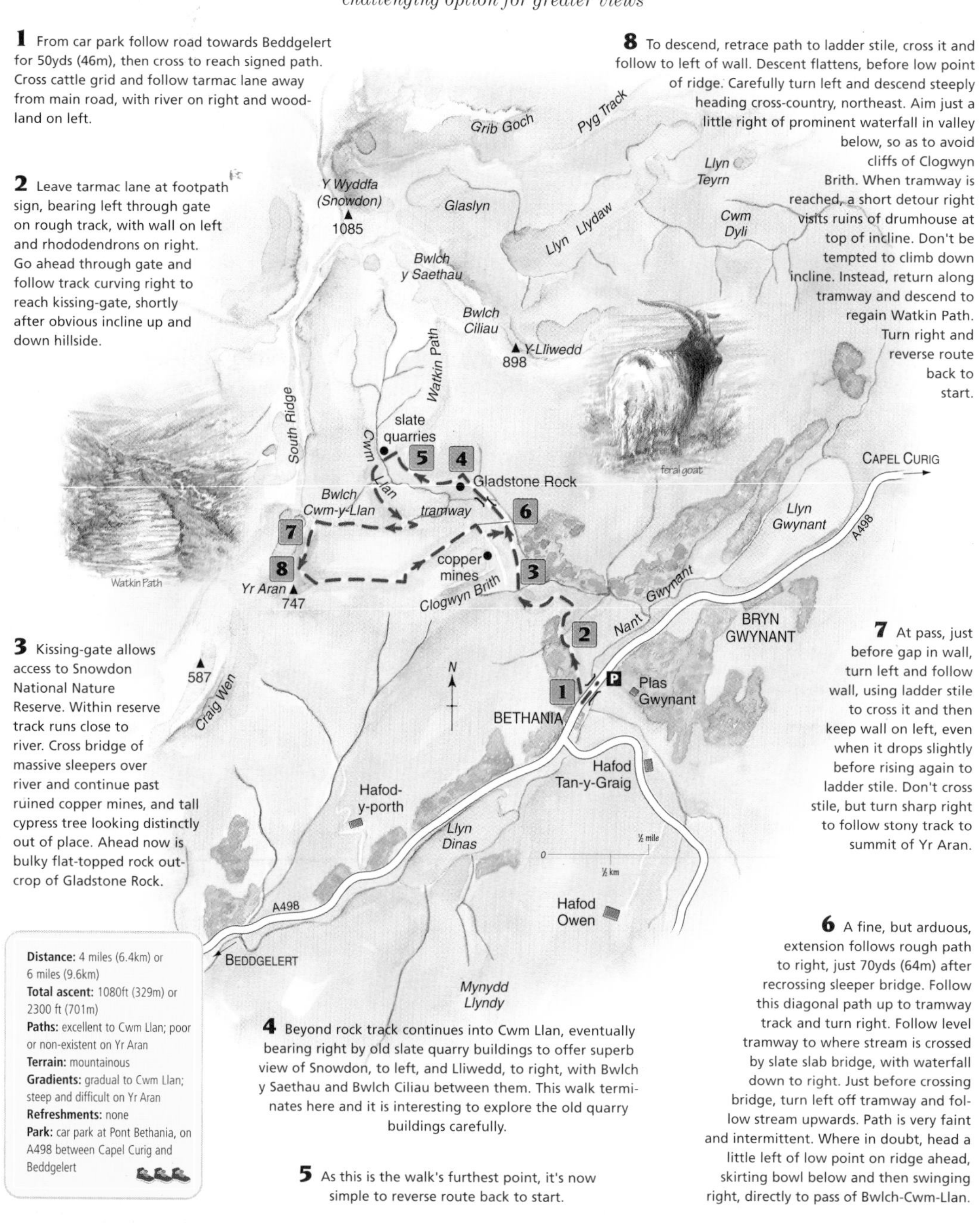

Distance: 4 miles (6.4km) or 6 miles (9.6km)
Total ascent: 1080ft (329m) or 2300 ft (701m)
Paths: excellent to Cwm Llan; poor or non-existent on Yr Aran
Terrain: mountainous
Gradients: gradual to Cwm Llan; steep and difficult on Yr Aran
Refreshments: none
Park: car park at Pont Bethania, on A498 between Capel Curig and Beddgelert

Lost Civilisations on Tal y Fan

The hinterland of the North Wales coast is dotted with mysterious stones and circles

Distance: 9½ miles (15.3km)
Total ascent: 1,725ft (526m)
Paths: mainly grassy and clear, but confusing in poor visibility
Terrain: mountain upland, hill pastures and rocky outcrops
Gradients: moderate
Refreshments: nothing near by; many places in Conwy.
Park: on roadside at the top of Sychnant Pass, the old hill road between Conwy and Penmaenmawr

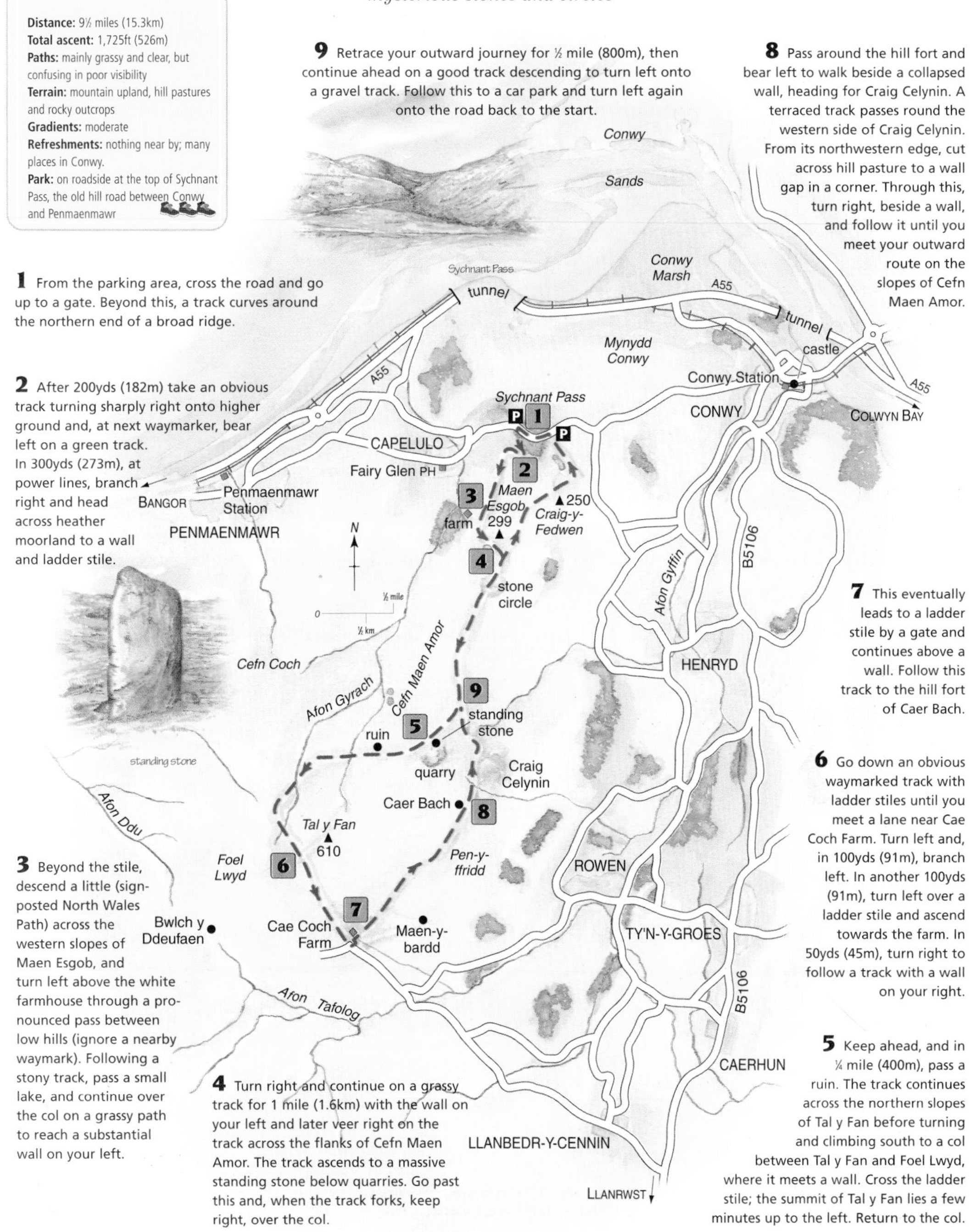

1 From the parking area, cross the road and go up to a gate. Beyond this, a track curves around the northern end of a broad ridge.

2 After 200yds (182m) take an obvious track turning sharply right onto higher ground and, at next waymarker, bear left on a green track. In 300yds (273m), at power lines, branch right and head across heather moorland to a wall and ladder stile.

3 Beyond the stile, descend a little (signposted North Wales Path) across the western slopes of Maen Esgob, and turn left above the white farmhouse through a pronounced pass between low hills (ignore a nearby waymark). Following a stony track, pass a small lake, and continue over the col on a grassy path to reach a substantial wall on your left.

4 Turn right and continue on a grassy track for 1 mile (1.6km) with the wall on your left and later veer right on the track across the flanks of Cefn Maen Amor. The track ascends to a massive standing stone below quarries. Go past this and, when the track forks, keep right, over the col.

5 Keep ahead, and in ¼ mile (400m), pass a ruin. The track continues across the northern slopes of Tal y Fan before turning and climbing south to a col between Tal y Fan and Foel Lwyd, where it meets a wall. Cross the ladder stile; the summit of Tal y Fan lies a few minutes up to the left. Return to the col.

6 Go down an obvious waymarked track with ladder stiles until you meet a lane near Cae Coch Farm. Turn left and, in 100yds (91m), branch left. In another 100yds (91m), turn left over a ladder stile and ascend towards the farm. In 50yds (45m), turn right to follow a track with a wall on your right.

7 This eventually leads to a ladder stile by a gate and continues above a wall. Follow this track to the hill fort of Caer Bach.

8 Pass around the hill fort and bear left to walk beside a collapsed wall, heading for Craig Celynin. A terraced track passes round the western side of Craig Celynin. From its northwestern edge, cut across hill pasture to a wall gap in a corner. Through this, turn right, beside a wall, and follow it until you meet your outward route on the slopes of Cefn Maen Amor.

9 Retrace your outward journey for ½ mile (800m), then continue ahead on a good track descending to turn left onto a gravel track. Follow this to a car park and turn left again onto the road back to the start.

WALK 98

Eastern Moorlands

The exhilarating open moorlands of Ruabon Mountain protect North Wales from the hubbub of English industry

1 Leave the car park at its top corner by crossing a stile and turning left along the road. Cross the road and in a few strides turn right onto a signposted track, which curves right and rises onto heather moorland.

2 A number of tracks soon branch from the main track. Keep to the highest, and after ¼ mile (400m) go on past an isolated tree. A second isolated tree stands near a path junction, where the most prominent track turns right and descends. Ignore this, and go forward on a narrow and boggy path through heather.

3 At a waymark post, keep forward into a rising gully, beyond which you emerge onto the open top of Ruabon Mountain. Go forward, descending easily in a south-easterly direction towards a clump of trees at Mountain Lodge, about ¾ mile (1.2km) away.

4 The path later veers north of Mountain Lodge, and finally eases down via a kissing-gate to a road. Turn right and follow the road across a stream and, later, the inflow to a small reservoir.

5 A few minutes further on leave the road for a bridleway on the right, going forward through a metal gate and along a delightful green track that soon rises to the left above a stream. As you near Newtown Mountain Plantation, watch for a path branching right, down to the stream, and taking you into the plantation.

6 Enter the plantation and follow the path with a stream on your right, to reach a clearing after ½ mile (800m). Cross the clearing to take the path on the right (now with a stream on your left). Shortly, at a fork, veer right uphill on a rocky path to the top of the plantation, ignoring the path from the left crossing the stream.

7 Beyond the plantation boundary, there is a steady haul on a narrow path across the heather moor, crossing the high point, veering right and descending to a waymark post at a path junction. Bear left and descend to another track. Turn right for 50yds (46m) passing a small pond, and then go left on a faint green path to pass around a circular bell pit after 100yds (91m).

8 Take an obvious path through a dip, and continue on the other side to join a good path parallel with a plantation boundary. Later, join the outward route just a few minutes from the start.

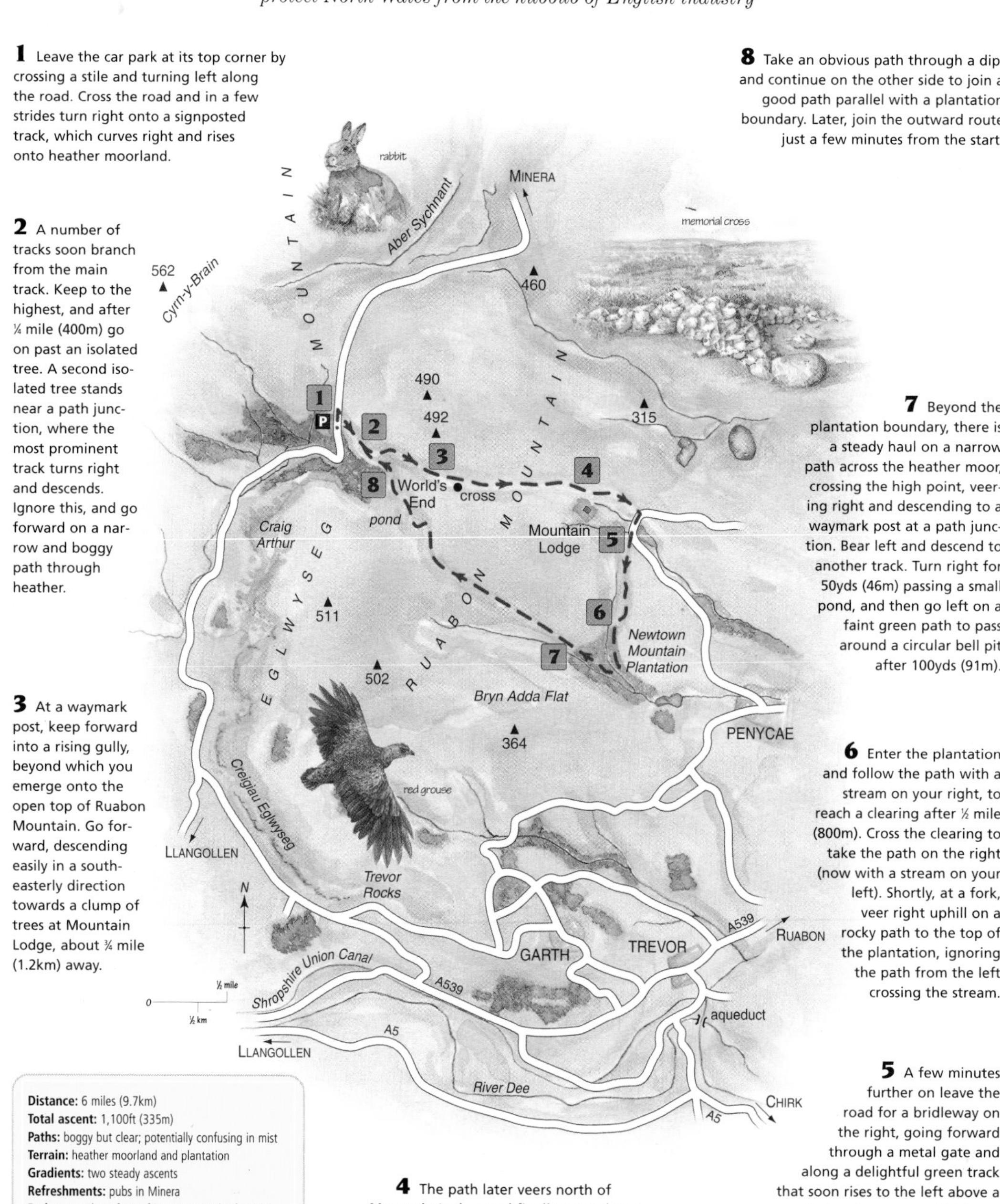

Distance: 6 miles (9.7km)
Total ascent: 1,100ft (335m)
Paths: boggy but clear; potentially confusing in mist
Terrain: heather moorland and plantation
Gradients: two steady ascents
Refreshments: pubs in Minera
Park: car park on forest fringe, just north of World's End, on hill road between Minera and A542, north of Llangollen

Scotland

Scotland displays many faces, even on first acquaintance: the rolling hills of the Southern Uplands, the industrial urban belt between the Clyde and the Forth, then the Highlands in all their splendour, breaking up west and north into a succession of headlands and sea lochs, islands and stacks. A tour of Scotland offers the chance to see Britain's landscape on a grand scale – all the island's highest mountains lie north of the border, along with an incredibly rugged coastline and vast tracts of wilderness. There is also a greater degree of freedom to roam than elsewhere, and a distinct culture and tradition evident wherever you travel.

The weather can be extreme on the high ground, so approach with due caution. You can approach the Cuillins from Sligachan on Skye without too much difficulty, but to grapple with the high ridges requires rock-climbing skills. You can wander in the wilds of the Flow Country, but you need to know when it's time to turn back. If the really high mountains look daunting, there are plenty of smaller hills you can climb.

The ancient Caledonian pine forest at Rothiemurchus is a mere remnant of a much more widespread wildwood. Even in the apparent wilds of Scotland most of the landscape is man-managed. The first rough highways through the glens and high passes were trodden by drovers, and the first attempt to establish a real road network came under the auspices of General Wade after the 1745 Jacobite Rebellion.

Wherever you look, you can find evidence of strife: Largs, Bannockburn, Stirling and Culloden all saw great and decisive battles. Then there are shameful episodes painfully seared into the folk memory: the Massacre of Glen Coe, and the brutal Clearances of the 19th century, in which thousands were evicted from the land.

Scotland is a land of conflicts and contrasts, of lovely scenery and loveless battlefields. Romantic-looking castles sit uneasily with their history of appalling bloodshed. Craggy peaks can look welcoming one moment, then threatening the next, as the weather clouds over. This endless variation is an essential part of Scotland's fascination.

Best of the Rest

Trotternish There is something surreal about the pillars and spikes of Quiraing, the intriguing end to the Trotternish uplands of northern Skye. Walkers who approach from the road crossing the centre of the island are rewarded by an unfolding view of towers and pinnacles. Although the pillars present problems to even the most experienced scrambler, there are good paths around the strange arenas created by this unique rock formation, making them accessible to most fit walkers.

Trossachs The Victorians were first drawn by the scenic splendours of the Trossachs, another point of entry from the lowland world to the upland wilds of the Highlands, and the area became a fashionable stopping place for tourists. As the road from Callander winds its way through forests and past lakes, the placenames turn from Anglicised lowland Scots to bewildering Highland Gaelic. The difference should not be lost on walkers who will find much to delight and challenge them here.

Glen Clova Glen Clova strikes out into the rising eastern Highlands, offering many Lowlanders the first glimpses of the great mountain ranges beyond the Highland line. Jock's Road is an ancient highway linking Kirriemuir with the splendour of Royal Deeside and can be used to access the Caenlochan National Nature Reserve.

Sandwood Bay Few places epitomise the essence of remote northwest Scotland than this spectacular sweep of sand on Sutherland's wild Atlantic coast. Accessible only on foot from a road end three miles (4.8km) away, walkers who make it this far (the drive out to the roadend is as challenging as the walking) are rewarded by solitude and a perfect beach.

Merrick The feral goats which loiter on the wild hillsides of the Southern Uplands are often the only company walkers have as they make their way up southern Scotland's highest peak, the Merrick. From the campsites and facilities in Glen Trool there is a good track, though very steep in places, to the upper parts of this lonely mountain, and the views in clear weather are unsurpassed.

Arran Often fêted as Scotland in miniature, there is a wealth of good walking at all levels on this Clyde island. For an introduction to Scottish mountain walking, the ascent of Goat Fell, the island's highest peak, from Brodick Castle by Glen Rosa and the Saddle, is hard to beat.

Edinburgh's Literary Past

A walk around the elegant streets of the Scottish capital, with a proud tradition of literature

Start: Edinburgh Waverley railway station
Distance: 5 miles (8km)
Paths: pavements throughout
Terrain: city streets
Gradients: a few short, steep sections
Refreshments: plenty in city centre
Park: Waverley Station

Edinburgh Castle

Morag Place, Newtown

1 From Waverley Station, turn right, then left into Princes Street. Walk down to the Scott Monument, cross over, continue down Princes Street, then right into Frederick Street. Take the second turning on your left, George Street, then next left into Castle Street.

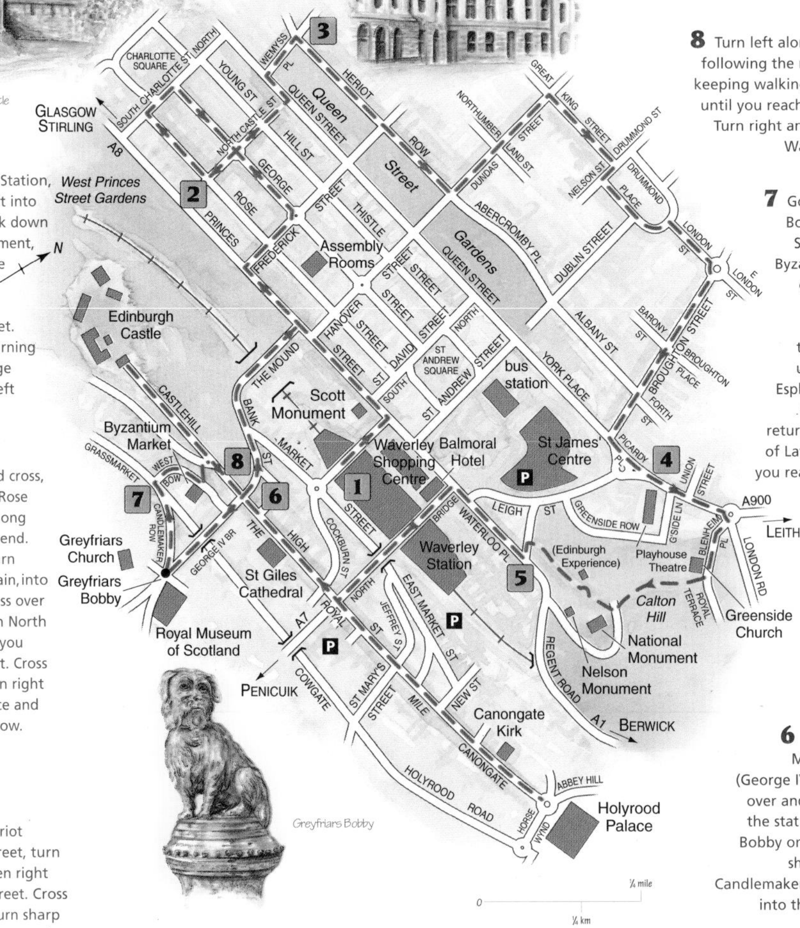

2 Walk down and cross, turning right into Rose Street. Continue along Rose Street to the end. At this junction, turn right and right again, into George Street. Cross over and turn left down North Castle Street until you reach Queen Street. Cross over, turn left, then right down Wemyss Place and right into Heriot Row.

3 Walk down Heriot Row to Dundas Street, turn left, cross over, then right into Great King Street. Cross at the end, then turn sharp right into Nelson Street, then left into Drummond Place. Follow Drummond Place into London Street, then turn right, up Broughton Street. Keep going to the main road junction at the top of the hill, then turn left into Picardy Place.

Greyfriars Bobby

4 Cross the road opposite the Playhouse, turn left, then right at the roundabout with the clock and immediately right up Blenheim Place. Take the path on the right by Greenside Church, climbing up to Calton Hill. Taking the the left hand path, walk across towards the Edinburgh Experience and descend by the path leading to Waterloo Place.

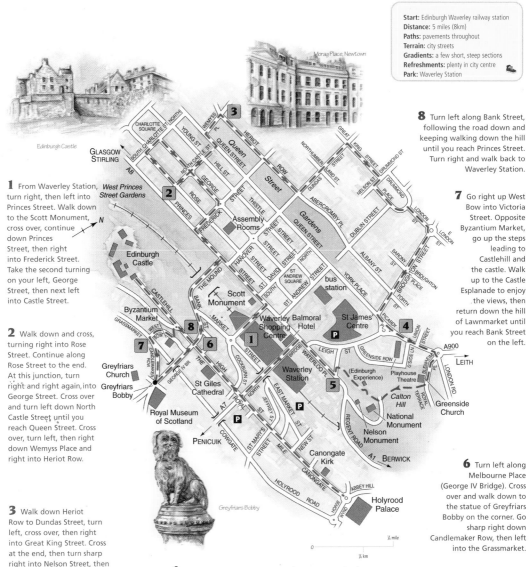

5 Turn right, cross over then turn left at the Balmoral Hotel and up North Bridge. Turn left down the High Street (Royal Mile) and walk down to Holyrood Palace. Walk back up the other side of the road.

6 Turn left along Melbourne Place (George IV Bridge). Cross over and walk down to the statue of Greyfriars Bobby on the corner. Go sharp right down Candlemaker Row, then left into the Grassmarket.

7 Go right up West Bow into Victoria Street. Opposite Byzantium Market, go up the steps leading to Castlehill and the castle. Walk up to the Castle Esplanade to enjoy the views, then return down the hill of Lawnmarket until you reach Bank Street on the left.

8 Turn left along Bank Street, following the road down and keeping walking down the hill until you reach Princes Street. Turn right and walk back to Waverley Station.

The Mysteries of Rosslyn

On the trail of the Holy Grail in a wooded glen near Edinburgh's suburbs

1 From the car park, take the path leading towards the river and cross the metal footbridge. Follow the path uphill and pass under the arch of the castle bridge. At the T-junction, turn left along Gardener's Brae.

2 Follow the path along the side of the river. This will take you uphill to a wall on the left. Keep the wall on your left as you follow the path back down towards the river, then continue over three stiles.

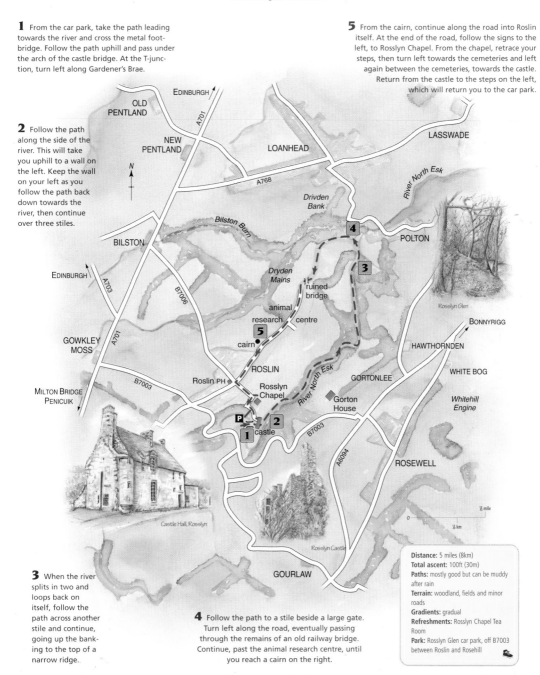

3 When the river splits in two and loops back on itself, follow the path across another stile and continue, going up the banking to the top of a narrow ridge.

4 Follow the path to a stile beside a large gate. Turn left along the road, eventually passing through the remains of an old railway bridge. Continue, past the animal research centre, until you reach a cairn on the right.

5 From the cairn, continue along the road into Roslin itself. At the end of the road, follow the signs to the left, to Rosslyn Chapel. From the chapel, retrace your steps, then turn left towards the cemeteries and left again between the cemeteries, towards the castle. Return from the castle to the steps on the left, which will return you to the car park.

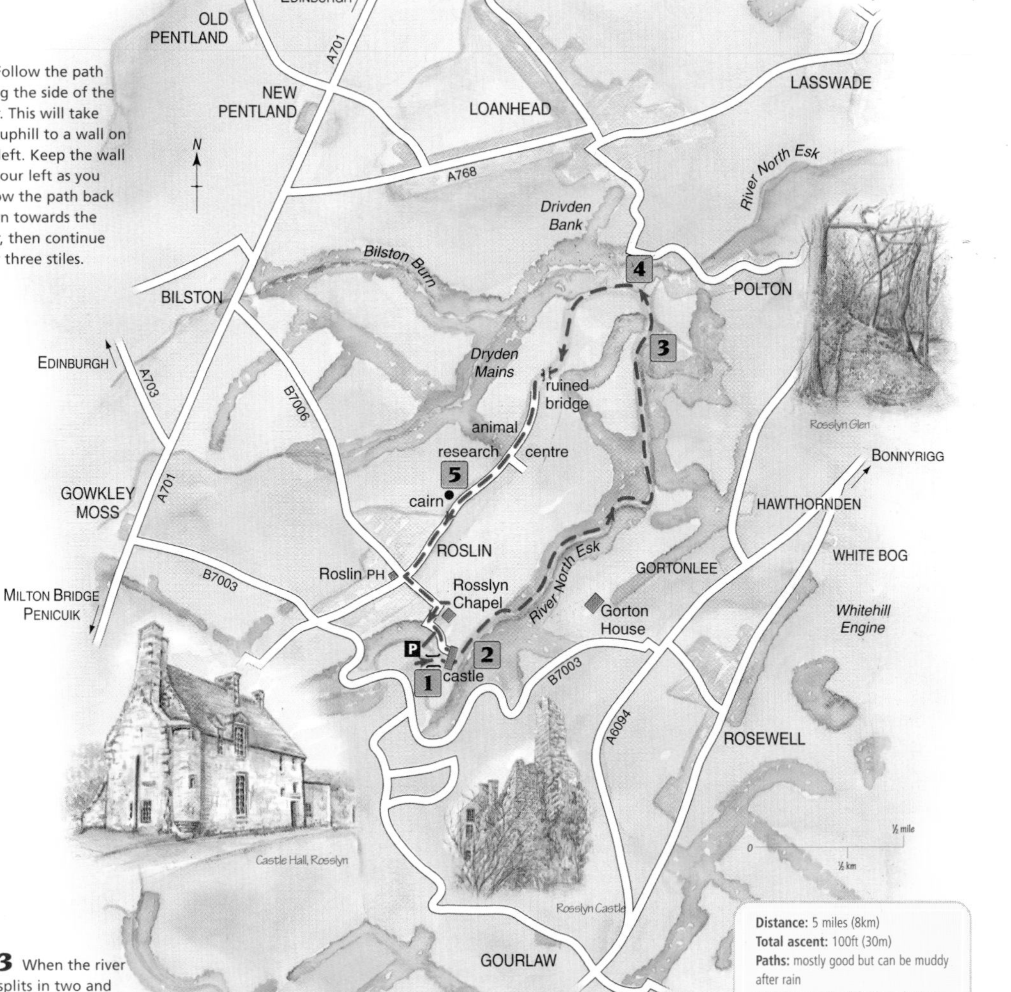

Distance: 5 miles (8km)
Total ascent: 100ft (30m)
Paths: mostly good but can be muddy after rain
Terrain: woodland, fields and minor roads
Gradients: gradual
Refreshments: Rosslyn Chapel Tea Room
Park: Rosslyn Glen car park, off B7003 between Roslin and Rosehill

Through the Wild Pentland Hills

A pleasingly gentle tour through the heart of this surprisingly severe little range of hills

1 From the car park, pass an information board on your left, turn left up the track, then immediately right along a footpath (Nine Mile Burn and Glencorse). After ¼ mile (400m), cross a stile and turn left into Bavelaw. Cross over a bridge and pass through the white gate to go uphill through an avenue of trees. Turn left at the junction, then follow drive to right. As the drive turns into private grounds of Bavelaw Castle, go straight ahead to a gate out onto moorland.

2 Go over the stile by the gate, then bear slightly left to follow marker posts across the open grassland until a path appears beside grassed old quarry scoops. Follow the path up into the hills, crossing two stiles. After the second stile, bear right and continue up to the head of the valley, then descend to the burn. Continuing downhill, keep to right of the burn until it meets a larger one by a waterfall.

3 Below the waterfall, cross the burn on stepping stones and follow right bank downstream. Cross a tributary and continue to The Howe.

4 Crossing a wooden bridge in front of the house, turn right down the lane, following the shore of Loganlea Reservoir and then Logan Burn down to Glencorse Reservoir. Continue along the lakeside for ½ mile (800m) until the shore is lined by pine trees.

5 Turn left through a gate, following a footpath signed to Balerno by Harlaw. After 300yds (275m) continue ahead, ignoring path to right. Continue up the valley, known as Maiden's Cleuch, to a stone stile near the summit of the pass.

6 Cross the stile and continue downhill across moorland. Further down the slopes, ignore a path to Currie and go straight ahead, crossing a stile and then along field paths to a T-junction. Turn right towards a belt of trees, then turn left, just before a gate, to a road. Follow the track to Warlaw House Rangers Centre (displays on local wildlife), passing through a gate to the cottage and ignoring sign to Balerno.

7 Beyond the cottage, follow the path to the right at the head of Harlaw Reservoir and, after crossing a dam, follow the track around to the left and along the shore. After ½ mile (800m), turn right along the side of a concrete spillway and follow the path as it swings left by Threipmuir Reservoir. Veering from the bank, the path turns right just before a hut. Pass through a gate and continue along a cinder track, which, after passing through another gate, continues to the car park.

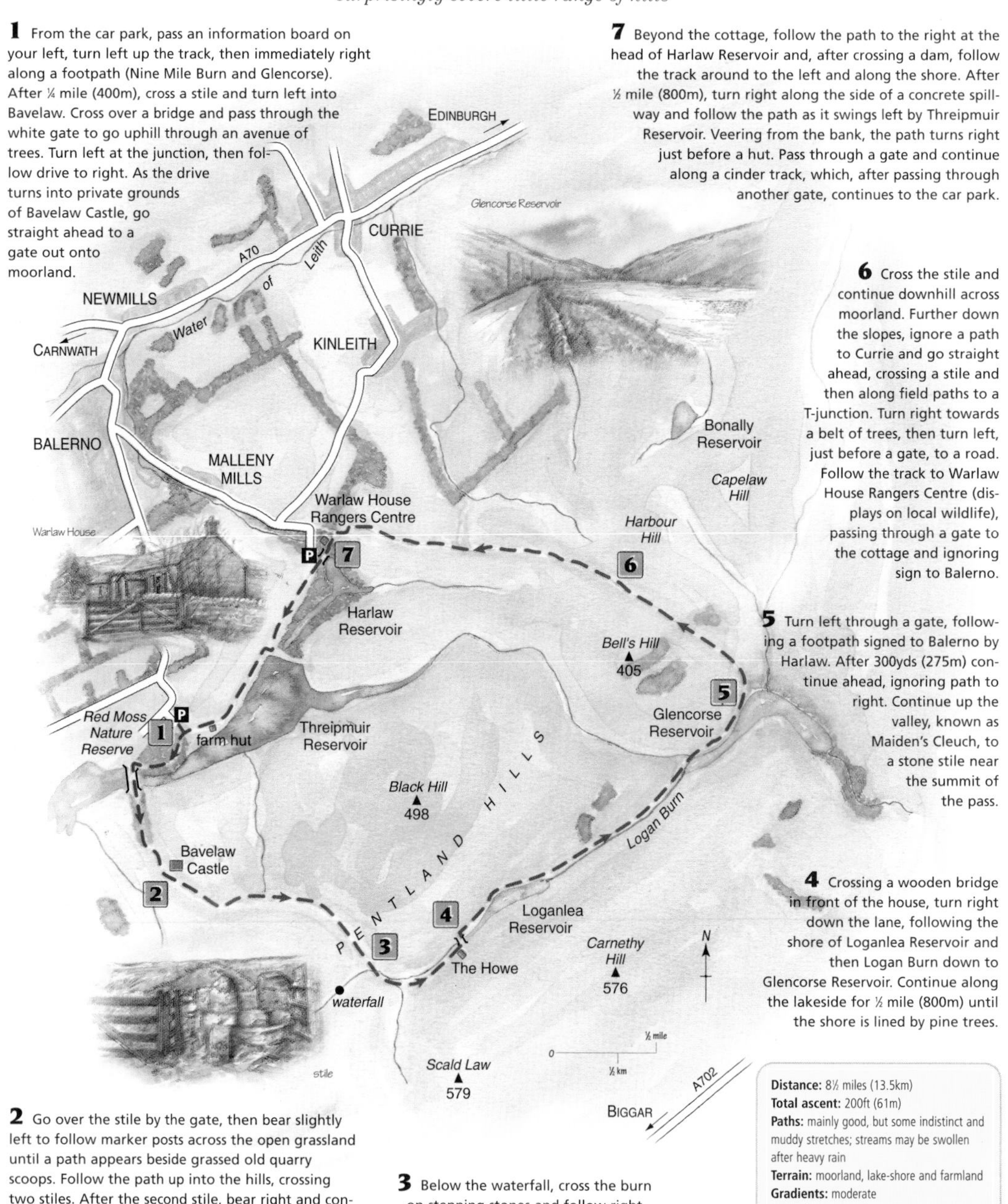

Distance: 8½ miles (13.5km)
Total ascent: 200ft (61m)
Paths: mainly good, but some indistinct and muddy stretches; streams may be swollen after heavy rain
Terrain: moorland, lake-shore and farmland
Gradients: moderate
Refreshments: pubs in Balerno
Park: Threipmuir car-park, on minor road south of A70 in Balerno

Magic Waters from Hart Fell

In the Southern Uplands with the magic of Merlin and the healing waters of the Hartfell Spa

Distance: 7 miles (11.2km)
Total ascent: 2,400ft (732m)
Paths: generally good but indistinct in places
Terrain: fields, riverbank and grassy mountain
Gradients: slight to moderate; one very steep section
Refreshments: Star Hotel, Moffat
Park: Annan Water Hall, near head of minor road north of A701 in Moffat

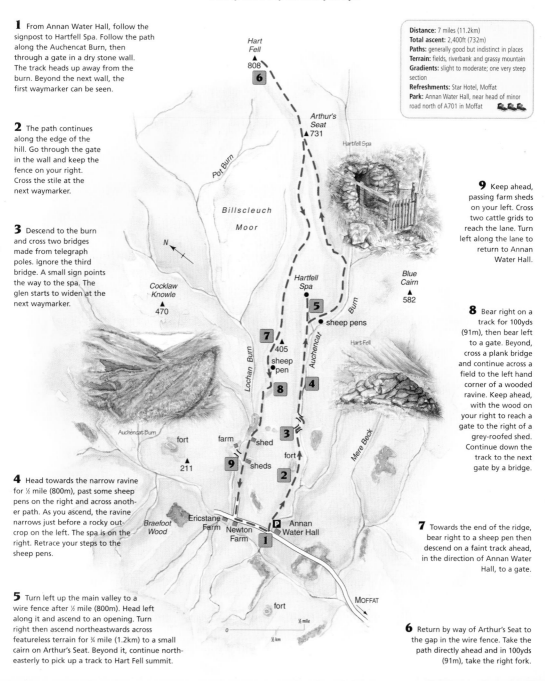

1 From Annan Water Hall, follow the signpost to Hartfell Spa. Follow the path along the Auchencat Burn, then through a gate in a dry stone wall. The track heads up away from the burn. Beyond the next wall, the first waymarker can be seen.

2 The path continues along the edge of the hill. Go through the gate in the wall and keep the fence on your right. Cross the stile at the next waymarker.

3 Descend to the burn and cross two bridges made from telegraph poles. Ignore the third bridge. A small sign points the way to the spa. The glen starts to widen at the next waymarker.

4 Head towards the narrow ravine for ½ mile (800m), past some sheep pens on the right and across another path. As you ascend, the ravine narrows just before a rocky outcrop on the left. The spa is on the right. Retrace your steps to the sheep pens.

5 Turn left up the main valley to a wire fence after ½ mile (800m). Head left along it and ascend to an opening. Turn right then ascend northeastwards across featureless terrain for ¾ mile (1.2km) to a small cairn on Arthur's Seat. Beyond it, continue north-easterly to pick up a track to Hart Fell summit.

6 Return by way of Arthur's Seat to the gap in the wire fence. Take the path directly ahead and in 100yds (91m), take the right fork.

7 Towards the end of the ridge, bear right to a sheep pen then descend on a faint track ahead, in the direction of Annan Water Hall, to a gate.

8 Bear right on a track for 100yds (91m), then bear left to a gate. Beyond, cross a plank bridge and continue across a field to the left hand corner of a wooded ravine. Keep ahead, with the wood on your right to reach a gate to the right of a grey-roofed shed. Continue down the track to the next gate by a bridge.

9 Keep ahead, passing farm sheds on your left. Cross two cattle grids to reach the lane. Turn left along the lane to return to Annan Water Hall.

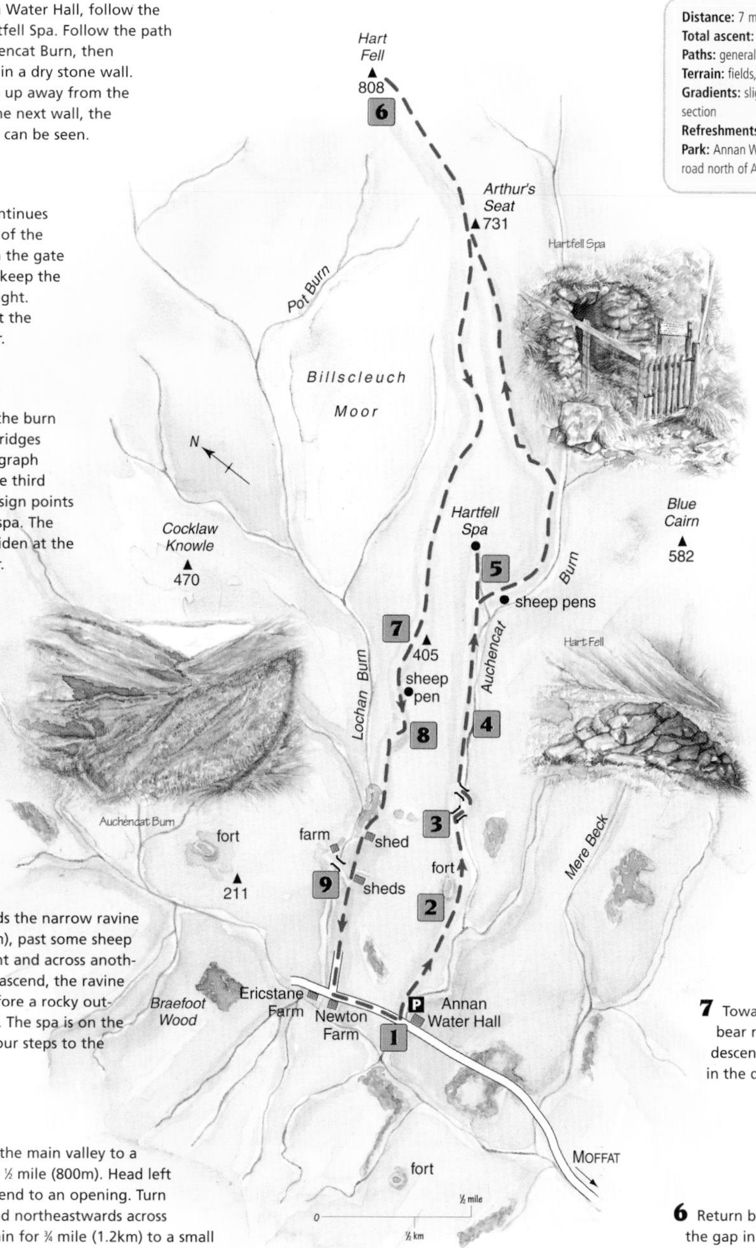

Caerlaverock and the Rich Solway Marshes

In the shadow of this unusual castle a nature reserve protects a rich marshland habitat

1 From the car park, turn back along the approach road for ½ mile (800m) then turn left, passing Scottish National Heritage's information point on your left.

2 In 300yds (275m), bear left by a house, along a hedged track to the edge of the Merse (saltmarsh). Turn right before the next fence and keep left for 150yds (136m) then turn right along a low bank for 1 mile (1.6km). Near the end, veer left to cross two wooden bridges and then a stile.

Distance: 6 miles (9.5km)
Total ascent: 310ft (95m)
Path: country roads, lanes and foreshore tracks; very muddy after rain
Terrain: flat estuary foreshore, saltmarsh, grassland
Gradients: one fairly gentle hill
Refreshments: tearoom at Caerlaverock Castle
Park: car park at the Wildfowl and Wetlands Trust's East Park Centre at Caerlaverock, signposted off the B725 nine miles (14.5km) south of Dumfries.
Note: entrance fees are charged for entry to the Wildfowl and Wetland Trust facilities and Caerlaverock Castle

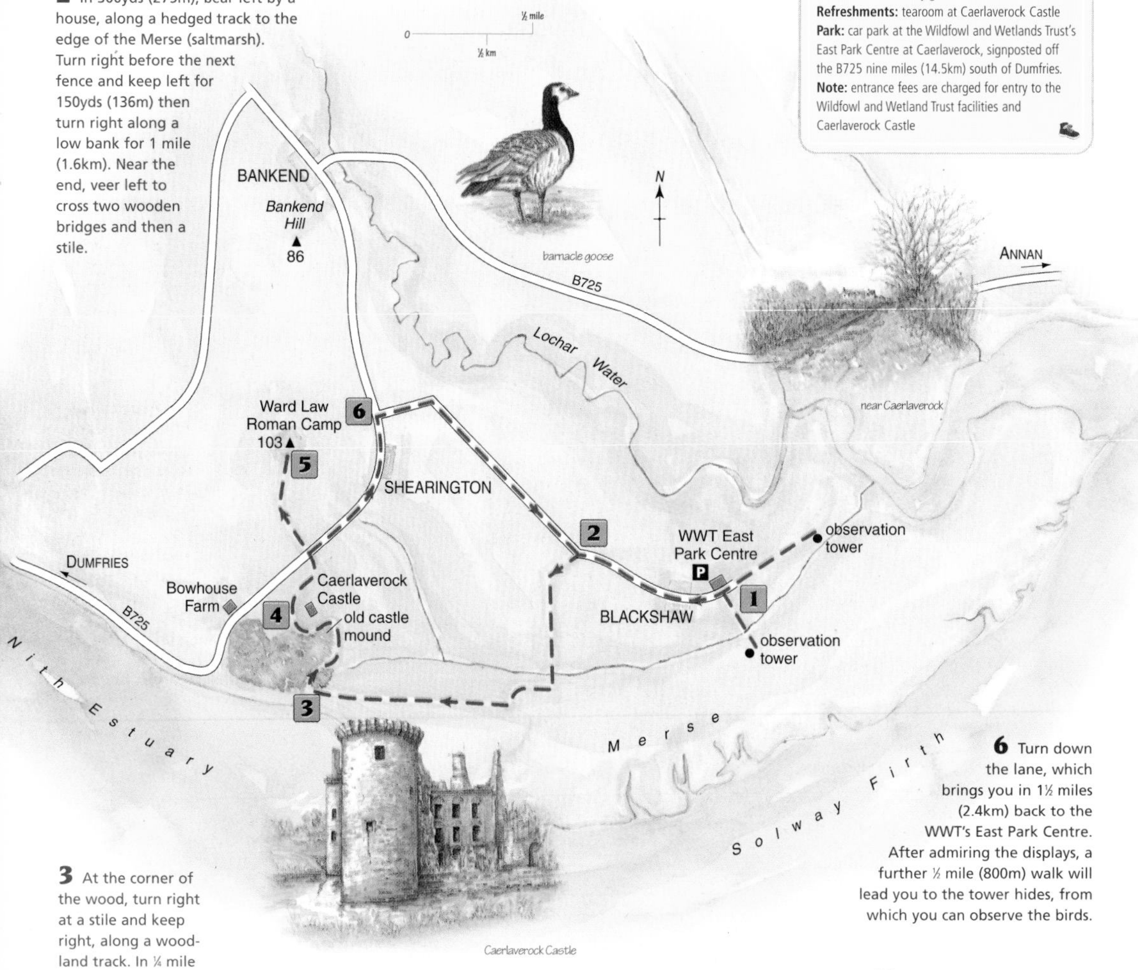

0 ½ mile ½ km
BANKEND
Bankend Hill 86
N
barnacle goose
B725
ANNAN
Lochar Water
near Caerlaverock
Ward Law Roman Camp 103
SHEARINGTON
WWT East Park Centre
observation tower
DUMFRIES
Bowhouse Farm
Caerlaverock Castle
old castle mound
BLACKSHAW
observation tower
Nith Estuary
Merse
Solway Firth

Caerlaverock Castle

3 At the corner of the wood, turn right at a stile and keep right, along a woodland track. In ¼ mile (400m), cross a footbridge and continue past some cottages to reach the old castle mound. Bear left here and follow the track to pass Caerlaverock Castle.

4 Continue up the castle drive, under the arch to cross B725, and take the track opposite. This climbs gently, and after passing through the gate, follow the field boundary, swing to the right and ascend a little more steeply to the ramparts of the roman camp on Ward Law Hill.

5 After taking in the splendid view of hills, forestry, green grazing lands and estuary marsh and water, return to B725. Turn left for ⅔ mile (1km) to reach a lane on the right with a Wildfowl and Wetlands Trust sign.

6 Turn down the lane, which brings you in 1½ miles (2.4km) back to the WWT's East Park Centre. After admiring the displays, a further ½ mile (800m) walk will lead you to the tower hides, from which you can observe the birds.

Four Kingdoms from Criffel

England, Ireland, Scotland and the Isle of Man are all visible from this looming moorland eminence above the Solway Firth

Distance: 9 miles (14.5km)
Total ascent: 1,867ft (569m)
Paths: mostly good; very boggy in winter and in wet weather
Terrain: road, fields, woodland, heather moorland and farm tracks
Gradients: very steep up Criffel
Refreshments: Abbey Tea Room at car park.
Park: Sweetheart Abbey car park off A710 in New Abbey

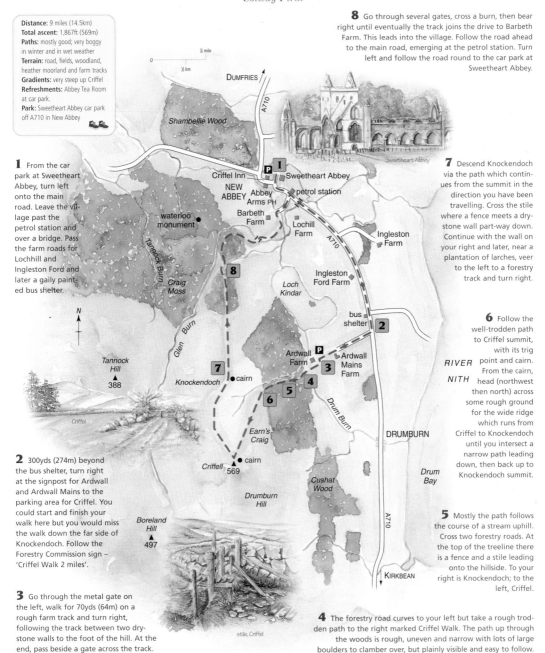

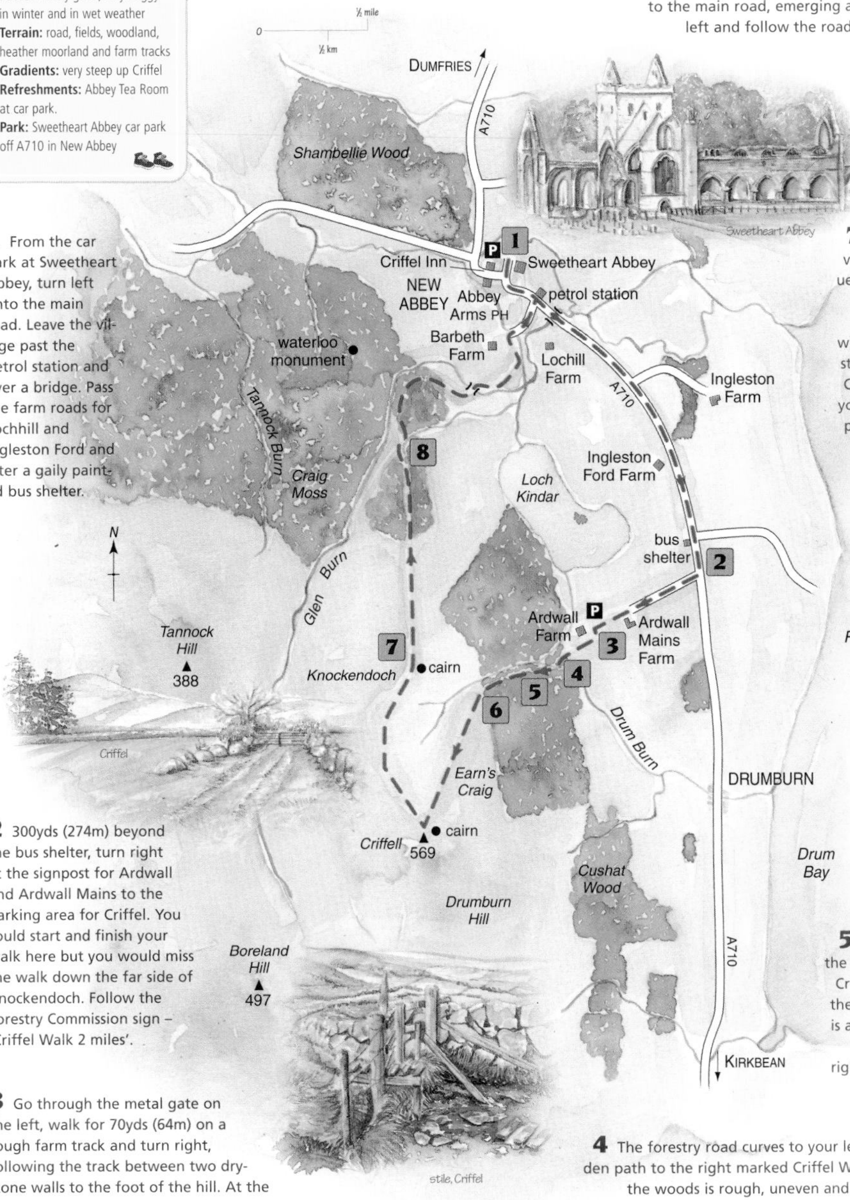

1 From the car park at Sweetheart Abbey, turn left onto the main road. Leave the village past the petrol station and over a bridge. Pass the farm roads for Lochhill and Ingleston Ford and later a gaily painted bus shelter.

2 300yds (274m) beyond the bus shelter, turn right at the signpost for Ardwall and Ardwall Mains to the parking area for Criffel. You could start and finish your walk here but you would miss the walk down the far side of Knockendoch. Follow the Forestry Commission sign – 'Criffel Walk 2 miles'.

3 Go through the metal gate on the left, walk for 70yds (64m) on a rough farm track and turn right, following the track between two dry-stone walls to the foot of the hill. At the end, pass beside a gate across the track.

4 The forestry road curves to your left but take a rough trodden path to the right marked Criffel Walk. The path up through the woods is rough, uneven and narrow with lots of large boulders to clamber over, but plainly visible and easy to follow.

5 Mostly the path follows the course of a stream uphill. Cross two forestry roads. At the top of the treeline there is a fence and a stile leading onto the hillside. To your right is Knockendoch; to the left, Criffel.

6 Follow the well-trodden path to Criffel summit, with its trig point and cairn. From the cairn, head (northwest then north) across some rough ground for the wide ridge which runs from Criffel to Knockendoch until you intersect a narrow path leading down, then back up to Knockendoch summit.

7 Descend Knockendoch via the path which continues from the summit in the direction you have been travelling. Cross the stile where a fence meets a dry-stone wall part-way down. Continue with the wall on your right and later, near a plantation of larches, veer to the left to a forestry track and turn right.

8 Go through several gates, cross a burn, then bear right until eventually the track joins the drive to Barbeth Farm. This leads into the village. Follow the road ahead to the main road, emerging at the petrol station. Turn left and follow the road round to the car park at Sweetheart Abbey.

Following St Ninian on the Isle of Whithorn

A coastal walk where St Ninian's early church thrived

1 At the harbour, beyond The Steampacket Inn, follow the signpost for St Ninian's Chapel. Follow the track through the children's play area and head for a cairn marking the end of the Pilgrims Way. Look for the chapel to your left.

2 Follow the path to a large, square, white tower which looks across the Solway to Cumbria. Then enter the chapel grounds via a kissing gate beside a cairn, raised in 1997 to celebrate the foundation of Ninian's church 1600 years earlier.

3 Retrace your steps, walking round the harbour past the tumbledown red village store, the parish church and the post office. At the Queen's Arms Hotel, turn left into Tonderghie Row, following the sign for Burrow Head Holiday Park past Cutcloy Farm.

4 ¼ mile (400m) beyond Cutcloy, keep left towards caravan park. At the flag poles, take the gate to your right, then keep directly ahead towards the sea. At the coast turn left through a kissing-gate by a coastal path sign pointing in the opposite direction.

5 Follow the path as it meanders around the coastline. A fence at the end of the holiday village is crossed via a gate. Follow the path over a rickety bridge, up the hill and along the coast to the left. Where a wall intersects the fence, cross a stile to the seaward side.

6 The path is easy to follow along the coast, although it may be overgrown at points. Keep close to the barbed-wire fence or cross it temporarily until the obstruction is passed.

7 Nearing a farm, where the path has fallen away, cross the fence into a field. Follow the track in the field through a gate between two dry-stone walls. Follow the right-hand wall along to another gate then turn left alongside the far wall and over a gate onto the farm road at Morrach and turn right onto a track.

8 Follow the road past Orfasey Cottage and on until it terminates at a T-junction beside an old barn. Turn right and, at the next junction, turn right again, following the road back round the harbour to your starting point.

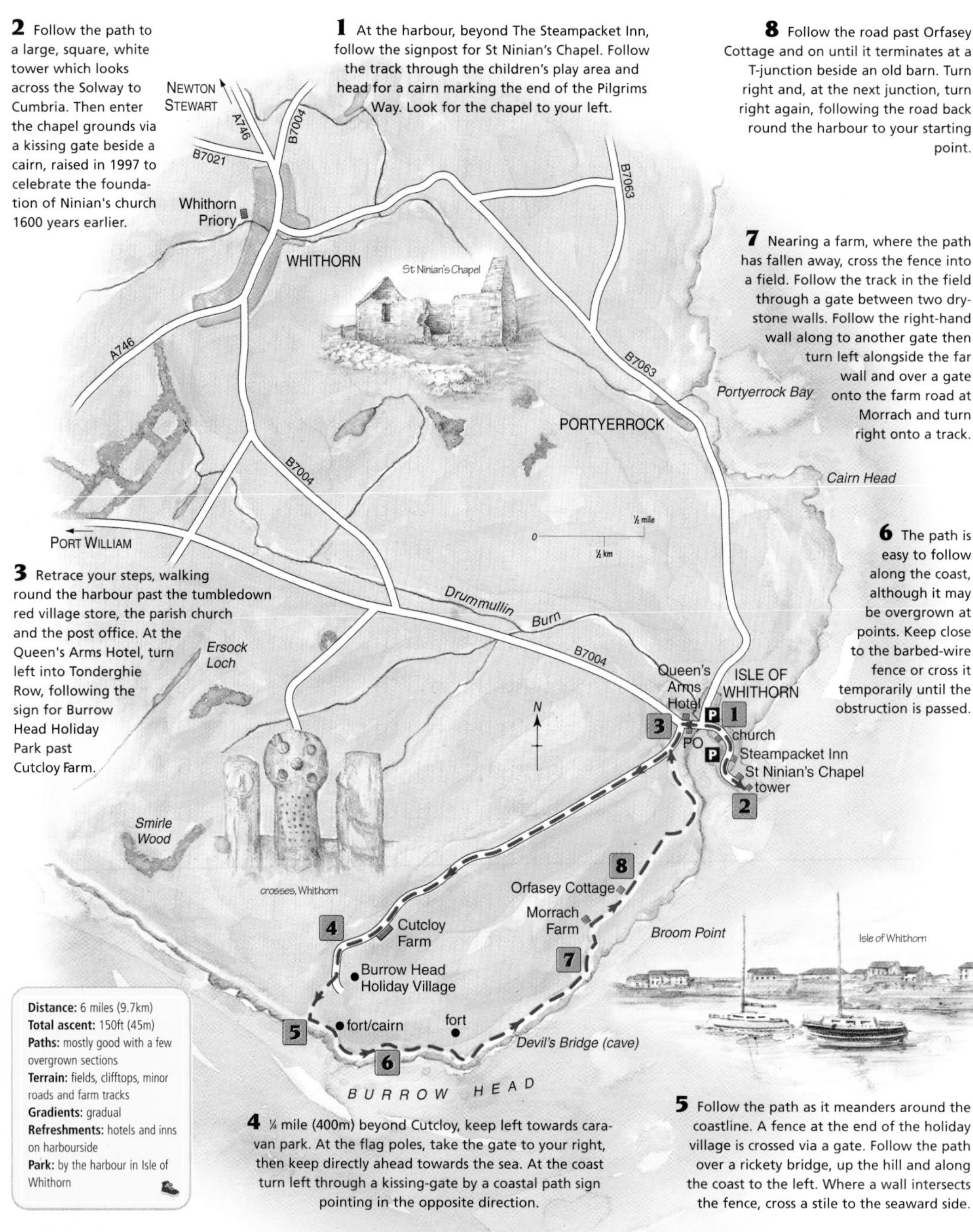

Distance: 6 miles (9.7km)
Total ascent: 150ft (45m)
Paths: mostly good with a few overgrown sections
Terrain: fields, clifftops, minor roads and farm tracks
Gradients: gradual
Refreshments: hotels and inns on harbourside
Park: by the harbour in Isle of Whithorn

Burns' Alloway and the Brig o' Doon

A landscape much changed, yet still recognisable as the one-time home of Scotland's national poet

Distance: 7 miles (11.3km)
Total ascent: negligible
Paths: good; can be muddy
Terrain: old railway, fields, beach, golf course and woodland
Gradients: some steps
Refreshments: visitor centre at car park
Park: Tam O'Shanter Experience car park, Alloway, near Ayr

1 From Tam O'Shanter Experience, walk to end of car park, furthest from entry road. Go right down path into Burns Monument Gardens. Follow path anti-clockwise around monument then towards Auld Brig (Brig o'Doon) ahead. Visit Statues House, then continue to top of steps down to right. Descend to road, turn right and cross over. Just short of large white hotel, go down steps on left into Riverside Gardens.

2 Walk around gardens by river towards Auld Brig. Leave by steps back up to road, turn right and cross Auld Brig. Continue up path, under old railway bridge to top, swinging right on to main road.

3 Turn right and follow main road back over river. Just over newer bridge, cross over and turn left, up steps, into Auld Alloway Kirkyard (opposite parish church) to Burns' parents' graves.

4 Leaving kirkyard by steps, turn left and go along the road until level with Tam O'Shanter Experience. Cross right into Murdoch's Lone and go left immediately beyond a low white pumping station, steeply down to old railway line. Turn left through two tunnels and beyond.

5 Eventually, emerge on main road at Burton Farm road end. Turn right and follow road over old railway, then turn left on other side into lane, turning back on itself before swinging right towards sea. Continue past estate house on left to cottages at end of track.

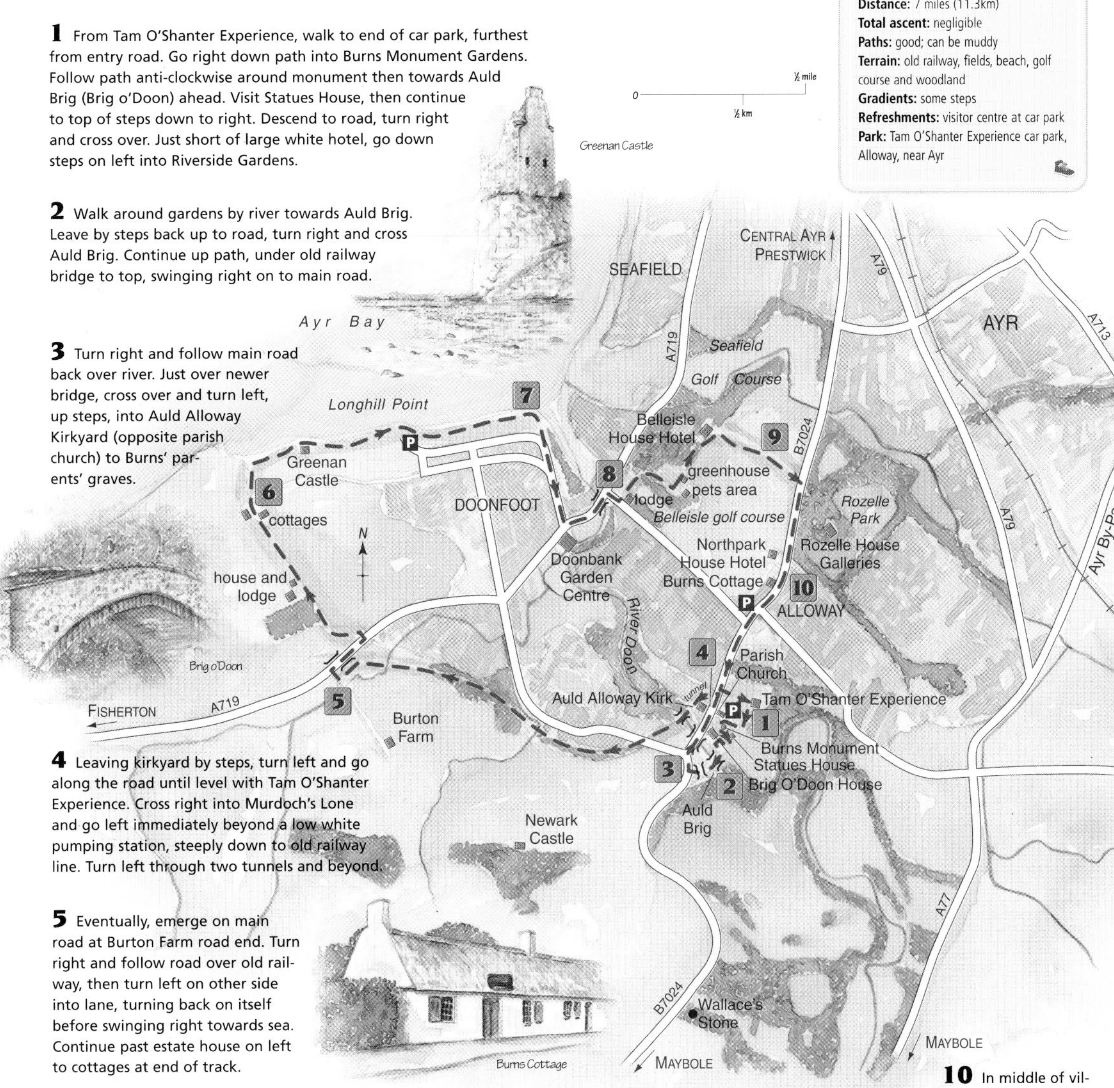

6 Go between cottages and leave lane as it swings right, going through gate and down field, through gate to beach. Turn right along beach past Greenan Castle and car park to river mouth.

7 Turn right up road with river to left, to T-junction, opposite garden centre. Turn left over river bridge and cross road, turning right into Greenfield Avenue.

8 As Greenfield Avenue curves, go left through gates by lodge into Belleisle Park. Continue with golf course on right, through trees and then curve off right to pets area. Just before this, turn left into walled garden and carry on into second garden with large greenhouse. Leave by path from far left corner, up to rear of Belleisle House Hotel. Pass in front of golf shop and in 150yds (136m) turn right across golf course, following signs to Practice Area.

9 At path's end, go through green gates to main road and turn right. Follow past Rozelle Park on left and Northpark House Hotel on right, until road curves right into Alloway.

10 In middle of village, pass Burns Cottage on right and continue on main road (B7024) past cricket ground to return to Tam O'Shanter Experience on left.

Glasgow's Not-so-mean Streets

Architectural wealth softens the edges of Scotland's biggest city

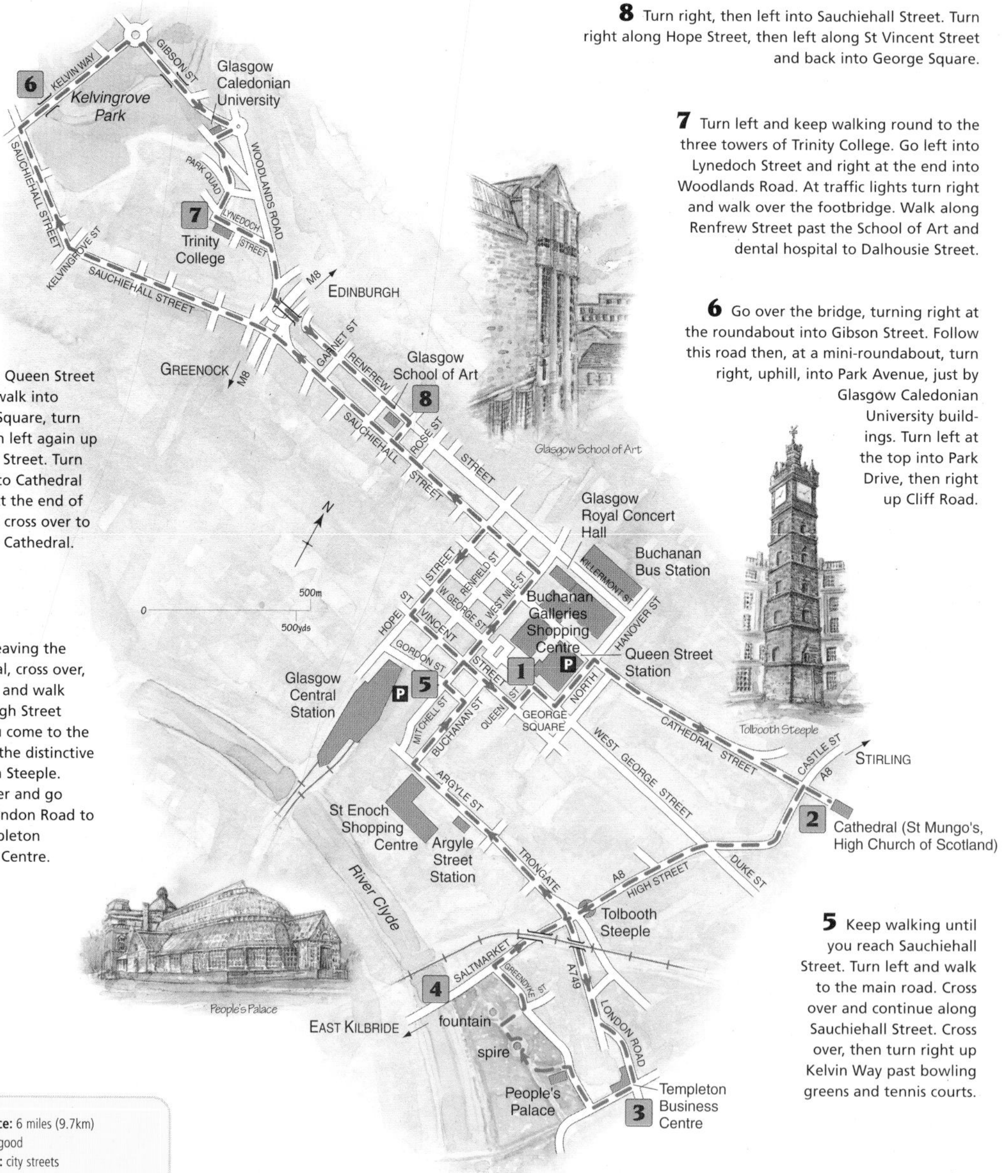

1 From Queen Street Station walk into George Square, turn left, then left again up Hanover Street. Turn right onto Cathedral Street. At the end of the road cross over to Glasgow Cathedral.

2 On leaving the Cathedral, cross over, turn left and walk down High Street until you come to the clock of the distinctive Tolbooth Steeple. Cross over and go along London Road to the Templeton Business Centre.

3 Walk right round the building, turning right and up the path on the other side. Just past the People's Palace, take the track on the left across Glasgow Green. Pass the spire, go right onto Greendyke Street then left to Saltmarket.

4 Turn right, then go left at the Tolbooth Steeple to walk along Trongate, into Argyle Street, then go right into Buchanan Street. Walk up until you reach Gordon Street. A short way along turn right into West Nile Street.

5 Keep walking until you reach Sauchiehall Street. Turn left and walk to the main road. Cross over and continue along Sauchiehall Street. Cross over, then turn right up Kelvin Way past bowling greens and tennis courts.

6 Go over the bridge, turning right at the roundabout into Gibson Street. Follow this road then, at a mini-roundabout, turn right, uphill, into Park Avenue, just by Glasgow Caledonian University buildings. Turn left at the top into Park Drive, then right up Cliff Road.

7 Turn left and keep walking round to the three towers of Trinity College. Go left into Lynedoch Street and right at the end into Woodlands Road. At traffic lights turn right and walk over the footbridge. Walk along Renfrew Street past the School of Art and dental hospital to Dalhousie Street.

8 Turn right, then left into Sauchiehall Street. Turn right along Hope Street, then left along St Vincent Street and back into George Square.

Glasgow School of Art

Tolbooth Steeple

People's Palace

Distance: 6 miles (9.7km)
Paths: good
Terrain: city streets
Gradients: some short steep sections
Refreshments: plenty in city centre
Park: Buchanan Galleries multi-storey, Cathedral Street, behind Queen Street Station

Kilmartin Glen, Valley of Ghosts

Exploring the glen which may well prove to be the cradle of civilisation in the Highlands

Distance: 9 miles (14.5km)
Total ascent: 200ft (61m)
Paths: mostly tracks and forest roads
Terrain: fields and forest
Gradients: moderate
Refreshments: Kilmartin House vistor centre; Kilmartin Hotel
Park: Lady Glassary Wood car park, on junction of A816 and B8025, 1 mile (1.6km) south of Kilmartin

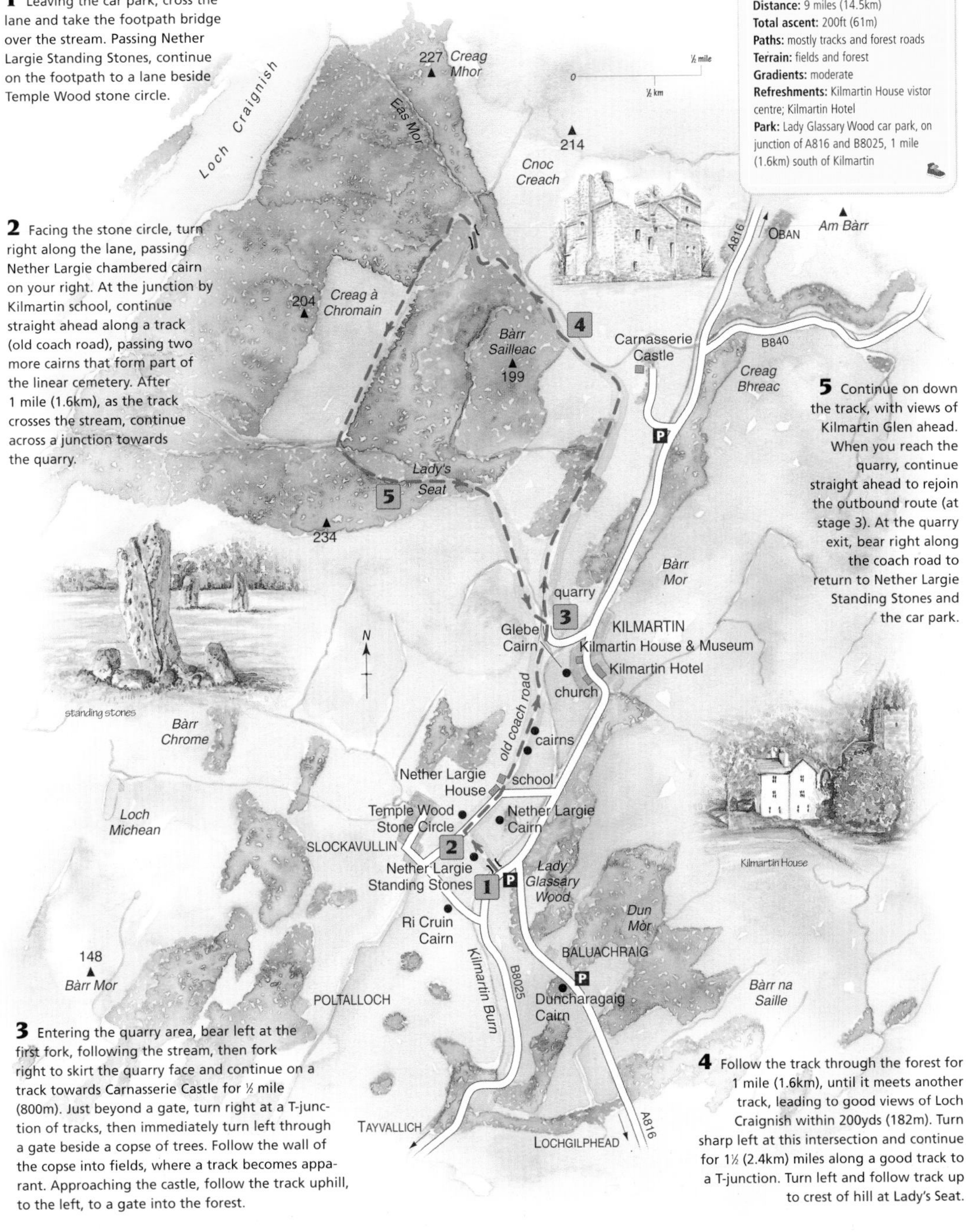

1 Leaving the car park, cross the lane and take the footpath bridge over the stream. Passing Nether Largie Standing Stones, continue on the footpath to a lane beside Temple Wood stone circle.

2 Facing the stone circle, turn right along the lane, passing Nether Largie chambered cairn on your right. At the junction by Kilmartin school, continue straight ahead along a track (old coach road), passing two more cairns that form part of the linear cemetery. After 1 mile (1.6km), as the track crosses the stream, continue across a junction towards the quarry.

3 Entering the quarry area, bear left at the first fork, following the stream, then fork right to skirt the quarry face and continue on a track towards Carnasserie Castle for ½ mile (800m). Just beyond a gate, turn right at a T-junction of tracks, then immediately turn left through a gate beside a copse of trees. Follow the wall of the copse into fields, where a track becomes apparant. Approaching the castle, follow the track uphill, to the left, to a gate into the forest.

4 Follow the track through the forest for 1 mile (1.6km), until it meets another track, leading to good views of Loch Craignish within 200yds (182m). Turn sharp left at this intersection and continue for 1½ (2.4km) miles along a good track to a T-junction. Turn left and follow track up to crest of hill at Lady's Seat.

5 Continue on down the track, with views of Kilmartin Glen ahead. When you reach the quarry, continue straight ahead to rejoin the outbound route (at stage 3). At the quarry exit, bear right along the coach road to return to Nether Largie Standing Stones and the car park.

Rob Roy and Balquhidder

Legend and reality merge in the tales of a Highland hero on the braes of these lovely mountains

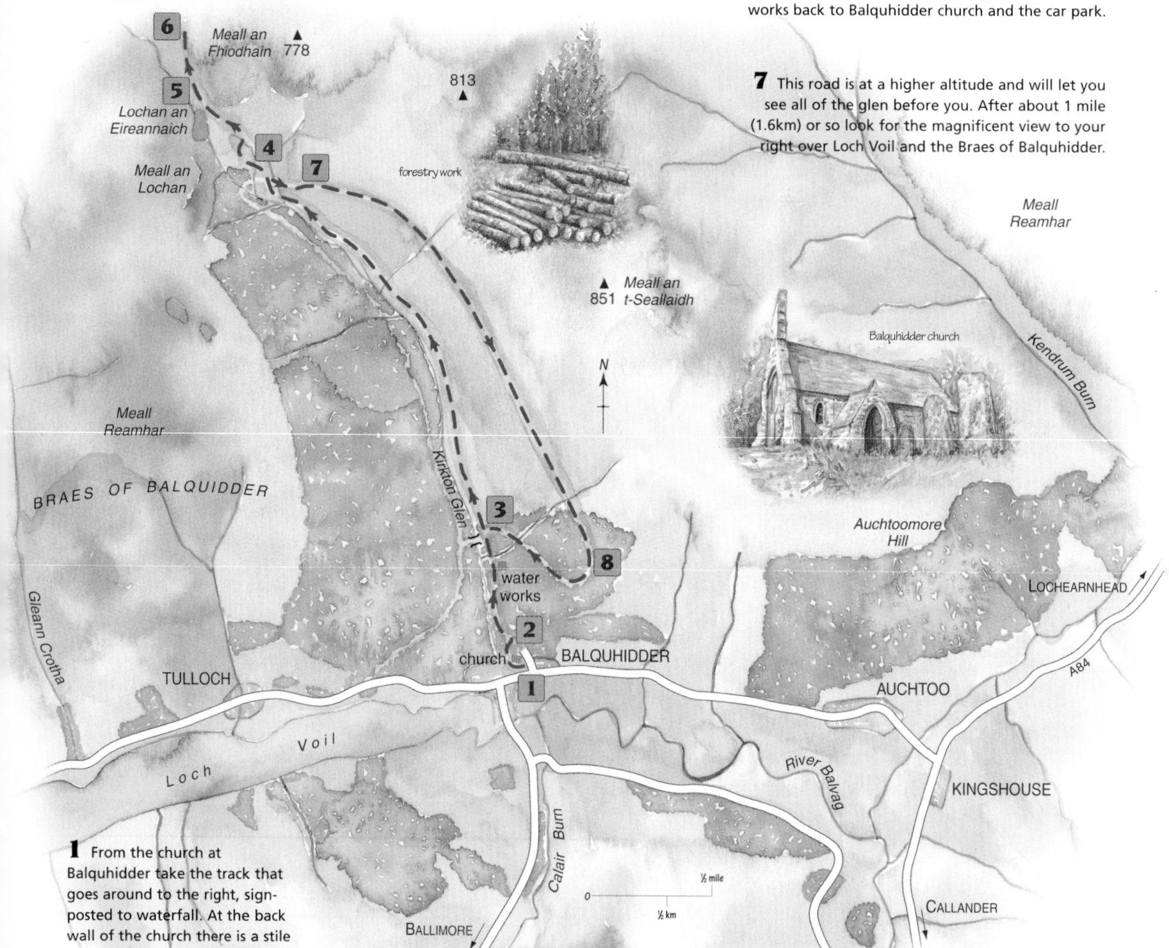

Distance: 7 miles (11km)
Total ascent: 1,750ft (533m)
Paths: good but boggy on hillside
Terrain: mostly forestry roads; some hillside
Gradients: moderate to steep
Refreshments: Kingshouse Hotel
Park: Balquhidder church, Balquhidder, off A84 between Callander and Lochearnhead

1 From the church at Balquhidder take the track that goes around to the right, signposted to waterfall. At the back wall of the church there is a stile over a fence and a Forest Enterprise sign for Kirkton Glen.

2 Follow the path uphill, through the woods and past the water works, keeping the burn on your left. A newly made logging road crosses the burn from the left. Continue uphill with burn on the left. There has been a lot of felling work here and it is now possible to see the shape of the Glen.

3 The road follows the line of the burn. It forks after 1½ miles (2.4km) and to your right there is a sign for Glen Dochart Pass. Follow a narrow but well-trodden path going uphill to the left of the sign.

4 Follow the path, crossing the burn at a fence then over the fence at a stile further up, and head for a range of crags as the path becomes indistinct. Follow it as it turns right then curve up to the left through the crags to the Lochan an Eireannaich.

5 From here cut across the shoulder of Meall an Fhiodhain, the hill on your right, keeping to the high ground and going through a ruined fence. Your reward is the spectacular view along the course of the Ledcharrie Burn to Glen Dochart.

6 Retrace your steps down the hill to rejoin the forestry road. Here you have the choice of three directions. Take the turning to the left and head off down the glen.

7 This road is at a higher altitude and will let you see all of the glen before you. After about 1 mile (1.6km) or so look for the magnificent view to your right over Loch Voil and the Braes of Balquhidder.

8 Eventually this road turns back on itself and goes downhill to join the road beside the burn. Turn left, continuing past the bridge on your right and the water works back to Balquhidder church and the car park.

The Lost Valley of Glen Coe

Hidden in the mountainous walls of this famous Highland glen, a hanging valley once sheltered the Macdonald's cattle from raiders

1 Start on the path leading down from the car park, to join the main path through the Pass of Glencoe. Walk down east, then turn south to cross the footbridge over the River Coe, located just downstream of the Meeting of Three Waters. Climb the opposite bank, go through the birch scrub and up over a ladder stile at fencing.

Distance: 3½ miles (5.2km)
Total ascent: 855ft (261m)
Paths: rough but clearly defined on ascent; less obvious on the short circuit around the Lost Valley
Terrain: confined, steep-sided gorge through woodland giving way to more open mountainous aspect at the top
Gradients: short but steep over rocks although no serious difficulties
Refreshments: Clachaig Inn, 3 miles (4.8km) west of car park
Park: westernmost car park in the Pass of Glencoe on A82 between Tyndrum and Ballachulish

2 After a further 100yds (91m) or so, leave the main path and climb a zigzagging path rising steeply off to the right. This leads up to the higher path, the one above the tree-fringed gorge of the Allt Coire Gabhail. Having enjoyed a gentle stroll for a while, and just before a large boulder, descend through the trees to make the crossing of the river. Take care traversing a few awkward rocks and roots on the way down.

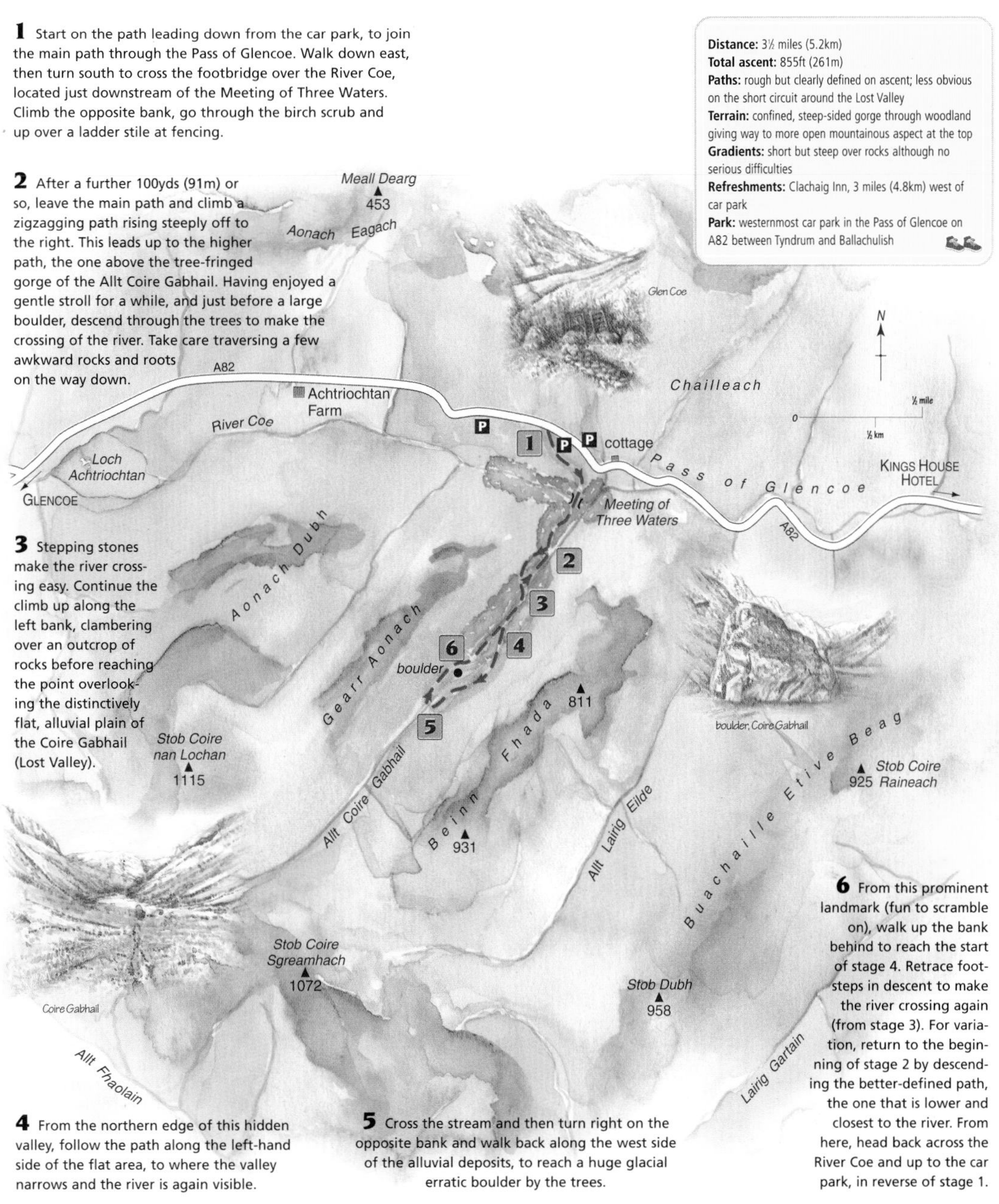

3 Stepping stones make the river crossing easy. Continue the climb up along the left bank, clambering over an outcrop of rocks before reaching the point overlooking the distinctively flat, alluvial plain of the Coire Gabhail (Lost Valley).

4 From the northern edge of this hidden valley, follow the path along the left-hand side of the flat area, to where the valley narrows and the river is again visible.

5 Cross the stream and then turn right on the opposite bank and walk back along the west side of the alluvial deposits, to reach a huge glacial erratic boulder by the trees.

6 From this prominent landmark (fun to scramble on), walk up the bank behind to reach the start of stage 4. Retrace footsteps in descent to make the river crossing again (from stage 3). For variation, return to the beginning of stage 2 by descending the better-defined path, the one that is lower and closest to the river. From here, head back across the River Coe and up to the car park, in reverse of stage 1.

Remote Moidart's Citadel

By the peaceful lochside at Castle Tioram, once home to a Clan Ranald chieftain

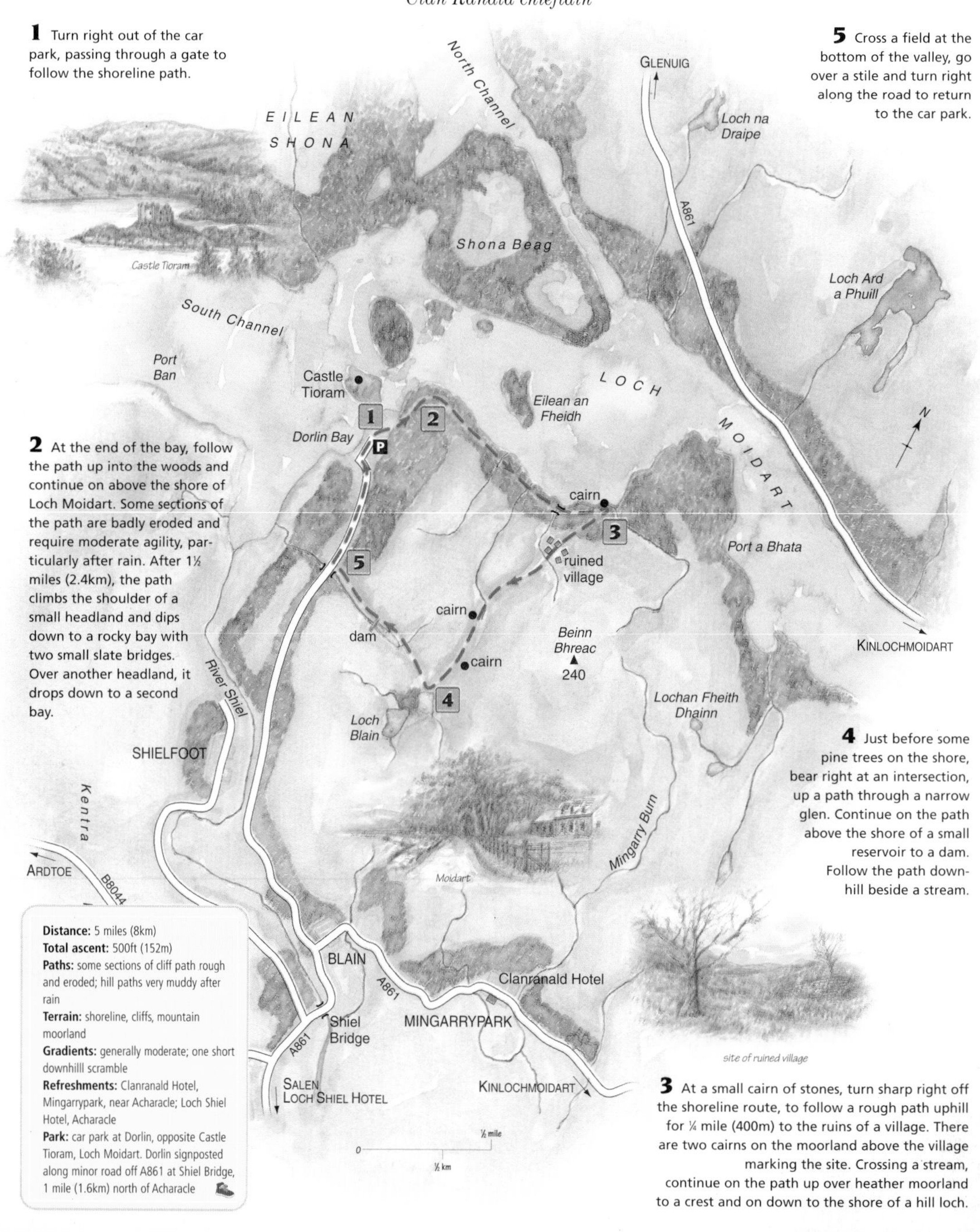

site of ruined village

1 Turn right out of the car park, passing through a gate to follow the shoreline path.

2 At the end of the bay, follow the path up into the woods and continue on above the shore of Loch Moidart. Some sections of the path are badly eroded and require moderate agility, particularly after rain. After 1½ miles (2.4km), the path climbs the shoulder of a small headland and dips down to a rocky bay with two small slate bridges. Over another headland, it drops down to a second bay.

3 At a small cairn of stones, turn sharp right off the shoreline route, to follow a rough path uphill for ¼ mile (400m) to the ruins of a village. There are two cairns on the moorland above the village marking the site. Crossing a stream, continue on the path up over heather moorland to a crest and on down to the shore of a hill loch.

4 Just before some pine trees on the shore, bear right at an intersection, up a path through a narrow glen. Continue on the path above the shore of a small reservoir to a dam. Follow the path downhill beside a stream.

5 Cross a field at the bottom of the valley, go over a stile and turn right along the road to return to the car park.

Distance: 5 miles (8km)
Total ascent: 500ft (152m)
Paths: some sections of cliff path rough and eroded; hill paths very muddy after rain
Terrain: shoreline, cliffs, mountain moorland
Gradients: generally moderate; one short downhilll scramble
Refreshments: Clanranald Hotel, Mingarrypark, near Acharacle; Loch Shiel Hotel, Acharacle
Park: car park at Dorlin, opposite Castle Tioram, Loch Moidart. Dorlin signposted along minor road off A861 at Shiel Bridge, 1 mile (1.6km) north of Acharacle

In the Executioner's Shadow, Deep in the Cuillins

Am Bàsteir means 'the Executioner' in Gaelic, but this is a relatively gentle walk beneath its awesome profile

1 From the Sligachan Hotel, walk along the A863 for about 200yds (182m). Take one of the paths on the left, opposite the top of a slip road to the hotel. Most lead across boggy ground to cross the Allt Dearg Mor at the footbridge. Walk south on the gently rising footpath towards Sgurr nan Gillean, the easternmost peak of the mountains seen clearly on the skyline ahead.

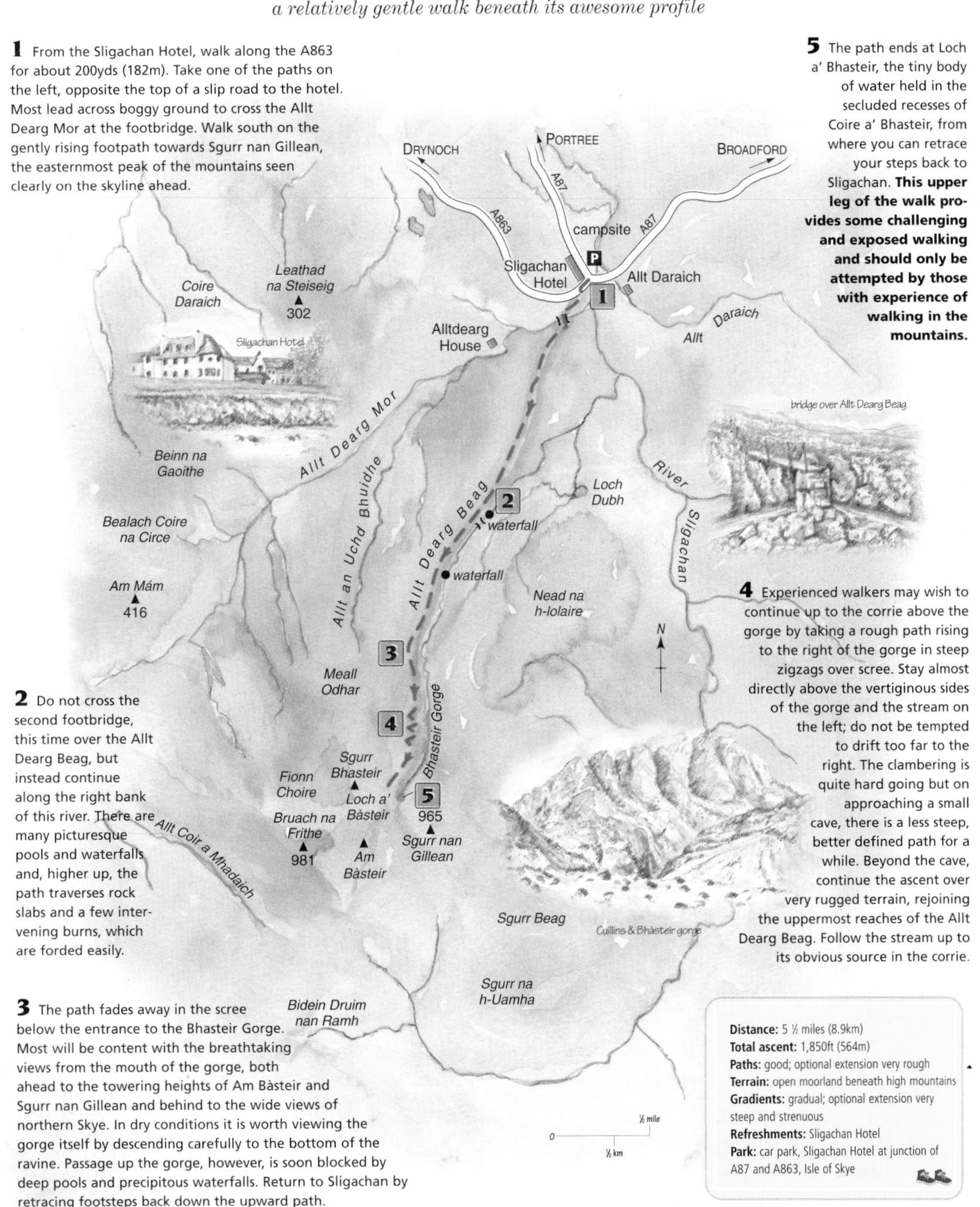

2 Do not cross the second footbridge, this time over the Allt Dearg Beag, but instead continue along the right bank of this river. There are many picturesque pools and waterfalls and, higher up, the path traverses rock slabs and a few intervening burns, which are forded easily.

3 The path fades away in the scree below the entrance to the Bhasteir Gorge. Most will be content with the breathtaking views from the mouth of the gorge, both ahead to the towering heights of Am Bàsteir and Sgurr nan Gillean and behind to the wide views of northern Skye. In dry conditions it is worth viewing the gorge itself by descending carefully to the bottom of the ravine. Passage up the gorge, however, is soon blocked by deep pools and precipitous waterfalls. Return to Sligachan by retracing footsteps back down the upward path.

4 Experienced walkers may wish to continue up to the corrie above the gorge by taking a rough path rising to the right of the gorge in steep zigzags over scree. Stay almost directly above the vertiginous sides of the gorge and the stream on the left; do not be tempted to drift too far to the right. The clambering is quite hard going but on approaching a small cave, there is a less steep, better defined path for a while. Beyond the cave, continue the ascent over very rugged terrain, rejoining the uppermost reaches of the Allt Dearg Beag. Follow the stream up to its obvious source in the corrie.

5 The path ends at Loch a' Bhasteir, the tiny body of water held in the secluded recesses of Coire a' Bhasteir, from where you can retrace your steps back to Sligachan. **This upper leg of the walk provides some challenging and exposed walking and should only be attempted by those with experience of walking in the mountains.**

Distance: 5 ½ miles (8.9km)
Total ascent: 1,850ft (564m)
Paths: good; optional extension very rough
Terrain: open moorland beneath high mountains
Gradients: gradual; optional extension very steep and strenuous
Refreshments: Sligachan Hotel
Park: car park, Sligachan Hotel at junction of A87 and A863, Isle of Skye

Ullapool and the Drove Roads

Following the tracks of drovers bringing cattle across from the isles

1 From the car park next to Safeway supermarket, exit to Latheron Lane and turn left into Quay Street. At the Riverside Hotel, where the road curves right, turn left into Castle Terrace. Go down the steps to the river on the right and cross a bridge.

2 At the far side, turn right and follow the path along the side of the river. Continue by the riverside to a wooden bridge and up some steps. Turn right at a cattle grid to the main road.

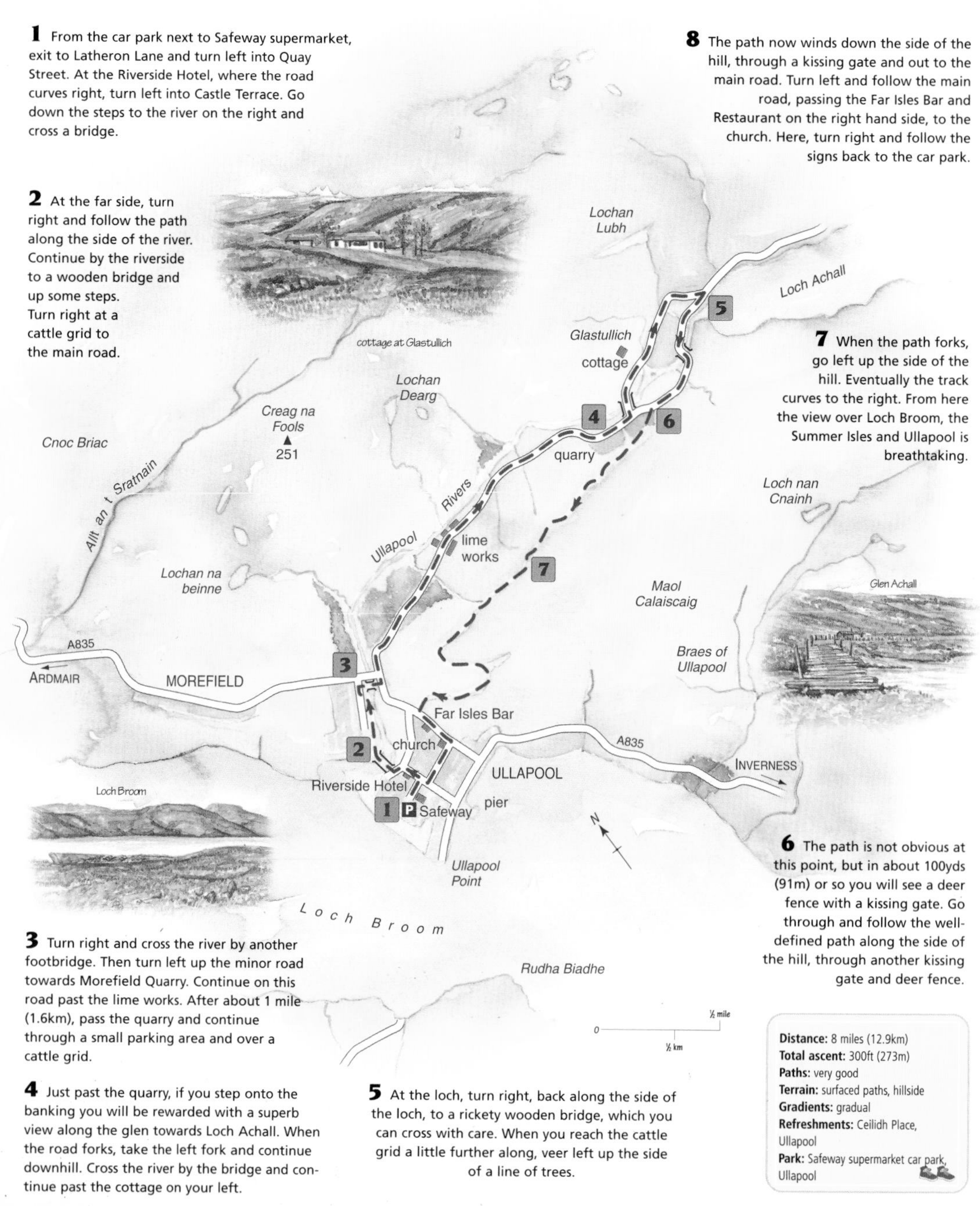

3 Turn right and cross the river by another footbridge. Then turn left up the minor road towards Morefield Quarry. Continue on this road past the lime works. After about 1 mile (1.6km), pass the quarry and continue through a small parking area and over a cattle grid.

4 Just past the quarry, if you step onto the banking you will be rewarded with a superb view along the glen towards Loch Achall. When the road forks, take the left fork and continue downhill. Cross the river by the bridge and continue past the cottage on your left.

5 At the loch, turn right, back along the side of the loch, to a rickety wooden bridge, which you can cross with care. When you reach the cattle grid a little further along, veer left up the side of a line of trees.

6 The path is not obvious at this point, but in about 100yds (91m) or so you will see a deer fence with a kissing gate. Go through and follow the well-defined path along the side of the hill, through another kissing gate and deer fence.

7 When the path forks, go left up the side of the hill. Eventually the track curves to the right. From here the view over Loch Broom, the Summer Isles and Ullapool is breathtaking.

8 The path now winds down the side of the hill, through a kissing gate and out to the main road. Turn left and follow the main road, passing the Far Isles Bar and Restaurant on the right hand side, to the church. Here, turn right and follow the signs back to the car park.

Distance: 8 miles (12.9km)
Total ascent: 300ft (273m)
Paths: very good
Terrain: surfaced paths, hillside
Gradients: gradual
Refreshments: Ceilidh Place, Ullapool
Park: Safeway supermarket car park, Ullapool

The Flow Country

A unique landscape of extensive peatlands is glimpsed from its northern edge

1 From the lay-by to the southeast of Melvich, cross the road and head up a farm track to the left of a small loch. The track goes through a gate and curves to the left behind a derelict cottage. You will encounter two gates across the track close together.

2 Midway between the two gates, take the rough peat-cutters track that goes uphill on your left. Continue to follow this track, keeping left when it forks, until it disappears. Then continue in this direction heading for the highest point, where you will see Loch Sgiathanach slightly to your left.

3 Head for the left-hand edge of the loch and follow the course of the Allt a Ghlasraich burn, which flows from here to Achridigill Loch.

4 Where the burn meets the loch, turn 90 degrees to the right. You should be heading to the mid-point between two small hills. Loch Baligill lies at the foot of the hills. Follow the shore-line along the right-hand side of the loch.

5 At the end of the loch, turn right and, keeping the hills on your left, head for the highest point in front of you. Climb a short, steep slope and from the top you should see the hill of Cnoc Eipteil ahead of you.

6 Trace the line of Cnoc Eipteil to the left; just before the horizon starts to rise again a notch is visible. This is a peat-cutters' track. Head for it through the peat beds and trenches and continue through it.

7 When you reach the fence, follow it past the gate and as it turns right. When the fence ends, you will see an aerial mast on the horizon ahead. Turn left about 45 degrees and you should see a peat-cutters' track in the distance.

8 If you don't spot it, walk in that direction and eventually you will cut across it. This track will take you back to the main road. Turn right and follow the road through the village and beyond, to where you started.

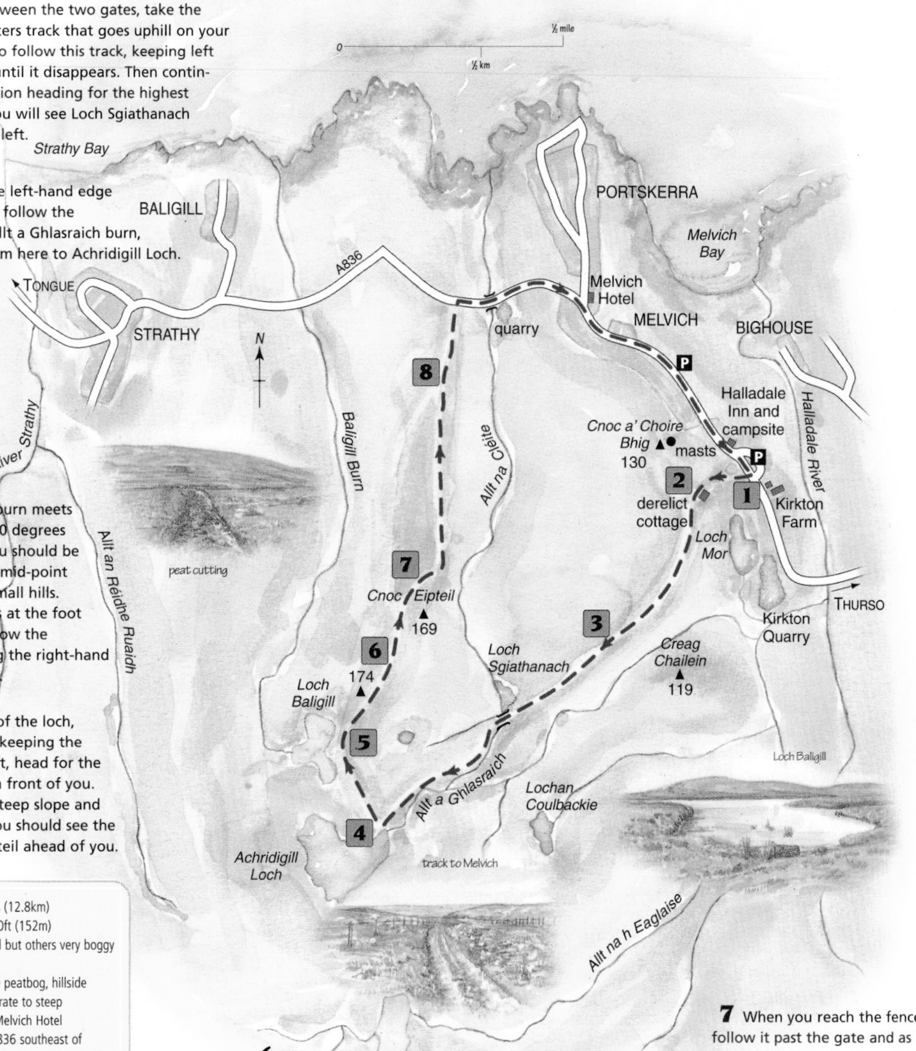

Distance: 8 miles (12.8km)
Total ascent: 500ft (152m)
Paths: some good but others very boggy or indistinct
Terrain: extensive peatbog, hillside
Gradients: moderate to steep
Refreshments: Melvich Hotel
Park: lay-by on A836 southeast of Melvich
Note: this is remote and difficult terrain and the walk should not be attempted in wet weather or poor visibility

The Stuarts' Last Stand at Culloden

Around the woods and moors of Culloden, where the Stuart cause died in battle

Distance: 6½ miles (10.5km)
Total ascent: negligible
Paths: mostly good but can be muddy after wet weather
Terrain: moorland, woodland, fields, forestry road and minor roads
Gradients: none
Refreshments: visitor centre
Park: Culloden battlefield visitor centre car park, off B9006 between Inverness and Croy
Note: the battlefield site is owned by the National Trust for Scotland and an entrance fee is payable

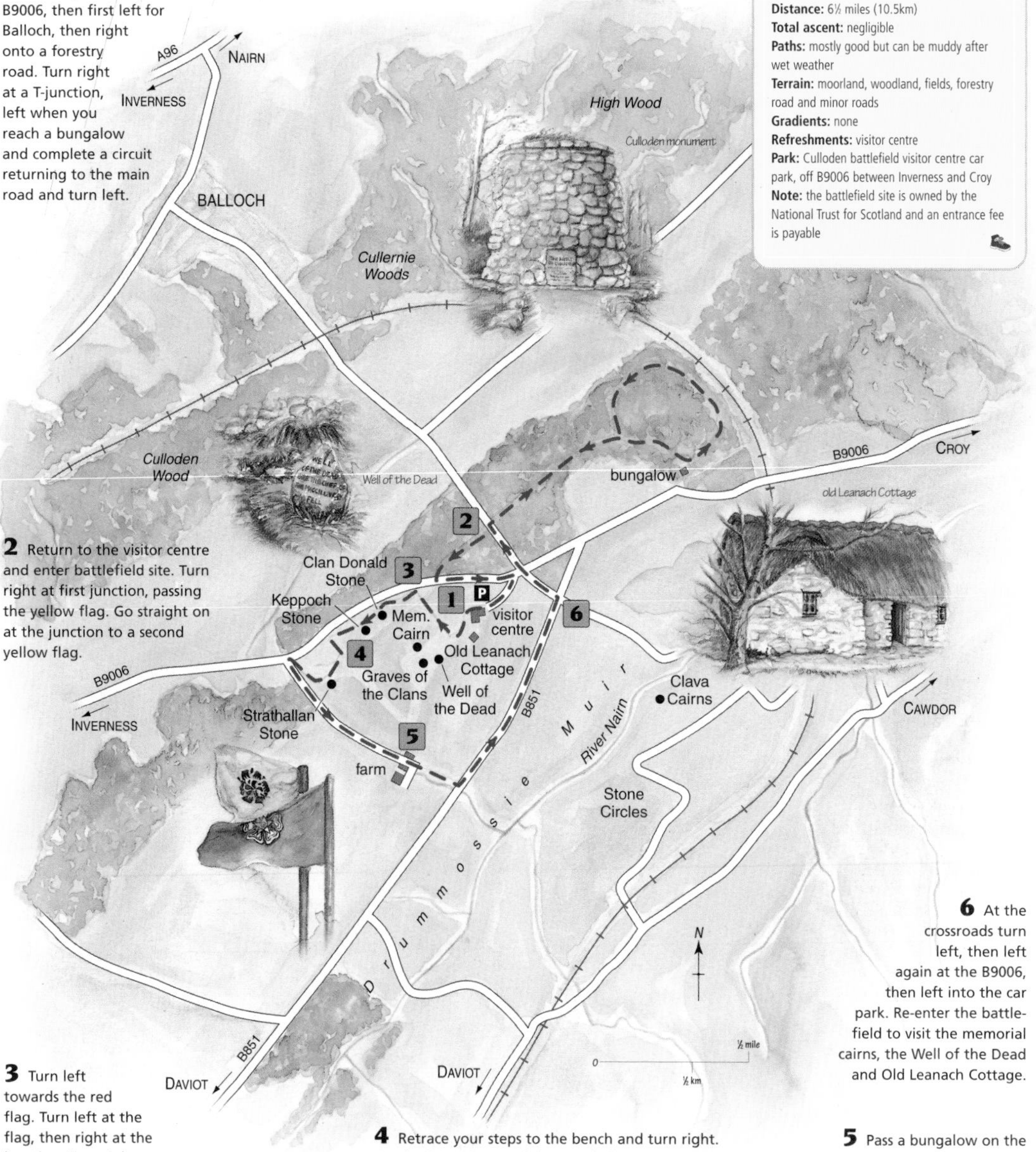

A96
NAIRN
INVERNESS
High Wood
Culloden monument
BALLOCH
Cullernie Woods
Culloden Wood
Well of the Dead
bungalow
B9006
CROY
old Leanach Cottage
Clan Donald Stone
Keppoch Stone
Mem. Cairn
visitor centre
Old Leanach Cottage
Graves of the Clans
Well of the Dead
Strathallan Stone
farm
B9006
INVERNESS
B851
Clava Cairns
River Nairn
Drummossie Muir
Stone Circles
CAWDOR
N
DAVIOT
B851
DAVIOT
0 ½ mile
½ km

1 Turn right onto the B9006, then first left for Balloch, then right onto a forestry road. Turn right at a T-junction, left when you reach a bungalow and complete a circuit returning to the main road and turn left.

2 Return to the visitor centre and enter battlefield site. Turn right at first junction, passing the yellow flag. Go straight on at the junction to a second yellow flag.

3 Turn left towards the red flag. Turn left at the flag, then right at the junction. Turn right at the bench and head for the vantage point for a view over the battlefield.

4 Retrace your steps to the bench and turn right. At the T-Junction, and the Strathallan Stone, turn right and follow the path. Go through a gate, turn left and head up a farm road for 650yds (592m) with the battlefield on your left.

5 Pass a bungalow on the left, climb a gate and follow the track along the left of the field. Exit over a fence onto a minor road and turn left.

6 At the crossroads turn left, then left again at the B9006, then left into the car park. Re-enter the battlefield to visit the memorial cairns, the Well of the Dead and Old Leanach Cottage.

Rothiemurchus – Heart of the Caledonian Pine Forest

A memorable ramble through ancient woodland

1 Start on the footpath immediately to the right of the Rothiemurchus Camp and Caravan Park entrance, signposted Public Path to Braemar by the Lairig Ghru. Walk south along the track into the forest, then on through a gate by Lairig Ghru Cottage.

2 Where the track divides take the right fork, signposted for Gleann Einich, passing a large cairn on the left. Soon after, go over a stile at the cattle grid. The track then rises to more open country.

3 Having gained about the highest point along the track, turn sharp right for another track leading up over the heather. Reach a tarmac lane by a cattle grid, turn left and continue to where the lane terminates at Whitewell Croft. From there, bear left down a path for Rothiemurchus footpath. A short deviation leads first to a large memorial cairn on the left.

4 Walk down from the cairn and, on regaining the track for Gleann Einich, turn right for 700 yds (637m) to arrive at a major crossroads of estate tracks. There are fire beaters and signposts here. Follow the Lairig Ghru track to the left, passing pine-fringed Lochan Deo and walking beyond where the other path from Coylumbridge joins from the left. Soon after, reach the Cairngorm Club footbridge over the Allt na Bheinn Mhor.

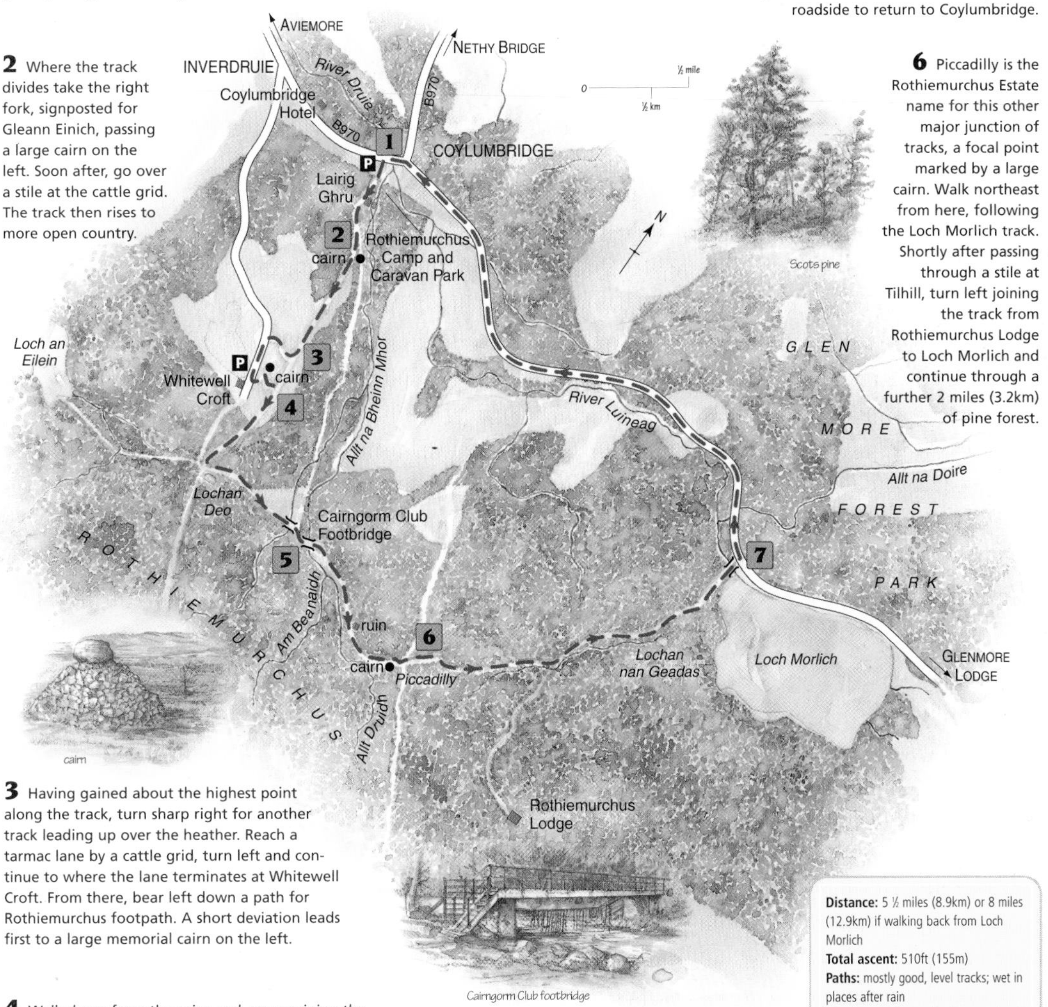

5 Go over the bridge and turn right on a rough track heading upstream of the river. From where the waters of the Am Beanaidh and the Allt Druidh join forces, veer southeast, passing close to a ruined house on the left before rising gently up to Piccadilly.

6 Piccadilly is the Rothiemurchus Estate name for this other major junction of tracks, a focal point marked by a large cairn. Walk northeast from here, following the Loch Morlich track. Shortly after passing through a stile at Tilhill, turn left joining the track from Rothiemurchus Lodge to Loch Morlich and continue through a further 2 miles (3.2km) of pine forest.

7 Join the road to Glen More and the ski centre by the western shore of Loch Morlich. At certain times of the year the road is served by buses connecting with Aviemore (check with local tourist information), which offers a convenient return; alternatively it is a further 1 hour of walking by the roadside to return to Coylumbridge.

Distance: 5 ½ miles (8.9km) or 8 miles (12.9km) if walking back from Loch Morlich
Total ascent: 510ft (155m)
Paths: mostly good, level tracks; wet in places after rain
Terrain: pine forest, heather moorland
Gradients: gradual
Refreshments: Coylumbridge Hotel and in Aviemore
Park: by roadside, just west of entrance to Rothiemurchus Camp and Caravan Park, near Coylumbridge, 2 miles (3.2km) southeast of Aviemore

On General Wade's Road

Discovering a section of the great military occupation road near Newtonmore

1 From the visitor centre car park at Ralia turn right and walk 330yds (300m) to the road that runs parallel to the A9. When the A9 exit for Newtonmore joins this road, cross over and take the minor road (signposted to Ralia and Nuide) to the right.

2 A short distance along here on the right, at the gap in the trees, climb a gate and follow the track uphill. Cross another gate and turn left onto the A9. About 350yds (320m) further along you reach Ralia Kennels (unmistakable but unsigned).

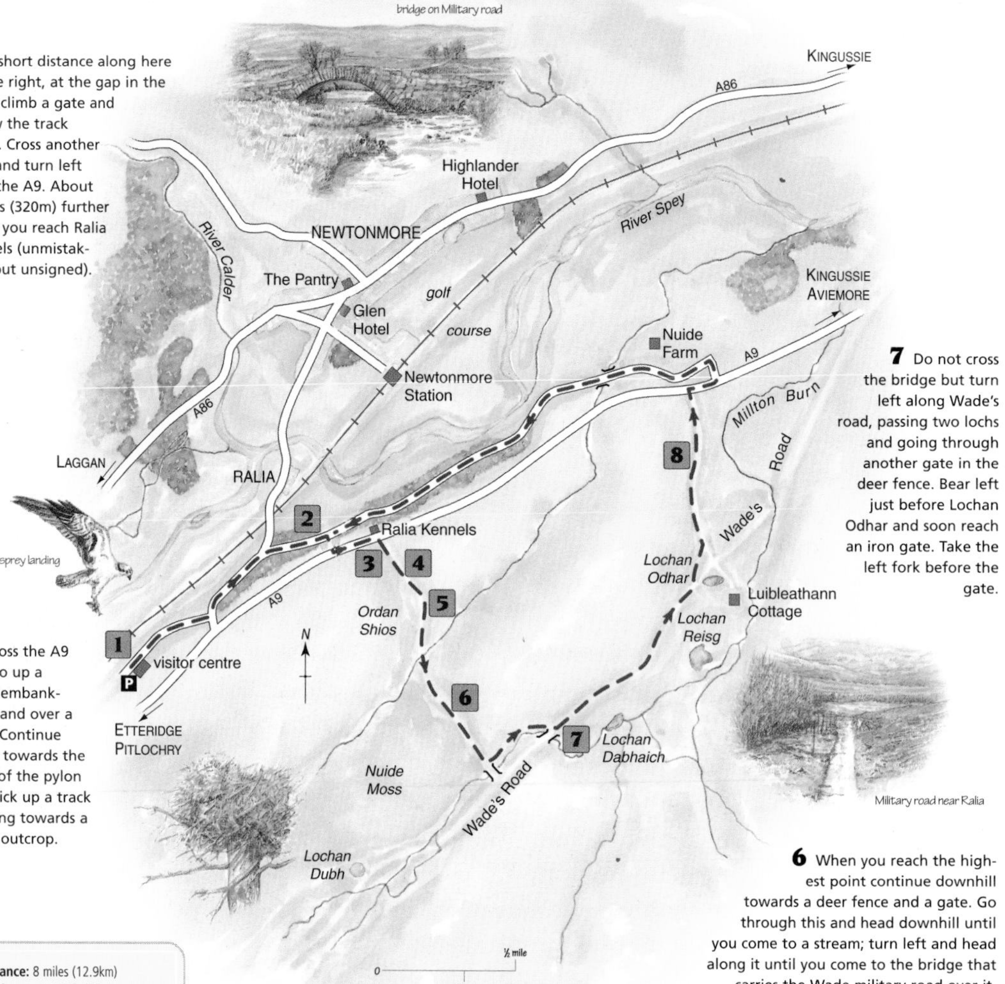

3 Cross the A9 and go up a steep embankment and over a gate. Continue uphill towards the right of the pylon and pick up a track heading towards a rocky outcrop.

4 Cross a stile at the fence and continue on the track towards the left-hand side of the hill. On a good day it is worth detouring up to the summit to enjoy the panoramic views of the surrounding area.

5 Follow the path round the back of the hill and then turn left. Go downhill and across some boggy ground before rising again to meet a farm track passing in front of you. Cross this and continue on a line uphill.

6 When you reach the highest point continue downhill towards a deer fence and a gate. Go through this and head downhill until you come to a stream; turn left and head along it until you come to the bridge that carries the Wade military road over it.

7 Do not cross the bridge but turn left along Wade's road, passing two lochs and going through another gate in the deer fence. Bear left just before Lochan Odhar and soon reach an iron gate. Take the left fork before the gate.

8 Continue on this road towards the A9. Cross the A9 and turn right, then take the first left onto a minor road, signposted from the A9 'Farm Access 200yds'. Continue down this road, past the lane to Nuide Farm, until you return to the car park at Ralia.

bridge on Military road

osprey landing

Military road near Ralia

Distance: 8 miles (12.9km)
Total ascent: 230ft (70m)
Paths: Wade's road very good; approach path can be boggy in parts
Terrain: hillside, military road
Gradients: moderate
Refreshments: visitor centre
Park: Ralia visitor centre, off A9 near Newtonmore

Great Birnam Wood to Dunkeld

With overtones of Macbeth in the wooded Tay Valley

Distance: 6 miles (9.7km)
Total ascent: 200ft (61m)
Paths: good; can be muddy after rain
Terrain: woodland with some riverbank and pavements
Gradients: gradual
Refreshments: Birnam Hotel, opposite Beatrix Potter Garden
Park: car park at end of Athol Street

1 From the car park at Dunkeld walk along Athol Street and turn right into High Street. From the square you can investigate the fountain, rectory, cathedral and surrounding historic buildings. Retrace your steps to Athol Street and turn right.

2 Cross the bridge and walk down the steps on the left-hand side of the bridge. At the bottom follow the path to the right, downstream along the river. Just past the Birnam Oak turn up the steps signposted to Birnam, following the path round to the road. Cross to the Beatrix Potter Garden. Leaving there, turn left along the main road.

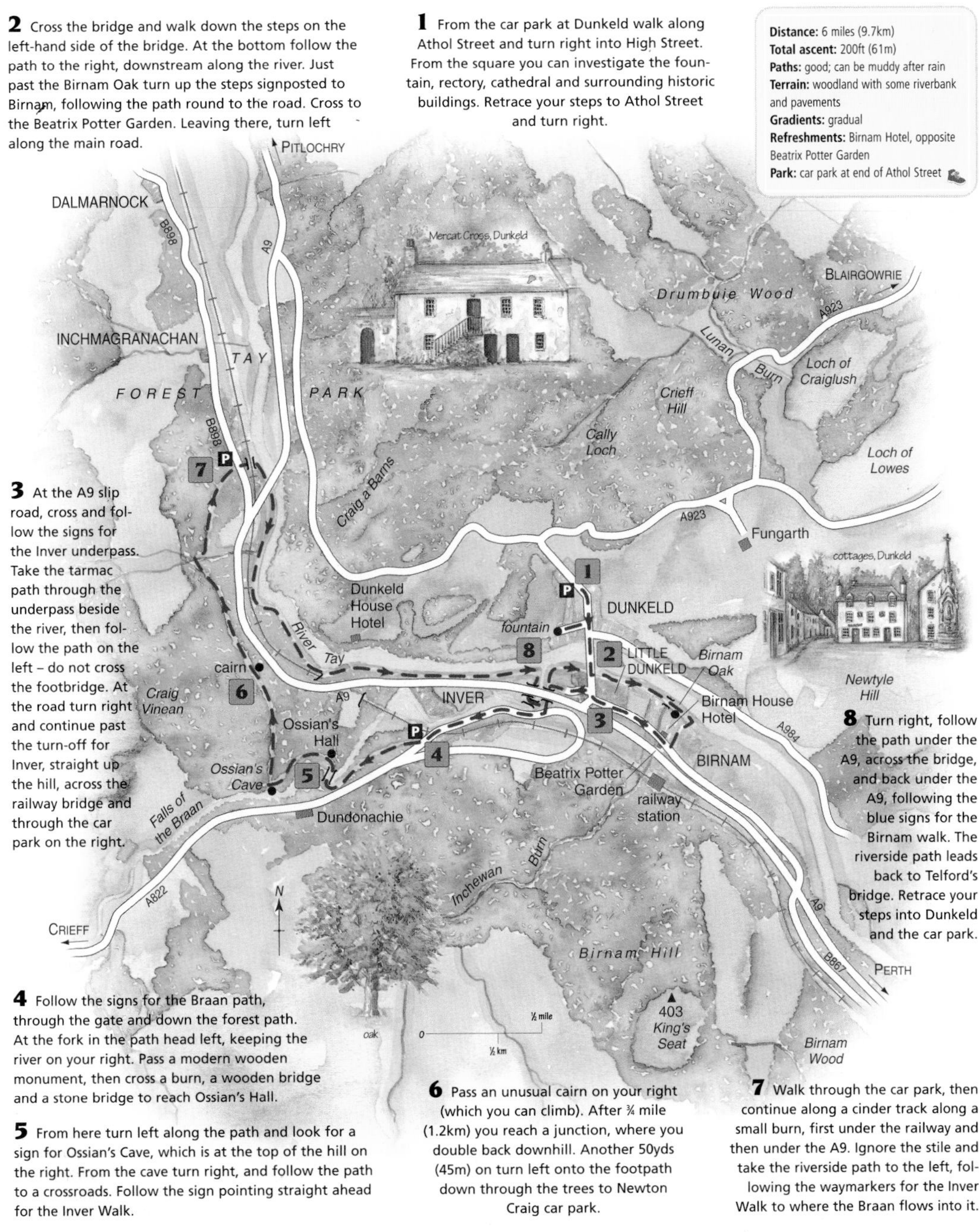

3 At the A9 slip road, cross and follow the signs for the Inver underpass. Take the tarmac path through the underpass beside the river, then follow the path on the left – do not cross the footbridge. At the road turn right and continue past the turn-off for Inver, straight up the hill, across the railway bridge and through the car park on the right.

4 Follow the signs for the Braan path, through the gate and down the forest path. At the fork in the path head left, keeping the river on your right. Pass a modern wooden monument, then cross a burn, a wooden bridge and a stone bridge to reach Ossian's Hall.

5 From here turn left along the path and look for a sign for Ossian's Cave, which is at the top of the hill on the right. From the cave turn right, and follow the path to a crossroads. Follow the sign pointing straight ahead for the Inver Walk.

6 Pass an unusual cairn on your right (which you can climb). After ¾ mile (1.2km) you reach a junction, where you double back downhill. Another 50yds (45m) on turn left onto the footpath down through the trees to Newton Craig car park.

7 Walk through the car park, then continue along a cinder track along a small burn, first under the railway and then under the A9. Ignore the stile and take the riverside path to the left, following the waymarkers for the Inver Walk to where the Braan flows into it.

8 Turn right, follow the path under the A9, across the bridge, and back under the A9, following the blue signs for the Birnam walk. The riverside path leads back to Telford's bridge. Retrace your steps into Dunkeld and the car park.

WALK 119

Stirling, Cockpit of Scottish History

The history of Scotland has been played out on the streets of this strategic burgh

Distance: 5 miles (8km)
Total ascent: 100ft (30m)
Paths: good; mostly paved but some dirt tracks
Terrain: town trail and riverside
Gradients: gentle, one short steep section
Refreshments: Castle Tea Room
Park: car park, Castle Esplanade, Stirling

1 From the castle car park, head downhill, passing the visitor centre on your left. Follow the sign to the right for the Back Walk, passing the old Grammar School, now a hotel called the Portcullis. On the Back Walk, the cemetery is to the left and the Pyramid to the right.

2 Turn into the cemetery by the iron gates opposite the Pyramid. Climb the Ladies' Rock for a view over the historic sites of Stirling and the Forth Valley and exit by the back gate. Turn right and continue until you see a fork to the left.

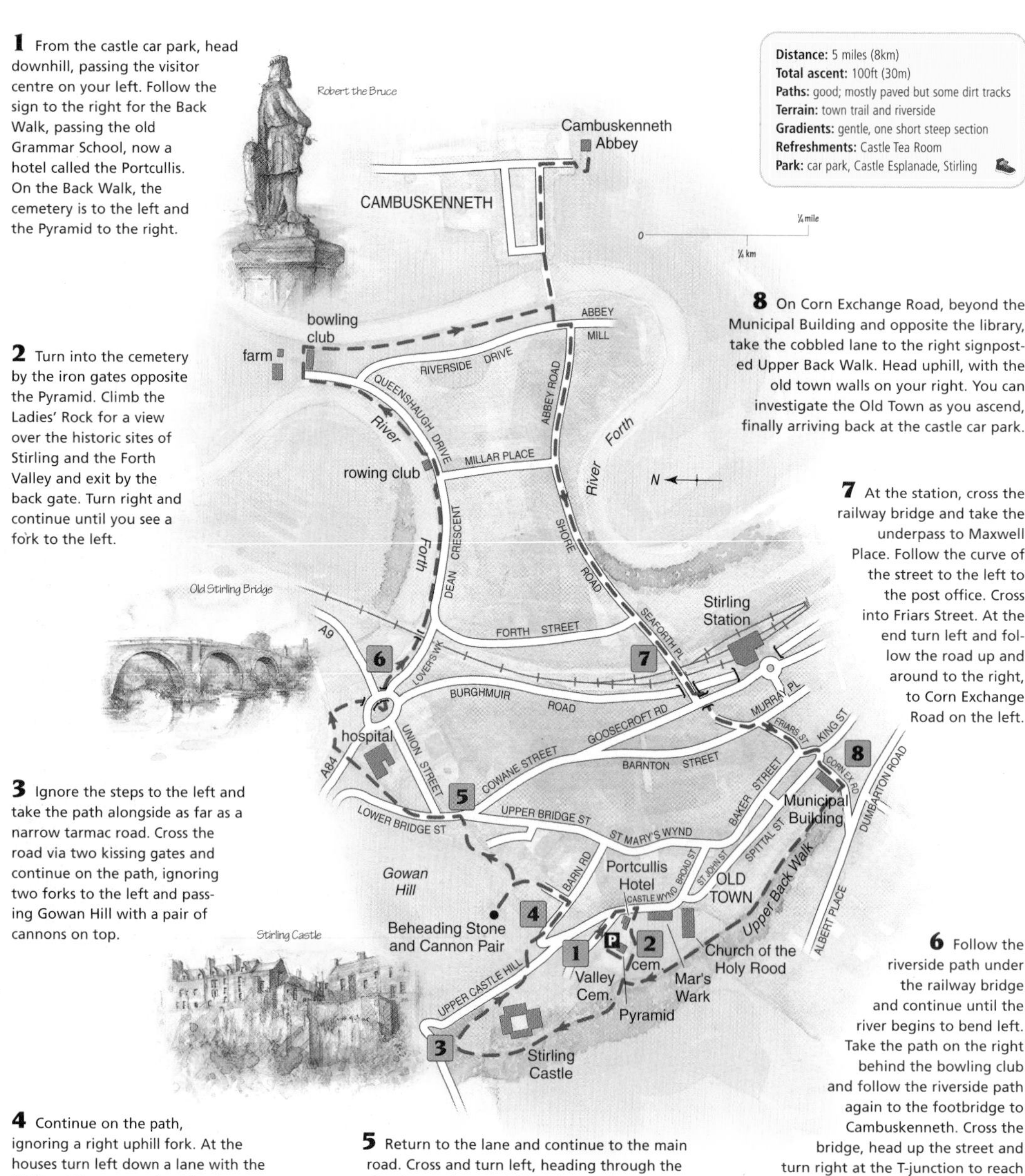

3 Ignore the steps to the left and take the path alongside as far as a narrow tarmac road. Cross the road via two kissing gates and continue on the path, ignoring two forks to the left and passing Gowan Hill with a pair of cannons on top.

4 Continue on the path, ignoring a right uphill fork. At the houses turn left down a lane with the Wallace Monument ahead in the distance. At the T-junction bear left on a lane, then take the narrow, grassy track on your left up to Gowan Hill.

5 Return to the lane and continue to the main road. Cross and turn left, heading through the pedestrian underpass. Old Stirling Bridge is to your left and accessible through the hospital grounds. Retrace your steps from the bridge and turn left into an underpass to the centre of the roundabout. Turn left again through another underpass which exits beyond the road bridge.

6 Follow the riverside path under the railway bridge and continue until the river begins to bend left. Take the path on the right behind the bowling club and follow the riverside path again to the footbridge to Cambuskenneth. Cross the bridge, head up the street and turn right at the T-junction to reach Cambuskenneth Abbey. Retrace your steps back over the bridge and turn left, then right to continue along Abbey Road towards the town.

7 At the station, cross the railway bridge and take the underpass to Maxwell Place. Follow the curve of the street to the left to the post office. Cross into Friars Street. At the end turn left and follow the road up and around to the right, to Corn Exchange Road on the left.

8 On Corn Exchange Road, beyond the Municipal Building and opposite the library, take the cobbled lane to the right signposted Upper Back Walk. Head uphill, with the old town walls on your right. You can investigate the Old Town as you ascend, finally arriving back at the castle car park.

The Lomond Hills of Fife

Topping out on the highest point of the ancient Kingdom of Fife

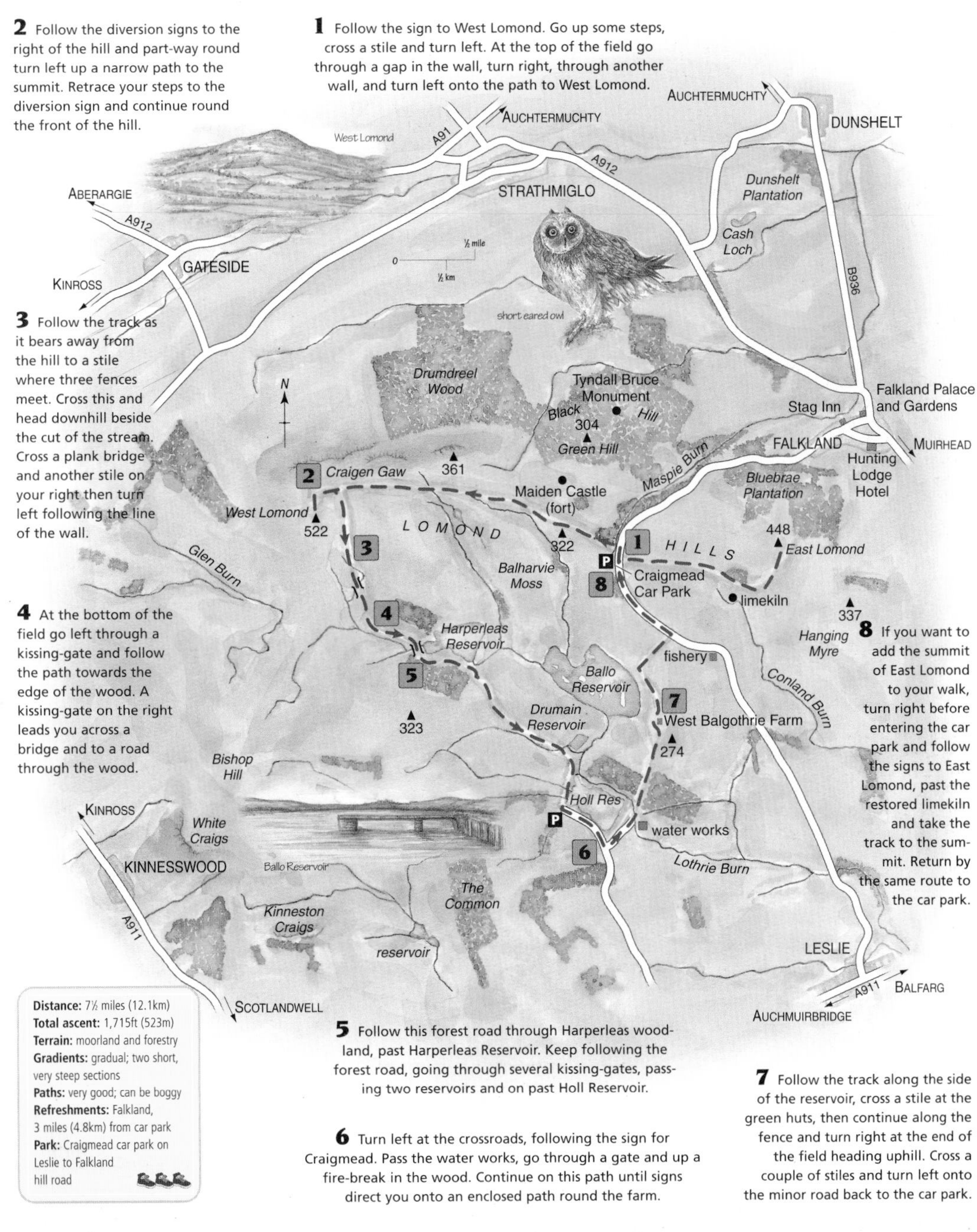

1 Follow the sign to West Lomond. Go up some steps, cross a stile and turn left. At the top of the field go through a gap in the wall, turn right, through another wall, and turn left onto the path to West Lomond.

2 Follow the diversion signs to the right of the hill and part-way round turn left up a narrow path to the summit. Retrace your steps to the diversion sign and continue round the front of the hill.

3 Follow the track as it bears away from the hill to a stile where three fences meet. Cross this and head downhill beside the cut of the stream. Cross a plank bridge and another stile on your right then turn left following the line of the wall.

4 At the bottom of the field go left through a kissing-gate and follow the path towards the edge of the wood. A kissing-gate on the right leads you across a bridge and to a road through the wood.

5 Follow this forest road through Harperleas woodland, past Harperleas Reservoir. Keep following the forest road, going through several kissing-gates, passing two reservoirs and on past Holl Reservoir.

6 Turn left at the crossroads, following the sign for Craigmead. Pass the water works, go through a gate and up a fire-break in the wood. Continue on this path until signs direct you onto an enclosed path round the farm.

7 Follow the track along the side of the reservoir, cross a stile at the green huts, then continue along the fence and turn right at the end of the field heading uphill. Cross a couple of stiles and turn left onto the minor road back to the car park.

8 If you want to add the summit of East Lomond to your walk, turn right before entering the car park and follow the signs to East Lomond, past the restored limekiln and take the track to the summit. Return by the same route to the car park.

Distance: 7½ miles (12.1km)
Total ascent: 1,715ft (523m)
Terrain: moorland and forestry
Gradients: gradual; two short, very steep sections
Paths: very good; can be boggy
Refreshments: Falkland, 3 miles (4.8km) from car park
Park: Craigmead car park on Leslie to Falkland hill road

Acknowledgements

Walks written and compiled by: Chris Bagshaw, Nick Channer, Paddy Dillon, Martin Dunning, Rebecca Ford, John Gillham, David Hancock, Alison Layland, Laurence Main, Terry Marsh, Julie Meech, John Morrison, Brian Pearce, Richard Sale, Hamish Scott, Roly Smith, Christopher Somerville, Hugh Taylor and Moira McCrossan, Hilary Weston, Stephen Whitehorne, Angela Wigglesworth, Nia Williams, David Winpenny.

Map illustrations: chrisorr.com

Page layout: Graham Dudley

We would like to thank Janet Tabinski and Nick Reynolds for their editorial input, and Jenny Gill of Skelley Cartographic Services for compiling the maps.